'Strangely, American federalism has been largely absent from American political development scholarship. Jared Sonnicksen's insightful, stimulating, and ambitious book represents a significant contribution to filling this gap. Building on the concept of immanent fragmentation as an institutional reality and regulative idea, this innovative account of American federal democracy "in" and "through" time has a lot to offer, for students of American politics and comparative federalism alike.'

Jörg Broschek, *Associate Professor and Canada Research Chair in Comparative Federalism and Multilevel Governance, Wilfrid Laurier University, Canada*

Cover image: © Getty Images

First published 2022
by Routledge
2 Park Square, Milton Park, Abingdon, Oxon OX14 4RN

and by Routledge
605 Third Avenue, New York, NY 10158

Routledge is an imprint of the Taylor & Francis Group, an informa business

British Library Cataloguing-in-Publication Data
A catalogue record for this book is available from the British Library

Library of Congress Cataloging-in-Publication Data
Names: Sonnicksen, Jared, 1978- author.
Title: Tensions of American federal democracy : fragmentation of the state / Jared Sonnicksen.
Description: Abingdon, Oxon ; New York, NY : Routledge, 2022. | Series: Federalism studies | Includes bibliographical references and index.
Identifiers: LCCN 2021039806 (print) | LCCN 2021039807 (ebook) | ISBN 9781032067452 (hardback) | ISBN 9781032067445 (paperback) | ISBN 9781003203674 (ebook)
Subjects: LCSH: Federal government--United States. | Divided government--United States. | Democracy--United States.
Classification: LCC JK325 .S68 2022 (print) | LCC JK325 (ebook) | DDC 320.473--dc23
LC record available at https://lccn.loc.gov/2021039806
LC ebook record available at https://lccn.loc.gov/2021039807

ISBN: 978-1-032-06745-2 (hbk)
ISBN: 978-1-032-06744-5 (pbk)
ISBN: 978-1-003-20367-4 (ebk)

DOI: 10.4324/9781003203674

Typeset in Bembo
by SPi Technologies India Pvt Ltd (Straive)

TENSIONS OF AMERICAN FEDERAL DEMOCRACY

Fragmentation of the State

Jared Sonnicksen

Routledge
Taylor & Francis Group
LONDON AND NEW YORK

Federalism Studies
Series Editor: Soren Dosenrode

The end of the Cold War profoundly altered the dynamics between and within the various states in Europe and the rest of the World, resulting in a resurgence of interest in the concept of federalism. This shift in balance has been further fuelled by the increase in the number of conflicts arising from the disaffection of the diverse ethnic or religious minorities residing within these states (e.g. Sudan, Iraq). Globalization is forcing governments not only to work together, but also to reconsider their internal roles as guarantors of economic growth, with regions playing the major part. Federalism Studies offers academics a complete and in-depth understanding of federalism and intergovernmental relations in historical, theoretical and comparative contexts. Intended to be international and interdisciplinary in scope, the books in the series are designed to build a common framework for the constructive analysis of federalism. Contributions are welcome on topics which explore federalism as a theory; as a political system and as a form of conflict management.

Federalism, Secession and International Recognition Regime
Iraqi Kurdistan
Alex Danilovich

Comparative Paradiplomacy
Jorge A. Schiavon

Tensions of American Federal Democracy
Fragmentation of the State
Jared Sonnicksen

For more information about this series, please visit: https://www.routledge.com/Federalism-Studies/book-series/FEDSTUD

TENSIONS OF AMERICAN FEDERAL DEMOCRACY

Tensions of American Federal Democracy uses an original analytical framework combined with comparative perspectives – including those of other modern federal democracies – to explore the jigsaw puzzle that is the state of American federal democracy.

The USA has a complex political system prone to "divided government", which has become highly polarized in recent years. The reasons for this extend further and deeper than party diversification or rising populism. This book provides an original contribution encompassing the US polity and its overall development. The author explores how the US constitution has predisposed branches and levels of government to multiple forms of separation of power and constituency; and how developments in democratic and federal government over time have fostered more competition, diffusion, and decoupling, despite earlier trends to more cross-branch and cross-level cooperation. The book thus addresses a multifaceted inquiry, interrogating and conceptualizing the connections between institutions, ideas, and political development, while exploring the interlinkage between the institutional parameters of multidimensional division of powers, constitutional political ideas and their contestation, and the limitation of the state in the US federal democratic system.

This book will appeal to students and scholars of political science, American government and constitutional politics, federalism, comparative politics, and political theory.

Jared Sonnicksen is a senior researcher in the Institute for Political Science at the Technical University of Darmstadt, Germany.

To Michaela, Julius, and Samuel

CONTENTS

FIGURES

ACKNOWLEDGMENTS

I plead guilty. I have written a book about democracy, federalism, the state, *and* the constitution of the USA. And if that were not reckless enough, I also deal here with ideas, institutions, historical developments, constitutional interpretations, comparisons with other political systems, cross-cutting themes like popular and state sovereignty, liberty, slavery, and the two-party duopoly in American politics and political development, as well as the occasional side note (did you know that Moses had a speech impairment?). In my defense, the original manuscript was nearly twice as long. But thank goodness for you, dear reader, that the publisher demanded that I revise and shorten the text. This has made the resultant book, if not good, then certainly better. Quite seriously, the book does cover a seemingly large spectrum, but this study and this student are more limited. Of course there are many books out there that already examine the American constitution, federalism, democracy, the state, and their historical development and current states. The goal here is not to cover each of those dimensions in their entirety, but rather to provide a big picture, one regarding the overarching pattern of fragmentation of the US polity. I also hope to offer a new perspective, one that builds on prior and copious work on the USA, but which is also particularly shaped by comparison with other federal democracies.

Which brings me to an expression of profound gratitude to Arthur Benz. He served as my mentor for several years at the Technical University of Darmstadt as well as a partner in several projects. I learned tremendously from his expertise and scholarship in multiple areas as well as from him personally. This book originated as a book-length thesis as part of the arduous – and somewhat arcane – *Habilitation* in the German higher education system. On this note, in addition to Arthur, I would like to thank Professors Ursula Münch and Roland Lhotta for generously serving as external reviewers of my *Habilitation* thesis in 2019. I owe a further debt of gratitude to Dirk Jörke, who became my de facto second adviser in Darmstadt and has challenged and supported me in numerous ways. On that note, I would also like to thank the entire Institute for Political Science in Darmstadt, with special thanks to Björn Egner, Michèle Knodt, and Nicole Ungermann for their immeasurable amount of time and support. Space forbids me from acknowledging everyone I should and would like to thank. For numerous intellectual exchanges, encouragement, and critique, as well pleasant work together over the past several years as either direct colleagues and/or in joint ventures, I would like to especially thank Nathalie Behnke, Jörg Broschek, César Colino, Timothy Conlan, Hideto Hiramatsu, Thomas Hueglin, Jörg Kemmerzell, Sabine Kropp, Sean Mueller, Veith Selk, Anna Wenz-Temming, and the one and only Mahir Tokatlı. Last but not least, I would like to thank Routledge, its Federalism Studies series editor, Søren Dosenrode, the anonymous reviewers for constructive critique, as well as editorial assistant Hannah Rich and editor Emily Ross for all of their time and effort.

Finally, I would like to thank my wife and partner Michaela and our sons Julius and Samuel, most of all for their existence, which they fortunately share with me. I am hesitant to say thanks for letting me work or "putting up with" me: for one, to Michaela, because you are equally busy and we equally challenge, help, and support each other; for another, to all three of you, because we lost a lot of time together thanks to this book and my apparent inability to pursue a more normal job. Sorry for that. At the same time, you are the main cause of my being an "ex pat"' for over two decades now. This circumstance has not only made my life richer, but also this book.

PROLOGUE

The US federal elections of 2008 ushered in a sweeping electoral victory for one party. With a sizeable majority for the Democrats in both the House of Representatives and the Senate, the presidency was to be occupied by a Democrat president-elect Barack Obama, the latter having campaigned no less upon a platform of "Change". With the stage set for "unified government", conditions were rather favorable to governing and for political reforms in particular. The year 2008 had, if not all, most of the trappings for a window of opportunity conducive to extensive legislating at the federal level. For one, the US economy found itself in the midst of the worst economic crisis since the Great Depression of the late 1920s to early 1930s. That earlier critical juncture had elicited in response a "New Deal" era, with a massive expansion of federal government programs and its scope of regulation. Such changes were achieved without any new amendment to the constitution. They transpired within the same formal constitutional order of separation of powers, including those of the federal government, which also continue to apply predominantly unchanged to this day. In the year running up to the 2008 election, the bursting of the "housing bubble" had triggered drastic convulsions across multiple markets but also numerous countries. The USA alone was witnessing a veritable implosion of housing market prices coinciding with a credit default swap crisis, and then a massive wave of home foreclosures. This culminated into an even more severe financial and economic downturn with record-breaking bankruptcies and the highest amount of job loss in the post-World War II era. These internal disruptions came in addition to a difficult state of international affairs. This stemmed not least from the embroilment of the USA in several military conflicts as part of a protracted War on Terror. None of these domestic and international developments were products of fate. They were instead connected to political decisions and polices, many if not all of them federal ones.

All the more so, it would appear at the bottom line – and did so for many after the elections of 2008 – that significant changes in federal government, akin to a new "New Deal", could have been expected. And as history had demonstrated, it would not even have been necessary to amend the constitution to achieve them. While big things like financial bailouts and some major reforms were achieved, most notably in expanding healthcare coverage, a comparable sort of transformation did not come about. This should seem puzzling.

1

INTRODUCTION

Exploring the limited state

The following study explores the concept of the limited state in the USA. It addresses the tensions of federalism and democracy, the complexity of the American polity, and the dynamic interplay of institutions and ideas over time. Of particular concern are how tensions and recurring contestation relate to the democratic and federal dimensions of government, in both their original constitutional and evolved structural-functional arrangements. In addition to the multifaceted division of powers, this study captures another major, if somehow peculiar, source of tension in the USA. It stems from the constitution in general, its interpretation and politicization, and its strict reading in particular. I conceptualize a pattern of interpretation as "text immanence" and a regulative idea. The institutional parameters of manifold divided government affect how constitutional politics unfolds. But the latter also affects the development of the former. The American Constitution has predisposed the political order toward contestation and tensions in many ways from the outset. Yet how this occurs varies, at times by design, by intention, by accident, or via unforeseen changes adapted under and to the constitutional framework. The study examines how the resultant pattern of a limited state may derive from an *immanent fragmentation* of the US polity, which includes multiple levels and branches of government as well as a multitude of constituencies.

Exploring the limited state will entail a complex analytical expedition. It will require navigational tools and an appropriate map and compass. To this end, the study delves first into the theoretical foundations of institutionalism and especially its historical and ideational institutionalist variants (Chapter 2). This provides for analytical perspectives suitable to understanding and explaining the complexities of political development. Furthermore, the analytical framework is specified by drawing from comparative federalism and federal dynamics, particularly in federal democracies. With this frame in mind, the second and main part (Chapters 3 to 7) explores the following: institutional and ideational dynamics underlying

DOI: 10.4324/9781003203674-1

the evolution of the US Constitution; patterns of its political interpretation; the formation and development of the American state; the dual dimensions of the division of powers (i.e. in federal and democratic government); and the corresponding politics of the Constitution. These comprise the institutional settings within which the democratic and federal tensions between power separating and sharing, cooperation, competition, and coercion unfold between the levels and branches of government as well as multiple constituencies. This book undertakes a case study (see e.g. Gerring 2004) that is implicitly comparative in character while also aiming to make a case. To borrow from Charles Tilly, this study will tackle questions concerning some "big structures" and "large processes" (Tilly 1984), and for the purposes here, about the complex interplay between institutions and ideas over time in the US federal democracy. Accordingly I will seek to capture and explain the immanent fragmentation of the US polity and the American state which are apparently limited by it.

Some further preliminary remarks are warranted. First of all, what lies ahead provides an original perspective. However, it builds on the work and insights of numerous others. In addition to the theoretical analytical foundations, the relevant state of the art encompasses copious research on various aspects of American federalism, democracy, and the state. There are also many studies that address the complexities of the US polity in its long scope of political development and other analogous "big pictures", like the one presented here. By no means an exhaustive review, several such works of importance and influence in general, and for the study at hand in particular, include:

- Studies dealing with the character of US government due to its origins in a late-18th-century context (see e.g. Huntington 1966; Ware 2011), the implications this has on a relatively distinct concept of the American state (see e.g. Nettl 1968), on the operation of government in the USA (see e.g. Cammisa and Manuel 2014), and the constraints on democracy and democratization (see e.g. Dahl 2003), or how a "pathological" development of the US presidential system of government ensued with related, but misleading, notions of "presidential democracy" (Ackerman 2005, 2013; Lowi 1969, 1994);
- Studies on the concurring legacies of *negative* beliefs in government as a necessary evil to be limited by the separation of powers versus the *positive* reformist intentions of division of powers for effective, consensus-seeking government (see Zvesper 1999);
- Studies on tensions between "self" and "shared" rule, and between the cooperative and the conflictual, to meanwhile polarizing tendencies in American federalism (Beer 1973, 1993; Conlan 1998, 2017; Elazar 1962, 1987);
- Studies on various features and myths of "American exceptionalism", including the supposed "statelessness" of its society and government (see e.g. Appleby 1992; Bellah et al. 1985; King 1973; Lipset 1991);
- On constitutional dilemmas embedded in US politics and society, e.g. between "institutions and ideals" (Huntington 1982), between different and, in parts,

contradicting political traditions of egalitarianism, liberalism, and republicanism (see e.g. Smith 1993), between "freedom and slavery" and hence equality and liberty for one, and institutions of state power and coercion, not least including enslavement, for another (see e.g. Gerstle 2009; Morgan 1972; Shklar 1991);
- And on how many of these contradictions have resulted in an overarching "irony" of American political history (Niebuhr 1952 [2008]), its state (King and Lieberman 2009), an "impoverished" polity (Roelofs 1992), or a deceptively "stateless" (King and Lieberman 2008) and "submerged" state (Mettler 2011).

In short: there is much illuminating research out there to work with already. This may beg the question of what then this study has to contribute. The most elementary contribution lies in bringing these multiple strands of theory, description, and explanation together. This would amount to a tall order already. But there is more in store than that.

Multiple scholarly predecessors have theorized about the ambivalences, paradoxes, and even ironies and pathologies of the US Constitution in a strict sense and of constitutional development in a broad sense. On the other hand, one finds many myths, misconceptions, and omissions being perpetuated. The approach taken here attempts to deal with both. My own reading ties various strands of theoretical, social science, and historical analysis together. In doing so, it provides for new insights, plot twists, as well as corrections and addenda to scholarly conventional wisdom, among other things. Some of the most influential common theories to be put in a new perspective include the US Constitution as a "federal bargain" (Riker 1964) and a "coming-together" type (Stepan 1999), American constitutional development as one of a dualism between phases of "constitutional" and "ordinary" politics (Ackerman 1991), and the US polity as seemingly "stateless" government and society. This study aspires to capture the fragmentation of the US polity through a compound theoretical-analytical perspective that also draws from comparative federalism and democracy research. Again, the USA represents the case at hand, but a comparative perspective is informative from the outset.

Surely one may still ask whether a theory of immanent fragmentation is necessary in order to solve different puzzles or paradoxes of American federalism, democracy, and the state. The following study will not only help to make sense of them. It can also provide for a relative explanation of the case at hand, but also for potential insights and lessons pertinent for comparison with other federal democracies. As a preliminary overview of the approach to the study and its thrust of argumentation, the following are the underlying main premises and components.

First, a new composite theoretical perspective is required in order to make better sense of the complexity of US federal democracy. To this end, I draw on comparative federalism and democracy research. Historical institutionalism and ideational institutionalism provide further suitable theoretical foundations.

Second, any modern state, and especially a federal and democratic one, is a limited one. All federal democracies face inherent tensions that arise between different and, at times, countervailing principles and logics of how their respective institutions are organized and supposed to work. *But* these ascriptions apply in part, and appear to apply in other parts, to the USA in peculiar ways.

Third, the two concepts proposed here of a "limited state" and "immanent fragmentation" refer to the overarching pattern in the evolution of the US polity from the outset to the present. Immanent fragmentation of the US polity is, to an extent, quite familiar with a view to the institutional default settings of the US Constitution: e.g. both democratic and federal separation of powers with checks and balances. The combination of these features in one political order would, again, tend to limit any state. But decisive for fragmentation is how these constitutional settings as much as the understanding of them have developed over time. Immanent fragmentation extends further than the division of powers. As process, it refers also to how dynamics of federal and democratic government evolve within and reproduce these constitutional settings in a way that can perpetuate and even intensify divisions. This may especially become the case on account of patterns of strict, literal, and *immanent* interpretation of the constitution as a whole or individual provisions, norms, or principles construed therein.

Fourth, constitutional immanence can be conceived as a regulative idea, or an ideational orientation that regulates interpretation. A strict to literal reading of the constitutional text and respective beliefs in the norms purported to be attached to a constitution may be found in different contexts or systems. But this regulative idea underlies American political development from the very beginning.

Fifth, key factors behind the dynamics of an immanent constitutional interpretation are multiple constituencies of federalism as much as the constituent multitudes of democracy. They are entangled with popular and state sovereignty, two foundational and *egalitarian* referents of democracy and federalism respectively in the USA. These egalitarian referents too pose default settings – as ideational orientations underpinned by formal institutions – for the establishment of the early federal republic. They become enshrined, contradicted, and over time integrated into the US Constitution also through *immanent* interpretation.

Finally, the ensuing path of analysis will help tie together how tensions and frictions, but also fragmentation, are immanent in the US polity. Historical legacies both of structural-functional institutional settings (i.e. rules and organization of formal institutions) for one, and ideas and ideational patterns (i.e. interpreting how they (are supposed to) work) for another, reveal that *fragmentation* does not just emerge in phases of polarization or on account of intensifying contestation. They are also reflective of a wider pattern I refer to as institutional and ideational *thinking in the box*. This "box" has been inherited from the late 18th century. Its evolution has brought about far-reaching changes, but has remained complexly bound to and limited by its points of departure to this day.

The US polity comprises a system of complex – i.e. multidimensional – and divided government as much as a highly diffuse and decentralized political order by predisposition. These structural conditions on their own are important. They are not, however, solely determinative. Even without formal constitutional change, the dynamics of governance, political contestation, and constitutional interpretation can take various directions and exhibit different patterns. Like any federal democracy in a modern, constitutional, and rule-of-law state, governments in the USA can cope with the tensions and navigate the multifarious divides inherent to its compound political order. However, they can also wind up intensifying the divisions and thus encumbering cooperation between branches and levels of government. Over time the latter particularly appears to recur, generating the overarching pattern of a limited state. I seek to make a case for why this is so.

The US government in comparison

The USA is a peculiar case in multiple ways. While every system is special and in sum a unique case, the USA can be particularly difficult to categorize. As a simple initial illustration, the USA, taking the time since independence as a measure, is neither young nor old. As a nation, it tends to be considered a rather young one, especially compared with most other civilizations or peoples in the world. On the other hand, its constitution of 1789 and thus its system of government stands by most accounts as the oldest continuous republic in the world. The same could apply regarding continuity in democratic government. Most democratic systems in the world were not established or democratized until after World Wars I and II and in another wave after the Cold War. Yet looking at universal suffrage alone, the USA was behind a number of countries in introducing the right to vote for women. Moreover, the USA also practiced slavery within its own country longer than most modern states and, despite emancipation in the 1860s, did not even abolish racial segregation until the 1950s or secure equal voting rights until the 1960s. Hence, the USA represents a rather young democracy too. From another perspective, the USA belongs to the group of (post-)industrialized and OECD countries. It continues to lead globally in multiple technological, education, and research areas, and has the largest economy by gross domestic product in the world. At the same time, it demonstrates rather below-average performance of its welfare and healthcare systems. Other metrics would seem to place the USA outside the group of most developed countries entirely, evident in the notoriously high percentage of gun ownership and violence, but even more drastically the usage of capital punishment and appalling levels of incarceration. This already reveals much ambiguity. Whether these matters are explainable by political culture are surely open to debate. What is certain though, and more relevant here, is that they undoubtedly relate to politics and political systems, the constitution, and even the types of separation of powers. A brief view of the USA, more specifically from comparative government, provides an overall similarly ambivalent account.

Democratic government

According to one of the most definitive typologies of democracy, that between majoritarian and consensus democracies by Lijphart (2012) for instance, the USA defies clear classification altogether: its system of government is highly majoritarian in the dimension of the horizontal separation of powers and party systems. Features of the "Westminster model" include a simple majoritarian electoral system for nearly all political offices at all levels and an almost impervious two-party system, one-party executive cabinets as a typical presidential government, and a nearly prototypical pluralist system of interest mediation. At the same time, with regard to the dimension of the vertical separation of powers, the USA amounts to an almost superlatively consensus model. In addition to having one of the apparently most rigid constitutions in the democratic world by multiple counts (Lorenz 2005),[1] and an obviously federal and decentralized composition of the polity, the US Congress is a symmetric bicameral legislature, the Supreme Court (along with lower federal courts) has developed extensive powers of judicial review, and the Federal Reserve clearly qualifies as an independent central bank. Yet, this composite picture could hardly lead to classifying the USA as a consensus – nor consociational and concordant – democracy. If it has at times exhibited features or practices of consensus or "negotiation democracy" (see e.g. Lehmbruch 1996; Lijphart 2002; Schmidt 2002),[2] the intense and increasing polarization of the party system of the last few decades have (re-)shifted the USA toward majoritarianism and highly competitive democratic dynamics. These circumstances have rendered it often difficult if not impossible – as the recent presidential administrations of Obama (2009–2017) and Trump (2017–2021) illustrated – to govern through the ordinary legislation process at federal level.

To take another classic dualism between Madisonian and populistic democracy by Dahl (1956), the USA with its sophisticated system of separation of powers and checks and balances represents a virtual ideal type of Madisonian democracy. Limited government by intricate division of authority, designed with a motivation to constrain dual tyrannies – of an overly powerful, potentially despotic government as much as of the perceived dangers of the majority or mob rule – are not only illustrated by the Constitution or the famous writings of the *Federalists Papers* (Rossiter 1961 [1999]). The complex system of democratic and federal government represent a distinct hallmark of the US constitutional political order. And yet, it would seem that few modern democracies demonstrate such a profound and extensive propensity to populism as the USA (see e.g. Kazin 1998; Lipset 1991: 20–35). Among many other things, the party system proves revealing. Tendencies toward relatively lower "partyness" of government and society and more populist politics are evident not only in a long history of populist movements. They apply over time to the spread of direct-democratic instruments (below federal level) and an unparalleled proliferation of directly elected offices: from municipal councilors, mayors, and school board directors to county commissioners, sheriffs, and judges, along with state executives and bicameral legislatures as well as members of both chambers of the US Congress (see e.g. Bowler and Donovan 2006; Clemens 1997). Furthermore, the structural-functional composition of the party and electoral systems has contributed to weak party representative democracy and rather catch-all as well as populist competitive politics. The pertinent components range from the plurality, winner-takes-all voting systems to the rather subordinate position of political parties as organizations. The latter is fostered in turn by their highly decentralized organization as well as the institution of primaries (see e.g. Ansolabehere et al. 2010; Pomper 1977). The latter essentially deprive – or at least severely limit – American parties even of *the* function that ultimately separates them from any other organization of political and civic life in established democracies, namely the recruitment of personnel under the auspices of their own organization in the competition for elected public offices.

Simultaneously idiosyncratic is the absence of regional parties, despite the highly decentralized order of the party system, in stark contrast to other political systems with strong regional parties, such as Canada, India, or the UK with almost identical first-past-the post electoral systems. Further indicative is that, in most modern democracies, parties tend to denote even by name a political program. By contrast, to this day, the only two significant American parties operate under the utterly vacuous – and incidentally synonymous – monikers of Democrats and Republicans, competing in largely candidate-centered contests within separated plurality electoral systems at all levels of government. The exception to the rule ultimately confirms these circumstances, namely that the only "third party" candidates to win public office are almost always those running as independents, who thus belong to no party at all (Fawcett et al. 2017). This ambivalence emerges in that all the while these, in many ways, quite plebiscitary-democratic and majoritarian features coincide or coexist with a counter-majoritarian, Madisonian, strict separation of powers and checks and balances, likewise to be found among all government branches at all levels.

A further classic typology concerns the differences between presidential and parliamentary democracies, for which the USA again has served as the chief basis for an ideal type, that is the presidential model (Bagehot 1867 [1974]; Steffani 1979; Verney 1959). The US form of government represents the first of its type in the world of modern republican government. Having been founded already in the late 18th century, the USA took a marked departure from the path taken by Great Britain and much of Europe toward democratization within constitutional monarchy (see e.g. Ziblatt 2006). The US form of government merged the offices of head of state and government into one chief executive, installed simultaneously but separately from the legislature, serving a fixed term of office independent of the latter's "confidence". This arrangement of the separation of powers has been emulated at state level in the USA, with governors elected and endowed with a tenure of office independent of the state legislatures, the latter being, except in Nebraska, all bicameral ones.

Looking at democracies around the world, it would appear however that the US model has not really served as much of a role model. Even those systems that adopted presidentialism during the independence movements of the 19th century in Central and South America have meanwhile diverged significantly, not least by transitioning from electoral colleges to a directly popularly elected head of state (Blais, Massicotte, and Dobrzynska 1997). Furthermore, the much stronger trend of democratization as of the late 19th century onward has been to adopt a form of parliamentary democracy with a head of government dependent on the confidence of the legislature.[3] This applies to most modern democracies: to nearly all of Europe (except Cyprus and Switzerland), Israel, Japan, Australia, New Zealand, India, Botswana, Cape Verde, Mauritius, South Africa, Canada, and Barbados, among others. Of course, these circumstances most likely have more to do with historical developments, timing, and the occurrence of constitutional change and evolution (see e.g. Cheibub, Elkins, and Ginsburg 2014) than conscious choices of avoiding the "perils of presidentialism" as phrased by Linz (1990), such as the propensity to political stalemate, executive overstretch, or backsliding into authoritarianism. Nonetheless, in contrast to the many parliamentary systems with heads of government responsible to parliaments, or the maintenance of an electoral college unlike almost all other presidential democracies which have directly elected chief executives, not to mention the persistent lack of multipartyism, the USA appears to represent a quite unusual case among modern and consolidated democratic governments.

Federal government

Analogously, a certain ambivalence may be postulated with regard to federalism in the USA. For one, the USA was long purported to serve as the standard bearer of federalism. As with the presidential system of government, the US federal system represents the first of its kind in modern history, that is, within a republican form of government. But similarly akin to its presidential model, few federal systems actually resemble the institutions and practices of US federalism, or more precisely, most have meanwhile diverged significantly from them. Nonetheless, after its founding, the US case stood (with the exception of Switzerland as of 1848) in a league of its own as a democratic federal system for many decades. This prototypical standing had perhaps invited the association, if not the downright equation of American-style federalism, with analytical and normative understandings of what federalism more generally was and supposed to be (see Hueglin 2013: 27ff.). This finds reflection in Riker's (1964) classic and often referenced notion of a "federal bargain" for explaining the origins and emergence of federalism. This was based on the US experience of aggregating sovereign units to transfer limited authority to a central government in order to fulfill certain interests, most notably security and common defense. Derived from the US experience of federalism were also once dominant notions of a need for the strict separation of powers in the vertical division of authority and with powers allocated symmetrically among the constituent units (see e.g. Wheare 1963), or the purpose of fostering liberty, policy innovation, and competition as echoed in the economic theory of federalism (see e.g. Buchanan 1995; Oates 1972).

In contrast, as illustrated by Stepan in a landmark article on "Federalism and Democracy" (1999), most federations actually diverge from the US model in multiple ways. They include the feature of symmetry or asymmetry of the constituent units, the relations between levels of government, ranging from power separating (self-rule) to more power sharing (shared rule), and even with regard to the motives and processes of federalization. Here, the US case represents not *the* mode of founding a federation, but rather only one type, namely "coming together" federalism. And as Ziblatt (2004) demonstrated in a seminal study on state building in Germany and Italy, the concept of a federal bargain is indeed informative, but has limited trajectory beyond the US case. More generally, for most cases of federalization, particularly since the 19th century to the present, the dynamics of "holding together" – e.g. accommodating regional groups or minorities, preventing secession and/or dissolution of the polity – have been as, if not more, prevalent than "coming together" federalism. Moreover, had one taken the US case and the experience of African Americans in particular up to the 1960s as an example, one could have hardly inferred that federalism comprises an arrangement for protecting minorities – and one could certainly consider a number of other minorities, not least Native Americans, to illustrate this point. On the whole, the expansion and protection of minority rights were achieved in the USA despite, rather than because of, federalism. Instead, it would be much more appropriate and necessary to look at the federal experience of other countries like Belgium, Canada, India, and Spain to conceptualize features of federalism serving to accommodate diversity (Gagnon and Tully 2001; Petersohn 2013). There are meanwhile multiple other persistent idiosyncrasies of US federalism. They include its type and comparatively limited scope of intergovernmental relations (Bolleyer 2006; Elazar 1993), its fiscal federalism with few, and no constitutionally prescribed, revenue-sharing arrangements, and an utter lack of a specific fiscal equalization scheme either vertically between levels of government or horizontally among the states (Béland and Lecours 2014; Pierson 1995).

What complicates the US federal case in comparative perspective all the more is its variability, particularly over time. Of course federal systems, like most political systems, are not static but rather dynamic, especially with regard to the distribution of powers or the extent of centralization and decentralization, again over time, but also by policy area. Furthermore, federal systems in general are predisposed to "federal dynamics" and tensions between continuity and change, given the inherent division of powers over multiple levels of government in federal arrangements (Benz and Broschek 2013). But in the US case, federalism does not quite conform to the model that its system of federalism is generally considered to stand for, namely *dual* federalism. A case in point here is provided by *cooperative* federalism. The latter concept is usually viewed as the ideal-typical contrast to dual federalism.

For dual federalism, the USA provides the classic example, involving the strict separation of spheres of (partial) sovereignty with specific powers delegated to the national and remaining powers reserved to the states (Watts 2006: 204). Yet originally, the concept of cooperative federalism was actually conceived precisely with regard to the US case. For instance Corwin (1950) posited, and seemingly lamented, a "passing of dual federalism" with reference to the shifts from autonomy and competition among states, as well as between them and the national government, toward more cooperation. Moreover, Elazar (1962) for instance elaborated a specific theory of "cooperative federalism", drawing not only on developments in the wake of the New Deal era but rather beginning in the 19th century.[4] The concept also helped to more aptly capture changes in multiple areas of government such as regulation, policy making, and public finances and expenditures, much of which were adapting in the 20th century to meet the growing demands and needs on public services for a changing society as well as the transformed role of the USA internationally.

A curious simultaneity becomes apparent in that the US system and practices of federalism have given birth to both the concepts of dual and cooperative federalism. The latter features, by and large, have been integrated or superimposed upon the structural-functional composition of the former, with the USA remaining overall a system of separated government, not only in the horizontal but also the vertical division of powers (Fabbrini 1999). The USA on the whole continues to demonstrate an institutionally dual federal predisposition. There remains a redundancy or double concurrence of institutions and functions of government; that is the states are not institutionally interlocked with each other or with the national government, and each have responsibilities and institutions for operating government (taxing, spending, lawmaking, implementation, adjudication, and enforcement) within their own spheres of limited sovereignty.

At the same time, US federalism has transformed in practice into a system of extensive multilevel interdependence. It diverges, however, significantly from arrangements of cooperative federalism found in most other federal systems, again given the non-existence of a fiscal equalization scheme or a lack of joint-decision making as typical, for instance in Germany's system of cooperative federalism (Benz 1999; Scharpf 1988). Nor has the US Constitution adopted a set of joint or common tasks to be shared between states and federal governments, though in practice they abound. If anything, the opposite may even be the case with regard to the Constitution. One formal cooperative-federal institution in the US federal order linking state and national governments, the appointment of US senators by their respective state legislatures, was even abolished in the early 20th century and replaced by their popular election. Thus, about the time that the "passing of dual federalism" was claimed to have set in, the structural-functional dualism of US federalism was constitutionally reinforced. Instead, the perhaps most major sources propelling cooperative federalism in the USA have been a more expansive usage of Congress's delegated powers, judicial review by the Supreme Court, and through federal spending, most prominently the grants-in-aid programs. It is especially the latter mechanism by which the operation of US federalism came to be viewed rather as *coercive* than cooperative (Kincaid 1990). The inherent asymmetry of this relationship had already been implicated by Corwin (1950), by which the federal government, Congress in particular, regulates in otherwise state policy areas 'through the backdoor' by attaching conditions to funding. This, in combination with different phases and instances of judicial review by the Supreme Court, among other things, have contributed to highly altering patterns of the making, implementation, and enforcement of law in the US federal system.

In actuality, the US case of federalism is of course even more complex. The system may demonstrate comparatively fewer or a low degree of formal institutional interconnection between state and federal governments. They do abound, however, in numerous areas of public policy and policy-making processes (Karch and Rose 2019). Moreover, the institutions of the national level of government alone, not just the second chamber, remain thoroughly permeated by aspects of federalism. They are found in the "lower" or "popular" chamber, the House of Representatives, in that its membership is determined solely by elections in separate constituencies and is thus highly non-centralist and local in character. Also, the chief executive, the president, to this day is elected through an electoral college, generating an election not just by popular vote but rather ultimately by states. This federal dimension is reflected likewise in the nomination procedures (e.g. primaries, caucuses) for the head of the national executive in the first place. The judiciary branch is likewise thoroughly federal in its multilevel composition, with the Supreme Court serving not only as a functional equivalent of a constitutional court but also as the highest instance of the judiciary system as a whole.

An ambivalent polity

Institutional frameworks make a difference. But this premise does not reveal in which ways and how. Ideas and how they interlink with institutional development may also contribute to why and how institutional frameworks matter. The preceding survey of the US federal democracy in comparative perspective points already to why the complex link between ideas and institutions can matter. At the bottom line, all of the features briefly depicted above are somehow related to the US Constitution. Yet most of their developments have precious little to do with formal constitutional change, that is in the specific sense of amendments. Whether US federalism for its part is to be construed as dual, cooperative, or coercive, not to mention state or nationally dominated or balanced, or US democracy as majoritarian and competitive, or rather geared toward consensus-seeking and compromise, presents difficult questions. What is certain though right away is that instances and phases of more expansive usage of Congressional and presidential powers, as well as, vice versa, their recurring contestation and limitation, have by and large occurred without a single formal amendment to the Constitution for over a century now.[5] As a result, contractions and dilations of federal government, policies, scope of power, and the like have been borne by politics and the contested interpretation of the purposes, needs, and demands of government for one, and the meaning of what the Constitution has to say about them for another. Consequently, when looking to the US Constitution to locate the numerous changes in the vertical and the horizontal division of powers: *seek and ye shall not find*. At the same time, at the very heart of these developments and coinciding disputes lies precisely the Constitution, its text per se, as well as contestation over its meanings, intentions, and adaptability.

Thus re-enter the brief narrative in the Prologue. By considering the interplay between ideas and institutions, we can make more sense of the tensions that abounded and the severely limited scope of change achieved after the national elections of 2008, which triggered substantial political backlash and resistance among political actors, large portions of the citizenry, as well as the states. Underpinning this opposition was not only party politics, but also ideas about the Constitution, and its strict interpretation in particular. More generally for the study at hand, it is against this backdrop that we may explore what makes US federal democracy and its "state" in fact, or by comparison at least, a peculiar case.

Outline and approach to the study

The previously illustrated features of American government, along with the introductory narrative of limited and failed reform of the 2000s, focus on its peculiarities and do so in admittedly simplified, cursory fashion. However, they introduce important points of departure that tap into the deeper issues at hand. For the big idea behind this study is to explore the limited state in the USA, but with a fresh perspective. The modern state, but also democracy, federalism, the rule of law, and constitutionalism, one may say, each form different dimensions of political rule, and each for its own part limits the state. All the more limited should be a political system that combines all of these features, whether construed as multiple "veto players" (Tsebelis 1995) or "veto points" (Immergut 1990), into one polity. Such is the case in the USA. From that perspective then, one could argue that it is no wonder that governing in the USA is difficult and so the puzzle is already solved. But if only our case were so simple.

Federal democracy in the USA has manifold dimensions of divided government. Yet this complex polity has demonstrated enormous adaptability in expanding the scope and functions of government, and this largely without changing the Constitution. The latter appears all the more striking in comparison with other multilevel systems, where constitutional change can prove difficult, but nonetheless possible, and in some cases even common (see e.g. Behnke et al. 2011; Benz and Colino 2011). What is more, the dearth of amendments to the US Constitution also makes for a stark contrast *within* the USA, that is compared with state constitutions where not only the propensity to change is much higher but also the constitutions have become much more specific and longer (see e.g. Hammons 1999; Lutz 1988, 1994; May 1987; Tarr 1996). For the more general point, the complexity of US federal democracy alone cannot explain change in the one or other direction, nor continuity. Conversely, the same compound institutional parameters and the same constitutional text equally allow for contestation of government, limiting the federal level, or returning power to the states as opposed to "the state" – though it bears mentioning, and specifying further on, that it is altogether a thorny issue to equate the superordinate or federal level with "the state" in the USA (or perhaps in any federal system for that matter). To this day, whether the US federal government or the states are responsible for regulating matters such as welfare, healthcare, education, reproductive rights, ownership of guns, or environmental pollution cannot be answered definitively. On these and many other issues, the answer may be either yes, no, both, or "it depends" (e.g. on time, place, policy, or parties in power). This may have much to do with the ambiguity of the state in the USA for one, and the tensions between its expansion and limitation for another.

The state in the USA has developed several particularities. There are of course numerous aspects and meanings linked to the wider concept of an "American Exceptionalism", not least in the context of political culture (see e.g. Hart 1907; Hofstadter 1964; Lipset 1975; Smith 1993). Yet, US statehood appears especially distinctive in a "huge comparison" (Tilly 1984) with political development in other countries and regions of the (post-)industrialized world, especially in Europe (see e.g. Dyson 2009; Skowronek 1982). Modernization and, increasingly, globalization and transnationalization affect numerous spheres of social, economic, and political life, intensifying adaptive pressures on governments. These developments and dynamics have spurred the emergence and expansion of cross-, multi-, and supranational governance, though also inverse and reactive trends of nationalism, populism, and regionalism. But in stark contrast to Europe or even Canada, the USA is hardly characterized by any comparable tendencies to a "new regionalism" (Keating 2008) or "peripheral nationalisms" (Gourevitch 1979) along the lines of secessionist movements or growing demands for regional autonomy for ethnic, linguistic, or other minorities. In parallel contrast, the USA, while a member in a plethora of international organizations, has stood out in the context of "statehood in transition" in lacking any noteworthy shift toward integration in the arrangements of multilevel government (see e.g. Benz 2008: 49–54; Blatter 2001; Fabbrini 2003). Thus another ambiguity emerges from a macro-comparative perspective with transformations of the state and transitions to multilevel governance for one (see e.g. Leibfried et al. 2015), and the global proliferation of regionalisms challenging the central state for another: the state would appear to be largely safe and sound in the USA. Yet, the political system of the country remains remarkably characterized by an ongoing problematic, tense relationship to its own central state or federal level of government in particular.

The past few years alone have seen a great deal of contestation surrounding issues of federal authority, legislation, and regulation in numerous areas. This has provoked debates on, among other things, the legitimate scope of federal government, its relationship to the states, and even on the proper role of government in general. More recent political turbulence against expanding federal competences and "big government" – most notably reflected in the 'Tea Party' movement (see e.g. Skocpol and Williamson 2013) and the national elections of 2016 – is neither wholly novel, nor strictly a matter of partisan conflict. On the contrary, one may find the "generational rhythm of American politics" (Elazar 1978). These rhythms comprise a long line of shifts not only in the horizontal (between institutions or branches of government) but also in the vertical (between levels of government) dimensions of the separation of powers. Moreover, they underline long-standing and recurring tensions with "the state" in general and with the federal level of government in particular. The widely same constitutional parameters in the USA have allowed for facilitating and hampering the federal government. All the while, the constitutional framework of multidimensional divided government in the US persists. But how it is constituted in practice and over time appears rather dynamic, both in institutional and ideational terms.

These federal and democratic complexities, dynamics, and peculiarities are by no means unfamiliar to social science scholarship. But their combination begs for further investigation, certainly in light of continuing and seemingly increasing tensions. The following study explores the connection between institutional frameworks, political development, and constitutional interpretation. The latter refers not only to judicial review, but rather, and especially here, to political and "popular" constitutional understandings. The connections between constitutional compounded government and constitutional interpretation may help solve the problem of why the federal government in the USA, under the same constitutional framework, can govern and regulate effectively – e.g. in times of permissive understandings or loose interpretations of the constitution – and at other times cannot. This study seeks to demonstrate that the immanent fragmentation of US federal democracy and its limited state connects to dimensions of the division of powers for one, and to the ideational construction of the Constitution for another. Both coincide with the limitation of further development and expansion of a (national) state in the USA. Constitutional immanent interpretation should be conceptualized in the context of political development in particular. This study conceives immanence or a close reading of the Constitution as a regulative idea – a concept that is not an ideal or constitutional principle in and of itself, but rather an orientation that regulates patterns of interpretation. This raises the question as to the extent to which this notion plays a role in the dynamic and yet limiting development of the US state. A further question is whether or in which ways this regulative idea is institutionalized or interlinked with the institutional framework of government in the USA. Thus, these inquiries call for examining the link between ideas and institutions in connection with the development of the state in the US federal democracy.

A novel contribution is to conceptualize *immanent fragmentation* as both inherent to the Constitution of federal democracy in the USA and as a political regulative idea entailing "text immanence" or a close reading of the Constitution. The approach and its underlying analytical premises build upon theoretical strands of (neo-)institutionalism, its historical and ideational perspectives, as well as related research from comparative government and federalism. Combining them will provide for an analytical framework for studying the development of American statehood in a federal and democratic compounded political order. Accordingly, the study follows these primary interests: exploring the composite paths of development of the state, federalism, and democracy in the USA; conceptualizing immanence as a generic term for "text-based" "high-fidelity" approaches to constitutional interpretation; and the exploration of this ideational orientation in connection with the tensions of US federal democracy and its multidimensionality of divided government. We need to determine how they can couple to generate an overall pattern of limiting the state.

This exercise in conceptualization and complex institutional analysis builds upon a number of theoretical premises and considerations. Furthermore, this inquiry subscribes to the idea that ideas have something to say about political developments. With that in mind, constitutional political ideas in the USA make up one of the main objects of investigation. More precisely, a guiding question is why or to what extent the politicization of the constitutional text relates to the evolution of the institutional framework of the US multidimensional separation of powers, and their combined contribution to both the development and limiting of the American state. The underlying proposition, the hunch of the argument, is that text immanent orientation to the Constitution may have the overall effect of reinforcing the fragmentation that is already immanent in the US constitutional order. In other words, if politics, according to the classic definition by Lasswell (1936), represent an endeavor of "who gets what, when, and how", then this study is concerned with whether politics and political developments in US federal democracy can be a matter of who reads what in the Constitution, when and how.

Approach to the study

The following study explores and conceptualizes the connections between institutions, ideas, and political development. Specific to the case, the study examines the interlinkage between the institutional parameters of the multidimensional division of powers, constitutional political ideas, and their contestation, and the limitation of the state in the US federal democratic polity. The overarching aspiration in the remaining chapters is to assess the ties and tensions between constitutional rules, ideas, and understandings on the one hand, and their politicization within a complex institutional framework on the other. In particular, the notion of immanent fragmentation warrants novel attention. This should prove fruitful for illuminating arrangements of interlinkage between democracy and federalism in the USA. The approach at hand builds on a wealth of existing research on the various aspects of concern here. However, through its conceptual synthesis, and a number of refinements, the study provides an innovative analytical contribution: by interlinking the institutional and ideational dimensions of the political order; by forming the concepts of immanent fragmentation and constitutional text immanence; and by exploring their intertwining with American political development, its system of multilevel divided government, and the overall pattern of a limited state.

To this end, this study builds upon much historical and social science groundwork and theoretical foundations. They make up the focus of the first part of the second chapter and include the theoretical strands of institutionalism, especially its historical and ideational variants. This by no means discounts the significance of interests and other related instrumentalist or "rational" motives, but they will be rather placed in connection with the bounds of institutions. In addition, this section will dig deeper into the motives and mechanisms driving the social construction of political reality, bounded in multidimensional institutional settings. This allows for conceiving, all the more plausibly, regulative ideas and patterns of interpretation. The second part of the chapter establishes the analytical framework. Proceeding from the previously theoretical foundations, it builds upon the research state of the art comprising the main components for the framework: federal dynamics (Benz and Broschek 2013) and the concept of coupling between federalism and democracy (see e.g. Benz and Sonnicksen 2017). Along these lines it will also be demonstrated how the interplay between institutions and ideas provides a fruitful theoretical perspective or lens for the study of continuity and change in democratic federal systems. The combined framework is developed from a comparative perspective, with the purpose of its focused application on the USA.

Chapter 3 explores regulative ideas, and their institutionalization and constitutionalization in the USA in particular. The chapter provides the first application of the analytical framework on the historical evolution of institutional and ideational constellations. Accordingly, it elaborates first the emergence and evolution of regulative ideas, with a view to popular and state sovereignty especially. It then reframes the contested forging of the US Constitution in the context of the already evolving egalitarian referents of both sovereignties and their ideational and institutional underpinnings. Subsequently, contestation of constitutional interpretation is addressed, focusing on a set of different movements or orientations that in parts contradict and in parts overlap one another, namely originalism, textualism, living, and popular constitutionalism. Drawing on these various strands of constitutional-political thinking, a concept of text immanence is elaborated, as regulative idea for interpreting the Constitution. This will be conceived, again, not only as a jurisprudential orientation, but especially as a *political* regulative idea. Consequently, a matter of analytical concern is the ambivalence, the interpretative openness, of the American Constitution. This is certainly given, as with any constitution ultimately. A general survey of the multiplicity and variance of constitutional meanings are beyond the scope of investigation here. Rather the focus lies much more on literal readings and constitutional text faithfulness. What needs to be assessed is what 'high fidelity' to constitutional text entails, in order to capture how it becomes a source of tension and political contestation and a form of political or politicizing interpretation in the US democratic federal order. Thus, Chapter 3 is dedicated to exploring the development of regulative ideas, constitutionalization, and institutional and ideational path dependencies in the USA. This also provides an underpinning for the subsequent analysis of the US political development of a limited state.

The next chapters connect institutional and ideational dimensions in keeping with the analytical framework, in order to assess the parameters of federal and democratic government and their bounded evolution. They provide a condensed analysis on historical and political development of the multidimensional US polity, which will be sorted into three main dimensions, each with a respective chapter: the state and statehood as an overarching linchpin of the political order (Chapter 4), and two further dimensions of government, namely the horizontal, democratic and the vertical, federal division of powers (Chapters 5 and 6 respectively). It is also here that the framework of coupling helps capture tensions and frictions in a democratic federal system. One underlying premise to this concept gained from comparative federal research is how federalism and democracy do not necessarily represent inherently compatible, nor opposing, division-of-power arrangements. However, a state with such high institutional dispersion of powers as the USA may be particularly prone from the outset to generating frictions in democratic contestation across multiple levels of government. Moreover, this may be especially the case when certain political ideas, and constitutional-political text immanence in particular, become activated or preponderant under the framework of a constitution inherited from a late-18th-century context, and thus an increasingly distant time and space.

Building on the preceding analytical steps, Chapter 7 weaves these components together in order to explore how political development is subject to dynamics and mechanisms of immanent fragmentation, why this appears to be increasingly the case, and how they in turn couple with the politics of constitutional contestation. The purpose is to traverse these objects with a particular view to interlinkages, dynamics, and tensions between federal and state governments and with respect to the politicization of the constitution in processes of democratic contestation.

Common to the politics of contesting the federal government is a distinctly constitutional-political perspective that is oriented toward the strict adherence to the text of the Constitution. As such, assorted political groupings find themselves linked, not so much by a particular partisan programmatic-ideological core, as by a political orientation to the constitution – and as will be shown, one that may not necessarily be easy to translate into terms of left and right, or in the US case, simply Democrat and Republican partisan preferences, certainly not over time. The politics of the Constitution underpinned by immanent interpretation can overlap with multiple anti-statist, grass-roots democratic, and republican sentiments and resentments directed chiefly against "Washington" and the institutions of government at the national level. Constitution politics following text faithfulness, however, can likewise gravitate toward different directions such as precisely the expansion of federal governance in the pursuit of realizing constitutional principles, equality in particular. At the same time, these constitutional orientations and their concomitant political movements represent for their part manifestations of more general, deeper lying phenomena. They can be followed far back into the 19th and even 18th centuries, accompanied by recurring shifts in the horizontal and vertical separation-of-powers dimensions. On the one hand, phases and programs extending the powers of and their exercise by the US government have been carried by, and have been even fundamentally reliant on, a respective constitutional interpretation instead of formal amendments. On the other hand, there emerge time and again inverse contesting and competing processes shaped by state and popular sovereignty motives into the present, across multiple political issues, and likewise underpinned by an interpretation of the very same constitutional text.

Finally, the study will conclude with a dual discussion (Chapter 8). In a first step, the threads of analysis will be tied together into a composite picture of immanent fragmentation and its implications regarding American political development and the limited state. Moreover, potential lessons for comparison from a more or less peculiar case will be drawn.

In summary: What lies ahead is a case study that is focused on the USA, but implicitly comparative in its overall approach. A comparative perspective has already been taken above to introduce the points of departure, and comparative reflection will be reapplied intermittently throughout. Comparison will serve as the method of *control*, to construct analytically meaningful concepts and to assess findings as generalizable, or rather distinctive (Sartori 1991; Schmitter 2009). The study derives premises from several theoretical foundations to construct concepts that allow us to make sense of a complex system and its complexly bounded development. To this end, it is also informed by social science and comparative political research, taking mechanistic and macro-configurational approaches to assess context, contingencies, and complex causation (Falleti and Lynch 2009; Gerring 2008; Mahoney and Thelen 2015; Tilly 1984). Translated into terms of a model, the outcome is the limited state in the USA. Complex institutional parameters can certainly explain this, but they cannot explain – especially given the absence of formal constitutional change – why some change regarding the expansion or limitation of federal democratic governance has, at times, occurred. The institutions of multidimensional divided government alone cannot provide the answer for both directions of change, that is the expansion of federal government, its limitation, or even reversal. Additional factors – namely constitutional political ideas and an evolved *thinking in the box* – must be considered in order to grasp these dynamics of immanent fragmentation.

Consequently, the purpose is not to determine one single factor of causality or one direction of causation. The approach embarks on this exploration to pinpoint missing links that can explain change and continuity in US federal democracy and the limited state by its immanent fragmentation. The path of analysis is: elaborating the underlying theoretical foundations and establishing the analytical framework; reconstructing the emergence of the Constitution (its institutional and ideational underpinnings) and forming an ideational concept (text immanence as a regulative idea); exploring the institutional parameters (of the state, federalism, democracy, the politics of the constitution), their intermingled and bounded evolution that reinforces fragmentation of the US polity; assessing how this approach elucidates the ambiguous political development of US federal democracy, but also provides for further comparative potential.

The approach to this study, as applies ultimately to any study, irrespective of the methodological approach (Gerring 2012), amounts to an *argumentation* or a set of arguments. Thus, this study is also ultimately designed to make a case in multiple senses: one which is about the tensions between continuity and change in the American federal democracy, the interplay between ideas and institutions in a complexly bounded constitutional evolution between persistence and fragmentation, and how and why they are compounding to generate a pattern of limiting the state.

Notes

1 Indicative of this constitutional rigidity are not only the comparatively high thresholds for amendments (Art. 5, US Const.), but also the relatively few number of amendments: 27 in over 225 years, the first ten of which comprised the bill of rights added shortly after the ratification of the constitution, leaving just 17 amendments since then.

2 The US system, particularly on account of the presidential system vis-à-vis a bicameral legislature, has been described in comparable terms with negotiation democracy, e.g. as reflected in Neustadt's (1960) dictum of "separate institutions sharing powers" or Sundquist's (1988) concept of "coalition government".

3 While there is much discussion in comparative government on whether semi-presidentialism is a distinct form of government (see e.g. Duverger 1980; Elgie 2011; Lijphart 1992), it is sufficient to point out that I regard semi-presidential systems as a type of parliamentary system of government since, despite the popular election of the head of state, the head of government remains responsible to parliament and its majority in particular.

4 For a more detailed discussion on the emergence of this concept in research on US federalism and in comparative federalism, see e.g. Zimmerman (2001) and Watts (2006) respectively.

5 Constitutional change is addressed further on. In short though, there have been amendments during the 20th century. But since the introduction of a federal income tax and the direct election of senators (16th and 17th amendments respectively, both in 1913), the remaining amendments, with the exception of prohibition (and its repeal), have not concerned specific "federal-state matters", but rather mostly the office of the presidency (e.g. term limits, succession of office) or suffrage rights (e.g. enfranchisement of women, reduction of voting age to 18).

References

Ackerman, Bruce. 1991. *We the People. Volume 1, Foundations*. Cambridge, MA: Belknap, Harvard University Press.

——— 2005. *The Failure of the Founding Fathers. Jefferson, Marshall, and the Rise of Presidential Democracy*. Cambridge, MA: Belknap, Harvard University Press.

——— 2013. *The Decline and Fall of the American Republic*. Cambridge, MA: Belknap, Harvard University Press.

Ansolabehere, Stephen, John M. Hansen, Shigeo Hirano, and James M. Snyder. 2010. "More Democracy: The Direct Primary and Competition in U.S. Elections." *Studies in American Political Development* 24 (2): 190–205.

Appleby, Joyce. 1992. "Rediscovering America's Historic Diversity: Beyond Exceptionalism." *Journal of American History* 79 (2): 419–31.

Bagehot, Walter. 1867 [1974]. *The English Constitution: The Collected Works of Walter Bagehot, Vol. 5*. London: The Economist.

Beer, Samuel. 1973. "The Modernization of American Federalism." *Publius* 3 (2): 49–95.

——— 1993. *To Make A Nation. The Rediscovery of American Federalism*. Cambridge, MA: Belknap, Harvard University Press.

Behnke, Nathalie, Bettina Petersohn, Andrea Fischer-Hotzel, and Dominic Heinz. 2011. "Measuring Success of Constitutional Reforms: Evidence from Territorial Reforms in Eight Western Democracies." *Regional & Federal Studies* 21 (4–5): 447–77.

Béland, Daniel, and André Lecours. 2014. "Fiscal Federalism and American Exceptionalism: Why is there no Federal Equalisation System in the United States?" *Journal of Public Policy* 34 (2): 303–29.

Bellah, Robert, Richard, Madsen, William, Sullivan, Ann Swidler, and Steven Tipton. 1985. *Habits of the Heart. Individualism and Commitment in American Life*. Berkeley: University of California Press.

Benz, Arthur. 1999. "From Unitary to Asymmetric Federalism in Germany: Taking Stock after 50 Years." *Publius* 29 (4): 55–78.

——— 2008. *Der Moderne Staat: Grundlagen der Politologischen Analyse*. 2nd ed. Munich: Oldenbourg.

Benz, Arthur, and Jörg Broschek, eds. 2013. *Federal Dynamics: Continuity, Change, and the Varieties of Federalism*. Oxford: Oxford University Press.

Benz, Arthur, and César Colino. 2011. "Constitutional Change in Federations: A Framework for Analysis." *Regional & Federal Studies* 21 (4–5): 381–406.
Benz, Arthur, and Jared Sonnicksen. 2017. "Patterns of Federal Democracy: Tensions, Friction, or Balance between Two Government Dimensions." *European Political Science Review* 9 (1): 3–25.
Blais, André, Louis Massicotte, and Agnieszka Dobrzynska. 1997. "Direct Presidential Elections: a World Summary." *Electoral Studies* 16 (4): 441–55.
Blatter, Joachim. 2001. "Debordering the World of States: Towards a Multi-Level System in Europe and a Multi-Polity System in North America? Insights from Border Regions." *European Journal of International Relations* 7 (2): 175–209.
Bolleyer, Nicole. 2006. "Federal Dynamics in Canada, the United States, and Switzerland: How Substates' Internal Organization Affects Intergovernmental Relations." *Publius* 36 (4): 471–502.
Bowler, Shaun, and Todd Donovan. 2006. "Direct Democracy and Political Parties in America." *Party Politics* 12 (5): 649–69.
Buchanan, James. 1995. "Federalism as an Ideal Political Order and an Objective for Constitutional Reform." *Publius* 25 (2): 19–27.
Cammisa, Anne M., and Paul Manuel. 2014. *The Path of American Public Policy. Comparative Perspectives*. Lanham: Lexington Books.
Cheibub, José A., Zachary Elkins, and Tom Ginsburg. 2014. "Beyond Presidentialism and Parliamentarism." *British Journal of Political Science* 44 (3): 515–44.
Clemens, Elisabeth. 1997. *The People's Lobby: Organizational Innovation and the Rise of Interest Group Politics in the United States, 1890–1925*. Chicago: University of Chicago Press.
Conlan, Timothy. 1998. *From New Federalism to Devolution. Twenty-Five Years of Intergovernmental Reform*. Washington, DC: Brookings Institute.
——— 2017. "Intergovernmental Relations in a Compound Republic: The Journey from Cooperative to Polarized Federalism." *Publius* 47 (2): 171–87.
Corwin, Edward. 1950. "The Passing of Dual Federalism." *Virginia Law Review* 36 (1): 1–24.
Dahl, Robert. 1956. *A Preface to Democratic Theory*. Chicago: University of Chicago Press.
——— 2003. *How Democratic is the American Constitution?* 2nd ed. New Haven: Yale University Press.
Duverger, Maurice. 1980. "A New Political System Model: Semi-Presidential Government." *European Journal of Political Research* 8 (2): 165–88.
Dyson, Kenneth. 2009. *The State Tradition in Western Europe: A Study of an Idea and Institution*. Colchester: ECPR Press.
Elazar, Daniel. 1962. *American Partnership: Intergovernmental Co-Operation in the Nineteenth-Century United States*. Chicago: University of Chicago Press.
——— 1978. "The Generational Rhythm of American Politics." *American Politics Quarterly* 6 (1): 55–94.
——— 1987. *Exploring Federalism*. Tuscaloosa: University of Alabama Press.
——— 1993. "International and Comparative Federalism." *PS: Political Science and Politics* 26 (2): 190–95.
Elgie, Robert. 2011. "Presidentialism, Parliamentarism and Semi-Presidentialism: Bringing the Parties Back in." *Government and Opposition* 46 (3): 392–409.
Fabbrini, Sergio. 1999. "The American System of Separated Government: An Historical-Institutional Interpretation." *International Political Science Review* 20 (1): 95–116.
——— 2003. "A Single Western State Model?: Differential Development and Constrained Convergence of Public Authority Organization in Europe and America." *Comparative Political Studies* 36 (6): 653–78.

Falleti, Tulia, and Julia Lynch. 2009. "Context and Causal Mechanisms in Political Analysis." *Comparative Political Studies* 42 (9): 1143–66.

Fawcett, Paul, Matthew, Flinders, Colin, Hay, and Matthew Wood, eds. 2017. *Anti-Politics, Depoliticization, and Governance*. Oxford: Oxford University Press.

Gagnon, Alain, and James Tully, eds. 2001. *Multinational Democracies*. Cambridge: Cambridge University Press.

Gerring, John. 2004. "What is a Case Study and What is it Good for?" *American Political Science Review* 98 (2): 341–54.

——— 2008. "The Mechanismic Worldview: Thinking Inside the Box." *British Journal of Political Science* 38 (1): 161–79.

——— 2012. "Mere Description." *British Journal of Political Science* 42 (4): 721–46.

Gerstle, Gary. 2009. "The Resilient Power of the States across the Long Nineteenth Century: An Inquiry into a Pattern of American Governance." In *The Unsustainable American State*, eds. Lawrence Jacobs and Desmond King. Oxford: Oxford University Press, 61–87.

Gourevitch, Peter. 1979. "The Reemergence of "Peripheral Nationalisms": Some Comparative Speculation on the Spatial Distribution of Political Leadership and Economic Growth." *Comparative Studies in Society and History* 21 (3): 303–22.

Hammons, Christopher. 1999. "Was James Madison Wrong? Rethinking the American Preference for Short, Framework-Oriented Constitutions." *American Political Science Review* 93 (4): 837–49.

Hart, Albert B. 1907. "Growth of American Theories of Popular Government." *American Political Science Review* 1 (4): 531–60.

Hofstadter, Richard. 1964. "The Paranoid Style in American Politics." *Harper's Magazine November*: 77–86.

Hueglin, Thomas. 2013. "Comparing Federalism: Variations or Distinct Models?" In *Federal Dynamics: Continuity, Change, and the Varieties of Federalism*, eds. Arthur Benz and Jörg Broschek. Oxford: Oxford University Press, 27–47.

Huntington, Samuel. 1966. "Political Modernization: America vs. Europe." *World Politics* 18 (03): 378–414.

——— 1982. "American Ideals versus American Institutions." *Political Science Quarterly* 97 (1): 1–37.

Immergut, Ellen. 1990. "Institutions, Veto Points, and Policy Results: A Comparative Analysis of Health Care." *Journal of Public Policy* 10 (4): 391–416.

Karch, Andrew, and Shanna Rose. 2019. *Responsive States. Federalism and American Public Policy*. Cambridge: Cambridge University Press.

Kazin, Michael. 1998. *The Populist Persuasion: An American History*. Ithaca: Cornell University Press.

Keating, Michael. 2008. "Thirty Years of Territorial Politics." *West European Politics* 31 (1–2): 60–81.

Kincaid, John. 1990. "From Cooperative to Coercive Federalism." *Annals of the American Academy of Political and Social Science* 509: 139–52.

King, Anthony. 1973. "Ideas, Institutions and Policies of Governments: a Comparative Analysis: Part III." *British Journal of Political Science* 3 (4): 409–23.

King, Desmond, and Robert Lieberman. 2008. "Finding the American State: Transcending the 'Statelessness' Account." *Polity* 40 (3): 368–78.

King, Desmond. 2009. "Ironies of State Building: A Comparative Perspective on the American State." *World Politics* 61 (3): 547–88.

Lasswell, Harold. 1936. *Politics: Who Gets What, When, How*. New York/London: Whittlesey House, McGraw-Hill.

Lehmbruch, Gerhard. 1996. "Die korporative Verhandlungsdemokratie in Westmitteleuropa." *Swiss Political Science Review* 2 (4): 1–24.
Leibfried, Stephan, Evelyne Huber, Matthew Lange, Jonah Levy, Frank Nullmeier, and John Stephens, eds. 2015. *The Oxford Handbook of Transformations of the State*. Oxford: Oxford University Press.
Lijphart, Arend, ed. 1992. *Parliamentary versus Presidential Government*. New York: Oxford University Press.
———, ed. 2002. "Negotiation Democracy Versus Consensus Democracy: Parallel Conclusions and Recommendations." *European Journal of Political Research* 41 (1): 107–13.
———, ed. 2012. *Patterns of Democracy. Government Forms and Performance in Thirty-Six Countries*. 2nd ed. New Haven: Yale University Press.
Linz, Juan. 1990. "The Perils of Presidentialism." *Journal of Democracy* 1 (1): 51–69.
Lipset, Seymour M. 1975. "The Paradox of American Politics." *The Public Interest Fall*: 142–65.
Lipset, Seymour M.. 1991. *Continental Divide: The Values and Institutions of the United States and Canada*. New York: Routledge.
Lorenz, Astrid. 2005. "How to Measure Constitutional Rigidity." *Journal of Theoretical Politics* 17 (3): 339–61.
Lowi, Theodore. 1969. *The End of Liberalism*. New York: W.W. Norton.
——— 1994. "Presidential Democracy in America: Toward the Homogenized Regime." *Political Science Quarterly* 109 (3): 401–15.
Lutz, Donald. 1988. "The United States Constitution as an Incomplete Text." *Annals of the American Academy of Political and Social Science* 496 (1): 23–32.
——— 1994. "Toward a Theory of Constitutional Amendment." *American Political Science Review* 88 (2): 355–70.
Mahoney, James, and Kathleen Thelen, eds. 2015. *Advances in Comparative-Historical Analysis*. Cambridge: Cambridge University Press.
May, Janice. 1987. "Constitutional Amendment and Revision Revisited." *Publius* 17 (1): 153–79.
Mettler, Suzanne. 2011. *The Submerged State: How Invisible Government Policies Undermine American Democracy*. Chicago: University of Chicago Press.
Morgan, Edmund. 1972. "Slavery and Freedom: The American Paradox." *Journal of American History* 59 (1): 5–29.
Nettl, J. P. 1968. "The State as a Conceptual Variable." *World Politics* 20 (4): 559–92.
Neustadt, Richard. 1960. *Presidential Power. The Politics of Leadership*. New York: Wiley.
Niebuhr, Reinhold. 1952 *[2008]. The Irony of American History: With a New Introduction by Andrew J. Bacevich*. Chicago: University of Chicago Press.
Oates, Wallace. 1972. *Fiscal Federalism*. New York: Harcourt, Brace and Jovanovich.
Petersohn, Bettina. 2013. *Konfliktregulierung in multinationalen Demokratien: Föderalismus und Verfassungsreformprozesse in Kanada und Belgien im Vergleich*. Baden-Baden: Nomos.
Pierson, Paul. 1995. "Fragmented Welfare States: Federal Institutions and the Development of Social Policy." *Governance* 8 (4): 449–78.
Pomper, Gerald. 1977. "The Decline of the Party in American Elections." *Political Science Quarterly* 92 (1): 21–41.
Riker, William. 1964. *Federalism: Origin, Operation, Significance*. Boston: Little, Brown and Co.
Roelofs, H. M.. 1992. *The Poverty of American Politics. A Theoretical Interpretation*. Philadelphia: Temple University Press.
Rossiter, Clinton, ed. 1961 *[1999]. The Federalist Papers. Alexander Hamilton, James Madison, John Jay.: With a new Introduction and Notes by Charles R. Kessler*. New York: Penguin.
Sartori, Giovanni. 1991. "Comparing and Miscomparing." *Journal of Theoretical Politics* 3 (3): 243–57.

Scharpf, Fritz. 1988. "The Joint-Decision Trap: Lessons from German Federalism and European Integration." *Public Administration* 66 (3): 239–78.
Schmidt, Manfred. 2002. "Political Performance and Types of Democracy: Findings from Comparative Studies." *European Journal of Political Research* 41 (1): 147–63.
Schmitter, Philippe. 2009. "The Nature and Future of Comparative Politics." *European Political Science Review* 1 (1): 33–61.
Shklar, Judith. 1991. "Redeeming American Political Theory." *American Political Science Review* 85 (1): 3–15.
Skocpol, Theda, and Vanessa Williamson. 2013. *The Tea Party and the Remaking of Republican Conservativism*. Oxford: Oxford University Press.
Skowronek, Stephen. 1982. *Building a New American State: The Expansion of Administrative Capacities, 1877–1920*. Cambridge: Cambridge University Press.
Smith, Rogers M. 1993. "Beyond Tocqueville, Myrdal, and Hartz: The Multiple Traditions in America." *American Political Science Review* 87 (3): 549–66.
Steffani, Winfried. 1979. *Parlamentarische und Präsidentielle Demokratie*. Opladen: Westdeutscher Verlag.
Stepan, Alfred. 1999. "Federalism and Democracy: Beyond the U.S. Model." *Journal of Democracy* 10 (4): 19–34.
Sundquist, James. 1988. "Needed: A Political Theory for the New Era of Coalition Government in the United States." *Political Science Quarterly* 103 (4): 613–35.
Tarr, G. A., ed. 1996. *Constitutional Politics in the States: Contemporary Controversies and Historical Patterns*. Westport, CT: Greenwood.
Tilly, Charles. 1984. *Big Structures, Large Processes, Huge Comparisons*. New York: Russell Sage Foundation.
Tsebelis, George. 1995. "Decision Making in Political Systems: Veto Players in Presidentialism, Parliamentarism, Multicameralism and Multipartyism." *British Journal of Political Science* 25 (3): 289–325.
Verney, Douglas. 1959. *The Analysis of Political Systems*. London: Routledge.
Ware, Alan. 2011. *Political Conflict in America*. New York: Palgrave Macmillan.
Watts, Ronald. 2006. "Origins of Cooperative and Competitive Federalism." In *Territory, Democracy and Justice: Regionalism and Federalism in Western Democracies*, ed. Scott Greer. Basingstoke: Palgrave Macmillan, 201–23.
Wheare, Kenneth. 1963. *Federal Government*. Oxford: Oxford University Press.
Ziblatt, Daniel. 2004. "Rethinking the Origins of Federalism: Puzzle, Theory, and Evidence from Nineteenth-Century Europe." *World Politics* 57 (1): 70–98.
——— 2006. "How Did Europe Democratize?" *World Politics* 58 (2): 311–38.
Zimmerman, Joseph. 2001. "National-State Relations in the Twentieth Century." *Publius* 31 (2): 15–30.
Zvesper, John. 1999. "The Separation of Powers in American Politics: Why We Fail to Accentuate the Positive." *Government and Opposition* 34 (1): 3–23.

2

TOWARDS AN ANALYTICAL FRAMEWORK

An inquiry into the tensions of American federal democracy and the fragmentation of the state touches on several governmental dimensions in a compound polity. They include democracy and federalism as well as the Constitution, their respective developments, and dynamic interplay. Their analysis will build upon a theoretical foundation. The following lays bare an institutionalist-theoretical way of thinking about and studying the political. It bridges more than chooses between a mechanistic and an evolutionary approach. The first part of this chapter revisits theories of neo-institutionalism, and the variants of historical institutionalism and ideational institutionalism, drawing from them a series of premises and concepts. Building on this, the analytical framework, in the second part, conceptualizes the dimensions and the dynamic political development of a democratic federal system of government.

Institutions and ideas: theoretical foundations

With their "rediscovery" several decades ago (March and Olsen 1984, 1989), institutions have come to be viewed not only as objects or phenomena to be captured through rich description, as in "classic institutionalism", they were also to be conceived as variables or other factors and mechanisms influencing the social world (see e.g. Peters 1998). From *neo*-institutionalist perspectives, institutions have interpretive and explanatory capacity regarding the change and continuity of policy, and political and polity outcomes. This complex notion is succinctly epitomized in the well-known dictum that "institutions matter" (Weaver and Rockman 1993). Yet, exactly how institutions really matter is framed in various ways.

A definitive outline of new institutionalism schools by Hall and Taylor (1996) sorts different strands into historical, sociological, and rational-choice institutionalism. They share several precepts on how institutions structure and shape society and politics, but differ on their focuses and understandings of what is embedded

DOI: 10.4324/9781003203674-2

in institutions: historical legacy, immanent values, frames and ways of thinking, or equilibriums and incentive structures (see e.g. Hay 2006; Sanders 2006; Shepsle 2006). Nevertheless, it is possible to infer their basic cross-cutting premises.

Accordingly, institutions can be said to govern, co-determine, or structure social behavior and rules and patterns of decision making (North 1991a). This inference has lent itself to critiques of viewing structures as overly deterministic of human agency (see e.g. Radaelli, Dente, and Dossi 2012). However, no branch of institutionalism reduces social, political, or economic decisions and developments solely to products of institutions. The processes of individual and collective actors reaching decisions and making choices (or not, as the case may be) are understood to be embedded in institutional parameters and a multiplicity of rules (Crawford and Ostrom 1995; Ostrom 1986). Their influence ranges from constraining to enabling, incentivizing to deterring, or shaping, transforming, and even socializing (see e.g. March and Olsen 1996; Scharpf 2000). Institutions thus co-regulate actions, choices, performance, and even thinking.

"Institutions" encompass formal and informal ones and have a basis of legitimacy (see e.g. Lownpes 1996). As the term *institution* already implies, institutionalist approaches are concerned with various *established* things, be they rules, codes of conduct, standard operating procedures, or frames and norms. *Institutionalization* suggests processes that make things static, rigid, or fixed, but institution-centered approaches are concerned with more than impediments to change, or the permanency or immutability of institutions themselves. In addition to the origins and development of institutions, institutionalisms seek to examine the dynamics of processes, continuity, *and* change, and reform or innovative capacity within a given environment (North 1991b). Against this backdrop, an institutionalist approach is particularly suitable for inquiries concerned with the embeddedness of causal factors in complex, multidimensional contexts, including the dimension of time.

History and institutions

From a historical institutionalist perspective, political institutions form through adaptive processes of development over time (Pierson 2000a, 2000b, 2004; Thelen 1999; Thelen and Steinmo 1992). In short, *history matters* for the political world and thus for how to understand and explain it. Choices of the past and institutional legacies are significant for the present and innumerable points in between (see e.g. Béland 2005). Without considering this, one could not really explain many unexpected outcomes or unintended consequences in the present. Taking a longitudinal perspective may imply a dilemma of "infinite regress" (Pierson 2000a: 262–63), as there is no definitive answer on when or to which point in time an analysis should return. Periodization within and comparison between cases though can help address this problem (see e.g. Falleti and Mahoney 2015; Lieberman 2001). Historical institutionalism, as with other neo-institutionalisms, postulates a structuring of politics by institutions, but in particular by institutional legacies. They can contribute for instance to continuity within cases or to persistent divergences between different cases (see e.g. Hall and Taylor 1996: 937–39; Immergut and Anderson 2008). Yet, as Mahoney points out, the claim that *history matters*, on its own, does not reveal much; all social sciences would concur that the past somehow shapes the present (Mahoney 2006: 129–30). The historical institutionalist purpose is not to study history for the sake of studying history. Here, historical analysis serves rather to enable and improve analytical description and explanation of the political present and of how history impacts on politics.

How history matters

Incrementalism and gradual change, timing and sequencing, and, especially, path dependence represent significant concepts of different ways historical development matters for politics. Incrementalism, impediments to large-scale change, or other tendencies to "muddling through" have long been of interest to the study of politics (Lindblom 1959). Tendencies of political inertia, complexity, and limits on ability to achieve change are also relevant for diverse institutionalist analyses. They are conceived in historical institutionalism as part of a general "stickiness" of institutions and structural factors, including their temporality or embeddedness in time (Pierson 2004: 8–9). Interests, preferences, and ideas are important. Yet, they unfold and interact together over time within a larger institutional setting. This "eclectic" view (Hall and Taylor 1996: 940; see also Thelen 1999) means taking ideas, preferences, and interests seriously, but also as contingent upon institutional frameworks. Institutions may be established solutions to collective action problems, and thus products of human choices, though also power relations, and are products of accumulated experience. Once established, institutions tend to be difficult to change for multiple reasons (e.g. high thresholds to reach consensus for reform). Institutions may be said to "take on a life of their own" (Lecours 2005: 9), though not in a vacuum, independent from socio-political action.

Consequently, as argued by Pierson, effects can become causes: institutions, as outcomes or "effects" from a previous point in time, may wind up as the, or at least *a*, "cause"; they do not preclude individual or collective actors' choices, but rather form "the conditions that frame their decisions", providing "strong inducements to make particular choices" (Pierson 1993: 598). As for changing these conditions, Hall and Taylor assert in a similar vein that "institutions are resistant to redesign ultimately because they structure the very choices about reform that the individual is likely to make" (Hall and Taylor 1996: 940). This reflects in part the quintessence of historical-institutionalist thinking on the macro-structural foundations of politics and the significance of temporality. However, while focus is placed on time, and the limits and boundaries of change, institutions are construed, as Immergut points out, as more than mere "products of the sediment of time" (Immergut 2006: 238).

Institutions and institutional frameworks, including rules (formal and informal), procedures, and norms, are established in political structures and the larger political order. Yet, they evolve over time. From this follows a certain "artefactuality" of politics (Immergut and Anderson 2008), with institutions constituting "carriers of history" (David 1994) in general and of allocations (e.g. of power, rules, ideas) "congealed" through experience (Lehmbruch 2000a). Experience accumulates in turn through political contestation around myriad distributions, like goods, values, powers, and rights. These iterative processes tend to render institutions more solidified over time. Change is not absent, but rather *bounded*.

Rationalist-type perspectives see institutions as neutral arbiters, equilibriums of preference distributions, or sets of rules designed purposively for reducing uncertainty or managing complexity. Historical institutionalism does not refute these notions, but views institutions as *more than that*. Institutions are co-determinants of political development and practice. The establishment of institutions and especially a framework for government, as with a constitution, proves formative. History matters, not because the "past" determines the "future", but rather that a formative institutional arrangement like a constitution sets a framework, structuring further development. They entrench rules, distributions and *asymmetries* in powers, and many other structural *biases* – and this in ways that often diverge from institutional intent or design and tend to be difficult, though not impossible, to change.

Mechanisms causing continuity and change

Path dependency makes up a central theoretical concept adopted by and applied in historical institutionalism. The course of institutional evolution is characterized as tending toward gradual change in the long term, but also by a sequence of phases, events, and, intermittently, "critical junctures" (Capoccia and Kelemen 2007; Soifer 2012). Following a formative period of a political system such as drafting the constitution, path dependencies impact the further course of institutional development (see e.g. Broschek 2009: 25ff.; Mahoney 2004: 91ff.). Path dependency easily invites distortions or over-simplifications, like a conflation with the inevitability of a particular development route. But the past per se does not determine political developmental paths. Path dependency is generated over time through interactions within institutions which provide for positive and negative feedback to which actors respond, learn, and adapt. The link between feedback and "increasing returns" (see e.g. North 1991a), positive feedback, and lock-in effects contribute to the consolidation and persistence of particular political paths.

Path dependence, as a concept, as Pierson elaborates, helps us to see beyond the limits of rational, functionalist, or consequentialist explanations:

> In a world of purposive actors, it may indeed be the case that the effects of an institution have something to do with an explanation for its emergence and persistence. Arguments about increasing returns, however, suggest the large dangers in any assumption that an institution arose because it serves some particularly useful purpose. ... Many alternatives to the outcome in question might have been possible, and a dynamic of increasing returns may have

> locked in a particular option even though it originated by accident, or the factors that gave it an original advantage may have long since passed away. Rather than assume relative efficiency as an explanation, we have to go back and look.
>
> (Pierson 2000a: 263–64)

Many factors and mechanisms affecting individual and collective political behavior can be conceived as *endogenous* to the respective system, order, institution, or set of institutions generating path-dependence (Rixen and Viola 2015). Variation and continued divergence abounds in the observable world, as opposed to the convergence toward best models long theoretically expected, in economics in particular. Precisely this had prompted the development of path dependency theory in the first place.

At the same time, as seminally formulated by Bendix, political developments should not be read "backwards", but need to be conceived as fundamentally uncertain; and this applies:

> in the past as well as the present. We do not know where currently observed changes may lead in the long run; hence we must keep the possibility of alternative developments conceptually open. For the present this is relatively easy to do, since we are genuinely uncertain. But the same consideration applies to the past, and here we must be on our guard against the "fallacy of retrospective determinism." The task is complicated by our knowledge of the historical outcome, which makes us more knowing than we have a right to be. The fact is that the eventual development of past social structures was uncertain as well.
>
> (Bendix 1964: 16)

The endpoint of a succession of experiences should not be reconstructed as the definite or inevitable destiny of that path. The "effect" can likely be the incremental consolidation of the path within which the further development had proceeded up to the present. Other "presents" (the futures of the past) could have resulted. At any given point, other decisions or directions of development could have been possible, even if they tended to become decreasingly likely.

Path dependence points towards complex causation within cases as well as between cases and thus "different worlds" of politics, that is the variety among different systems that persists despite the possibilities and practices of cross-country or otherwise cross-border and cross-environment diffusion, learning, or adaptation (see e.g. Berman 1998; Broschek 2014; Hall and Soskice 2001; Pierson 1995; Thelen 2004). These detected paths represent more "corridors" of available options and routes in further development, though which tend to become more restrictive or constricted over time (see e.g. Broschek 2012a: 105; Immergut and Anderson 2008: 359). This result is explainable by choices too, but ones embedded in self-reinforcing endogenous mechanisms at play.

Between critical junctures and gradual change

"Critical juncture" refers to events or instances that interrupt or disturb a development course. These types of events, turning points, crises, or similar represent a relatively short period in time which opens a window of opportunity for larger change. This bears resemblance to the concept of "punctuated equilibrium", a notion of change adopted chiefly from evolutionary theories, aiming primarily to capture dynamics of policy-making processes (Baumgartner and Jones 1993). For historical institutionalism and path dependency theory in particular, critical junctures may punctuate, shift, or alter a path of development. The effect of a critical juncture rather is to weaken or loosen the constraining effects of path-dependent institutions (Capoccia and Kelemen 2007: 342) which are generally prone to inertia, "stickiness", and continuity or resistance to change. Critical junctures can elicit new conditions or circumstances that open room for maneuver to change power structures, rules, or other institutional parameters.

The contestation that plays out under these circumstances, moreover, is not only limited to conflicts of interests and the (re-)allocations of powers. They can also revolve – and often do – around ideas and norms (Capoccia 2015: 160–65). The existing institutions remain all the while in place until change is achieved, or they manage to persist in the end. This intersection or crossroads does not cause, but rather can facilitate, change. As Capoccia and Kelemen point out further, "if an institution enters a critical juncture, in which several options are possible, the outcome may involve the restoration of the pre-critical juncture status quo" (Capoccia and Kelemen 2007: 352). Consequently, it may be difficult or impossible to determine critical junctures in retrospect. The critical events can (and often do) result in little to no noticeable change, while large changes can (and often do) emerge out of rather 'ordinary' times. Critical junctures and path dependence are different things (Pierson 2000a: 263; Rixen and Viola 2015: 316–18). Change in a critical juncture involves an intervention in those mechanisms otherwise causing path dependence. As Soifer posits, the "permissive conditions" triggered by a critical juncture need to be transformed into "productive conditions" to elicit change (Soifer 2012: 1573–76). Constitutional amendment procedures may be necessary when constitutionally entrenched rules are the object of revision; or if instead such rules require revision in order to attain other aspired changes.

In addition to critical junctures and surrounding conditions at a certain point in time, the "critical antecedents", that is the preceding factors, conditions, and developments impact on political developments (Slater and Simmons 2010). Whether a critical or otherwise momentous event is experienced or perceived as such in the first place is fundamentally context dependent. For whatever constitutes a critical juncture in one period may be utterly unspectacular in other ones, even under the same or similar conditions. The effect of an *exogenous* cause will depend on *endogenous* factors. This points toward contingency, particularly between "politics in time" (Pierson 2004) and institutions, and between, not only *which*, but also *when* political things happen, and *where* (cf. e.g. Tilly 1984). Context conditions can become permissive or restrictive to change. They are not limited to the conditions at or around one time, but include multiple background conditions, for example structural, institutional, as well as temporal ones, those prior, preceding, or *antecedent* in particular.

Summary

A historical-institutional approach takes a diachronic perspective to explain change and continuity. The two are not merely results of purposive action and design, but also gradual and incremental developments, which may lead to unintended consequences. As such, historical institutionalism bears some affinity to evolutionary theories (Lustick 2011). The usage of "evolution" in institutionalist scholarship though is often more metaphorical and interpretive in its usage (Cairney 2013; Ma 2016). There are nevertheless parallels, given the analytical attention to the origins, variety, and continuity of institutions as well as their interruption or "punctuation" by critical junctures where responses, change, and adaptation do occur, but not necessarily for conscious functional reasons. The evolutionary perspective is likewise underlined by the conceptualization of gradual change, sequences, and paths of development that can take different types of change (Falleti and Lynch 2009; Hacker, Pierson, and Thelen 2015). Changes and adaptations do not follow necessarily a logic of optimization or some "survival of the fittest" (the latter incidentally also represents a common misconception of evolutionary theory). This understanding of complex causation renders the context of developmental processes all the more important.

An historical institutional approach places an emphasis on the factor of time and the manifold contingencies of political development. We may still posit that "things always happen for a reason". Yet what that cause is cannot necessarily be isolated from a larger context, particularly in the complex world of politics and political systems. Furthermore, continuity in political systems may tend overall to outweigh observable change. What we in the long term or over time construe as continuity demands differentiation nonetheless. Institutional continuity is actually generated in constant tensions between learning, change, and adaptation on the one hand, and an array of mechanisms fostering persistence and inertia on the other. Path dependency is not limited to persistence alone, but also to change within institutional arrangements and particular types or directions of change and further development.

Ideas also constitute an additional dimension and set of mechanisms at play (Hall and Taylor 1996: 942, 957; 1998). They can be pivotal not least with regard to institutional persistence. Interpretations and collective ideas emerge that can rationalize the status quo. They may legitimize the distribution of power and relations between bodies and levels of government. All the while, fundamental rules become entrenched in constitutional law, and patterns of interaction consolidate through repeated, habitualized collective action that follows standard operating procedures – all of which contribute to forming ways of thinking about and within given institutional arrangements (Lecours 2005: 3–18). This ties into historical legacy as the explanation for political development as various preferences, ideas, and interests among individual and collective actors operating within institutional settings are somehow conditioned by those very settings.

Ideas and institutions

The classic definition by Easton sees politics as "the authoritative allocation of values" (Easton 1953) within or for a society. In addition to material, socio-economic ones, politics is concerned with immaterial values, whether as norms, beliefs, principles, or myriad moral, ethical, and identity orientations. Politics also involves the contestation of concepts, meanings, and "semantic struggle" (Koselleck 1982: 410–15). Institutions establish and, over time, shape rules and various distributions (e.g. of power, power asymmetries, and resources). But they also comprise distributions of immaterial values and patterns or "constellations of meanings" (Broschek 2016). This points to a complex nexus between ideas, institutions, and political development.

These preliminary remarks run deep and wide. Sociological, psychological and social-psychological findings are foundational for conceptualizing and analyzing social institutions. This bears relevance not only for the study of e.g. political culture, electoral behavior, political trust, or identity, but also for neo-institutionalism specifically. Like historical institutionalism, ideational-institutional approaches emphasize complexity of causation, as institutions bound or shape choices and preferences and even the scope of *imaginable* alternatives (Lecours 2005: 9–11). Ideational here serves as an umbrella term for diverse approaches focusing on "ideas", be they meanings, frames, discourses, or paradigms (see e.g. Koning 2016). The following extracts theoretical premises – on social construction and cognition, bounded rationality, and the logic of appropriateness – and outlines ideational institutionalism.

Social construction

Facts and knowledge are embedded in social contexts (Abbott 2004: 162–91). The "facts of life" can only be deemed as such when attributed value or meaning by and within a social context (see e.g. Searle 2005). This represents at least part of the gist of social construction. Theories of social construction draw from a diverse foundation of social scholarship. The variety of perspectives is concerned with interconnections between social structures, forms of and paths to knowing, social discourse, and relations of power. They draw, on the other hand, quite different inferences on the shaping and bounding effects of these interlinkages and their (trans)formative potential.[1] Rather than choose sides, basic cross-cutting premises of social construction can be adopted for analyzing the (perceptions of) institutional developments. I will proceed in this vein.

Path-dependency or rational-purposive choices offer important frames for assessing patterns of politics. However, making and following rules, decisions, or similar can likewise be explained in terms of *learning* and *socialization*. Such processes entail the internalization of norms, values, and other cognitive patterns of orientation. This suggests at least two types of contingencies: temporal and structural ones. The transmission, perception, interpretation, and ultimately production of reality are collectively and relationally mediated (see e.g. Berger and Luckmann 1966; Searle 1995). Thus knowledge and knowing are structured spatially, temporally, and intersubjectively, and in a continuous exchange between internalization and externalization (Berger and Luckmann 1966: 19–34). In brief, actions and interactions (externalizations) take place in institutionalized settings. Institutional arrangements do not solely determine them, nor are institutions static as they are made and evolve precisely through externalizations.

Social construction encompasses multiple specific mechanisms of "social cognition" (Bless, Fiedler, and Strack 2004; Kunda 1999). They operate in the interactions of social life. They include forms of *communication*, *representations*, *attributions*, *identity formations*, and *legitimations* (see e.g. Hewstone and Augoustinos 1998; Moscovici 1988). These processes occur repeatedly and on individual, intersubjective, and collective bases. How these processes play out relates to human and interpersonal traits, but they are also contingent upon contexts, situations, and environments, which also include "shared beliefs", that is collective ideas shared in (parts of) society (Bar-Tal 2000). Social construction mechanisms apply in general across space and time. Their manifestations also depend though on the complexity of the given society and political order (Berger and Luckmann 1966: 163–73), a particularly important point for political institutional analysis (cf. e.g. Tilly 1984; Tilly and Goodin 2006). To understand political development also warrants grasping further *why* these mechanisms have impact.

Rationality and its bounds

The motives of social construction and cognition do not necessarily contradict the classic rational-actor model. They rather point to different logics and motives of decision and sense making such as *consistency*, *explanation* and *prediction*, and *conservation* (Fiske and Taylor 2013). These mechanisms suggest that "thinking is for doing" (Fiske 1992).[2] However, *doing* can involve different purposes, such as: to reduce complexity and make sense of a host of others (people, places, phenomena, things) and one's relation to them; to fulfill various roles; or to adapt any of the above under different settings (Fiske and Taylor 2013; Kunda 1999). Multiple motives and mechanisms are exhibited not just across but rather also within individuals and in more or less automatic or controlled fashions (Banse and Greenwald 2007; Kahneman 2011). These insights and premises also suggest that potentials for conflicts and dilemmas loom in countless situations and settings. This is especially pertinent in the context of a *bounded rationality* in political institutional life.

The classic rational model views decision making as a sequence of setting goals, formulating strategies, and predicting likelihoods of the outcomes they could have. The theory of bounded rationality integrates constraints, pertaining to information and calculation, and organizational complexity in the case of collective actors (Simon 1959). These bounds are particularly relevant for theories of social choice, political game, and principal-agent theories, which precede from the rational utility motive, but under complex conditions and institutions (see e.g. Austen-Smith and Banks 1998; Jones 1999; Miller 2005). Yet, as postulated by Simon, actors also often opt to "satisfice", or make do with "enough", and apply mental shortcuts to reduce problem and problem-solving complexity, save time, or for information gathering and processing efforts, instead of seeking more or the optimum.

However, social cognition and its mechanisms point to various other purposes like making sense, finding consistency, or fulfilling roles. From the institutionalist perspective too, the bounds to rationality include, but also extend beyond, circumstances or conditions otherwise constraining rationality in a utility-oriented sense (see e.g. Schweers Cook and Levi 1990) – e.g. factors like limited information, computational errors, or goal conflicts. Other motives, logics, and norms – from justice, equality, fairness, or "what is right", to roles and identities – are at play. These premises point to how the logic of appropriateness affects the very "life" of and in political institutions.

Appropriateness and institutional logics

As March and Olsen summarize, rational and utilitarian perspectives tend to frame social and political dynamics and outcomes as matters of calculated choice, with instrumentalist logics of competition, efficiency, and optimization in general, and with the direction of institutional development viewed as explainable in functional terms (March and Olsen 1989: 4–16). The logic of appropriateness, on the other hand, conceives rule-based behavior as organized in institutions (March and Olsen 2009). It accommodates the mechanisms of social cognition, rule interpreting and following, and the role of sense making in decision making, interpretation, and other forms of action.

The neo-institutional concept of logics of appropriateness aims to extend rather than replace other perspectives (see e.g. Olsen 2001: 191). Divergences from rational-consequential expectations are not just deficits or disturbances, but rather *features* of behavior in institutional frameworks. Norms, rules, roles, and routines contribute to shaping decision making and more generally interpretation and judgment, each with its own rationality (March 1994). Thus problem, task, or other decisional contexts are also approached in attempts to comply with the appropriate behavior, which may be variably defined. The logic of appropriateness is concerned more with obligation (rules, roles, norms, identity), and thus the search for correctness or suitability of actions in situations (March and Olsen 1989: 23ff.). Conceiving actors as maximizers of utility suggests their preferences are *endogenous* and their interactions resemble more exchanges and "games", with institutions posing *exogenous* "rules of the game". From the appropriateness perspective, action and interaction are oriented toward for example norms, roles, and rules, which are shaped by institutions. The heuristics and corresponding searches are applied to achieve *consistency*, for example between current and past situations, norms and practice, and rules and problems at hand, to assess appropriate options (March and Olsen 1989: 160–62).

The referents of appropriateness are embedded in the institutions themselves: for example temporally, structurally, ideationally (Hall and Taylor 1996: 948–50). They evolve out of accumulated social interactions and experiences that become represented, encompassed, and institutionalized, for example in formal and informal rules and habitualized practices (Lownpes 1996: 191–92). Viewed together with historical institutionalism, institutions foster particular patterns of assessing appropriateness. These institutional parameters provide for a set of limiting "bounds" as much as a "breeding ground" for ideational dynamics. Bounds are as much boundaries and limits as they are features and environs. Legitimacy becomes possible, not only through outcomes (ends justifying means), but rather through processes and practices themselves embedded in institutions. This adds a normative dimension to institutions, especially political ones, which structure and regulate life in a polity. This also warrants taking ideas and their interconnection with institutions seriously.

Ideational institutionalism

The evaluations, values, and even interests of actors vis-à-vis institutions and each other are formed and transformed by experiences and interactions within institutional frameworks (see e.g. Hay 2011). A vast growth of research addresses the impact of ideas on political developments (Béland and Cox 2011: 4ff.). While there are multiple strands, I adopt the umbrella term *ideational* institutionalism (cf. e.g. Koning 2016).[3] Ideas have been considered as a co-influencing factor in other strands of theory, whether as contingent upon historical developments and the respective structural-functional path dependencies, or rather as subject to instrumentalization by actors (e.g. their strategic 'usage' of ideas to advance political interests). The "ideational turn" (Blyth 1997, 2003) in political science implies instead a concept of ideas as significant in their own right.

That "ideas matter" does not imply that they pose solely determinant factors, resist change, or cause persistence on their own. How they matter for political outcomes and development depends likewise on conditions, circumstances, constellations of actors and institutions, and their interplay with these ideas (see e.g. Mehta 2011). Ideational approaches take a more intermediary approach between structure and agency, tying in ideas for example as norms, beliefs, and worldviews – which are certainly held at the micro-level by individual and collective actors – into a more macro-structural study of political developments (see e.g. Berman 2001). Ideas can take on myriad types of influence, from stabilizing the status quo to fostering change. Accounts taking ideas seriously, as posited by Lieberman, tend less to be "a story of variables", but more "of configuration, not of ordered patterns of ideas *or* institutions in equilibriums, but of disjunction, friction, and overlap among ideational and institutional elements" (Lieberman 2002: 709). While ideational dynamics and political developments may appear in synch at times, they reveal, perhaps more often than not, a *Gleichzeitigkeit des Ungleichzeitigen*, or simultaneity of unsimultaneous things, "lags", and contradictions.

What constitutes ideas in the first place is ultimately ambiguous (Schmidt 2008: 304ff.). All the same, it is necessary to determine what ideas are as much as, or as far as possible, what ideas do. As proposed by Parsons, ideas can be construed as some form of claim about something else, in descriptive, analytical, explanatory or normative terms, or combinations thereof (Parsons 2002: 48ff.). They describe what is, ascribe qualities or features, or explain how something relates, for instance causally or otherwise correlationally, to other things. Ideas can also have imaginative facets, or normativity with regard to evaluating others or even the ideas themselves (e.g. "good" or "bad" ideas). Moreover, ideas individually and in sets, as with ideologies, work or operate in compounded fashions (see e.g. Freeden 2008). This applies also on account of developments over time, for one, and from individual as well as social learning, for another (Matthijs and Blyth 2018: 111ff.). This does not preclude viewing ideas or ideational elements in isolation. However, especially vis-à-vis politics, ideas need to be comprehended together with other factors. Political ideas as part of worldviews, ideologies, or party programs serve to connect individuals and groups of people to political communities and institutions (Berman 2011: 105ff.). They become embedded in an interrelational and trans-subjective political dimension.

Some ideas are more at an individual level, others at a collective or macro-level, or at multiple levels simultaneously (Berman 2013: 223–27). From the institutionalist perspective, even individual "beliefs" are interlinked with the broader institutional framework, endowed with its own "institutional memory", which shapes how actors gain experience and ultimately "interpret the world" (March and Olsen 1989: 40–46). Ideas may also be conceived as *explicit* and salient, or rather *implicit* and in the background. Ideational approaches also confront puzzles, for example referring to the persistence of differences across cases facing similar circumstances or challenges; within cases as to why under comparable circumstances changes occurred at one time, but not later; or why change occurs against all the odds in certain cases. In addition to temporal, structural, and functional dimensions, institutions also have an ideational one and, as such, serve as "carriers" or "repositories" of ideas. This theoretical perspective endogenizes both power and ideas within institutional bounds, as well as contestation revolving around meanings (Schmidt 2008, 2010).

Finally, three main premises on ideas and institutions can be summarized. *First*, ideas have power (Béland 2010; Parsons 2016), but not necessarily due to their plausibility, objectifiable validity, or some normative (moral, ethical) superiority they must demonstrate in order to exude such power. Their impact can also manifest, *secondly*, through and due to their institutionalization. Those ideas are not necessarily stable, but rather prone to induce contestation or develop through incremental change (see e.g. Carstensen 2011, 2012). *Third*, the coupling between institutions and ideas ultimately amounts to *political order*, that is as "a regular, predictable, and interconnected pattern of institutional and ideological arrangements that structures political life in a given place at a given time" (Lieberman 2002: 702). A political order does not always resist change, nor is continuity in the aggregate necessarily the product of stability. Instead, institutional arrangements, embedded in larger political orders, likewise comprise "meaning constellations" (Broschek 2016). They shape, prompt, and reinforce particular patterns and ways of thinking. These constellations also invite political contestation, especially since they host multiple, concurring, and contradicting ideas which can change over time.

Summary: the complex dynamics of institutions and ideas

Institutions matter, while patterns of meaning, interpretation, and thinking about politics are also matters concerning institutions. Diverse rules in a political community and logics of appropriateness are embedded in institutional settings that have evolved over time, through experience and with a dynamic interplay between norm and rule establishment in tensions between change and continuity. Ideas range from frames, referents of appropriateness, accounts and narratives, or regulative ideas among many others, for one, while they may combine to form patterns of interpretation and meaning constellations, for another. The theory of social construction defines institutionalization as an intersubjective phenomenon, but also one evolving over time, yet dependent on historical legacy. Institutionalization couples the dimensions of micro-, intersubjective, and structural levels with space and temporality. Hence, in short: "It is impossible to understand an institution adequately without an understanding of the historical process in which it was produced" (Berger and Luckmann 1966: 54-55). This points to the nexus of ideas, institutions, and powers.

Ideas and ideational orientations may become locked in at a certain point in time, and subsequently take on a life of their own. That life, however, is a dynamic one. It unfolds in tensions with multiple forces over time – new empirical challenges, new information, altering ideas and ways of thinking. At the same time, institutionalization implies that a distribution of the powers of the past has been entrenched. The way things *are* often tend to be considered in terms of how they also *should* be. This complicates matters all the more so in the political realm. Issues regarding reform, change, or other adaptations of the existing rules are not resolved by the "best" idea or argument alone, but become intertwined with questions of power and the assessment of its (im)balance or (re)distribution.

Political things are interpreted and reinterpreted over generations by myriad actors: for example individuals and groups of citizens, and collective actors like political parties, officers in government and public administrations, and civil society organizations. The spectrum of interpretations is vast. How they manifest ranges from a rather seamless internalization of the given order's ideas, to its being called fundamentally into question, or rather giving new meanings to and legitimizing established ways of organizing and doing politics. The institutionalization of a particular distribution (of values, norms, powers) may be widely deemed legitimate at some time. However, changing social, economic, and political conditions, or changing values, attitudes, and perceptions can call their appropriateness into question. This may bring different and new actors into contestation. That process in all likelihood will transpire due to conflicts of interest, but also differences in the evaluation of the appropriateness, correctness, and ultimately legitimacy of a particular institutional arrangement, specific rules, norms, or distribution of powers. How political order develops, as these theoretical foundations suggest and substantiate, is both complexly bounded and dynamic.

The linkage between institutions and ideas is manifold. To capture this invites a recourse to neo-institutionalism theory, and historical and ideational institutionalisms in particular. As Blyth asserts, social and political life constitute "a world of knots and spheres, but without attending to ideas, social scientists are equipped to see only right angles and squares" (Blyth 2011: 83). The above review of neo-institutionalism exposed further knots and spheres in political life. We can conceive them as multiple dimensions of boundedness. They derive from processes of institutionalization in general and historical development in particular. As succinctly posited by Hay: "Institutions are built on ideational foundations that exert an independent path-dependent effect on their subsequent development" (Hay 2011: 69). The trajectory of path dependency in institutions affects ideas, but extends much further.

Time, history, and historical legacy impact on politics and the political order, and on how rules and many ideas become embedded in institutional arrangements: from the constitution and constitutional norms, to specific institutions, and formal and informal rules. Institutions, as "carriers of history" and accumulated experience (David 1994), also consolidate distributions – of powers, resources, as well as values, including immaterial ones. Institutions shape the corridors of political development, due to their high thresholds to change, or other factors like increasing returns, lock-in effects, or processes of socialization and learning over time. Institutional settings bound subsequent adaptation processes and the dynamic interplay between change and continuity. Hence institutions also provide settings toward and within which adaptation transpires over time, as well as the "grammar" underlying these processes.

Patterns of interpretative, descriptive, analytical, and normative orientations are constructed over time and become embedded within their own institutional contexts. Institutions are formed by ideas which in turn are shaped by and evolve within institutional settings. These co-evolutionary processes are characterized by, and thus understandable and explainable by, interdependence and mutual influence. From this follows, drawing on Olsen, a complex understanding of and a "way of thinking about" politics and political development (Olsen 2009, 2013). The corresponding political analysis accepts the complex causal premise of "it depends" (Tilly and Goodin 2006). Complex causation means that various dimensions and multiple contingencies make up the boundedness of politics. These contingencies include temporal, structural, and functional as well as ideational ones.

Finally, I derive another premise from the prior review of ideas, institutions, their historical development, and dynamic interplay: there is a difference between what an institution *does* and what it is *there for*. "Does" (e.g. action and function) and "there for" (e.g. purpose and origin) often tend to be treated synonymously. But an institution is not there *just because* it does something, and not necessarily on account of what it *is doing* now. This may become apparent when also asking why *something else* is not there to do it. Herein lies a knot located in a sphere. The origins of institutions do not necessarily match their purposes, functions, and meanings in the present. However, that does not always stop us from assuming otherwise.

Scholars and citizens continuously (re-)evaluate, (re-)interpret, attribute purposes and even causes, and find and give meaning to political institutions, irrespective of where they come from, how they changed, whether they fulfill their intents, or not. Attributions and inferences can be and are constantly made with awareness and knowledge of how things came into being and evolved, or rather on the surface of things. At the same time, awareness of what lies beneath the surface fails to guarantee that it rests on an accurate description or valid inference. The language of institutions can be spoken with or without consciously knowing the rules, while also knowing the rules does not mean they are easy to change, even when "better" rules are not only imaginable, but also readily available for adoption. Last but not least, *democratic* systems endogenize principles and notions of equality and liberty and link them to inclusion, representation, and participation in particular. They make mass affairs out of participation in the polity, as well as in the processes of finding meaning in, forming, having, and expressing opinions, values, preferences, or myriad types of ideas. Similar in principle, but with different points of reference, this also applies to federal systems.

Framing federalism and democracy: linkages and dynamics

The Prologue raised the question of why change in the wake of the 2008 elections in the USA wound up so limited, despite prior instances of major reform under comparable and such seemingly favorable political conditions. A readily available answer could lie in the Constitution and the multiple divisions of powers in US federal democracy. But this would leave unanswered why extensive changes can also occur under the very same constitution. To address the deeper question on the limited state in the USA requires an adequate analytical framework. To this end, neo-institutional theories, historical and ideational institutionalism in particular, have been elaborated. Building on those premises, the following lays out the analytical framework for the rest of the study. To this end, it draws on comparative federalism and government research, the dynamic institutional approach to federal dynamics, and on concepts of the interlinkage or "coupling" between federalism and democracy.

Dynamic institutionalism

The concept of *federal dynamics* (Benz and Broschek 2013b) provides a theory of "dynamic institutionalism". It integrates multiple levels of analysis. It also draws on comparative federalism and government insights in general and institutionalism theories in particular (Benz and Broschek 2013a). The view of federal systems as dynamic is hardly an obvious or standard outlook. For a long time, a more static view of the layers of government was predominant, with sparse differentiation between federalism as a system or process. By that token, federal systems were considered inherently prone to rigidity and immobility, given their multiple levels of government, each endowed with partial sovereignty, the scope of authority and competences, or checks and balances. Earlier research instigating a shift in perspective did not discount these structural default settings of federal state organization, but considered them also as potentially *dynamic* features of federalism (Benz 1985; Elazar 1985; Friedrich 1968; Landau 1973). The dynamic institutionalism perspective expands the layers of federalism to include actor constellations, state–society relations, and normative–ideational relations, those deriving from the federal constitution in particular (Benz and Broschek 2013c).

Dynamic institutionalism echoes neo-institutional propositions which frame political development in more evolutionary terms. Movement is constant, and change in federal systems occurs. Paths of development and specific changes follow different, often competing and divergent, logics, but not necessarily toward optimization, advancement, or progress. Change may be prone to a gradual, incremental sort. Even when continuity in the long term appears, tensions and dynamics recur. They emerge on account of the multiple federal layers. We may construe these parameters in neo-institutional terms as multiple *bounds* and *contingencies* which shape political development. Accordingly, federalism can be conceived as a complex system of adaptation (see also Bednar 2011), in which the bounds are multiple and refer not only to territorial ones, but also to distribution of power, authority, and concrete policy-making competences. The ensuing dynamics unfold through collective action in various and recurring, though not necessarily synchronous and compatible, fashions.

Dynamic institutionalism posits an interconnection between actor-constellations, state–society relations, and the distribution of power in historically evolved and bounding institutional settings (Benz 2013; Benz and Broschek 2013c). Accordingly, the interplay between the multiple layers generates federal dynamics. With regard to the ideational layer:

> Institutions are formed by collective ideas legitimizing the allocation of power in a federal polity, by patterns of interaction consolidated in standard operating procedures through repeated collective action and by rules usually entrenched in a federal constitution.
>
> (Benz and Broschek 2013a: 369)

This inference underlines mutual influence, co-evolution, and boundedness for one. It factors in the mechanisms causing change and continuity as in historical institutionalism for another.

The ideational layer, though, as framed above appears somewhat ambivalent. It is formulated as a distinct layer, but linked particularly to the federal constitution. This points to a gap regarding the ideational dimension of and complex interlinkage with other sources in federal dynamics. One ideational source, again, is the constitution and its federal ideas in particular. Adding *interpretation* as a mechanism of federal dynamics is decisive for the analytical framework here. Different mechanisms link in different ways the society, individual and collective actors, and levels as much as various branches of government in a federal system. This proposition holds on account of the multilayered configuration of federalism, whether in federal systems proper or in other "non-centralistic" (Elazar 1985, 1987) polities. These mechanisms warrant a more explicit delineation here, and with a specific view to democracy.

Democracy and multiple facets of democratic politics are considered in the *federal dynamics* framework, but without translating them into a specific dimension or layer. This is neither surprising nor inconsistent, given its focus on *federal* dynamics, which are also relevant to authoritarian or other non-democratic federations. Despite a long-held inference in political science on the compatibility between federalism and democracy (cf. e.g. Lijphart 1979; Watts 2008), federalism is both conceptually and empirically possible in authoritarian regimes and other non-democratic systems (Gibson 2013; Obydenkova and Swenden 2013). The dynamic institutionalism framework, while not limited to democracy outright, does consider the special complexity for federal dynamics with democracy:

> [F]ederalism and democracy have different implications for actors and different effects on policy-making which often produces conflicts. Federalism constitutes an arena of intergovernmental relations characterized by territorial interests. In the arena of democratic government, politics is predominantly conducted by competing parties, as well as executives responsible to parliaments and the electorate. Hence a democratic federation is characterized by built-in tensions between arenas of inter- and intra-level governance.
>
> (Benz and Broschek 2013a: 372)

This points to the analytical appropriateness of an explicit and systematic delineation of federalism and democracy as distinct dimensions of government. For another, it depicts their relationship in differentiated terms, that is neither normative advantages nor propensities to mutual enhancing effects are presumed. For the analytical approach at hand, a resort to an additional framework is necessary that places precisely those dynamics and tensions between federalism and democracy at the forefront.

Federal and democratic government

There is a long tradition in political thought according to which federalism and other non-centralistic divisions of powers harmonize with and even reinforce democracy (see e.g. Burgess and Gagnon 2010; Gerring, Thacker, and Moreno 2005: 567–69). The US model, as the forerunner of modern federalism combined with a republican government, contributed to the emergence of this view (cf. also e.g. Hueglin 2013). In theory as well, a federal system's multiple levels of government has been said to provide comparatively more opportunities for "voice" and participation than unitary systems.[4] In addition to voice, federalism may offer more opportunities for "exit", both of which can engender competition fostering policy innovation and "laboratories of democracy" (Kochen and Deutsch 1969; Oates 1972).[5] Other democratic-promoting features attributed to federalism include stronger safeguards to liberty and the rule of law (see e.g. Hueglin and Fenna 2015: 41ff.; Levy 2007) and a built-in capacity to accommodate diversity and minority groups (see e.g. Kincaid 2010; Kymlicka 2001). However, there is substantial potential for tensions and incongruities between federalism and democracy.

Federal democracies face complex dynamics, tensions, and frictions. At the bottom line, federalism neither automatically facilitates, nor deteriorates, democracy, and the inverses apply, or rather do not, with regard to the impact of democracy on federalism (Benz and Sonnicksen 2015). The US case already has exemplified various types of outcomes, including the extremely undemocratic and abominable one of slavery. The relationship between federalism and democracy is rather a complex, even tense, one. Combining federalism and democracy in one political system means, in turn, combining different institutional arrangements, logics, and mechanisms. As Benz proposes, the types and modes of their interlinkage can be subsumed under the concept of the *coupling* (Benz 2009, 2015) of federalism and democracy. To comprehend these interlinkages, it is imperative to distinguish, first, the federal and democratic dimensions distinctly, their respective institutional arrangements, and their coinciding mechanisms.

A full elaboration of federalism and democracy would present a monumental task. Each exhibits different theoretical and practiced models as well as diverse mixtures. Such an exhaustive survey is beyond the scope of this analytical framework. Instead, by drawing from the relevant comparative research (see e.g. Benz 2009, 2013, 2015; Benz and Broschek 2013a, 2013c; Benz and Sonnicksen 2015, 2017; Sonnicksen 2018), it is possible to delineate compactly the democratic and federal government dimensions and their own structural-functional logics.

Democracy and federalism are not the same as the separation of powers, but they each constitute a type thereof. They represent two different arrangements or ordering principles for the division of powers: *democracy* as a *horizontal* division of powers between branches in one government, *federalism* as a *vertical* division between governments. The democratic dimension is rather *intragovernmental*, regulating relations within one government (i.e. between the legislative, executive, and judicial branches), and federalism rather *intergovernmental*, organizing relations between levels of governments (i.e. between the superordinate or central and the constituent-unit or state governments). The dichotomy between the horizontal and intragovernmental for democracy, and that between the vertical and intergovernmental for federalism, refer chiefly to structural ordering. In political processes and practices, the lines between intra- and intergovernmental or horizontal and vertical intersect.

This outline of federalism and democracy requires the further conceptual differentiation of each dimension too. The separation of power already implies its partition. Yet this alone reveals little about specific distributions of powers, which can take variable forms. Following the federal dynamics framework, federal arrangements can be distinguished on a spectrum between "shared rule" and "self-rule" (Benz and Broschek 2013a, 2013c). Shared and self-rule coincide with more cooperative or interlocking and more competitive or separating in federalism respectively. A similar situation can apply to differentiating democracy. The spectrum of the division of powers in democratic government analogously spans between shared rule and self-rule or rather power-separating and power-sharing forms (Benz and Sonnicksen 2017: 8–10; cf. also Nagel 2000). While the lines between the different core propensities blur in many institutional features and certainly in practice, the following outline should provide a useful frame for mapping democratic and federal institutional arrangements.

The democratic governmental dimension

The variety of democratic systems and certainly theories is almost inexhaustible. For the context at hand though, and institutionally viewed, democratic *government* is understood as relating primarily to the organization of relations between executive and legislative institutions grounded in recurring popular elections. The spectrum of division of powers spans from the strict *separation* between the legislative and executive branches to the more fluid, fused, and *shared* ones. Drawing on comparative government literature (see e.g. Cheibub and Limongi 2002; Elgie 2011; Lijphart 1992; Samuels and Shugart 2010; Shugart and Carey 1992; Steffani 1979), we can locate, on the former pole, presidential systems, where chief executives and legislatures are installed via separate elections and endowed with independent institutional survival, and on the latter pole, parliamentary systems, in which the "government" (i.e. premier and cabinet) emanates from the popularly elected parliament and depends on its majority's confidence to remain in office while the executive usually has some power to have parliament dissolved. Another typical variant is a "semi-presidential system" with popularly elected heads of state in an otherwise parliamentary system (see e.g. Decker 2010; Duverger 1980; Elgie 1998). There are also rare cases that do not fit any of these types, like Switzerland (Siaroff 2003) or the European Union (Sonnicksen 2017).

There are of course further institutional features directly connected to democratic government. They include the electoral (e.g. (simple) majoritarian vs. proportional) and party (e.g. two vs. multiparty) systems (though also many other possible ones like direct democracy or even interest group mediation). Regarding these features, "patterns of democracy" (Lijphart 2012) as either majoritarian or consensus refer to their power-concentrating or rather power-sharing disposition respectively (cf. also Ganghof 2010; Vatter 2009). These institutional arrangements have also been framed in dichotomous categories such as a competitive, winner-takes-all type democracy versus a more consociational, consensus democratic type (Benz 2015; Daalder 1974; Lehmbruch 1967; Lijphart 1969). These distinctions refer to formal institutions, but which have own logics of politics. The cooperative or competitive dynamics of democratic governing interlink, albeit in diverse patterns, with the power-separating or power-sharing character of institutional arrangements. In short, the institutional settings matter for how democratic government works.

Another approach to analyzing types as much as levels of democracy is provided by Dahl's seminal *Polyarchy*, with a two-dimensional framework constructed around participation for one and opposition for another (Dahl 1971). Participation and inclusiveness are generally one elemental side of democratic typologies. Other concepts vary concerning the second side, being conceived, for instance, as *responsibility* in the sense of accountability (Lundell 2011), *authority* pertaining to capacity to govern (Gerring and Thacker 2008), or *contestation* as opposition but also public debate (Coppedge, Alvarez, and Maldonado 2008). Dualisms between responsibility, accountability, authority, or opposition on one side, and inclusion and citizen participation on the other, do not match fully the distinction here between self and shared rule, or power separating and sharing. However, there is considerable overlap.

Contestation and inclusion are reflected in the distinctions between competition and cooperation, between (simple) majoritarian and non- or super-majoritarian governance, and between separating and sharing power. The democratic government dimension is configured foremost by the *form* of democratic government with regard to either executive-legislative separation (e.g. a presidential system) or fusion of powers (e.g. a parliamentary one). Regarding political party systems, competitive party politics can be considered typified most by a two-party system. Systems of party pluralism or multipartyism are inclined comparably toward cooperative or concordant patterns on account of the common necessity to form coalitions at all (e.g. even minimum-winning ones). Though not determined alone, the number of relevant parties tends to coincide with the type of election procedures, which can range from plurality (simple majority) and majoritarian to (partially to fully) proportional.

In summary, democratic government is itself multifaceted. Even when condensed into a one-dimensional perspective (i.e. a democratic-government dimension), there is a variety of possible arrangements for the horizontal division of powers, though variance can occur within democratic governments over time. Democratic institutional settings and certainly political dynamics may tend toward power-concentrating "majority rule" patterns, with winner-takes-all elections and highly competitive party politics among a few effective parties; or more toward power sharing, consensus-seeking patterns with proportional electoral rules, multipartyism, and cross-branch negotiation. In turn, we also find a range of different types of division of power arrangements in the federal dimension.

Federal governmental dimension

The variety of federal systems and concepts are both extensive. Like democracy, federalism encompasses theoretical, structural, as well as procedural dimensions, not to mention numerous concurring and competing meanings. Such multiplicity derives from the currently observable diversity of federalism, but also the historical evolution and transformation of related concepts. Following the federal dynamics framework (Benz and Broschek 2013a, 2013b, 2013c), federalism as a dimension of government relates to the organization of relations between levels of government. All modern governments exhibit some form or degree of a vertical distribution of powers, competences, structures, and functions. In federalism though, the division is chiefly between the federal (or national-level) government and the constituent units – be they cantons, *Länder*, provinces, or states. Focusing on institutional, structural features, a federal system is a de-central or non-central arrangement based on a compact (typically a constitution) between constituent units, their governments and "peoples", and a superordinate level of government that maintains their institutional and legal integrity (e.g. (partial) sovereignty). This holds irrespective of centralization and decentralization, which refer to processes and degrees and may vary in any polity over time or at any one time by policy area.

Regarding the antecedent processes *toward* a federal system, we also find different types, most notably in the dichotomy between "coming together" and "holding together" federalism (Stepan 1999). This dualism refers to *federalization* either by aggregation of sovereign or independent constituents, or by disaggregation of a unitary order into superordinate and sub-state governments respectively. Whether formed by aggregation or disaggregation, the type of compact between levels of governments (how powers are allocated, conferred, or transferred as it were) can have a long trajectory of impact on the ensuing federal dynamics (Broschek 2012a, 2012b). The further distinction between "demos-enabling" and "demos-constraining" federalisms (Stepan 1999; cf. also Watts 2006) points to different impacts the federal order can have on democratic politics.

Federal institutional arrangements can be distinguished between self or shared rule, or rather power separating and power sharing *between* levels of government. The ideal-typical models of *dual* and *cooperative* federalism refer to strictly separated powers emphasizing more *self-rule* or the sharing of powers, and *shared rule*, respectively (see e.g. Hueglin 2013; Watts 1998, 2008). Dual type federal orders exhibit a strict enumeration of powers among levels exercised independently by governments within their own ambits. This arrangement may more likely be found in "coming together" federal systems that have brought formerly sovereign entities into a union. At the other side of the federal spectrum lie cooperative-type federal systems, which have an enumeration of powers (as in any federal constitution), but include cross-level joint competences, and structural and/or functional intermingling between governments. A cooperative model may be established from the outset, or develop through constitutional changes.

Budgetary and other fiscal powers of the purse are pivotal to modern government, but also indicate either the power separating or sharing character of federalism (see e.g. Anderson 2010; Hueglin and Fenna 2015: 166–203; Rodden 2006): fiscal autonomy, along with responsibility for their own revenues and expenditures, of the separate levels of government corresponds with dual federalism. Cooperative federalism exhibits assorted elements of common or joint fiscal policy. A similar situation applies to forms of fiscal equalization or the lack thereof. Horizontal fiscal equalization arrangements comply with cooperative federalism, while dual federalism exhibits few to no such arrangements. Grants and other vertical financial transfers, that is from federal to state governments, suggest cooperative federalism, though they can differ considerably in the discretion afforded to or conditionality imposed on the recipients.

Federalism is distinctly confronted with the challenge of reconciling unity and diversity and thus shared and self-rule (Elazar 1985: 23; 1987: 5). While the constitution prescribes a division of powers, multiple problems in practice cut across state boundaries and levels of government, requiring mutual responses and coordination (see e.g. Benz, Scharpf, and Zintl 1992; Scharpf 1988; Simeon 1972). As a result, all federal systems develop some form(s) and extent of intergovernmental coordination irrespective of the federal model. But *how* they are coped with can depend in many ways on the institutional character of the vertical division of powers as dualistic and power separating, or cooperative and power sharing. Accordingly, different federal models tend to have also a different organization of intergovernmental relations as either more loose and voluntary or more formally institutionalized and even mandatory (see e.g. Bakvis and Brown 2010; Bolleyer 2013; Hueglin and Fenna 2015: 238–74; Simeon 2005). Modern federal systems thus comprise systems of two-level or multilevel governance. But as in democratic government, the interactions between governments at different levels can range from more cooperation to more competition and separating or sharing patterns.

In summary, federalism as a dimension of government entails a division of powers among levels of government, with a variety of possible arrangements. Self and shared rule and more separating and sharing of powers respectively are paralleled in the dichotomy between dual and cooperative federalism. These distinctions refer to constitutional rules and formal institutions but also political practice, exhibiting different inclinations toward autonomy or cooperation. All the more complex is their interlinkage or *coupling* with democracy.

Coupling between federalism and democracy

Several basic models can be drawn according to the horizontal-democratic and vertical-federal dimensions of government, with each spanning from the separation to the sharing of powers. The model types of these combinations represent: democratic government with a stricter separation of powers between the executive and legislative branches, typified by the presidential government form, or a more fused sharing of powers, typified by parliamentary government. In the federal government dimension, the strict separating of governmental levels versus the sharing of powers and interlocking between levels is typified by dual and cooperative federalism respectively. Setting the separation of powers/self-rule and sharing of powers/shared rule as the cardinal directions streamlines complexity in order to capture it. However, it is necessary to bear in mind that concrete institutional arrangements that by design appear as either self or shared-rule oriented may still function quite differently in practice. This alludes to the different logics of politics more or less inherent in the different governmental dimensions. Their respective functional and mechanistic features should be spelled out more specifically.

For one, democratic and federal divisions of powers in one system implies that different principles and modes of democratic and federal representation become compounded (Lancaster 1999). In short, different norms and rules guide the representation of the people or citizenry and of territorial units (and/or "their" people(s)). For another, with these two dimensions of government come different types of institutions that can also function as veto "players" or "points", affecting the dynamics of governing (Immergut 1990; Tsebelis 1995). This points to the many potentials for friction and tension. Federalism and democracy may set the proverbial stage for an interplay of "rival institutional logics" (Sharman 1990) in government whose incongruity may be prone to frictions or "ruptures" (Lehmbruch 1978, 2000b). For example, democratic government may induce a particular logic of politics (e.g. party competition) that could contravene a "federal" logic of politics (e.g. cooperation between governments). Frictions thus emerge between the two institutional dimensions, in short, on account of the overlaps and ambiguities (Benz and Sonnicksen 2015). Logics of representation, accountability, constituency, and, more generally, *appropriateness* have different meanings and implications for federalism and for democracy. Federalism may refer chiefly to the territorial organization of a polity with constituent states, democracy to the form of government by popular rule. However, democratic government can engender competition, coalitions, or consensus-seeking among political parties and branches of government, while federalism can support contests or coordination, joint-decision making, or "doing one's own thing" among multiple governments or administrations. Multibranch and multilevel governance and contestation thus become compounded within one polity.

The dynamics of federal democratic government result from how these dimensions are organized for one, and how the logics of democratic and of federal politics are linked for another. The concept of *coupling* (Benz 2009; Benz and Sonnicksen 2017)[6] aims to capture these types of interlinkages between federalism and democracy. Coupling refers to the type and intensity of structural and functional linkage between levels and arenas of democratic and federal politics, and thus to features and mechanisms of the democratic and federal dimensions and how these institutional conditions combine and interact. *Uncoupled* and *tightly coupled* represent two such basic types, and *loose coupling* a third intermediary one. In an *uncoupled* arrangement, federal and democratic institutions are organized and tend to operate separately. This is underpinned by the separation of powers between executives and legislatures within governments (horizontal) and between levels of government (vertical). The formal institutional linkages between levels of government are rather disjointed, while fiscal relations are oriented toward autonomy of the governmental levels and constituent units (e.g. states). These separations can be linked in the processes of governing, though more likely through voluntary cooperative networks than formalized and mandatory arrangements. Decisions can be taken at different levels, which may be coordinated, but are not required to be. In contrast, *tightly coupled* federalism and democracy is characterized by the sharing or some extent of fusion of powers between branches of government, and cooperation and multiple institutional linkages between levels of government. In the "tightest" variant, the constitution prescribes joint tasks between levels of government, rendering cooperation and coordination mandatory, while fiscal relations are oriented toward joint or common revenue responsibilities. Finally, *loose coupling* can apply to an arrangement

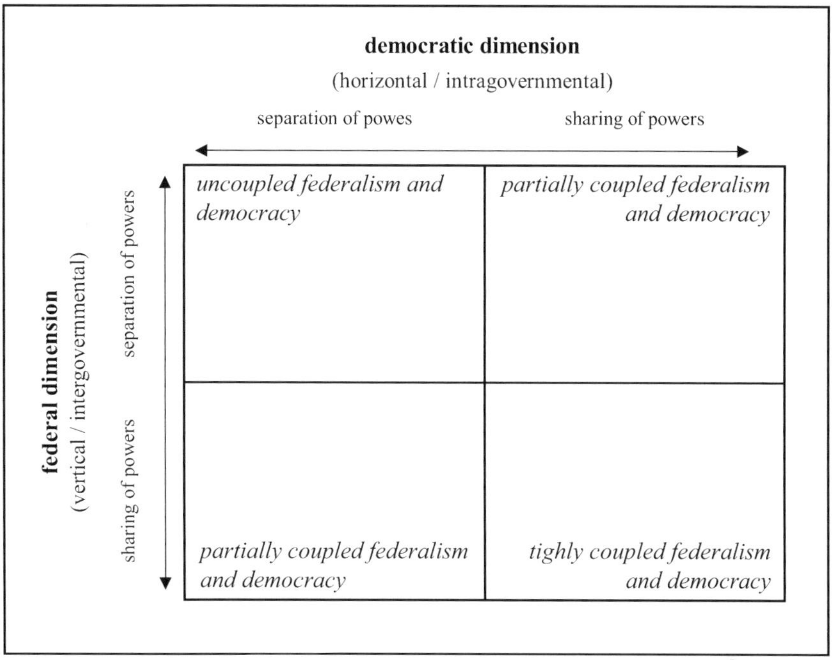

FIGURE 2.1 Coupling between federal and democratic government dimensions

of federalism and democracy with one dimension structured more toward separation and the other toward the sharing of powers. Moreover, tightly coupled and uncoupled types of federal democracy can develop loose coupling in practice. For instance, despite the mandatory cooperation in a tightly coupled system or the stricter separation of powers in an uncoupled system, the different levels of government find flexible ways to cooperate.

Basic types of coupling between the federal and democratic government can be framed as follows (Figure 2.1). With the *uncoupled* type, a stricter separation of powers is found in both dimensions, that is a mutual independence between branches and levels of governments (upper left quadrant); inversely, with the *tightly coupled* type, there is a mutual dependence between branches and levels of governments (lower right) and the respective mixtures of loose coupling (upper right and lower left).

At the same time, second chambers warrant brief attention as an institutional linkage between the democratic and federal dimensions. These chambers even intersect both dimensions. The relevance of bicameralism for federalism appears unambiguous, given that second chambers usually are based on some form of specifically territorial representation. However, they are also relevant for the *horizontal* division of powers (i.e. the *intra*-legislative separation of powers). Thus their position and composition reflect the character of the federal dimension, while a second chamber with legislative co-decision competences (from consultative to suspensive or absolute veto powers) affects the operation of democratic government (see e.g. Tsebelis 1995; Tsebelis and Money 1997). Bicameralism is of particular interest to coupling as well: a popular elected second chamber corresponds rather with an *uncoupled* federal democracy, and a council model second chamber, with representatives delegated or coopted by constituent-unit governments, more a *tightly coupled* one (i.e. as a formal institutional linkage between government levels).

The dynamics of political interaction vary between coupling types and thus between arrangements of sharing or separating powers in a structural and institutional, but also a more functional, regard. This framework allows for assessing multiple cases as well as the in-depth examination of an individual case in an implicit comparison with others. It also builds on several theory-building antecedents, as elaborated above. They pertain to potential tensions, frictions, and discontinuities between the federal and democratic dimensions that emerge in processes of governing. However, these earlier related works apply mainly to combinations of federalism with parliamentary democratic government, and their complex relations between executives and the (majorities in) parliaments they remain responsible to. This underlines the novelty of applying the framework elaborated up to now specifically to the USA as a non-parliamentary democratic federation. At the same time, gaps in the *federal dynamics* and *dynamic institutionalism* approaches have been identified above, namely with regard to the dimension of democratic government. The coupling framework, in turn, integrates both dimensions of government. Yet so far it lacks an explicit treatment of ideas and institutions. The following adds this into the analytical framework.

Ideas, institutions, and democratic federal dynamics

With the prior frameworks and the foundations of historical and ideational institutionalism again in mind, I propose more explicitly a complex linkage between ideas and institutions. In short, there is an institutional impact on ideas, but one that works both ways: ideas contributing to shaping institutions, but institutions, over time, impacting on ideas and ideational development. Institutions on the whole tend to be framed more as constraints on change, and ideas more as sources of dynamics. However, institutions and institutional complexity can serve as sources of innovation, while ideas can become bounds and constraints on political development. By this token, which comes first (Smith 2006) remains evasive.

Regarding federalism and democracy, we may maintain that they are distinct types of a division of powers and dimensions of government, and that from this follow different logics of politics. On the other hand, the two are connected to ideas, especially including constitutional governmental principles. There are actually several principles common to both federalism and democracy: that is the division of powers; self-rule and self-determination; shared rule and collective self-determination; and equality. Cross-cutting these principles are not only modes, but also particular ideas of representation and constituency. As elaborated above, potential discontinuities, tensions, and ambivalences are triggered in practice by the coupling of the two government dimensions. However, the concurrence of principles and ideas also raises dilemmas. Tensions arise conceptually and certainly in practice with regard to *what* and *how people think* federalism and democracy *are* and *should* be and work, whether toward competition or cooperation, separating or sharing, going it alone, or joining up.

The division of powers, self-rule, equality, representation, and constituency apply both to federalism and democracy. Their points of reference, on the other hand, differ fundamentally: democracy is predicated foremost on citizens as constituents, or "the people"; federalism is predicated on constituent territories or places (see Figure 2.2). A fundamental difference becomes apparent with a view to the, arguably most important, principle of equality: democratic equality implies the equal

Features	**Constitutional-governmental order**	**Democracy**	**Federalism**
division of powers		intragovernmental	intergovernmental
	horizontal	between branches and collective actors of government	among jurisdictions, states, constituent units, regions
	vertical	between citizens, intermediaries, and government	between levels of government and respective intermediaries
equality		civil liberties & rights; popular sovereignty; one person one vote	constituent unit liberties & rights; state sovereignty; one state, one vote
constituency		citizens, residents (individuals and groups)	territorial districts, regions
representation		citizen-/population-based constituents	territory-/state-based constituents
	descriptive	reflective of composition of citizenry; input by the people	reflective of territorial composition; input by constituent unit (gov't/'demoi')
	substantive	output for the people / interested groups	output for the constituent units / for the *demoi*
logic of politics		intragovernmental arena	intergovernmental arena
	self-rule	limited government, strict sep. of powers, checks & balances, safeguard inividual liberty	multilevel autonomy; competition; independence; own responsibility
	shared rule	cooperation, consensus-seeking; collective self-determination; foster outcome equality	comity; multilevel cooperation and coordination; joint responsibility; equalization

FIGURE 2.2 The institutional ordering principles of democracy and federalism

value of all citizens; federal equality that of constituent states. This may have different implications also for representation, for example the equal representation of people or places or both, and thus the potential for contradictions. The concurrence of similar principles but with different points of reference engenders interpretation and contestation on multiple questions, on for example: whether federalism should protect the autonomy of constituent units or foster comity and shared rule among levels of government; whether democratic equality should serve individual liberty or collective solidarity; and, not least, whether and when a federal principle takes precedence over a democratic one or vice versa.

Democratic and federal ordering principles find structural and functional expression, that is they take on concrete institutional forms. However, already established institutions frequently become infused with, or have imposed on them, respective ideas and principles. Irrespective of which comes first, institutions also encode into the polity respective notions inducing ideational dynamics, for example of understanding, making sense and meaning, and legitimation.

The ordering principles of federalism and democracy link with the arrangements of the division of powers, coinciding with the different logics of politics but also, over time, with the bases for different "institutionalized patterns of understanding" (Lieberman 2011: 211) and "meaning constellations" (Broschek 2016). Political order, including here the government dimensions of federalism and democracy, encompasses institutional and ideational constellations. They develop in a bounded but dynamic interplay over time. They do so not necessarily in congruence, but also with tensions and frictions, especially on account of discontinuities, ambivalences, and mismatches, that is when institutional change is pursued but ideational patterns constrain it, or vice versa, ideas change but institutional settings impede their conversion into actual change (Broschek 2009; Lieberman 2002: 701–2; Orren and Skowronek 1996). In a federal democracy, these ideational and institutional constellations are underpinned by a constitution, which provides a foundation for government as much as governmental principles, and thus the interpretation of their meanings. The interlinkage between institutions and ideas and their developmental processes contribute to the emergence of *regulative ideas* – ideas prescribing norms, rule-based behavior, logics of appropriateness, and similar. Accordingly, *interpretation* becomes a distinct *mechanism* causing dynamics which can take diverse directions of political development over time.

Against this backdrop, we can frame dynamics and tensions between ideas on the one hand, and institutions and processes of government on the other, as embedded in multidimensional bounds (see Figure 2.3). These bounds include temporality, ordering principles, structural-functional arrangements, and thus multiple institutions and institutionalizations. They make up the paths and corridors within which political development unfolds. While they always remain subject to potential change, these conditions and mechanisms can lead over time to structuring a proverbial "thinking in the box". Social construction processes, encompassing intrinsic mechanisms and motives, are embedded in formative institutionalized settings which have evolved over time. Logics of appropriateness develop out of such processes, but are diverse, both for different actors as well as different arenas. The dynamics of

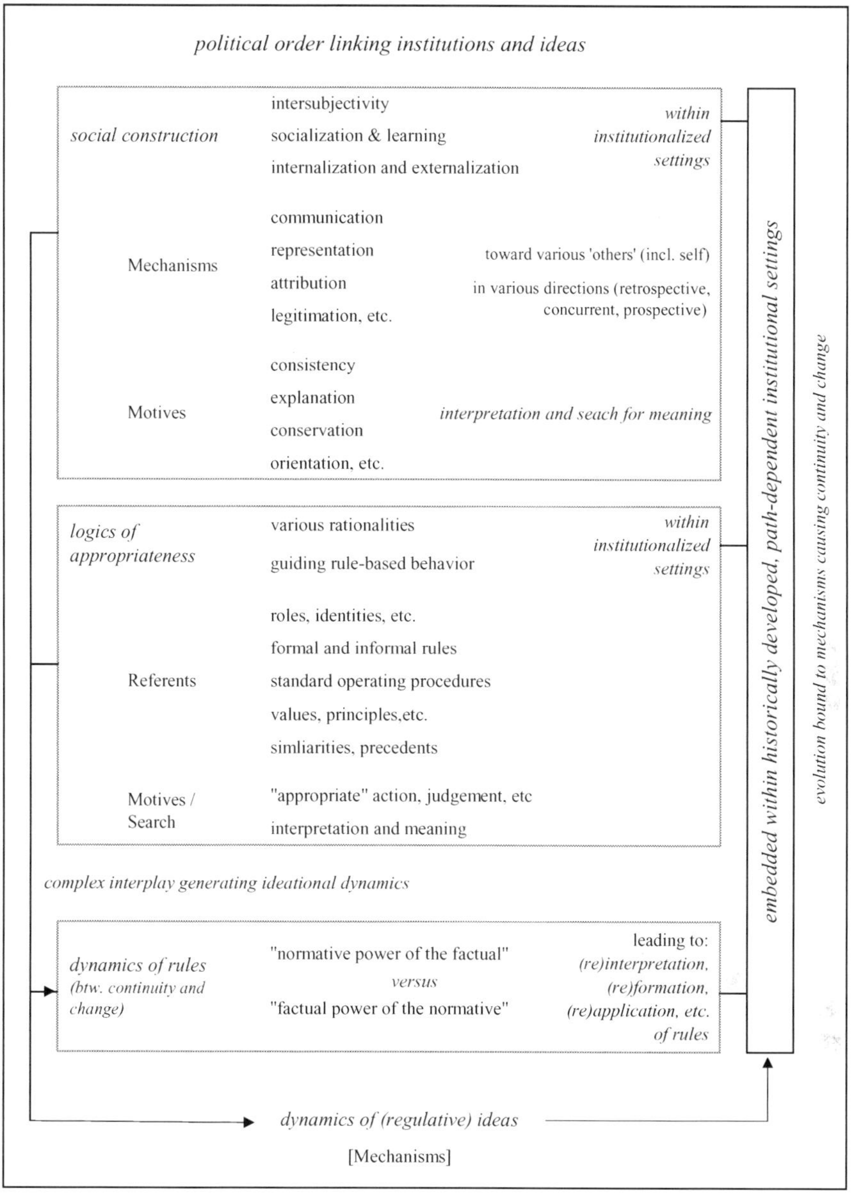

FIGURE 2.3 Coupling between ideational and institutional configurations

rules emerge between the establishment of rules, their interpretation, application, and contestation. Regulative ideas deriving from institutionalization (e.g. in the constitution, in formal institutions and practices of federal and democratic government) stimulate dynamics with the institutional framework and myriad "others" (e.g. collective actors, political intermediaries, government branches and levels).

Interpretation translates internalized political ideas into externalizations and thus manifests dynamics. While the lower arrows (depicted in Figure 2.3) point to one type of movement, and thus show ideas "acting on" institutional settings, these and other dynamics are understood as multidirectional and interlinked.

The settings and interlinkages within the institutional and ideational "box" depicted above amount to political order. This is not tantamount to equilibrium or an otherwise stable state. What lies within the comparatively small sub-box of "historically evolved institutionalized settings" (right-hand side, Figure 2.3) is much larger. It includes the federal and democratic dimensions of government. The coupling of governmental dimensions, concepts, and coinciding regulative ideas infuse additional complexity into the political order. The ideational and institutional configurations bound as well as induce different logics of government and collective action but also patterns of rules, norms, interpretations, and meanings. The resultant political order encompasses structural arrangements, a multitude of rules, as well as a "grammar" and "vocabulary". Yet even the same concepts or terms can imply different connotations and meanings. Their interpretations, in addition to conflicts of interests and multiple veto points and players, likewise invite contestation. This applies to such questions as: does democratic equality imply non-discrimination, fair rules, and opportunities, or commitment to reducing asymmetries in power and resources? Does federalism allow us to do our own thing or require us to work together? Does the constitution provide answers to these questions, and if so, which "reading" should be taken?

In sum: politics and government are bounded in a world of complexity of their own making over time. Change, reform, or capacities for "thinking outside the box" remain possible. These premises imply institutional and ideational path dependencies and many bounds and contingencies. This also helps to explain why attempts at conversions of ideas, practices, or rules, whether proposed anew or adopted from elsewhere, can face persistent rejection or, if passed and implemented, wind up "lost in translation". There are numerous anomalies to be found in political practice, whether the puzzles refer to when political change succeeds against all the odds and constraints or, conversely, the status quo persists despite permissive conditions favorable to change. They can start to appear less vexing when taking an historical institutional and ideational theoretical analytical approach. Multiple approaches to knowing things ultimately involve discovery but also construction – through description, interpretation, and explanation. Alas we can discover, for the most part, nothing without exploring. To this end, it surely helps to have a map, knowing full well that the map is not the territory, but that it allows for a more productive navigation. Against this backdrop, the remaining chapters explore the federal democratic dynamics between ideas and institutions in the US polity.

Notes

1 For an overview, see e.g. Finnemore and Sikkink (2001).

2 This common phrase, and the notion it encompasses, paraphrases William James's dictum of "my thinking is first and last and always for the sake of my doing" (James 1890:

Vol. I, Ch. 22). The apparent parallel to Deweyan pragmatist thinking is not coincidental. James was an influential contributor to the pragmatist school himself, and his *Principles of Psychology* had significant impact on Dewey (see Jörke 2003: 6–124).

3 This umbrella term for different idea-oriented approaches in discursive, constructivist, and sociological institutionalisms is likewise applied by Béland and Cox, in their respective overview, as "streams of ideational research" (Béland and Cox 2011: 6–8). In contrast, Vivien Schmidt for instance treats discursive institutionalism as a strand of new institutionalism, distinct from the sociological variant (see e.g. Schmidt 2010).

4 See also the classic work on *Exit, Voice, and Loyalty* by Hirschman (1970).

5 On the notion of a democratic experimentalism fostered by federalism more generally, as observed by James Bryce, and adopted by US Supreme Court Justice Brandeis regarding the virtue of the states to "serve as laboratory", see e.g. Hueglin and Fenna (2015: 42ff.).

6 This draws insights from earlier works on coupling; see e.g. Landau (1973) and Orten and Weick (1990).

References

Abbott, Andrew. 2004. *Methods of Discovery: Heuristics for the Social Sciences*. New York: W.W. Norton.

Anderson, George. 2010. *Fiscal Federalism: A Comparative Introduction*. Oxford: Oxford University Press.

Austen-Smith, David, and Jeffrey Banks. 1998. "Social Choice Theory, Game Theory, and Positive Political Theory." *Annual Review of Political Science* 1 (1): 259–87.

Bakvis, Herman, and Douglas Brown. 2010. "Policy Coordination in Federal Systems: Comparing Intergovernmental Processes and Outcomes in Canada and the United States." *Publius* 40 (3): 484–507.

Banse, Rainer, and Anthony Greenwald. 2007. "Personality and Implicit Social Cognition Research: Past, Present and Future." *European Journal of Personality* 21 (3): 371–82.

Bar-Tal, Daniel. 2000. *Shared Beliefs in a Society: Social Psychological Analysis*. London: Sage.

Baumgartner, Frank, and Brian Jones. 1993. *Agendas and Instability in American Politics*. Chicago: Chicago University Press.

Bednar, Jenna. 2011. "The Political Science of Federalism." *Annual Review of Law and Social Science* 7: 269–88.

Béland, Daniel. 2005. "Ideas, Interests, and Institutions: Historical Institutionalism Revisited." In *New Institutionalism: Theory and Analysis*, ed. André Lecours. Toronto: University of Toronto Press, 29–50.

——— 2010. "The Idea of Power and the Role of Ideas." *Political Studies Review* 8 (2): 145–54.

Béland, Daniel, and Robert H. Cox. 2011. "Introductions. Ideas and Politics." In *Ideas and Politics in Social Science Research*, eds. Daniel Béland and Robert H. Cox. Oxford: Oxford University Press, 3–20.

Bendix, Reinhard. 1964. *Nation-Building and Citizenship: Studies of Our Changing Social Order*. New York: Wiley.

Benz, Arthur. 1985. *Föderalismus als dynamisches System: Zentralisierung und Dezentralisierung im föderativen Staat*. Opladen: Westdeutscher Verlag.

——— 2009. "Ein gordischer Knoten der Politikwissenschaft? Zur Vereinbarkeit von Föderalismus und Demokratie." *Politische Vierteljahresschrift* 50 (1): 3–22.

——— 2013. "Dimensions and Dynamics of Federal Regimes." In *Federal Dynamics: Continuity, Change, and the Varieties of Federalism*, eds. Arthur Benz and Jörg Broschek. Oxford: Oxford University Press, 70–90.

——— 2015. "Lehmbruch versus Lijphart: Comparing Democratic Governments as Multidimensional Regimes." In *Complex Democracy: Variations, Crisis and Transformations*, eds.Volker Schneider and Burkhard Eberlein. Berlin: Springer, 69–82.

Benz, Arthur, and Jörg Broschek. 2013a. "Conclusion: Theorizing Federal Dynamics." In *Federal Dynamics: Continuity, Change, and the Varieties of Federalism*, eds. Arthur Benz and Jörg Broschek. Oxford: Oxford University Press, 367–88.

———, eds. 2013b. *Federal Dynamics: Continuity, Change, and the Varieties of Federalism*. Oxford: Oxford University Press.

——— eds. 2013c. "Federal Dynamics: Introduction." In *Federal Dynamics: Continuity, Change, and the Varieties of Federalism*, eds. Arthur Benz and Jörg Broschek. Oxford: Oxford University Press, 1–23.

Benz, Arthur, Fritz Scharpf, and Reinhard Zintl. 1992. *Horizontale Politikverflechtung; Zur Theorie von Verhandlungssystemen*. Frankfurt: Campus.

Benz, Arthur, and Jared Sonnicksen. 2015. "Federalism and Democracy – Compatible or at Odds with One Another? Re-examining a Tense Relationship." In *Citizen Participation in Multi-Level Democracies*, eds. Christina Fraenkel-Haeberle, Sabine Kropp, Francesco Palermo and Karl-Peter Sommermann. Leiden: Brill, 15–30.

——— 2017. "Patterns of Federal Democracy: Tensions, Friction, or Balance between Two Government Dimensions." *European Political Science Review* 9 (1): 3–25.

Berger, Peter, and Thomas Luckmann. 1966. *The Social Construction of Reality: A Treatise in the Sociology of Knowledge*. New York: Penguin.

Berman, Sheri. 1998. "Path Dependency and Political Action: Reexamining Responses to the Depression." *Comparative Politics* 30 (4): 379–400.

——— 2001. "Ideas, Norms, and Culture in Political Analysis." *Comparative Politics* 33 (2): 231–50.

——— 2011. "Ideology, History, and Politics." In *Ideas and Politics in Social Science Research*, eds. Daniel Béland and Robert H. Cox. Oxford: Oxford University Press, 105–26.

——— 2013. "Ideational Theorizing in the Social Sciences since "Policy Paradigms, Social Learning, and the State"." *Governance* 26 (2): 217–37.

Bless, Herbert, Klaus Fiedler, and Fritz Strack. 2004. *Social Cognition: How Individuals Construct Social Reality*. East Sussex: Psychology Press.

Blyth, Mark. 1997. "'Any More Bright Ideas?' The Ideational Turn of Comparative Political Economy." *Comparative Politics* 29 (2): 229–50.

——— 2003. "Structures Do Not Come with an Instruction Sheet: Interests, Ideas, and Progress in Political Science." *Perspectives on Politics* 1 (4): 695–706.

——— 2011. "Ideas, Uncertainty, and Evolution." In *Ideas and Politics in Social Science Research*, eds. Daniel Béland and Robert H. Cox. Oxford: Oxford University Press, 83–101.

Bolleyer, Nicole. 2013. "Paradoxes of Self-coordination in Federal Systems." In *Federal Dynamics: Continuity, Change, and the Varieties of Federalism*, eds. Arthur Benz and Jörg Broschek. Oxford: Oxford University Press, 321–42.

Broschek, Jörg. 2009. *Der Kanadische Föderalismus. Eine historisch-institutionalistische Analyse*. Wiesbaden: VS Verlag.

——— 2012a. "Historical Institutionalism and Comparative Federalism." *World Political Science Review* 8 (1): 101–28.

——— 2012b. "Historical Institutionalism and the Varieties of Federalism in Germany and Canada." *Publius* 42 (4): 662–87.

——— 2014. "Pathways of Federal Reform: Australia, Canada, Germany, and Switzerland." *Publius* 45 (1): 51–76.

——— 2016. "The Historical Construction of Social Order: Ideas, Institutions, and Meaning Constellations." In *World Culture Re-Contextualized: Meaning Constellations and Path-dependencies in Comparative and International Education Research*, ed. Jürgen Schriewer. Abingdon/New York: Routledge, 161–80.

Burgess, Michael, and Alain Gagnon, eds. 2010. *Federal Democracies*. London: Routledge.

Cairney, Paul. 2013. "What is Evolutionary Theory and How Does it Inform Policy Studies?" *Policy & Politics* 41 (2): 279–98.

Capoccia, Giovanni. 2015. "Critical Junctures and Institutional Change." In *Advances in Comparative-Historical Analysis*, eds. James Mahoney and Kathleen Thelen. Cambridge: Cambridge University Press, 147–79.

Capoccia, Giovanni, and R. D. Kelemen. 2007. "The Study of Critical Junctures: Theory, Narrative, and Counterfactuals in Historical Institutionalism." *World Politics* 59 (3): 341–69.

Carstensen, Martin. 2011. "Ideas are Not as Stable as Political Scientists Want Them to Be: A Theory of Incremental Ideational Change." *Political Studies* 59 (3): 596–615.

——— 2012. "The Relevance of an Incremental Approach to Ideational Change: A Rejoinder to Liam Stanley." *Political Studies* 60 (3): 720–28.

Cheibub, José A., and Fernando Limongi. 2002. "Democratic Institutions and Regime Survival: Parliamentary and Presidential Democracies Reconsidered." *Annual Review of Political Science* 5: 151–79.

Coppedge, Michael, Angel Alvarez, and Claudia Maldonado. 2008. "Two Persistent Dimensions of Democracy: Contestation and Inclusiveness." *Journal of Politics* 70 (3): 632–47.

Crawford, Sue, and Elinor Ostrom. 1995. "A Grammar of Institutions." *American Political Science Review* 89 (3): 582–600.

Daalder, Hans. 1974. "The Consociational Democracy Theme." *World Politics* 26 (4): 604–21.

Dahl, Robert. 1971. *Polyarchy: Participation and Opposition*. New Haven: Yale University Press.

David, Paul. 1994. "Why are Institutions the 'Carriers of History'? Path Dependence and the Evolution of Conventions, Organizations, and Institutions." *Structural Change and Economic Dynamics* 5 (2): 205–20.

Decker, Frank. 2010. "Der Semi-Präsidentialismus als unechtes Mischsystem: Eine Forschungsnotiz." *Zeitschrift für Politik* 57 (3): 329–42.

Duverger, Maurice. 1980. "A New Political System Model: Semi-Presidential Government." *European Journal of Political Research* 8 (2): 165–88.

Easton, David. 1953. *The Political System: An Inquiry into the State of Political Science*. New York: Alfred A. Knopf.

Elazar, Daniel. 1985. "Federalism and Consociational Regimes." *Publius* 15 (2): 17–34.

——— 1987. *Exploring Federalism*. Tuscaloosa: University of Alabama Press.

Elgie, Robert, ed. 1998. *Semi-Presidentialism in Europe*. Oxford: Oxford University Press.

———, ed. 2011. "Presidentialism, Parliamentarism and Semi-Presidentialism: Bringing the Parties Back in." *Government and Opposition* 46 (3): 392–409.

Falleti, Tulia, and Julia Lynch. 2009. "Context and Causal Mechanisms in Political Analysis." *Comparative Political Studies* 42 (9): 1143–66.

Falleti, Tulia, and James Mahoney. 2015. "The Comparative Sequential Method." In *Advances in Comparative-Historical Analysis*, eds. James Mahoney and Kathleen Thelen. Cambridge: Cambridge University Press, 211–39.

Finnemore, Martha, and Kathryn Sikkink. 2001. "Taking Stock: The Constructivist Research Program in International Relations and Comparative Politics." *Annual Review of Political Science* 4: 391–416.

Fiske, Susan. 1992. "Thinking is for Doing: Portraits of Social Cognition from Daguerreotype to Laserphoto." *Journal of Personality and Social Psychology* 63 (6): 877–89.

Fiske, Susan, and Shelley Taylor. 2013. *Social Cognition: From Brains to Culture.* 2nd ed. London: Sage.

Freeden, Michael. 2008. *Ideologies and Political Theory: A Conceptual Approach.* Oxford: Clarendon Press.

Friedrich, Carl J. 1968. *Trends of Federalism in Theory and Practice.* New York: Praeger.

Ganghof, Steffen. 2010. "Review Article: Democratic Inclusiveness: A Reinterpretation of Lijphart's Patterns of Democracy." *British Journal of Political Science* 40: 679–92.

Gerring, John, and Strom Thacker. 2008. *A Centripetal Theory of Democratic Governance.* Cambridge: Cambridge University Press.

Gerring, John, Strom Thacker, and Carola Moreno. 2005. "Centripetal Democratic Governance: A Theory and Global Inquiry." *American Political Science Review* 99 (4): 567–81.

Gibson, Edward. 2013. *Boundary Control: Subnational Authoritarianism in Federal Democracies.* Cambridge: Cambridge University Press.

Hacker, Jacob, Paul Pierson, and Kathleen Thelen. 2015. "Drift and Conversion: Hidden Faces of Institutional Change." In *Advances in Comparative-Historical Analysis*, eds. James Mahoney and Kathleen Thelen. Cambridge: Cambridge University Press, 180–208.

Hall, Peter, and David Soskice, eds. 2001. *Varieties of Capitalism: The Institutional Foundations of Comparative Advantage.* Oxford: Oxford University Press.

Hall, Peter, and Rosemary Taylor. 1996. "Political Science and the Three New Institutionalisms." *Political Studies* 44 (5): 936–57.

——— 1998. "The Potential of Historical Institutionalism: A Response to Hay and Wincott." *Political Studies* 46 (5): 958–62.

Hay, Colin. 2006. "Constructivist Institutionalism." In *The Oxford Handbook of Political Institutions*, eds. R.A.W. Rhodes, Sarah Binder and Bert Rockman. Oxford: Oxford University Press, 56–74.

——— 2011. "Ideas and the Construction of Interests." In *Ideas and Politics in Social Science Research*, eds. Daniel Béland and Robert H. Cox. Oxford: Oxford University Press, 65–82.

Hewstone, Miles, and Martha Augoustinos. 1998. "Social Attributions and Social Representations." In *The Psychology of the Social*, ed. Uwe Flick. Cambridge: Cambridge University Press, 60–76.

Hirschman, Albert. 1970. *Exit, Voice, and Loyalty.* Cambridge, MA: Harvard University Press.

Hueglin, Thomas. 2013. *"Comparing Federalism: Variations or Distinct Models?" In Federal Dynamics: Continuity, Change, and the Varieties of Federalism*, eds. Arthur Benz and Jörg Broschek. Oxford: Oxford University Press, 27–47.

Hueglin, Thomas, and Alan Fenna. 2015. *Comparative Federalism: A Systematic Inquiry.* 2nd ed. Toronto: University of Toronto Press.

Immergut, Ellen. 1990. "Institutions, Veto Points, and Policy Results: A Comparative Analysis of Health Care." *Journal of Public Policy* 10 (4): 391–416.

——— 2006. "Historical Institutionalism in Political Science and the Problem of Change." In *Understanding Change: Models, Methodologies, and Metaphors*, eds. Andreas Wimmer and Reinhart Kössler. Basingstoke: Palgrave Macmillan, 237–59.

Immergut, Ellen, and Karen Anderson. 2008. "Historical Institutionalism and West European Politics." *West European Politics* 31 (1-2): 345–69.

James, William. 1890. *The Principles of Psychology.* New York: Henry Holt and Company.

Jones, Bryan. 1999. "Bounded Rationality." *Annual Review of Political Science* 2: 297–321.

Jörke, Dirk. 2003. *Demokratie als Erfahrung: John Dewey und die politische Philosophie der Gegenwart*. Wiesbaden: Westdeutscher Verlag.

Kahneman, Daniel. 2011. *Thinking, Fast and Slow*. New York: Farrar, Straus and Giroux.

Kincaid, John. 2010. "Federalism and Democracy.: Comparative Empirical and Theoretical Perspectives." In *Federal Democracies*, eds. Michael Burgess and Alain Gagnon. London: Routledge, 299–324.

Kochen, Manfred, and Karl Deutsch. 1969. "Toward a Rational Theory of Decentralization: Some Implications of a Mathematical Approach." *American Political Science Review* 63 (3): 734–49.

Koning, Edward. 2016. "The Three Institutionalisms and Institutional Dynamics: Understanding Endogenous and Exogenous Change." *Journal of Public Policy* 36 (4): 639–64.

Koselleck, Reinhart. 1982. "Begriffsgeschichte and Social History." *Economy and Society* 11 (4): 409–27.

Kunda, Ziva. 1999. *Social Cognition: Making Sense of People*. Cambridge, MA: MIT Press.

Kymlicka, Will. 2001. *Politics in the Vernacular: Nationalism, Multiculturalism, and Citizenship*. Oxford: Oxford University Press.

Lancaster, Thomas. 1999. "Complex Self-identification and Compounded Representation in Federal Systems." *West European Politics* 22 (2): 59–89.

Landau, Martin. 1973. "Federalism, Redundancy and System Reliability." *Publius* 3 (2): 173–96.

Lecours, André. 2005. "New Institutionalism: Issues and Questions." In *New Institutionalism: Theory and Analysis*, ed. André Lecours. Toronto: University of Toronto Press, 3–26.

Lehmbruch, Gerhard. 1967. *Proporzdemokratie. Politisches System und politische Kultur in der Schweiz und in Österreich*. Tübingen: Mohr Siebeck.

——— 1978. "Party and Federation in Germany: A Developmental Dilemma." *Government and Opposition* 13 (2): 151–77.

——— 2000a. "Föderalismus als entwicklungsgeschichtlich geronnene Verteilungsentscheidungen." In *Die deutschen Länder: Geschichte, Politik, Wirtschaft*, ed. Hans-Georg Wehling. Opladen: Leske + Budrich, 299–314.

——— 2000b. *Parteienwettbewerb im Bundesstaat. Regelsysteme und Spannungslagen im politischen System der Bundesrepublik Deutschland*. 3rd ed. Wiesbaden: Westdeutscher Verlag.

Levy, Jacob. 2007. "Federalism, Liberalism, and the Separation of Loyalties." *American Political Science Review* 101 (3): 459–77.

Lieberman, Evan. 2001. "Causal Inference in Historical Institutional Analysis: A Specification of Periodization Strategies." *Comparative Political Studies* 34 (9): 1011–35.

Lieberman, Robert. 2002. "Ideas, Institutions, and Political Order: Explaining Political Change." *American Political Science Review* 96 (4): 697–712.

——— 2011. "Ideas and Institutions in Race Politics." In *Ideas and Politics in Social Science Research*, eds. Daniel Béland and Robert H. Cox. Oxford: Oxford University Press, 209–27.

Lijphart, Arend. 1969. "Consociational Democracy." *World Politics* 21 (2): 207–25.

——— 1979. "Consociation and Federation: Conceptual and Empirical Links." *Canadian Journal of Political Science* 12 (3): 499–515.

———, ed. 1992. *Parliamentary versus Presidential Government*. New York: Oxford University Press.

———, ed. 2012. *Patterns of Democracy. Government Forms and Performance in Thirty-Six Countries*. 2nd ed. New Haven: Yale University Press.

Lindblom, Charles. 1959. "The Science of "Muddling Through"." *Public Administration Review* 19 (2): 79–88.

Lownpes, Vivien. 1996. "Varieties of New Institutionalism: A Critical Appraisal." *Public Administration* 74 (2): 181–97.
Lundell, Krister. 2011. "Accountability and Patterns of Alternation in Pluralitarian, Majoritarian and Consensus Democracies." *Government and Opposition* 46 (2): 145–67.
Lustick, Ian. 2011. "Taking Evolution Seriously: Historical Institutionalism and Evolutionary Theory." *Polity* 43 (2): 179–209.
Ma, Shu-Yun. 2016. "Taking Evolution Seriously, or Metaphorically? A Review of Interactions between Historical Institutionalism and Darwinian Evolutionary Theory." *Political Studies Review* 14 (2): 223–34.
Mahoney, James. 2004. "Comparative-Historical Methodology." *Annual Review of Sociology* 30: 81–101.
——— 2006. "Analyzing Path Dependence: Lessons from the Social Sciences." In *Understanding Change: Models, Methodologies, and Metaphors*, eds. Andreas Wimmer and Reinhart Kössler. Basingstoke: Palgrave Macmillan, 129–39.
March, James. 1994. *A Primer on Decision Making. How Decisions Happen*. New York: Free Press.
March, James, and Johan Olsen. 1984. "The New Institutionalism: Organizational Factors in Political Life." *American Political Science Review* 78 (3): 734–49.
——— 1989. *Rediscovering Institutions: The Organizational Basis of Politics*. New York: Free Press.
——— 1996. "Institutional Perspectives on Political Institutions." *Governance* 9 (3): 247–64.
——— 2009. "The Logic of Appropriateness." In *The Oxford Handbook of Political Science*, ed. Robert Goodin. Oxford: Oxford University Press, 478–97.
Matthijs, Matthias, and Mark Blyth. 2018. "When Is It Rational to Learn the Wrong Lessons? Technocratic Authority, Social Learning, and Euro Fragility." *Perspectives on Politics* 16 (1): 110–26.
Mehta, Jal. 2011. "The Varied Roles of Ideas in Politics. From "Whether" to "How"." In *Ideas and Politics in Social Science Research*, eds. Daniel Béland and Robert H. Cox. Oxford: Oxford University Press, 23–46.
Miller, Gary. 2005. "The Political Evolution of Principal-Agent Models." *Annual Review of Political Science* 8: 203–25.
Moscovici, Serge. 1988. "Notes Towards a Description of Social Representations." *European Journal of Social Psychology* 18 (3): 211–50.
Nagel, Jack. 2000. "Expanding the Spectrum of Democracies: Reflections on Proportional Representation in New Zealand." In *Democracy and Institutions. The Life Work of Arend Lijphart*, eds. Marcus Crepaz, Thomas Koelble and David Wilsford. Ann Arbor: University of Michigan Press, 113–27.
North, Douglass. 1991a. "Institutions." *Journal of Economic Perspectives* 5 (1): 97–112.
——— 1991b. *Institutions, Institutional Change and Economic Performance*. Cambridge: Cambridge University Press.
Oates, Wallace. 1972. *Fiscal Federalism*. New York: Harcourt, Brace and Jovanovich.
Obydenkova, Anastassia, and Wilfried Swenden. 2013. "Autocracy-Sustaining Versus Democratic Federalism: Explaining the Divergent Trajectories of Territorial Politics in Russia and Western Europe." *Territory, Politics, Governance* 1 (1): 86–112.
Olsen, Johan. 2001. "Garbage Cans, New Institutionalism, and the Study of Politics." *American Political Science Review* 95 (1): 191–98.
——— 2009. "Change and Continuity: An Institutional Approach to Institutions of Democratic Government." *European Political Science Review* 1 (1): 3.
——— 2013. "The Institutional Basis of Democratic Accountability." *West European Politics* 36 (3): 447–73.

Orren, Karen, and Stephen Skowronek. 1996. "Institutions and Intercurrence: Theory Building in the Fullness of Time." *Nomos* 38: 111–46.

Orten, J. D., and Karl Weick. 1990. "Loosely Coupled Systems: A Reconceptualization." *Academy of Management Review* 15 (2): 203–23.

Ostrom, Elinor. 1986. "An Agenda for the Study of Institutions." *Public Choice* 48 (1): 3–25.

Parsons, Craig. 2002. "Showing Ideas as Causes: The Origins of the European Union." *International Organization* 56 (1): 47–84.

——— 2016. "Ideas and Power: Four Intersections and how to Show them." *Journal of European Public Policy* 23 (3): 446–63.

Peters, B. G. 1998. "Political Institutions, Old and New." In *A New Handbook of Political Science*, eds. Robert Goodin and Hans-Dieter Klingemann. Oxford: Oxford University Press, 205–20.

Pierson, Paul. 1993. "When Effect Becomes Cause: Policy Feedback and Political Change." *World Politics* 45 (4): 595–628.

——— 1995. "Fragmented Welfare States: Federal Institutions and the Development of Social Policy." *Governance* 8 (4): 449–78.

——— 2000a. "Increasing Returns, Path Dependence, and the Study of Politics." *American Political Science Review* 94 (2): 251–67.

——— 2000b. "The Limits of Design: Explaining Institutional Origins and Change." *Governance* 13 (4): 475–99.

——— 2004. *Politics in Time: History, Institutions, and Social Analysis*. Princeton: Princeton University Press.

Radaelli, Claudio, Bruno Dente, and Samuele Dossi. 2012. "Recasting Institutionalism: Institutional Analysis and Public Policy." *European Political Science* 11 (4): 537–50.

Rixen, Thomas, and Lora A. Viola. 2015. "Putting Path Dependence in its Place: Toward a Taxonomy of Institutional Change." *Journal of Theoretical Politics* 27 (2): 301–23.

Rodden, Jonathan. 2006. *Hamilton's Paradox. The Promise and Peril of Fiscal Federalism*. Cambridge: Cambridge University Press.

Samuels, David, and Matthew Shugart. 2010. *Presidents, Parties, and Prime Ministers: How the Separation of Powers Affects Party Organization and Behavior*. Cambridge: Cambridge University Press.

Sanders, Elizabeth. 2006. "Historical Institutionalism." In *The Oxford Handbook of Political Institutions*, eds. R.A.W. Rhodes, Sarah Binder and Bert Rockman. Oxford: Oxford University Press, 39–55.

Scharpf, Fritz. 1988. "The Joint-Decision Trap: Lessons from German Federalism and European Integration." *Public Administration* 66 (3): 239–78.

——— 2000. "Institutions in Comparative Policy Research." *Comparative Political Studies* 33 (6/7): 762–90.

Schmidt, Vivien. 2008. "Discursive Institutionalism: The Explanatory Power of Ideas and Discourse." *Annual Review of Political Science* 11 (1): 303–26.

——— 2010. "Taking Ideas and Discourse Seriously: Explaining Change through Discursive Institutionalism as the Fourth 'New Institutionalism'." *European Political Science Review* 2 (1): 1–25.

Schweers Cook, Karen, and Margaret Levi, eds. 1990. *The Limits of Rationality*. Chicago: University of Chicago Press.

Searle, John. 1995. *The Construction of Social Reality*. New York: Free Press.

——— 2005. "What is an Institution?" *Journal of Institutional Economics* 1 (1): 1–22.

Sharman, Campbell. 1990. "Parliamentary Federations and Limited Government: Constitutional Design and Redesign in Australia and Canada." *Journal of Theoretical Politics* 2 (2): 205–30.

Shepsle, Kenneth. 2006. "Rational Choice Institutionalism." In *The Oxford Handbook of Political Institutions*, eds. R.A.W. Rhodes, Sarah Binder and Bert Rockman. Oxford: Oxford University Press, 23–38.

Shugart, Matthew, and John Carey. 1992. *Presidents and Assemblies: Constitutional Design and Electoral Dynamics*. New York: Cambridge University Press.

Siaroff, Alan. 2003. "Comparative Presidencies: The Inadequacy of the Presidential, Semi-Presidential, and Parliamentary Distinction." *European Journal of Political Research* 42 (3): 287–312.

Simeon, Richard. 1972. *Federal-Provincial Diplomacy: The Making of Recent Policy in Canada*. Toronto: University of Toronto Press.

——— 2005. "Plus ça change: Inter-governmental Relations Then and Now." *Policy Options* 26 (3): 84–87.

Simon, Herbert. 1959. "Theories of Decision-Making in Economics and Behavioral Science." *American Economic Review* 49 (3): 253–83.

Slater, Dan, and Erica Simmons. 2010. "Informative Regress: Critical Antecedents in Comparative Politics." *Comparative Political Studies* 43 (7): 886–917.

Smith, Rogers M. 2006. "Which Comes First, the Ideas or the Institutions?" In *Rethinking Political Institutions. The Art of the State*, eds. Ian Shapiro, Stephen Skowronek and Daniel Galvin. New York: New York University Press, 93–113.

Soifer, Hillel D. 2012. "The Causal Logic of Critical Junctures." *Comparative Political Studies* 45 (12): 1572–97.

Sonnicksen, Jared. 2017. "Democratising the Separation of Powers in EU Government: The Case for Presidentialism." *European Law Review* 23 (6): 509–22.

——— 2018. "Federalism and Democracy. A Tense Relationship." In *Calidad democratic y organización territorial*, eds. José Tudela, Mario Kölling and Fernando Reviriego. Madrid: Marcial Pons, 31–52.

Steffani, Winfried. 1979. *Parlamentarische und Präsidentielle Demokratie*. Opladen: Westdeutscher Verlag.

Stepan, Alfred. 1999. "Federalism and Democracy: Beyond the U.S. Model." *Journal of Democracy* 10 (4): 19–34.

Thelen, Kathleen. 1999. "Historical Institutionalism in Comparative Politics." *Annual Review of Political Science* 2: 369–404.

——— 2004. *How Institutions Evolve. The Political Economy of Skills in Germany, Britain, the United States, and Japan*. Cambridge: Cambridge University Press.

Thelen, Kathleen, and Sven Steinmo. 1992. "Historical Institutionalism in Comparative Politics." In *Structuring Politics: Historical Institutionalism in Comparative Analysis*, eds. Sven Steinmo, Kathleen Thelen and Frank Longstreth. Cambridge: Cambridge University Press, 1–32.

Tilly, Charles. 1984. *Big Structures, Large Processes, Huge Comparisons*. New York: Russell Sage Foundation.

Tilly, Charles, and Robert E. Goodin. 2006. "It Depends." In *The Oxford Handbook of Contextual Political Analysis*, eds. Robert Goodin and Charles Tilly. Oxford: Oxford University Press, 3–32.

Tsebelis, George. 1995. "Decision Making in Political Systems: Veto Players in Presidentialism, Parliamentarism, Multicameralism and Multipartyism." *British Journal of Political Science* 25 (3): 289–325.

Tsebelis, George, and Jeannette Money. 1997. *Bicameralism*. Cambridge: Cambridge University Press.

Vatter, Adrian. 2009. "Lijphart Expanded: Three Dimensions of Democracy in Advanced OECD Countries?" *European Political Science Review* 1 (1): 125–54.

Watts, Ronald. 1998. "Federalism, Federal Political Systems, and Federations." *Annual Review of Political Science* 1: 117–37.

——— 2006. "Origins of Cooperative and Competitive Federalism." In *Territory, Democracy and Justice: Regionalism and Federalism in Western Democracies*, ed. Scott Greer. Basingstoke: Palgrave Macmillan, 201–23.

——— 2008. *Comparing Federal Systems*. 3rd ed. Montréal: McGill-Queen's University Press.

Weaver, Kent, and Bert Rockman, eds. 1993. *Do Institutions Matter?* Washington, DC: Brookings Institute.

3

CONSTITUTIONAL IMMANENCE IN THE USA

Politics transpires in spaces of meaning. Democracy populates that space, while federalism multiplies it. The constitution frames it. These premises comprise a complex quartet. They each and surely taken together demand differentiation.

The constitution in the strict sense typically stands for a written compact establishing the political order, its instruments and institutions of government, the distribution of powers and competences, and a catalog of basic rights. But it pertains in a broader sense to the make-up of that order in practice. Over time a constitution may come to encompass and mean much more, or in parts much less, than what is written on the pages. A host of purposes, functions, and even effects are commonly attributed to constitutions. However, it should be obvious that a constitution in its strict sense does not really do anything other than just "be there". Thus, enter interpretation. Who performs this can depend on the constitution in the strict sense, but ultimately on what is made of it in its broader sense: whether it is put into practice, sustained, perceived as legitimate, held to contain truths that are self-evident, considered in parts obsolete but innocuous, or instead warranting amendment. A federally constituted system establishes not only a multilevel order, but also the constituent status and rights of its integral parts and their governments. They possess an entitlement and a vested interest in having a say in what goes into the constitution in the strict sense and certainly what comes out of it in the broader sense. Moreover, a federal order engenders from the outset a veritable recipe for turning many ensuing political matters into constitutional ones. That can also be the case with a democracy, which necessarily grounds itself in a multitude of constituents. They have extensive rights to partake in the polity and in the interpretation of the very compact that binds them to a *people*. The constitution authorizes a government. A democratic one derives its authority from the people on the presupposition of their equality.

To assert that politics unfolds in spaces of meaning would appear to restate the obvious. But the claim applies with profound and extensive implications for politics

DOI: 10.4324/9781003203674-3

in a democratic, federal constitutional order. Such is the case in the USA, which combines these dimensions in its polity. Democratic, federal, and constitutional premises and principles undoubtedly belong to the facts of political life in the US polity. They build at the same time on fictions. Therein lies part of their power.

This chapter examines the emergence of constitutional ideas, their institutionalization, and the dynamics of interpretation regulated, surely among other things, by ideas. It pursues two chief ends: to conceptualize with comparisons and to specify the US case. It needs to be shown how these processes are compounded in a democratic and federal order and in the USA in particular. This will provide some first insights into how the fragmentation of the US polity is constitutive from the outset and ideationally reinforced through constitutional political interpretation and contestation.

The concept and evolution of a regulative idea

Democratic and federal constitutional principles rest upon certain fictions. This is not meant in the sense of falsehoods and fairytales. Rather, as accounts and narratives, fictions can be quite real, or, more precisely, when they are believed, followed, or prompt the realization of something else. In this regard, fiction can also imply more of a pretending, or *tun als ob*, a doing *as if*. Conceptual contestation, politics in spaces of meaning as it were, recurs for multiple reasons and in multiple respects. Ideas and their interpretation contribute to the dynamics of the "real world" of politics. Those dynamics, the things that happen, in turn provide referents for the imagined, the conceptual, and their further development. History, as a process of the past leading to the present, is entangled with conceptual development (Ball 1998; Koselleck 1982; Palonen 2002). We can detect such an entanglement in constitutions.

As for their origins and development, the concept of sovereignty represents one example, and a pivotal one. Its emergence and conceptualization is interlinked with the development of modern states and their constitutions (see e.g. Troper 2012). A similar thing could be said of *popular* sovereignty regarding the constitutions of a democracy. State and popular sovereignty are among the cornerstones of constitutionalism, while those concepts are interwoven with the development of further things like the "imaginations" of a peoplehood, self-government, and political territory (see e.g. Anderson 1983; Held 1989; Urbinati 2006). In short, there is a complex interlinkage between political and conceptual development on the path to constitutions, as with the US founding. Popular sovereignty poses a loaded term, laden with equality in particular. Like many political concepts (e.g. representation, democracy, power), equality is also an "essentially contested" (Gallie 1956) one. Contested political concepts invoke multiple meanings, with varying normative as well as institutional implications at *one time*, as well as tensions with changing conditions *over time*. Again, paths of historical developments include conceptual ones. This is relevant for the conditions in which popular sovereignty became a guiding idea for the constitution.

Emergent popular sovereignty as idea and precursor to the US case

The power play between the House of Commons and the monarch in 16th and 17th-century England proved foundational. It constitutes an antecedent for path dependencies of institutional and ideational evolution, as it did for the latter US case. This particular interplay, as reconstructed by Morgan, fostered the "invention of the people" and popular sovereignty (Morgan 1989), in parts by strategy, in parts inadvertently, and with an extensive trajectory of impact.

Dislodging power from monarchs supposed to be endowed with the divine right to rule is observable in other times and places (Bendix 1980). Distinct to the English case in the early 17th century was however a particular strategy. Parliament was not disputing the status of monarchs as vicar of the divine and thus of perfection (i.e. like God, "the King can do no wrong", itself an old and powerful fiction). Doing so would have likely provoked its dissolution, followed by the imprisonment of unruly parliamentarians, if not worse. Royal divine authority rather became increasingly employed *as an argument* by Parliament to wrest power from the King and in some cases to overturn royal councils' decisions (e.g. erroneous royal decisions must have resulted from poor advice). Such actions were presented as a means to "protect" the king, leaving Parliament no choice but to assume the duties of ordinary earthly and thus fallible government. More importantly, in lieu of divine royal authority, the appeal to the *people* came increasingly to serve as the purported source of authority for Parliament.[1]

This appeal constituted a *fiction* in Morgan's terms, not least since only a small minority of English subjects were enfranchised at the time. Yet, since at least some form of suffrage was already established, "only a stretch of the imagination was required to envisage parliamentary elections as the act in which *the* people endowed Parliament with their sovereign power" (Morgan 1989: 60). Similarly fictitious was the invention of consent of the governed in the formation of government. Partially analogous or related notions already existed, while the wars of religion in early modern Europe, the catastrophes and disorder they wrought, helped shatter in the long run the moral order in which the Church and Christendom provided its bedrock. More specifically, elaborate reconstructions of a "social contract" appeared in the midst and end of the English civil wars. Most notable were Hobbes's *Leviathan*, which argued for the need for an absolute sovereign incorporating the body politic to maintain peace, order, and ultimately the "commonwealth" (Hobbes 1651 [1985]), and Locke's (at first anonymously published) *Two Treatises of Government*, which was positioned against patriarchal and divinely legitimated absolutist rule for one, and for government by consent of the governed, created as equals, and the protection of their inalienable rights to life, liberty, and property, for another (Locke 1689 [2000]).

Common to both theories was not only their logical refutation of the foundation of a centuries-old medieval order (granted, one whose deterioration was already well underway). They also supposed a societal compact establishing its government, based on accounts – and of course fabrications – of a state-of-nature society had left in order to rationally consent to its subjugation in a polity to serve certain ends. This sort of account was employed as justification in the politics of Parliament's claim to rest upon and embody some primordial transfer of power from a sovereign people (Morgan 1989: 58 ff.).[2]

What is even more remarkable, and important for our purposes here, is not only that Parliament managed to get away with this in the end,[3] but that the idea also *got away from Parliament*. These contestations had wider implications, many of them inadvertently, for the evolution of popular sovereignty, democratic equality, and representation. While fictions, the related ideas and arguments were not fantasy. To have effect, which they apparently did, they needed some grounding in "facts". These ideas and claims also induced expectations far beyond what Parliament intended. It only took a short time for more radical calls for "narrowing the gap" between normative claims and actual circumstances to erupt (Morgan 1989: 66). The concrete manifestations of these dynamics are most salient in the emergence of the "Levellers" and the even more radical-democratic "Diggers" in the midst of the 17th century, demanding a more consistent realization of popular sovereignty through for example expanding the suffrage, increasing the frequency of elections, imposing imperative mandates on representatives, and even abolishing private property.[4]

Hence it did not take long for the pretense of authority by the people in the context of a power struggle within Parliament against the Royalists, and Parliament against (Catholic-friendly) kings, to be turned back on Parliament. It soon came to face demands for, what we may call in contemporary terms, representative democracy and popular rule by the many. Similarly, whether Locke, with the idea of government by consent, meant actually recurring elections and regular renewals of that popular consent is irrelevant here. More certain and telling is that the concept wound up being interpreted *that way*. Ideas constructed and communicated in a specific political context thus came to be taken out of context and nonetheless, or for this reason, taken seriously and, by many, quite literally. Moreover, comparable dynamics unfolded when claims to popular sovereignty, inalienable rights, representation, and self-government were turned against Britain in colonial America. That contest culminated in the formation of an independent republic by those former British subjects less than a century after the establishment of parliamentary sovereignty and constitutional monarchy in England (see e.g. Kenyon 1962; Morgan 1989: 239–306).

The contestation and ensuing changes triggered by perceived contradictions between ideational claims, particularly of those in power, and political practices reveal politics in spaces of meaning. This does not preclude the incidence of contradictions by reformers, "revolutionaries", or others seeking change either. Of course interests or ulterior motives may drive a contestation around ideas, while various participants may sincerely hold concurrent but inconsistent ideas. It should come as no surprise that people, irrespective of their erudition and eloquence, can square noble principles with gross violations of them in practice. This becomes all too evident in the founding of the USA, where in the act of declaring independence, slaveholders could claim that "all men are created equal".

Persons or parliaments propagating ideas and contravening them in parts does not negate the relevance of ideas and dynamics of interpretation. The idea of equality and the claim of "all men are created equal" were invoked. The notion was not forfeited due to the appalling contradiction in the formation of the USA and for many decades thereafter. It would become instead one of the most influential ideas and referents of the American "creed" and "identity" despite persistent contradictions (Smith 1988). It has been channeled in multiple political movements for expanding suffrage (e.g. on the basis of race, gender, age), countless other calls for political reforms, and even into the definition of citizenship and democracy (see e.g. Appleby 1992; Smith 2001). For more than two centuries in the USA, "it was precisely the commitment to democratic ideology that, at each step in the redefinition of rights, enabled critics of the limited scope of citizenship to accuse their opponents of hypocrisy", allowing, even empowering, agents of reform and change to appeal to "democracy's capacity to democratize itself" (Dorf and Sabel 1998: 452). Like the idea of popular sovereignty invoked by Parliament in the England of the 17th century, the idea of equality, its trajectory of change and impact, escaped the late-18th-century US authors of independence and the Constitution.

The ideas of popular sovereignty and equality and their early institutionalization were to be followed by a veritable democratization of interpretation. Political contestation and discourses vis-à-vis policies and the polity itself would become mass affairs of "the people". Constitutional politics was rendered more complex. The interplay between facts and fictions, as paraphrased from Morgan for the English case and in its transfer to the early USA, is informative. But how to conceptualize these tensions needs further examination.

From fictive to regulative idea

A rule, such as regarding the age of majority, may be conceived as a "legal fiction" – i.e. it serves as a construct for effectively regulating e.g. consent and liability matters. However, it is misleading to subsume numerous others norms and ideas under "fictions". Many ideas signify commandments or commitments for practice. Human equality is such an idea. Its presupposition may require, to certain extents and at certain times, a leap of faith. However, the ideas of equality in democracy, or comity in federalism, autonomy, or shared rule in either of them, can set guidelines, foster logics of appropriateness, and induce people to find meaning and take actions. Political ideas have not only imaginative qualities, but can also take on a *regulative* character, especially those enshrined in a constitution.

Ideas can contribute to shaping behavior. A *regulative idea* has particular implications. This specific term finds its origination in Kantian philosophy.[5] For our purposes, one may underline that a *regulative* idea is contrasted with a *constitutive* one, the latter referring to understanding (*Verstand*), and regulative more to reason (*Vernunft*) (see e.g. Dister 1972; Friedman 1992). Reason, in short, follows different practical and theoretical logics (Lahat 2013: 64–94). A theoretical interest may concern "knowing for knowledge's sake", while practical interest can be analogized with the social cognition theoretical claim of "thinking is for doing" (Fiske 1992). Here the term fiction comes into play, with particular relevance for ideas like freedom. Accordingly, whether there is such a thing as freedom or whether we are free or not is ultimately beside the point for "practical reason" as, theoretically, freedom's existence can be either proven or falsified. However, for living in the world, especially in the hope of attaining a just, fair, and peaceful one, reason may dictate, or it may be reasonable, to *tun als ob*, to assume and proceed *as if* humans are free (Schönecker 2005: 55–60; Vaihinger 1924 [2000]: 289 ff.). Acting *as if* or in predication on "practical beliefs", furthermore, serves to achieve purposive ends, not only (self-)interests, but also, and more importantly, moral ones (Goldman 2012: 504–6). These propositions are grounded in a wider Enlightenment model. However, a regulative idea can also be adopted chiefly with regard to its functions (Kleingeld 2008). Accordingly, regulative ideas are understood here as attached to mechanisms like reasoning, by which people can interpret ideas, norms, and principles and use them as guidelines for thinking and action.

Diverse strands of scholarship follow this understanding of regulative idea, treating or equating with regulative idea, for instance: key elements of constitutionalism, the constitution itself, and the concept of a social contract (Grimm 2016; Loughlin 2010; Post 1990); the entrance into a "covenant" for example to balance diversity and unity in theories of pluralism, federalism, and multilevel governance (Elazar 1987; Hueglin 1985; Requejo and Caminal 2010); the "rationality" of public discourse and deliberation (Habermas 1992); the "veil of ignorance" (Rawls 1971) prescribed in a theory of justice, as well as for deliberation in political arenas, including constitutional conventions (Elster 2000); or with regard to democracy, or again the explicit notion that "all humans are created free and equal" (Laserson 1947; Michelman 1999; Post 2006; Sørensen and Torfing 2005). Regulative idea in these cases suggests ideas requiring more belief and *tun als ob* than proof. They are embedded in institutions and help guide interaction and operation within institutional settings, including critical reflection.

The idea itself, as vision or belief, eschews perfect realization. Whether as "thick" and "dense" principles or "thin" and "loose" understandings thereof, regulative ideas provide orientation *toward* their fulfillment. The interpretation and contestation connected to regulative ideas are also contingent upon institutional settings, the polity and society, and their interconnected development. Thus regulative ideas are not necessarily stable or permanent. Equality, and the commitments it may entail, for example, as a common fundamental principle of democracy and democratic governments, can be construed in different ways at one time in different systems or interpreted differently than in the past. Regulative ideas can be interpreted with diverse implications in time and space.

The "invention" of popular sovereignty and its subsequent development in the founding of the USA illustrates the dynamics of conceptual contestation as well as regulative ideas. They are reflected in what Morgan (1989) depicts as "stretching the imagination" versus "narrowing the gap" between fact and fiction: for example Parliament claiming political authority as derived from *the people* (the "stretch") in contrast with their actual inclusion in determining their government, which triggered movements to reform *toward* more popular sovereignty ("narrowing the gap"). A congruent premise on the concept and dynamics of regulative ideas is also provided in Scharpf's thesis on the primary challenge confronting modern government: between the *Utopie* of democracy and the *Anpassung* (adaptation) to the complexities of government (Scharpf 1970). Not only the idea or vision, but also the *adaptation*, is decisive. Adaptations arise on an individual and collective basis, and can work both ways. They may involve adjusting and refining concepts to fit changing circumstances and conditions of society and governing. Conversely, adaptation may entail pursuing reforms and adjustments of circumstances and conditions to fulfill claims and norms better. All the while, the quality of the dynamics and the trajectory of change can diverge from original intentions and understandings. Popular sovereignty emerged and evolved into a regulative idea in interplay with institutions and political dynamics, which contributed to further institutional development. This points to the formation of a path of institutional and ideational development that was contingent on the antecedent and surrounding circumstances in the founding and Constitution of the USA.

The US constitutional quandary

The founding of the USA and its Constitution have, for many reasons, enduring significance for American federal democracy. They formed particular institutional and ideational paths, as well as several dilemmas, both for government under the Constitution and for constitutional interpretation. The following delves into the formative process of the Constitution, and its surrounding and antecedent institutional and ideational development. This is prefaced by a brief discussion of the slavery issue in the context of the Constitution, which ushered in a foundational set of institutional and ideational path dependencies in the USA that cut across its democratic and federal legacies.

Two foundational legacies

The US Constitution unites two unique legacies: that of the first modern republican and federal government in the world for one, and the only modern government to include slavery in its constitution for another. To consider slavery an exception in the US Constitution and one limited to the Southern States is a severe distortion in multiple respects. The institution of slavery affected the entire political order in numerous structural-institutional and complex ideational ways. Slavery is not explicitly mentioned, but is alluded to, in the Constitution. Aside from the sunset clause in Article 1(9) withholding from Congress the power to prohibit the "importation of persons" prior to the year 1808, the most tangible reference to slavery is found in the Three-Fifths-Clause. Article 1(2) regulates the apportionment of both representatives in the House of Representatives and of taxation based on the population of "free persons" and three-fifths of "all other persons", a circuitous term for slaves.[6]

Focusing on just this provision, it is not difficult to identify how it embodies a flagrant denigration of persons as "three-fifths", but also the abysmal moral depravity of enslaving people in the first place. This institution became enshrined in a Constitution that was connected to a revolutionary legacy which included commitment to the Enlightenment vision of uplifting humanity. The latter assertion is clearly not the whole story, but not a romantic embellishment of US independence either. Referents to the "city on the hill" and ideals of progress that could be achieved by its own laws and practices, and even serve as role models to the world, had already permeated the ideational space of the American colonies and intensified in the run-up to the War of Independence (see e.g. Bell 1975; Bellah et al. 1985; Grey 1984; Smith 1988). One could resolve these contradictions if such a self-proclaimed idealism were construed rather as a strategy to cloak self-interests. The republican-liberty legacy in the Constitution would be easier to square with its slavery legacy. But to reduce things like the battle cry of "no taxation without representation" in the rally for independence to an exercise in tax evasion would distort matters.[7] It would also unduly alleviate the necessity to comprehend these intertwined foundational legacies. They are more than historically relevant too, as both unique American constitutional legacies affect politics to this day. Incidentally there should also be no doubt that the Founders, many of them already born and socialized in the early colonial ideational space as well as versed in Enlightenment writings, were not only quite capable of anticipating, but also explicitly confronted with, condemnations of slavery, including by their contemporaries (see e.g. Einhorn 2002; Ellis 2000: 80–88; Morgan 1972). The assumption that "for they knew not what they did", while perhaps relatively applicable to the republican polities of Ancient Greece and Rome that practiced slavery, fails to pass empirical muster in the case of the late-18th-century USA.

From an institutional-analytical point of view alone, one can only imagine how vastly different the routes American political development could have taken had the three-fifths compromise failed. It not only gave the practice of slavery constitutional protection. Its effect was to apportion a substantially larger share of Congressional representation to the slave-holding states for several more generations to come than they would have otherwise been entitled to – and this almost no matter which counterfactual scenario we take.[8] Moreover, the three-fifths clause managed to provide a genuinely "perverse effect" by incentivizing the expansion of the slave population for both economic *and political* gains in the following decades.

The institutional consequences are reflected in the continuation of the free–slave state divide in the American westward expansion – entailing yet another legacy of innumerable calamities inflicted on Native Americans – and the peculiar negotiation to incorporate new states by parity (e.g. the 1820 "Missouri Comprise", by which accession of a new free state had to be matched by a new slave state). While the free-vs.-slave state policy was part of the balancing of interests and power in the Senate, old and new slave states equally gained a disproportionate representation in their favor in the House of Representatives. As a further consequence, slaveholding states presided over a strong veto power in regular legislative processes and an insurmountable one against attempts to amend the constitution.[9] And as if that were not enough, the constitutional three-fifths rule also meant that those states had a substantially disproportionate influence in the Electoral College. Electoral votes are apportioned pursuant to the Constitution, to this day, on the basis of a state's number of senators (two irrespective of population; thus re-enters the balance of power at play in the politics of admitting new states) *and* representatives (population-based, including three-fifths of the respective and increasing slave populations). As a result, the slaveholding states were *also* endowed with a disproportionately strong say in determining the Presidency. And with that of course came more influence in determining the composition of the Judiciary, that is the presidential appointments to the Supreme Court and subordinate Federal Courts, which are also subject to Senate confirmation. Consequently, rather than an exception, a minor accident, or an ironic twist of history, this one constitutional provision, whether (some) framers intended it this way or not, facilitated and became entangled with an array of ramifications for *at least* seventy years of American politics and political development.

The ideational underpinnings and societal implications of slavery are manifold: for slaves and their posterity, but also for all citizens including those of the "Free North". For the evolution of American liberal ideas, there is a complicated legacy involved here as well.[10] Were the persistence and expansion of liberty and slavery explainable only by blatant racism and bigotry, which are evident and grave enough, the puzzle would be easier to solve. However, there is a particularly important legacy to note here, in US history and in many ways into the present it seems, especially since it cuts across race, nationality, gender, and more. It involves the association of values of equality, liberty, and independence as virtues of a free and self-governing people on the one hand, with the ownership of property on the other. Earlier electoral laws prescribing property as a criterion for suffrage rights in the USA, and in many other modern democracies, provide but one testament to a shared and less noble past. This linkage coincides, in turn, with the disdain for the poor and property-less (and thus the vast share of people at most times throughout human history) and, in concomitance, the fear of the disorder and decay their enfranchisement would supposedly wreak upon a republican "civil society". Such ideational patterns and reasoning united the Federalists and the framers with the likes of the otherwise "radical democrat" Thomas Jefferson, but also political philosophers theorizing toward a modern representative democracy, like Locke and Sieyes (see e.g. Jörke 2011), and many before them.

This provides a clue at least on how the circle of equality and liberty could be squared by its advocates with the continued exclusion and subjugation of those they perceived as "unworthy" of and "unfit" for citizenship. One gathers the disturbing insight that the existence and expansion of a permanent underclass may have had "productive effects" in economic as well as psychological, social, and political, and thus institutional and ideational, regards for the entire white population in the USA. Not only the colonial past but also slavery in their present provided a continuous and brutal reminder of what it meant to be unfree. American individualism and egalitarianism were allegedly inaugurated from the outset, with an apparent absence of the shackles of a feudal order that once bounded most European countries. Yet the unparalleled reality of a rapidly expanding legal and substantive equality to be found already in the early USA was also accompanied, even facilitated, by slavery. In the world of modern government, both of these legacies have made the American Constitution exceptional.

Forging the US Constitution: between the Convention and conventions

The institutional measures under deliberation when drafting a constitution go beyond technical issues for calibrating the machinery of government. They touch upon fundamental principles and questions with multiple interests and value conflicts (e.g. political, social, territorial, cultural). The constitutional quandary lies in not only having to reach a compromise that accommodates diverse ideas, but also to design the corresponding institutional rules to foster their realization. Forging the constitution entails a political, societal mediation and exchange and requires a "contingent consensus" (Levi 1998) in order to be adopted. This complex challenge confronted the Constitutional Convention at Philadelphia (1787) and the debate surrounding the establishment of a new and mixed, or "hybrid" (Ball 1995: 217; Lhotta 2010b), federal republic for the then thirteen United States.

The differences of opinion among Convention participants and the broader public discourse during the ratification process certainly revolved around competing interests. They included territorial-based interests, economic ones, and the cross-cutting issue of slavery.[11] However, votes in the Convention, and later in ratification, were not divided along *one* socio-economic cleavage, but rather varied between and at times within delegations by issues such as federalism, representation, and the distribution of powers in general (Jillson and Eubanks 1984; Pope and Treier 2015). Of particular concern were the interests of delegates' *constituents* and larger interests such as protecting the rights of democratic and federal participation, representation, and self-government (McGuire 2003). Given the salience of *property* in the Convention, the wider public debates, and certainly the *Federalist Papers*, they can easily read like material self-interest, decades to centuries later (Morgan 1957). Irrespective of how we may or should evaluate their ideas normatively, it would be inaccurate to construe ideational claims lodged by either of the sides as only a disguise for other ulterior motives (see also e.g. Schultz 1993). Taking the ideas in institutional context seriously, the extensive and profound inextricable link *believed* to exist between human liberty and property rights during the US founding,[12] which "no taxation without representation" also reflects, becomes as such ideationally and institutionally more comprehensible.

The debates in this formative era were grounded in various political philosophies, diverse "ideological origins" of the Revolution itself (Bailyn 1992), and multiple ideational underpinnings in the immediate political and evolved institutional context (see e.g. McDonald 1985). The Convention itself, deliberating as it did in secrecy, was initially detached from public scrutiny and appears to have provided an arena conducive to argumentation (see e.g. Elster 1995, 2000). How far the delegates conformed to arguing behind a "veil of ignorance", impartially following higher motives, need not be ascertained here. What is certain is that debates involved ideas and transpired, quite intensely, in a space of contested, even transforming, meanings.

As for the original constitutional quandary, the different Founders expressed different ideas on the issues under debate. They constituted, in parts, shared beliefs and concepts, but attached with different meanings shared among different camps. For simplicity's sake, one can summarize the supporters of the draft constitution more or less under the *Federalists'* camp, and the no less diverse camp of opponents under the (quite misleading, but common (Hutson 1981)) label of *Antifederalists*. The range of ideas encompassed various, concurring, and competing conceptions of a republic, a federation, and a duly compounded governmental order conducive to equality, liberty and security, property and prosperity, but also civil society, free association, autonomy, and self-government, among other things.[13] It also appears that many of the said concepts were transformed in the course of the debates themselves, within and beyond the Convention and in the ratification process (Ball and Pocock 1988; Jörke 2010). At the same time, by and large, there was almost a unanimous consensus on constitutionalizing these principles of *popular* but *limited* government in a *federal* union. Hence, at least *some* commitment to the Revolution united the contestants of the debate. However, there was considerably more consensus within the Convention, with few Antifederalists present, than outside of it. All the while these different "parties" disputed bitterly, voicing mutual suspicions and at times defamations on each other's sincerity and commitment to these principles.

One most noticeable and yet easily overlooked aspect may be that, for all political and public figures and the citizenry (outliers and some privately harbored preferences aside), monarchy was out of the question, as was a centralized unitary state. While this may seem self-evident now, it definitely should not be. For perhaps even more profoundly revealing is what is also *not there*. That is, there is an utter lack of proposals from the other side of the potential spectrum, such as anarchism or communalism and the abolishment of private property, and thus radical visions like those already proposed by the Levellers and the Diggers in mid-17th-century England – i.e. quite logical and consequential implications that people could, and already *did*, infer from claims to equality and liberty, especially in a critical juncture like the Convention.[14] Apparently much had changed in the early USA since the contest of the English Parliament and the House of Commons in their, in parts inadvertently, induced evolution of popular sovereignty that culminated in the Glorious Revolution a century prior to the American Revolution. Against this backdrop, though also in contrast to the dynamics that unfolded in the French Revolution shortly thereafter, we can conclude with all the more certainty that the scope of legitimate constitutional options had apparently become quite constricted.

The positions in the US constitutional debates for the large part involved variations predicated on already established and, in many instances, long practiced institutions of limited government in localities and states. Forging the US Constitution thus could transpire on the basis of an ample experienced, learned, and internalized substantiation for the regulative ideas of grounding a *non-centralized* government in the *people* through respective constituencies and some form of representation, separation of powers, the unalienable rights of life, liberty, happiness, and property – to which all sides of the constitutional debate laid claim. They differed considerably and contentiously on the choice of types of division of power arrangement, the proper balance between shared and self-rule, and the appropriate realization thereof.

Moreover, they all exhibited some degree of trust and distrust in government, as neither its necessity nor potential "evil" was disputed outright. The same can be inferred regarding trust and distrust in the people. Especially with regard to how they viewed the people and the government, the rival camps have been categorized as rather aristocratic or democratic, rather conservative or radical, rather liberal or republican. Yet the numerous supporting and opposing positions on the Constitution were drawing from many of the *same* ideational sources: from Locke's (1689 [2000]) *Treatises of Government* and Montesquieu's (1748 [1989]) *Spirit of the Laws* on for example the horizontal and vertical separation of powers and limited government, to the widely revered Blackstone's (1765 [2016]) *Commentaries on the Laws of England*, a host of ancient Greek and Roman philosophers and statesmen whose names, like Publius and Brutus, the contestants also donned for themselves, the English Glorious Revolution, and numerous, for them, deterrent references to monarchic and imperial examples throughout Europe (see also Hart 1907; Kenyon 1955, 1962; Levy 2006; Lutz 1984; Morgan 1948; Shalhope 1972; Tuckness 2003). This renders it all the more difficult to neatly compartmentalize the Founders in contemporary political theoretical terms that have transformed considerably over the last two centuries, transformations moreover to which these debaters contributed significantly.

In this context, the *Federalist Papers* by James Madison, Alexander Hamilton, and John Jay, published during the ratification debate, represent an influential as well as renowned documentation on the design and purpose of the (then still draft) Constitution. These essays provide insight into the debates of the time, constituting an essential second primary source, but also a much-referenced "theory" of the US Constitution (see e.g. Brunhöber 2015; Epstein 1984; Lhotta 2010a; Mahoney 1987; Pole 2005: 14–24; Zuckert 1992). However, it has not escaped scholars across multiple disciplines and theoretical-analytical perspectives that the Federalists also pursued a political strategy. They sought to prevail in the ratification debates with their much transformed vision of a compound republic. Consequently, equating the Federalists' theory of government with a far-sighted recipe for modern government, federalism and democracy, amounts to a fallacy of retrospective determinism. Their side "won". They were not predicting modern American federalism and democracy; they invented its framework. Like almost all inventions, theirs involved refining and redefining components and concepts that already existed. They actually did not veer far from the institutions of their time and place, certainly when one considers any number of alternative potential routes that constitutional drafts could have taken. Things simply could have gone differently. And they incidentally did, as the 1800 elections only one decade later demonstrated (addressed further below), ushering in a sweeping victory for the Democrat-Republicans, with further implications for the constitution and polity until the Civil War, and in complexly recurring ways into the present.

Finally, there are two further significant factors or rather parts of the ideational dimension to address. The divergences among the framers, their opponents, and other contemporaries are to an extent attributable to their various interpretations of historical experiences up to and of the circumstances at the time. In addition to different principles or rather interpretations thereof, perceptions gained through experience also contributed to Convention participants and protesters reaching different conclusions and lessons learned on how to design their democratic or republican federation (see e.g. Edling 2003; Jensen 1950; Sonnicksen 2010). To name just two intertwined areas: one is the perceived failure or inadequacy of the Articles of Confederation during the "critical period" between independence and the Convention, plagued by mountains of war debt and mounting dissatisfaction among indebted farmers, though also their creditors, precipitating in "Shay's Rebellion" in Western Massachusetts (see e.g. Morgan 1989: 265 ff.). Another area concerns the lessons from the colonial experience, for example regarding established practices in self-government worthy of emulation or evasion, or the potential tyrannies and threats to liberty, equality, and property imposed by governments deemed insufficiently controlled, be they unchecked executives or unchecked legislatures (whether in reference to the English Parliament or their own state assemblies). How the framers, Founders, and ordinary citizens reflected on and evaluated these experiences were bound in the institutional and ideational frames elaborated above, but these frames evolved also through such experiences.

The dynamics of the constitutional debates reveal a pattern of "thinking in the box", with particular and rather limited scope of democratic and federal preferences, but also an egalitarian orientation. The latter can be inferred from the ratification process itself and the intense debates including in and outside the Convention. They transpired in the shadow of the press, the local and state governments, the ratification conventions, and the public votes. Together, this indicates a highly dynamic space with – i.e. again, for that time – relatively broad participation and inclusion at multiple levels of the nascent federal republic that had evolved by the time of drafting and ratifying the US Constitution. These conditions and evolving institutions formed major parts of the "box" at the time of forging the Constitution. Another part of this box to address related to religion.

Religious dynamics as critical-institutional and ideational-antecedent

That colonists and newly independent citizens came to hold comparatively egalitarian views and expectations surely developed with rights and practices like the long-established local self-governments or, for the time, the remarkable scope of popular enfranchisement. In addition to political factors, socio-economic ones likely contributed to this outcome, such as exposure to and participation in an emerging market economy, or the abundance of land citizens settled, purchased, or violently acquired. However, another crucial part of the foundational "ideational-institutional box" are religious beliefs and practices. A caveat here is that there is vast scholarly research and debate on the correlations and different directions of causation, in general, and the US case specifically, between Protestantism (or Christianity in general) and the development of such phenomena as the market economy, democracy, individualism, and egalitarianism (see e.g. Acemoglu and Robinson 2012; Landes 1999; Mitchell 1992; Woodberry 2012), and also their interlinkage with the American "settler society" as seemingly unbounded by the relatively rapidly removed vestiges of European feudalism[15] and a single state Church. It is not the point here to confirm or reject one or the other theories on these nexuses. The point is rather that the respective constellation of these phenomena help us to understand and explain developments in cases where such a constellation applies. To comprehend the dynamics of constitutionalization in the USA, of further political development and constitutional political interpretation, it is necessary to consider this part of the box.

Multiple religious-related socio-political motifs like "American Creed", "American Exceptionalism", the "Protestant Ethic", the "Puritan Ethic", the "Covenant" (and the "Mayflower Compact"), and "Manifest Destiny" represent influential concepts that have been engaged to describe and explain US societal, economic and political development, self-understandings and identities, and pervasive beliefs or senses of mission (see e.g. Bell 1975; Huntington 1982; Lipset 1991; Morgan 1967; Weber 1905/06 [2010]). The concepts are not without pitfalls: for example analytically, given their inherent Anglo-Saxon biases and potentials for normative overload; politically, given their liability as regulative ideas to foster not just inclusion, but also legitimation of excluding, and in many cases dominating, myriad "others" (see e.g. Hodgson 2009; Shklar 1991a; Smith 1988). However, for descriptive analytical purposes, the prevalence and persistence of these concepts are informative. How they especially relate to egalitarian, individualist (rugged or otherwise), and religious institutions reveals insight into ideational constellations in the USA, and its politically inclusive and exclusive history and polity.

From the outset, religion plays a remarkably conspicuous part of the settlement, colonialization, and founding of the USA. This pertains to the Constitution as well, albeit somewhat indirectly. While some in both the Federalist and Antifederalist camps were non-sectarian "Deists", the vast majority of citizens were not, but rather apparently deeply religious and deeply attached to their religious group. The resultant constitutionalization of separation of church and state could then appear as a compromise in the face of obstacles to establishing a *national* religion. For instance, some states already had established churches, but different ones. Moreover, there were numerous religious groups: multiple confessions and denominations one could generically label Protestant (e.g. Congregationalists, Anglicans, Lutherans, Calvinists, Presbyterians, Huguenots, Baptists, Mennonites, Quakers), a large population of Catholics, a significant population of Jews, and more – and this just with a view to the European descendants in the 17th and 18th centuries (see e.g. Lepsius 2006; Owen 2007; Smith 2009). The multiplicity of religious groups may have been too large to allow for any other feasible compromise than separation of church and state.

In addition to "virtue by necessity" though, there were already established practices of tolerance. Ideas related to religious tolerance were hardly limited to the non-religious, but rather common as a regulative idea. It was espoused, and saliently exhibited, by a number of religious figures and church members, whether this developed out of the shared experiences of persecution (in England, France, Germany, the Netherlands, as well as *within* the colonies), the influence of Enlightenment philosophy, or the precedents set by colonies like Maryland, Pennsylvania, and Rhode Island, protecting the free exercise of religion (see e.g. Bejan 2015; Morgan 1983).[16] The institutionalization of tolerance, which by no means suggests it was lived up to from then on, may figure in the spread of egalitarianism, or at least claims to and beliefs in individual equality; but there is more.

The colonies together lacked *one* established Church, one headed by a monarch no less, so that an overarching fusion between *a* church and *the* state was absent. From this it does not follow, though, that the original colonies began as secular orders. Quite the opposite was often the case. Precisely the attempts to establish ecclesiastical and political orders may have made another path-dependent difference. The Mayflower Compact forged by the Pilgrims for the settlement of Plymouth in 1620 has taken on a somewhat mystical place in common narratives of US history (see e.g. Sargent 1988). However, unlike the social contract theorists' concept of an imaginary state-of-nature society left to form a government, this compact provided a precedent for collectively reimagining *real people* entering a *real* (though short-lived) social contract of their own design on their own, however appropriated, soil.

What is more, when establishing new and reforming existing colonies and communities, hundreds of charters, compacts, plans, covenants, combinations, ordinances, and agreements were forged as frameworks for regulating local and state governments, liberties, rights, and duties (for a comprehensive compendium and analysis, see Lutz 1980, 1998). These practices united such diverse cases from the originally, at times fanatically, theocratic Massachusetts Bay Colony to the original tolerance havens of Rhode Island and Pennsylvania. They obviously did not achieve Heaven on Earth, but the documents suggest that many were explicitly aspiring, or at least claiming, to do so (see also ibid.; Richards 1989; Wald and Calhoun-Brown 2014: 39–64). A critical difference here is that they wrote their own constitutions to this end. Whether the legacy of numerous "early constitutions" prior to the Revolution (Adams 1980) made *the* difference or not, they surely contributed precedents that could figure in the larger ideational and institutional "box".

There are some further indicators of attenuating hierarchies and intensifying individualization through religious-related dynamics. Without revisiting the history of religion and of religion and politics in the USA (for a comprehensive overview, see e.g. Wald and Calhoun-Brown 2014), a particularly significant development relates to the first "Great Awakening" in colonial America. This amounted to a critical juncture with far-reaching social-political implications, though it also rested on critical antecedents. The general idea of a direct, personal relationship to Scripture and Salvation already united many diverse confessions and denominations in colonial America. Apparently so did the persistence of strict hierarchies and strict social control. However, they became disrupted by the wave of revivalism and evangelicalism that affected not only Puritan, Congregationalist, and Presbyterian dominated New England, but rather swept through the colonies around the 1730s and 1740s. These developments instigated a pattern of challenging authority – a notion already inherited among Reformation ideas, e.g. the dogma of *sola scriptura*, the "Covenant theology", and the right to revolt (Wald and Calhoun-Brown 2014: 43–48) – as well as a pattern of an emerging "democratization of American Christianity" (Hatch 1989).

The ensuing dynamics included: an enormous wave of conversions (an act that beforehand commonly led to social ostracism, if not banishment from the community); reactions in various established religious communities to place demands on their preachers and their preaching styles and, failing that, to remove church leaders (a right that Covenant church congregations had before, but rarely dared to exercise); increasing reforms to separate the church from (local) worldly government, not so much as to preserve liberty as to preserve the purity of faith, so that the institution of separating church from state was reinforced all the same, including for the zealously faithful; sparking "demand", a "market", and competition for believers; and fervent encouragement of individual believers to take the interpretation of Scripture into their own hands and eyes, to seek and find meanings for their own daily lives, and similar (Heimert 1966; Kidd 2007; Langley 1996: 13–80; Morgan 1989: 295–303; Stout 1977). At the bottom line, the already proto-egalitarian institutions of local Covenant communities became further imbued with individualizing ideas and substance.

As many scholars emphasize (see the works cited immediately above here, plus Adams 1980 and Shain 1994), these evolving religious institutions, beliefs, and practices, and their complex interlinkage with wider societal and political ones, may point toward liberal individualism, but not unilaterally. They also (some argue even more so) entail regulative ideas and corresponding republican-type institutions and practices attached to communities. The socio-political reality in the run-up to the Revolution still differs significantly from the one of egalitarianism permeating multiple aspects of social and political life so famously observed by De Tocqueville in the 1830s and 1840s (Tocqueville 1835-40 [2003]).[17] However, this critical juncture and the dynamics that unfolded, while not singular causes, provide insight into how developments in understandings of equality and liberty could come about, also by the time of the constitutional debates. In addition to political and socio-economic factors, these antecedent religious dynamics contributed to facilitating an interpersonal and social *levelling*, but without threatening the sanctity of property.

None of the above is taken here to infer correlations between democracy and Christianity.[18] In a simplified, but pertinent, analogy: whether the Luther Bible which translated Scripture into the vernacular enabled its mass accessibility, or rather the invention of the printing press enabled its mass dissemination and mass literacy, whether either one caused the rise and spread of the Reformation as of the mid-15th century, or resulted rather on account of conflicts between ambitious rulers, this comprises a knot entangling development strands, and one of its sequences commenced with an intention to reform rather than break with an established institution. The conjunction in time of "propaganda, printed pages" (see e.g. Edwards 1994) and persons, and their embeddedness in antecedent historical developments and their wider institutional context (see e.g. Lindberg 2010; Zander 2016), help explain how critical events set off institutional and ideational path dependencies irrespective of any intended trajectory of change.

The conjunction of the above developments and factors in combination with other political and societal factors in colonial America help us to grasp a path of critical antecedents leading to US independence, its Constitution, and an ensuing democratization of its interpretation. A constitution resulting from this multidimensional process engenders a particular but ambivalent set of norms, rules, and regulative ideas. They have consequences for the polity and the different approaches to interpretation of its constitution far beyond their original time and place.

A preliminary foray into constitutional politics in the USA

The US Constitution, like any constitution, can be understood as the written document itself, its formal provisions, for one, and the constitution in a broader sense, its interpretation and adaptation in practice, for another. Both are relevant for constitutional politics. One approach to understanding the US Constitution in the strict and broad senses is provided by Ackerman's seminal "dualist democracy" theory. This frames American constitutional political development as unfolding in phases of "constitutional" or "higher politics" and "ordinary politics" (Ackerman 1991, 1998, 2007, 2014). By this scheme, the founding clearly represents a phase of constitutional or higher politics, as do changes to the Constitution in the strict sense, as do amendments. In ordinary phases, constitutional politics do not disappear, but continue in different modes in the complex division-of-powers system. Constitutional change occurs in the broader sense, and through "normal" party politics and judicial review, among others. This dualistic concept is widely influential and highly instructive. However, there is good reason *not* to equate constitutional with "higher" politics.

For one, the later Reconstruction Era after the Civil War provides a complicated case in point. The Congress, then dominated by the Republican Party, was on higher ground and the "right side of history" in ending slavery and introducing the 13th, 14th, and 15th amendments (on e.g. emancipation, enfranchisement, due process, and equal protection). From a moral standpoint, they were justified to use the permissive conditions of that critical juncture and require the defeated Confederacy to accept the amendments as stipulation for their readmission to the Union. From a conceptual analytical standpoint though, this achievement in formal constitutional change was enabled precisely by one-sided, disciplined party politics.[19] This is pivotal for comprehending the dynamics of constitutional politics in the USA.

For another reason, the conceptual distinction between higher and ordinary politics may also invite the problematic association of "party" with somehow "lower" politics. This distinction actually contravenes multiple "constitutional moments" in the USA. Reconstruction and the New Deal (1930s) for example were achieved in no small way *also* through the predominance of single parties, Republicans in the former, Democrats in the latter case. What is more, this pattern is already evident in the forging of the Constitution itself. The Convention was a predominantly *partisan* affair. Their proceedings took place under the circumstances of having almost no opponents to the then present Constitution. Granted, they largely excluded themselves by not participating. But the Convention could more easily achieve a setting conducive to deliberation and consensus in the absence of its opponents. The Convention could only look like a non-partisan arena precisely because it was dominated by one "party". Furthermore, it had, at best, questionable legitimacy to write a new constitution instead of reforming the existing one, the Article of Confederation, in the first place. One of the framers' ingenious tactics, moreover, was to unilaterally dictate the ratification rules for the Constitution to take effect by including these rules in the Constitution itself: they required nine of the thirteen states (Art. 7, US Constitution) instead of unanimity, that is the actual rule in place under the existing Articles of Confederation (Art. 13). It would be no exaggeration, but rather wholly legitimate, for opponents to view the framers' stratagem as a *coup d'état*, albeit a peaceful one. Thus they would likely not have seen a categorical difference to "ordinary" politics. Scholars should not either. The circumstances of the US founding politics, on the other hand, were of course *extraordinary*. The constitutional politics of formal constitutional change indeed differs in many ways from ordinary politics, no less when undertaken during or in the wake of critical junctures. Moreover, the rules of amendment already render these politics extraordinary, in requiring larger-than-usual consensus and coalition building. Constitutional amendments are often pursued in order to achieve "higher" things like expanding rights. But the higher goal is not necessarily tantamount to a higher pattern of politics. If one party happens to enjoy the requisite super-majority at the time of a constitutional juncture, they may resort to *partisan* politics to achieve *constitutional* change.

The dichotomy between constitutional and ordinary politics in the USA, while warranting differentiation, helps to identify several fundamental aspects to consider (see also Ackerman 2005). The "founding" extends beyond the Convention and ratification processes, and should include the preceding War for Independence and its 1776 Declaration (its main author, Thomas Jefferson, was among the opponents to the draft constitution and not even present at the Convention). If the "Revolution" is considered part of the founding, its conceptualization should also encompass the intense contestation for the meaning of and commitment to the revolution that persisted at least until the early 19th century. Then, the formative period of constitutional politics did not end with the Constitution's ratification in 1789, but also includes the "Revolution of 1800" when the Federalists lost power and many of the Democrat–Republican "other Founders" and their supporters came to dominate the federal executive, legislative, and increasingly judiciary branches (in addition to Ackerman, (2005) see also Horn, Lewis, and Onuf 2002).[20]

That Democratic–Republican transition ushered in changes to the Constitution in its broad sense, while also hindering constitutional change in the strict sense for a long time, and with implications for its interpretation into the present. Particularly noteworthy is the interpretation of the Constitution with regard to its very nature, not as a compound national Union, but as *treaty* or *compact* between sovereign states. This concept was ardently supported by many as the actual nature of the Union, and conventional understandings of federalism and small republics at the time of the Convention were actually closer to their positions (see e.g. Banning 1974; Crosskey 1953; Forsyth 1981; Jörke 2010; Tushnet 2015: 9–20). The Democrat–Republican transition helped firmly plant the seeds of interpreting the constitution as one emphasizing states' rights but also as prescribing the states as an, if not the, appropriate domain for protecting individual rights and popular sovereignty (see e.g. Brennan 1977). This regulative idea had extensive sway until the Civil War, and would resurge later. Its invocation is evident in opposition to the federal government's regulatory thrust, notoriously against desegregation in the 1950s, but also in many other policy areas into the present.

The thrust toward expanding the scope and reach of the federal government, in contrast, conforms to a different regulative idea of interpreting the Constitution in the vein of many of those Founders supporting the Constitution. It is likewise predicated on popular sovereignty, but oriented more toward "We the People" of the entire USA in a compound Union. This regulative idea, that the people created the US Constitution, entailed a shift in conventional meanings of federalism and republic toward large-scale representative democracy (see e.g. Ackerman 2007; Ball and Pocock 1988; Jörke 2010; Keller 1987; Post and Siegel 2009). Who has the right idea? Irrespective of how different people, in scholarship or citizenship, answer that question, both basic regulative ideas combine federal and democratic ideas, and each wind up permeating politics and constitutional interpretation into the present. The original ideas of the supporters of the US Constitution obviously matter, but the opponents to it also contributed significant ideas that would become part of it.

The original and the living Constitution

In the original Roe v. Wade (1973) case, one of the constitutional questions raised concerned whether states can prohibit abortion. The decision ruled against a Texan law and affirmed a constitutional right to privacy that included women's reproductive rights. Neither abortion nor this right to privacy are to be found verbatim in the Constitution. Whether the never-ending debate on abortion ever since has to do with American "culture" or not is another matter. Importantly here, the questions on responsibilities of state versus federal governments or on an expanded right to privacy reveal constitutional political "thinking in the box". Something leads people debating abortion, and many other issues, to consider whether one or the other is an *appropriate question* at all. That policy issues turn into constitutional ones in the USA is not unique. It is rather that numerous issues transform into certain *types* of constitutional questions. They are bound to the *constitution of the Constitution*, its evolved normative legal, political, and ideational make-up in a strict and broad sense.

For instance, the Constitution of 1787 also lacks anything explicitly, and unlikely intentionally, referring to digital forms of communication, providing no answer on regulating the internet. That is unless the internet, social media, and similar can be *construed* as some form of "commerce" or as some form of "speech", then a whole set of possible constitutional political questions emerge. This presupposes that people *believe* that the Constitution is the right place to visit for the answers. This is by no means self-evident since that would mean the Constitution and the political order it underlies enjoy legitimacy. The US Constitution grants Congress power to "regulate Commerce with foreign Nations, and among the several States, and with the Indian Tribes" (Art. 1(8)), but also prohibits Congress from "abridging the freedom of speech" (Amendment 1). Thus, barring a specific amendment vis-à-vis internet regulation, there are at least two substantially different norms to weigh. Political actors at the national level will have to figure out if any regulation would unduly infringe on free speech. If so, apparently nothing can be done at any level of government. But if internet communications and transactions are deemed matters of commerce, the next questions concern whether such commerce transpires "across the several States" ("several" meanwhile apparently accepted to apply as much to fifty as to thirteen), and whether commerce can be understood in the present sense, or whether one is compelled to retrace the meaning that would have been understood by citizens at the time of the founding or rather as intended by the constitutional authors.

These reflect actual questions and challenges that American politics faces. They are also ones that the Constitution and its interpretation in particular *create*. Because of tensions between upholding the original and adapting the living Constitution, numerous issues become a matter of determining compatibility with the Constitution. Yet what the Constitution has to say about that depends on what people say it says. The federal and democratic dimensions of the polity and corresponding logics of politics complicate these constitutional questions. This raises the overarching question of *who* decides on *how* to determine *who* answers these questions in the first place: the Congress, the states, the courts, the parties, the people, the present, or the past?

Between living and original approaches

In addition to rules and bounds, constitutions provide scripts and guidance for following the rules (see e.g. Holmes 2012). These scripts take on a special purpose and function in a federal polity, given the "compact" or "covenant" between governments at one time but also generations over time, which may take and have effect as well as adapt through re-reading and re-interpreting its text (see e.g. Baumgarten 1979; Elazar 1987, 1993; Hueglin 1985; Hueglin and Fenna 2015: 73–81). Interpretation, whether as part of deliberation or contest, becomes normatively and politically charged by consequence, and develops dynamically over time. Contestation around "parchment politics" (Levinson 2005, 2011), the sense and meaning of the constitution and various commitments it implies, recurs throughout US political development. Moreover, different interpretive approaches have emerged over time.

One basic interpretive approach can be referred to as textualism. In general this infers a binding effect of the text of the Constitution, as opposed to constructible norms derived through open, adaptive interpretation or the inclusion of other sources like philosophy or non-text sources. Interpretation orients toward the text itself, whether its "plain" or "ordinary" meanings, and its overall structure, while the courts rather than the law's authors determine what the law says (Eskridge 2001; Molot 2006; Rappaport 1999; Tushnet 2015: 245–50). Ambiguities may warrant consulting the framers' intents and meanings, or determining ordinary meanings at the time of drafting the Constitution. On the other hand, there are varying textualist views as to whether author intents can play a role at all in determining the meaning and implications of the Constitution (see e.g. Manning 1997; Molot 2006; Scalia 1997; Strauss 1996; Tushnet 1985).

Originalism represents another approach to constitutional interpretation. This has become a particularly influential and controversial one in the USA, and is oriented toward the original Constitution in multiple respects. The basic referents include the original text, the original intents, or the original meanings. Originalist approaches assert that, barring any amendments, it is necessary to determine the intentions of the framers of the Constitution, their understandings of the text (what did they *mean*?), or rather the common meanings at the time (how would contemporaries have understood words in the constitution?) – and on knowing these things, then to adhere to them as guidance for interpreting the Constitution (for further elaboration, see e.g. Eskridge 2001; Harris 1982; Powell 1985; Rakove 1997, 2011; for an argument in support, see Scalia 1989). Originalist approaches may offer one path to reducing ambiguity. They represent foremost legal doctrines and schools, and are relevant for historical scholarship as well, but they have also been highly prevalent in politics.

While originalist perspectives may have conservative appeal, there is a democratic idea in originalism concerning commitments to the will of the people. While one democratic view sees the collective will in the immediate present and the majority of the people or their representatives, the originalist perspective emphasizes, in cases of conflict, the larger popular will as embodied in the Constitution. From this follows the requisite to achieve a corresponding interpretation, for which the courts serve as "agents" of this latter will (see e.g. Höreth 2010). This notion of popular sovereignty implies that, were the popular will clearly in favor of a new right or regulation, it would materialize in a respective amendment. Until the Constitution as repository of this larger will is changed, the original one takes precedent.

An orientation to the text and the letter of the law unites virtually any interpretive approach to the Constitution. Likewise common is at least a certain restraint and deference toward democratically elected governments and the laws they have produced. However, the rise and spread of originalism's "conservative constitutionalism", with its claim to provide the only appropriate interpretative approach, emerged in reaction to the federal courts' "progressive constitutionalist" turn as of the 1950s and 1960s, and a "loose" interpretation of constitutional provisions deeming the expansion of rights and of the federal government's legislative and regulative activity constitutional (Post and Siegel 2006; West 1990). Emphasis on original constitutional text, intentions, and meanings has always been important for interpretation to some extent, whether by courts, politicians, or citizens. However, there has also long been dissent on how to weigh them against changing social, political, and economic circumstances, ideas, and values. Originalism has met with substantial critique on multiple counts: for example that it is susceptible to arbitrary interpretations because determining original intentions as well as earlier understandings, and given the contestability of determining whose intentions matter most or more, all amount to uncertain and ambiguous endeavors; many original meanings and intentions contradict modern democratic ones, so that it seems dubious why the former should override the latter; and such an approach to the constitution may, ironically, not even be compatible with many of the framers' and founders' intentions at all regarding how later generations should interpret the Constitution (Berman 2009; see e.g. Goodheart 2013; Post 1990; Post and Siegel 2006; Spiekermann and Goodin 2012; Sunstein 2009). These critiques, in turn, provide premises for alternative approaches.

The referents of plain text, ordinary meanings, and popular understandings are shared by another concept of interpretation, namely "popular constitutionalism", but with different implications. These readings and interpretative approaches in US constitutional-political discourse also emphasize textual faithfulness. Rather than conformity to origins, popular constitutionalism asserts the crucial value of the Constitution and its interpretation in a democratic society, not just by courts, but political actors and above all the citizens themselves, and thus democratized constitutional interpretation (see e.g. Kramer 2004; Levinson 2006; Post and Siegel 2009; Tushnet 1999). This idea bears a general affinity to the broader concept of a "living constitution" (see e.g. Ackerman 2007). This can imply a popular constitution in the strict sense of belonging to the people and broadly as an orientation for constitutional interpretation.

The notion of a living constitution originally developed as a legal doctrine.[21] Its emergence and spread in the course of the 20th century facilitated drastic changes in the Constitution in its broad sense of American political development, visible in the expansion of legal rights, liberties, and equal protection (see e.g. Gillman 1997). Moreover, various concepts related to the living constitution include, for example "reform textualism" (Ives 2018), "active liberty" (Breyer 2005), constitution as "law for the living" and the *real* original intent of the Founders (see e.g. Brennan 2017), or "constitutional authorship" as belonging to the people more than the framers (Michelman 1999). Furthermore, the Preamble and "We the People" in particular are taken as fundamental signifiers of establishing a compound Union of the *entire* people and the states, rather than a compact among states only. The idea of a living constitution points toward reformative and moral readings of the US Constitution. It also resonates with a (Deweyan-type) pragmatic, adaptive, democratic-emphasizing, and rights-expanding interpretative approach (see e.g. Dworkin 1975; Easterbrook 2008; Posner 2010, 2013; Post 1990: 15–26; Tushnet 2015: 192–98; West 1990). The guiding orientation is thus toward improvement (e.g. Preamble: "*to form a more perfect*

Union") and further actualizations of liberty, equality, and rights in fulfilling the "spirit" of the US Constitution (e.g. Preamble "establish Justice" and "secure the Blessings of Liberty"). Inherent to popular constitutionalism and the living constitution, like originalism, is a fundamental reference to popular sovereignty, but with more priority on the present over the past.

The conceptual lines between the original and the living can blur: the living constitution could equate to a variant of originalism, given its commitment to the US Constitution and constitutional legacies, the Revolution in the broader sense (including the Declaration of Independence), the promises of the Preamble, and the rights-expanding amendments. Inversely, originalism exhibits a living constitution approach with its fidelity to keeping the Constitution, the letter of the law, and the original meanings and intents alive through faithful interpretation (see e.g. Balkin 2009a, 2009b; Post and Siegel 2006). Each variant thus represents a kind of constitutional faithfulness, with one oriented toward upholding the letter of the Constitution in a strict sense and the other the spirit of the Constitution in a broader sense. There may be an irresolvable tension between the "people's" and the "lawyers'" constitution (Cornell 2011), and between a "forward-looking" constitutional politics of progressivism, reform, evolution, and adaptation on the one hand, and a "backward-looking" constitutional politics of conservation, continuity, coherence, stability, and limited government on the other (Gourevitch 2011). Loose and strict construction of the Constitution, commitments to the text itself and its legacies, and the significance of constitutional-legal laypersons (e.g. political actors and citizens) each make up important referents but in different ways to these interpretive approaches.

The layperson's understanding of the Constitution is significant for the originalist as well as the living and certainly the popular constitution perspectives. Similar applies to strict and loose construction as well as forward and backward looking orientations. The originalist interpretation relies on a strict construction of the text, but can imply necessities to look "outside it" into numerous other sources to assess a former contemporaneous understanding of a phrase or word in a constitutional provision. The idea of a living constitution can, in turn, imply the backward-looking imperative to read and uphold original preamble phrases, such as "form a more perfect Union" or "promote the general Welfare" strictly, even literally. The different constitutional interpretive approaches have tended to be associated with one or the other political orientation (e.g. liberal, libertarian, conservative, or progressive) and applied to achieve results that could be construed along those lines – and indeed, different interpretive approaches can lead to significantly different institutional consequences (see e.g. Sunstein and Vermeule 2003). As regulative ideas, and not just legal doctrines for judges and lawyers vis-à-vis a constitution that belongs to the people and the government it has established, these interpretive approaches span the political spectrum of democratic political dynamics.

At the bottom line and across the interpretive board, the constitutional text matters. While seemingly self-evident in a rule-of-law political system, this significance points to the power of several regulative ideas – of popular sovereignty, federalism, of the legitimacy of the constitution itself, and of the notion that the constitution bears meaning as a referent at all for everyday policymaking and politics. The one or other performance of interpretation can be attributed to strategy, for instance if a political party cloaks its pursuit of narrow interests in terms of a constitutional principle. The simple yet important point remains nonetheless that even constitutional "posturing" would have little effect and meaning, were the constitution, the ideas and norms appealed to therein, meaningless to the public. Consequently, interpreting the US Constitution has become clearly something *meaningful*. In the democratic-federal political order, a multitude of political actors revisit, recall, and reinterpret the Constitution on a recurring basis. The document as a whole and the text itself serve as referents for political contestations. This points to a collectively believed or conferred intrinsic or immanent value of this text.

Text immanence of constitutional meaning

The text of the US Constitution itself apparently holds an intrinsic value. Were it and its text deemed obsolete, it would then seem puzzling what all the trouble was about concerning interpreting the Constitution. That there are multiple legal schools and theories of interpretation, not to mention political controversies, underlines a seemingly given intrinsic value. The democratic politics of constitutional interpretation does not imply one particular political direction or trajectory of constitutional change, but simply that constitutional interpretations can be as diverse as the political spectrum itself. This diversity is augmented by a multiplicity of interpreters. This provides, in turn, an important point of departure to conceive text immanence as a regulative idea to interpreting the constitution.

The concept of immanence touches upon diverse legal, literary, cognitive, social, philosophical, and even existential territory.[22] Addressing what immanence means already raises such rudimentary questions as to what "is" could mean in the first place. The term *is* denotes usually some reference to some sort of "other". However, denoting others with "is" already amounts to imposing an attribute or a representation upon that other. This may sound or read as a bit esoteric at first glance, but, and especially with the theoretical foundations previously elaborated in mind,[23] it is rather straightforward.

For instance, if asking what is the US Constitution, one could respond that it is a piece of parchment produced in 1787 and currently on display in the National Archives, or rather the compact or covenant that provides a framework for federal and democratic government, and the rules and rights in the USA. Both views may obviously apply, but are not the only ones. It could be a pdf file too, or rather ideas about and interpretations of the rules and norms associated with the Constitution, even those of the Declaration of Independence (e.g. "the right to life, liberty and the pursuit of happiness" is often conflated with the Constitution). Yet *is* the pdf file the same document as the US Constitution *really* or a mere representation? Is the piece of parchment on display in the National Archives the real Constitution, or is it to be found in the *living one*, the one applied in practice, the one encompassing its meanings, implications, how things have developed and apply to the contemporary system of government? More importantly regarding the Constitution in practice: Does it make a difference which answer is correct? If so, does the person answering the question make the difference? How would a constitutional legal scholar answer that question? Or an originalist or a popular constitutionalist, a layperson, a Democrat or a Republican, a state representative, or a Congress member?

As a *first* point, the immanence of something can be deceivingly simple to detect. Capturing immanence conceptually turns out to be rather abstract and complex. Ambiguities arise already in searches for a description of *is*, and even more so for causal as well as evaluative and normative considerations (e.g. is something (un)fair or (un)just? Is Y a result of X? Is X immanent to the system?). Validity and meanings, sense or significance, are attributed to things like the US Constitution on the whole or its individual provisions. The same goes for innumerable others like situations and occurrences in everyday life (something *is* fate, a coincidence, an accident, a sign, a critical juncture), animate and inanimate objects (e.g. the constitution is old, short, far-sighted), and much more. The *second* point is rather this: perception – regardless of supposedly objective being or being-ness – is inextricably linked, directly or indirectly, to intersubjectivity. In addition to the capacity to perceive things at all, any one of the above example statements is predicated on some sort of value or quality and on institutional and personal capacities to generate meanings that are developed and learned. This takes on particular relevance and contingency for political "things". Accordingly, and as a *third* point, people, as individuals or groups, in societies, and over generations, construct the meaning of things over time. As phrased by Dowding with reference to rights, people manage to "feedback-loop" rights into existence which can only exist ultimately when "we think they exist" (Dowding 2017: 228). The same can be said of course for example for democracy, federalism, freedom, or sovereignty. Whether by "leaps of faith" or incrementally, this feedback-loop of meaning occurs in the multidimensional boundedness of institutional and ideational development and dynamics.

However, and *fourth*, there is actually nothing necessarily immanent to immanence. Coming back to the Constitution: what is deemed immanent to the text can just as easily be deep and wide as it could be thin and shallow, full or empty. The US Constitution is equally just a piece of parchment, as it is the compilation of over two centuries of development of rules, precedents, and meanings. Inherent to a text is ultimately nothing other than letters in ink or braille on paper or encoded 0's and 1's displayed on a monitor. And even they would be nothing, certainly not of any *meaning*, without senses to perceive them or electricity to make them appear, and no less minds to process them that have developed in social contexts by which some sort of meaning can be attributed to the text. Even at the most basic, proverbially particle-like level of textual matter, any sort of meaning presupposes intersubjectivity and a much larger context. How the code of the text is deciphered depends *fifthly* on the readers and the multiple levels of encoding in which they have been embedded.

This becomes patently obvious when considering the US Constitution: Why should the phrase "We the People" as constitutional provision mean *immanently* anything more than the power to "grant Letters of Marque and Reprisal"? One is but a mere snippet of the Preamble and thus not even a concrete provision at all, while the other appears *twice* in enumerating the powers of the federal government and limiting those of the states (Article 1, Secs 9 and 10 respectively). A reader bereft of any knowledge of either the original or evolved context of the constitutional text might not understand what those letter-whatchamacallits are, but could easily conclude that they must have been a pretty important thing for the authors (after all, they did take the effort to write about those letters twice). Of course *we know* that the three-word morsel of the Preamble is located, or rather has been *placed*, at the heart of debates on the constitutional nature of the Union as one of people or of states, as signifier of tenets of a living constitution, and embodiment of popular sovereignty, while the said twice-enumerated rule on letters of whatchamacallit is meanwhile veritably full of nothing significant for today's reader.

From the preceding discussion on immanence we arrive essentially at nothing. By this I do not mean any deeper philosophical notion of nothingness being something too, but rather the simple notion that immanence, in and of itself, entails nothing, or more precisely, nothing yet. By unraveling immanence all the way down, we arrive, *sixthly*, at the most fundamental point: what is actually or purportedly immanent can only become so *by interpretation*. Interpretation does not necessarily imply the discovery of something sublime, but rather a process of actualizing toward something other, for example a value, a principle, a truth, an understanding. Interpretation *can* orient toward grand or "higher" things, and this bears decisive relevance for interpreting constitutions. Thus immanent becomes an appropriate term, not as something in and of itself essential, but as a designator for qualities, attributes, traits, or values that are held to be inherent or intrinsic to the described other. Immanence so conceived does not require solipsism, quite the opposite for the complex world of politics. This specification and contextualization of immanence is based simply on thinking in social contexts and institutional settings. Consequently, immanence ultimately cannot be disentangled from context and multiple contingencies bounding the *interpretative* process, nor from the *interpreters* themselves.

Regulative ideas of personal and immanent reading of texts abound, or at least they do implicitly and often explicitly. Artists, literature teachers, popular constitutionalists, or evangelical revivalists in the Great Awakening, among many others, emphatically encourage readers to find their own meanings in the respective texts of concern (e.g. "What does the text *say* to *you*?"). This implies, *seventhly*, a personalizing, *levelling*, and even empowering approach to text. It divorces interpretation from authority and inherited contexts that various authorities (e.g. governors and judges, scholars, priests, the authors themselves) would otherwise impose on interpretation and the search for meaning. Again, the printed text cannot say much of anything on its own. Its reading induces a dialog with readers who bring along their own "imprints" generated out of dynamic processes of experience, learning, development, and interactions in social and institutionalized settings, all of which can change and develop further. Almost everyone *knows*, or is familiar with, this: for example reading the *same* text, be it the Constitution or the *Federalist Papers*, and how it *reads* differently later with more experience and learning, even though the text itself has not changed one bit. Through immanent reading and respective interpretation, the text and its discovered, though rather constructed, meanings can become one's individual or a collective own.

From the above it follows that text interpretation and derived meanings are institutionally, societally, and temporally *contingent*, and thus can also be *restricted*. The constitution of a society and political order make a difference. For the US Constitution, democracy and federalism become additional specific and significant factors in this respect. The very idea of participating in the interpretation and even more so the production of the laws, directly or via elected representatives, or rather the idea of viewing only certain levels responsible for these processes, may simply not occur as self-evident otherwise. Democratic and federal polities commit to respective ideas of self-government and equality. Their formal constitution can imbue, though not program on its own, the political order with these regulative ideas. The more democratic equality manages to become taken seriously and even *literally*, through dynamics of development between ideas and institutions over time, the more empowerment and entitlement to have an opinion that counts equally may emerge and spread. The federal constitution of the polity and the constitutionalization of the state(s) also develop dynamically. The different governments and their peoples over time become increasingly distanced from those peoples and governments of the past that once established the compact. But they can become so constituted, as territorially organized peoples and governments nonetheless, through continuing reinterpretation and the ongoing, explicit or implicit, recommitment to its rules, norms, and ideas.

Text immanence as a regulative idea, one that is relevant to constitutional political interpretative approaches, becomes particularly relevant on account of factors or circumstances of federalism, democracy, and constitutionalism. The conjunction of those three already invite the dynamics of immanent interpretive approaches. They can each, and certainly in combination, contribute to endowing a multitude of levels, branches, actors, and individuals with the right to, if not the very idea of, taking the interpretation of the constitution into their own hands, or eyes as it were. A further important factor though for the emergence of text immanence as a regulative idea stems from the widely perceived sanctity of the constitution.

With a view to constitutional interpretive debates, Goodheart points out how already Bryce's *American Commonwealth* (Bryce 1888 [1995]) underlined the parallels between the US Constitution and religious texts and anticipated the respective dynamics of constitutional interpretation, and concludes that the Constitution meanwhile constitutes such a "sacred text", that is one that is higher, extraordinary, awe-inspiring, and revered across different interpretive camps (Goodheart 2013: 540ff.). As Grey asserts, likewise in the context of debates on interpretive approaches (summarized there as between "textualists" vs. "supplementers"), the adoration of the US Constitution results in its resemblance more to sacred "Scripture" than secular literature, not least on account of the "authority" attributed to the Constitution, the *vox populi* it embodies in lieu of the *vox Dei*, thus comprising a powerful source of identity and meaning as much as the "sovereign Word" itself (Grey 1984). Conceptualizations of the US Constitution as "Scripture" have been substantially influenced by Levinson's seminal account of "civil religion": in addition to the longstanding proliferation of religious-type speech and analogies in American public life, Levinson explores the centrality of the US Constitution for the "American tribe" in secular "civil religion", the place of authority it and its interpreters inhabit, and not only parallels but also the attachment to Reformation legacies and the doctrine of *sola scriptura* in particular (Levinson 1979, 1988).

Such equations between the *vox populi* and *vox Dei* are hardly far-fetched, but rather historically substantiated in the USA. Already in one of the earliest decisions of the Supreme Court, reference is made to the people as the "sacred source" from which the state "derives its authority" (*Chisholm v. Georgia* (1793)). The historical evolution toward sublimation of the people as sovereign becomes apparent when reconsidering the dynamics of the particular "invention" of popular sovereignty in 17th-century England: the House of Commons in its contest with the monarch increasingly appealed in lieu of divine authority to its own (at first more or less "fictitious") basis of authority in the *people*. This set in motion dynamics of political change, not least when actual people began to take these ideas *literally*. Taken literally and further in the American colonies' march toward independence, many of the English parliamentarians, by now in an institution in which parliamentary sovereignty was the established norm, appear to have been appalled by how the US Founders became "crazy disciples" of British Glorious Revolution principles (Zink 2009: 447). However, the abstract people's authority points to only one dimension contributing to constitutional sanctification.

That the Constitution is sacrosanct would appear to unite various elements of different interpretive approaches (see e.g. Brennan 2017; Goodheart 2013). At many times, the fate of the federal government's or the states' powers to regulate in multiple policy areas has seemed to turn on the painstaking interpretation of individual words, such as whether "among" in the provision "To regulate Commerce…, among the several States" (Art. 1 (8)) is synonymous with "between" (suggesting commerce only crossing *between* state lines and thus *interstate* commerce) or rather "amid" and thus also within the states (see e.g. Balkin 1988; Tushnet 2015: 159–65). Beyond the contestation between legal doctrines and ordinary politics, this reveals an institutionalized pattern of taking the text itself seriously and *literally*. The US Constitution may be conducive to different immanent readings of the "text itself", as a means to coping with gaps, ambiguities, and tensions left over to constitutional interpretation in practice (see e.g. Balkin 1988; Turley 2015). Immanent readings in turn have a reinforcing effect of sanctifying the Constitution (Harris 1982: 35ff.; Murkens 2007: 747ff.), generating the processes of a feedback loop of complexly evolving meanings. Complex here refers to multidimensional processes and not necessarily the meanings themselves. Meanings can become more complex over time, but can just as well wind up "flattening" toward the verbatim of the original text. Both types of dynamics and trajectories of change can emerge, coexist, and foster even more tensions. Different *immanent* readings are possible at one time. However, change may occur over time in such a fashion that what appears to be *immanent* to an enduring constitution and its provisions has rather changed on account of transformed meanings, with or without awareness on the part of the interpreters.

To conceive text immanence and the however supposed immanent value of constitutional text requires taking the individual, the intersubjective, and especially the collective dimension into account. As briefly mentioned above, constitutionalism and the modern state evolved not only on the basis of political and legal concepts, but also community-related ones, and more specifically communities formed and bound by "shared beliefs" as well as notions of "peoplehood" and the respective myths or narratives of their origins. Religion has constituted another fundamental source of building and binding communities for one. As likewise shown previously, this also plays a multifaceted foundational part in the USA and its Constitution in a broad and, indeed, strict sense, for another.

To make an enormously long and complex story short again: the Reformation, the printing press, the mass proliferation of literacy, and further ensuing changes induced the onset of the path dependencies of "textual communities", and with that the relegation in value of "other sources" other than *the text* (for a comprehensive study, including on "text", see Zander 2016). *Faith* and *text* alone implied the sheer necessity of reading, again as individuals, but also in a community: in congregations, and, by the time of the first colonies in America, in Covenant congregations bound now by the Scripture as well as their own compacts. The societal significance of scripts, whether as oral or written narratives, are nothing special on their own. Written texts however are somehow different (see e.g. Bader 2012), since they can emancipate the "receiver" from the "sender", the readers from the authors, or rather their presence.

Constitutional laws and their reading can likewise be deemed "like literature" (Dworkin 2015), but invite mass interpretation in a free and democratic society and provide constitutive purpose and meaning for "textual communities" (Soifer 1995; West 1988). The evolution of participatory textual communities as a phenomenon has some origin in the above-mentioned Reformation developments, which permeated through the European settlement of America and in the later USA in particular. They apparently played a role in 17th-century England in the politics of religion and political reforms in conjunction with mass publications, pamphleteering, and "paper contestations" among for example Anglicans, Catholics, Puritans, Royalists, Parliamentarians, Levellers, and Diggers (Sauer 2005). Similar dynamics were foundational for much of the American ideational "box", not only in the ratification debates on the Constitution. Again in the realm of religion, societal developments over the 19th century appear quite indicative: with recurring "Great Awakenings" and intensifying mass publication of evangelical texts, read by tens of millions, taking Scripture *immanently* as guidance for finding purity in a secular world, ideas which would later "turn outward" and energize the progressive reform movements of the late 19th and early 20th centuries (see e.g. Brown 2004; Casper et al. 2007). This compact canvass of historical, political, and social developments provides important insights into the evolving elevation of the Constitution "as Scripture" (Grey 1984; see also Kammen 2006). This implicates an embeddedness in multidimensional dynamics of historical, institutional, and ideational developments in the USA.

Against this compounded background, not only does the higher value of the Constitution become more comprehensible. This also and finally shows why its immanent reading can be conceptualized as an own regulative idea guiding constitutional interpretation. It has evolved on account of, as well contributed to, the development of the institutional and ideational dimensions of the political order. "Egalitarian" poses an admittedly positively connoted term. But to infer a certain egalitarianism behind the logic of text-immanent reading suggests neither positive nor negative implications. It does however point to one of the answers to the questions posed in this chapter, namely *who* decides *how* to determine *who* answers the question of who interprets the Constitution. In the compound constitution of the US federal democracy, in its strict and broad sense, and almost irrespective of the constitutional political or theoretical perspective, the answer is likely to be: a multitude.

Summary: the Constitution as a matter of interpretation

The Constitution of the USA *means* multiple things. It is or is recurrently made a matter of interpretation, and the very matter which is to be interpreted. Constitutional meanings connect to ideas regarding federalism and democracy, further underlying principles such as state and popular sovereignty, as well as how to interpret the text itself. A multiplicity of meanings results from multiple factors and dimensions of development. They and their contestation contribute in turn to dynamics of development. Rather than equilibrium, political order is in flux and evolving. The constitution of the political order comprises at once a framework of rules (e.g. on representation, decision making), powers (e.g. between branches and levels of government), rights (e.g. held by the citizens or states), a carrier of history (e.g. the founding era, but also its antecedents), and a repository of ideas (e.g. on the intentions of the framers, the meanings of the text). The Constitution may seemingly fixate on these variegated sets of distributions, from which the various constituents of the political order withdraw. However, they are also deposited back in the ensuing changes. Those changes need not be, and more often are not evidenced or literally in the written Constitution.

Such complexity renders it necessary to differentiate between the US Constitution in a strict and broad sense and between formal and informal change. The postulated differences between the two refer, in short, to the formal, written Constitution on the one hand, and the Constitution in practice and development over time, including the wider ideational and institutional make-up of the political order on the other. Constitutional understandings and readings, be they strict, broad, originalistic, popular, or living, can relate to regulative ideas which guide action and interaction among branches and levels of governments, and by political actors from parties and individual politicians to civil society groups and citizens. A distinct regulative idea of constitutional text immanence has been derived from various concepts related to constitutional interpretative approaches and their overlaps in particular. Types of constitutional political interpretation follow different, in parts conflicting, notions on the proper ways to interpret the Constitution. Conceiving text immanence as a constitutional political regulative idea offers a frame for capturing the significance of literal or text-faithful interpretations of the Constitution in American politics and political development.

Constitutional faithful strands of interpretation like originalism, textualism, living, and popular constitutionalism are each concerned with constitutional fidelity (cf. e.g. Dworkin 1997; Fleming 1997). Text immanence does not encapsulate those strands or theories of interpretation. It rather bundles the "hi-fi" characteristics of these constitutional reading approaches. Text immanence thus stands for a regulative idea of interpretation found in various discourses and constitutional referents of US politics. It is grounded in a long arc of ideational and institutional development, especially the Constitution in a broad sense of the American polity. The latter incorporates antecedent developments of state and popular sovereignty, egalitarianism, and an early institutionalization of immanent orientations to text, also through religious dynamics which are also linked with early constitution-making in local communities. The text immanent orientation to the Constitution finds resonance in originalistic as well as living constitutional approaches, but such an approach does not lead in one particular direction. It may facilitate the adaptation to changing circumstances of governing and, intertwined with this, the further actualization of values and norms carried by the Constitution. It may also point toward strict preservation of the letter of the law and the prevention of change. Both fundamental motifs are found throughout US politics and history. Save several amendments, nearly the same constitutional parameters in the strict sense for over two centuries allow for both facilitating and limiting government. Thus, how the Constitution is interpreted also proves decisive for the dynamics and directions of change.

Finally, what something means and what something was meant to mean are two different things. What an institution does is not necessarily what it is there for. Those institutions may have been meant to work a particular way and to produce certain results, and their design followed certain ideas. On account of the necessity to reach compromises in a federal republic in the making, the constitutional product from the outset is necessarily a mixture – of motives, interests, ideas, and more. The mixture can mean different things to others at the time and its meaning can change over time. The once contingent compromise born out of contestation may over time come to look coherent, even visionary, and perfect as much as full of inconsistencies and inadequacies for the present. This is a matter of interpretation.

The different interpretations may even result from or lay claim to the same ideas. A concept, an idea, a phrasing, or a word may become filled with additional and different meanings. Neither institutions nor ideas literally take on a life of their own. They do become dynamic, or subject to dynamics between change and continuity. Tensions between principles and regulative ideas emerge through the interplay with political circumstances and institutional settings. Institutions and ideas impact on one another in and over time. Asymmetric changes and the perception of resultant incongruities between principles and practices may and, in all likelihood, will result. Recurring attempts to synchronize the two may look to the constitution again – through its formal or informal change to match institutions to ideas, or to steer divergent practices back so as to conform with the constitutions as it stands. Both quite distinct types of political orientation can be grounded in constitutional fidelity. Each can result from taking its ideas seriously, even literally.

Notes

1 In addition to Morgan, see also e.g. (Pocock (1957).
2 Of further interest is how this line of reasoning "made Parliament its own creator", which "had the great advantage of endowing Parliament not simply with a part of the powers of government, but with the people's inherent power to begin, change, and end governments. And however circular the reasoning, the attribution attained a degree of plausibility from the election of the House of Commons by what passed for a popular vote" (Morgan 1989: 59).
3 Though this process was an incremental one, including the execution of Charles I and the ensuing Civil Wars (three between 1642 and 1651), parliamentary sovereignty became institutionalized by 1688 with the Glorious Revolution, the Bill of Rights of 1689, and the 1701 Act of Settlement (regulating monarchic succession).
4 Skinner for instance cautions though that "radical democratic" bears the potential of misconstruing their ideas: since the Levellers were not completely against maintaining a monarchy and even one still at the head of the Anglican Church, while democratic, let alone radical democratic, would not have fit in the concrete ideology nor the terminology of the Diggers (Skinner 1969: 27 ff.). With this caveat in mind, we may still refer to them or rather at least their *ideas* accordingly (cf. e.g. Kenyon 1962).
5 The following cannot capture the complex underpinnings and embeddedness in Kant's theorization of human experience, knowledge, reason, and concepts (for a brief overview, see e.g. Ameriks 1999).
6 I.e. this predominantly meant slaves, though it also applied to persons bound to (temporary) servitude by punishment or contract.
7 On this argument against reducing these representation claims to a "tax evasion" attempt, see Morgan (1957: 5).
8 In one scenario, the ratification of the Constitution failed altogether, which branches off into other scenarios such as the creation of parallel republics: a "Northern" one under the new constitution and a "Southern" one (on the basis of a new compact or reformed Articles of Confederation), in which case perhaps no slaveholding states join the Union and thus are not represented in the US Congress at all. Ratification *without* the three-fifths clause entails two basic scenarios: one in which the slave population is counted entirely, which would increase the strength of the slaveholding states, while the other case, i.e. not counting slaves at all, would have reduced their countable population and thus their share of seats in the House of Representatives. Obviously the other alternative would have been to abolish slavery altogether. In this case, the countable population of (formerly) slaveholding states increases, though without much immediate effect on voting presumably since, as former slaves, the new citizens would likely not have any property and thus no voting rights yet. It would not take long until the male population, with or without property, could vote. How then they would have voted cannot be speculated

for certain, other than that their aggregate voting preferences may have diverged from those of their former slaveholders.

9 This is also reflected in the three constitutional amendments – the 13th (abolishing slavery), the 14th (defining citizenship, regulating apportionment by "counting the *whole number* of persons" in a state and thus repealing the three-fifths clause, establishing rights of due process and equal protection under the law), and the 15th amendment (prohibiting discrimination based on race or "*previous condition of servitude*" for the right to vote) – which were passed toward the Civil War's end and during the period of "Reconstruction" of the South, as Congress could require Southern States to ratify them as stipulation to restoring their right e.g. to send representatives to Congress. They were the first constitutional amendments after approximately six decades of the antebellum period and the largest wave of formal constitutional change since the Bill of Rights (the first ten amendments). For a historical and legal analysis of the "Reconstruction Amendments", see e.g. Richards (1993).

10 This complex interlinkage cannot be elaborated further here, but it has been drawn from related discussions and analyses: see e.g. Appleby (1992); Chaplin (1990); Gourevitch (2012); Huntington (1982: 2–15); Kateb (2003: 296–99); Morgan (1972); Myrdal (1944 [1996]); Neem (2013); Rothman (2005); Shklar (1991b); Smith (1988); van Cleve (2010); Young (1996).

11 A material-analytical approach to the US founding was provided by Beard's seminal *Economic Interpretation* of the Constitution (Beard 1913 [2013]), inspiring further affinitive studies (e.g. Jensen 1950; Rossiter 1966 [1987]), but also a backlash from scholars of various disciplines (see e.g. Buchanan and Tullock 1962; McDonald 1958; Wood 1969).

12 On this nexus, Morgan provides an informative summary: "Anyone who studies the Revolution must notice at once the attachment of all articulate Americans to property. 'Liberty and Property' was their cry, not 'Liberty and Democracy'. In the face of the modern dissociation of property from liberty, historians have often felt that this concern of the revolutionists for property was a rather shabby thing, and that the constitutional principles so much talked of, before 1776 as well as afterward, were invented to hide it under a more attractive cloak. But the Americans were actually quite shameless about their concern for property and made no effort to hide it, because it did not seem at all shabby to them. The colonial protests against taxation frankly and openly, indeed passionately, affirm the sanctity of property. And the passion is not the simple and unlovely passion of greed. For eighteenth century Americans, property and liberty were one and inseparable, because property was the only foundation yet conceived for security of life and liberty" (Morgan 1957: 11).

13 For respective analyses as well as different interpretations, see e.g. Allen and Cloonan 2000; Cornell 1999; Dahl 2003; Diamond 1973; Ellis 2000; LaCroix 2010a, 2010b; Main 2004; Onuf 1989; Riker 1987; Storing 1981; Wright 1949; Zehnpfennig 2010; Zink 2009.

14 Some communes, mainly Protestant religious and short-lived ones, were established in colonial America. For a historical overview of communal organized societies in America, see Oved (1993).

15 This brings up another contested concept. For a critical analysis of the feudal concept and its deficient suitability for European societal orders and certainly non-European ones, see e.g. Morillo (2003).

16 Notable examples include: Roger Williams, a Puritan expelled from Massachusetts who founded Providence Plantations; Anne and William Hutchinson, likewise Puritans expelled from Massachusetts who established Rhode Island (merged later with Providence Plantations); or William Penn, Quaker founder of Pennsylvania.

17 For the context here, see especially Chap. 6 (on the advantages of democratic government for society) of Vol. 1, Part 1. Nearly the entire Vol. 2 is immediately relevant here, with treatments of various democratic societal patterns, habits, ways of thinking, and cross-cutting connections to egalitarianism, individualism, among others. Regarding religious-related democratic tendencies, see in Vol. 2, Part 1, Chaps 5 and 6.
18 Analytical caveats are likewise warranted against overly inferring a peculiarity of the USA. For a recent historical comparative analysis of the Reformation in Europe focused on religious institutions, see e.g. Rublack (2017).
19 Legal scholars may find occasion to problematize the use of coercion (the former rebel states that seceded were for a time under occupation), and thus the legitimacy of accession by those states under such conditions. My point is a different one, namely *conceptual*.
20 Though again, as argued above, the three-fifths clause helped provide especially the slave-holding states dominated by the Democrat–Republicans a disproportionately high electoral weight.
21 For the judicial-review precedent in the USA of an explicit reference to a "living constitution", see the Supreme Court decision in *Missouri v. Holland* 252 U.S. 416 (1920).
22 Accordingly from various disciplinary perspectives (see e.g. Deleuze 1997; Dowding 2017; Quine 1991; Russell 1905; Urban 1944).
23 See again Chap. 2 on historical institutionalism and ideational institutionalism.

References

Acemoglu, Daron, and James Robinson. 2012. *Why Nations Fail. The Origins of Power, Prosperity and Poverty*. New York: Crown Business.

Ackerman, Bruce. 1991. *We the People. Volume 1, Foundations*. Cambridge, MA: Belknap, Harvard University Press.

——— 1998. *We the People. Volume 2, Transformations*. Cambridge, MA: Belknap, Harvard University Press.

——— 2005. *The Failure of the Founding Fathers. Jefferson, Marshall, and the Rise of Presidential Democracy*. Cambridge, MA: Belknap, Harvard University Press.

——— 2007. "The Living Constitution." *Harvard Law Review* 120 (7): 1737–1812.

——— 2014. *The Civil Rights Revolution. We the People, Volume 3*. Cambridge, MA: Belknap, Harvard University Press.

Adams, Willi P. 1980. *The First American Constitutions. Republican Ideology and the Making of the State Constitutions in the Revolutionary Era*. Lanham: Rowman & Littlefield.

Allen, W. B., and Keven Cloonan. 2000. *The Federalist Papers. A Commentary*. New York: Peter Lang.

Ameriks, Karl. 1999. "Immanuel Kant." In *The Columbia History of Western Philosophy*, ed. Richard Popkin. New York: MJF Books, 494–502.

Anderson, Benedict. 1983. *Imagined Communities: Reflections on the Origin and Spread of Nationalism*. London: Verso.

Appleby, Joyce. 1992. "Rediscovering America's Historic Diversity: Beyond Exceptionalism." *Journal of American History* 79 (2): 419–31.

Bader, Veit. 2012. "Post-Secularism or Liberal Constitutionalism?" *Erasmus Law Review* 5 (1): 5–26.

Bailyn, Bernard. 1992. *The Ideological Origins of the American Revolution*. Cambridge: Belknap.

Balkin, Jack. 1988. "Constitutional Interpretation and the Problem of History." *New York University Law Review* 63 (4): 911–54.

——— 2009a. "Fidelity to Text and Principle." In *The Constitution in 2020*, eds. Jack Balkin and Reva Siegel. Oxford: Oxford University Press, 11–24.

——— 2009b. "Framework Originalism and the Living Constitution." *Northwestern University Law Review* 103 (2): 549–614.

Ball, Terrence. 1995. "Reviewed Work(s): Federal Union, Modern World: The Law of Nations in an Age of Revolutions, 1776-1814 by Peter Onuf and Nicholas Onuf." *William and Mary Quarterly* 52 (1): 216–18.

——— 1998. "Conceptual History and the History of Political Though." In *History of Concepts: Comparative Perspectives*, eds. Ian Hampsher-Monk, Karin Tilmans and Frank van Vree. Amsterdam: University of Amsterdam Press, 75–86.

Ball, Terrence, and J.G.A. Pocock, eds. 1988. *Conceptual Change and the Constitution*. Lawrence: University Press of Kansas.

Banning, Lance. 1974. "Republican Ideology and the Triumph of the Constitution, 1789 to 1793." *William and Mary Quarterly* 31 (2): 168–88.

Baumgarten, Murray. 1979. "That Stutterer Moses." *Western Political Quarterly* 32 (2): 150–53.

Beard, Charles. 1913 [2013]. *An Economic Interpretation of the Constitution of the United States*. New York: Macmillan.

Bejan, Teresa. 2015. "Evangelical Toleration." *Journal of Politics* 77 (4): 1103–14.

Bell, Daniel. 1975. "The End of American Exceptionalism." *The Public Interest* Fall: 193–224.

Bellah, Robert, Richard Madsen, William Sullivan, Ann Swidler, and Steven Tipton. 1985. *Habits of the Heart. Individualism and Commitment in American Life*. Berkeley: University of California Press.

Bendix, Reinhard. 1980. *Kings or People: Power and the Mandate to Rule*. Berkeley: University of California Press.

Berman, Mitchell. 2009. "Originalism is Bunk." *New York University Law Review* 84 (1): 1–96.

Blackstone, William. 1765 [2016]. *Commentaries on the Laws of England*. Oxford: Oxford University Press.

Brennan, Timothy. 2017. "Thomas Jefferson and the Living Constitution." *The Journal of Politics* 79 (3): 936–48.

Brennan, William. 1977. "State Constitutions and the Protection of Individual Rights." *Harvard Law Review* 90 (3): 489–504.

Breyer, Stephen. 2005. *Active Liberty. Interpreting our Democratic Constitution*. New York: Alfred A. Knopf.

Brown, Candy. 2004. *The Word in the World. Evangelical Writing, Publishing, and Reading in America, 1789–1880*. Chapel Hill: University of North Carolina Press.

Brunhöber, Beatrice. 2015. *Die Erfindung 'demokratischer Repräsentation' in den Federalist Papers*. Tübingen: Mohr Siebeck.

Bryce, James. 1888 [1995]. *The American Commonwealth*. Indianapolis: Liberty Fund.

Buchanan, James, and Gordon Tullock. 1962. *The Calculus of Consent: Logical Foundations of Constitutional Democracy*. Ann Arbor: University of Michigan Press.

Casper, Scott, Jeffrey Groves, Stephen Nissenbaum, and Michael Winship, eds. 2007. *A History of the Book in America. Vol. 3, The Industrial Book, 1840–1880*. Chapel Hill: University of North Carolina Press.

Chaplin, Joyce. 1990. "Slavery and the Principle of Humanity: A Modern Idea in the Early Lower South." *Journal of Social History* 24 (2): 299–315.

Cornell, Saul. 1999. *The Other Founders. Anti-Federalism and the Dissenting Tradition in America, 1788–1828*. Chapel Hill: University of North Carolina Press.

——— 2011. "The People's Constitution vs. the Lawyer's Constitution: Popular Constitutionalism and the Original Debate over Originalism." *Yale Law Journal* 23 (2): 295–338.

Crosskey, William. 1953. *Politics and the Constitution in the History of the United States*. Chicago: Chicago University Press.

Dahl, Robert. 2003. *How Democratic is the American Constitution?* 2nd ed. New Haven: Yale University Press.
Deleuze, Gill. 1997. "Immanence. A Life...". *Theory, Culture & Society* 14 (2): 3–7.
Diamond, Martin. 1973. "The Ends of Federalism." *Publius* 3 (2): 129–52.
Dister, John. 1972. "Kant's Regulative Ideas and the 'Objectivity' of Reason." In *The Proceedings of the Third International Kant Congress*, ed. Lewis White Beck. Dordrecht: Springer, 262–69.
Dorf, Michael, and Charles Sabel. 1998. "A Constitution of Democratic Experimentalism." *Columbia Law Review* 98 (2): 267–473.
Dowding, Keith. 2017. "So Much to Say: Response to Commentators." *Political Studies Review* 15 (2): 217–30.
Dworkin, Ronald. 1975. "Hard Cases." *Harvard Law Review* 88 (6): 1057–1109.
——— 1997. "The Arduous Virtue of Fidelity: Originalism, Scalia, Tribe, and Nerve." *Fordham Law Review* 65 (4): 1249–68.
——— 2015. "How Law is Like Literature." In *Law and Literature. Text and Theory*, ed. Lenora Ledwon. London: Routledge, 29–46.
Easterbrook, Frank. 2008. "Pragmatism's Role in Interpretation." *Harvard Journal of Law and Public Policy* 31: 901–6.
Edling, Max. 2003. *A Revolution in Favor of Government. Origins of the US Constitution and the Making of the American State.* Oxford: Oxford University Press.
Edwards, Mark. 1994. *Printing, Propaganda and Martin Luther.* Berkeley: University of California Press.
Einhorn, Robin. 2002. "Patrick Henry's Case against the Constitution: The Structural Problem with Slavery." *Journal of the Early Republic* 22 (4): 549–73.
Elazar, Daniel. 1987. *Exploring Federalism.* Tuscaloosa: University of Alabama Press.
——— 1993. "Communal Democracy and Liberal Democracy: An Outside Friend's Look at the Swiss Political Tradition." *Publius* 23 (2): 3–18.
Ellis, Joseph. 2000. *Founding Brothers. The Revolutionary Generation.* New York: Random House.
Elster, Jon. 1995. "Forces and Mechanisms in the Constitution-Making process." *Duke Law Journal* 45 (2): 364–96.
——— 2000. "Arguing and Bargaining in Constituent Assemblies." *University of Pennsylvania Journal of Constitutional Law* 2 (2): 345–421.
Epstein, David. 1984. *The Political Theory of the Federalist.* Chicago: University of Chicago Press.
Eskridge, William. 2001. "All about Words: Early Understandings of the "Judicial Power" in Statutory Interpretation, 1776-1806." *Columbia Law Review* 101 (5): 990–1106.
Fiske, Susan. 1992. "Thinking is for Doing: Portraits of Social Cognition from Daguerreotype to Laserphoto." *Journal of Personality and Social Psychology* 63 (6): 877–89.
Fleming, James. 1997. "Fidelity to Our Imperfect Constitution." *Fordham Law Review* 65 (4): 1335–55.
Forsyth, Murray. 1981. *A Union of States. The Theory and Practice of Confederation.* New York: Leicester University Press.
Friedman, Michael. 1992. "Regulative and Constitutive." *Southern Journal of Philosophy* 30 (S1): 73–102.
Gallie, W. B. 1956. "Essentially Contested Concepts." *Proceedings of the Aristotelian Society* 56 (2): 167–98.
Gillman, Howard. 1997. "The Collapse of Originalism and the Rise of the Notion of the "Living Constitution" in the Course of American State-Building." *Studies in American Political Development* 11 (2): 191–247.
Goldman, Loren. 2012. "In Defense of Blinders: On Kant, Political Hope, and the Need for Practical Belief." *Political Theory* 40 (4): 492–523.

Goodheart, Eugene. 2013. "The Constitution: Dead or Alive." *Society* 50 (6): 535–42.

Gourevitch, Alex. 2011. "The Contradictions of Progressive Constitutionalism." *Ohio State Law Review* 72 (6): 1159–82.

——— 2012. "William Manning and the Political Theory of the Dependent Classes." *Modern Intellectual History* 9 (2): 331–60.

Grey, Thomas. 1984. "The Constitution as Scripture." *Stanford Law Review* 37 (1): 1–25.

Grimm, Dieter. 2016. *Constitutionalism. Past, Present, and Future.* Oxford: Oxford University Press.

Habermas, Jürgen. 1992. *Faktizität und Geltung. Beiträge zur Diskurstheorie des Rechts und des demokratischen Rechtsstaats.* Frankfurt: Suhrkamp.

Harris, William. 1982. "Bonding Word and Polity: The Logic of American Constitutionalism." *American Political Science Review* 76 (1): 34–45.

Hart, Albert B. 1907. "Growth of American Theories of Popular Government." *American Political Science Review* 1 (4): 531–60.

Hatch, Nathan. 1989. *The Democratization of American Christianity.* New Haven: Yale University Press.

Heimert, Alan. 1966. *Religion and the American Mind. From the Great Awakening to the Revolution.* Eugene: Harvard University Press.

Held, David. 1989. *Political Theory and the Modern State: Essays on State, Power, and Democracy.* Stanford: Stanford University Press.

Hobbes, Thomas. 1651 [1985]. *Leviathan.* London: Penguin.

Hodgson, Godfrey. 2009. *The Myth of American Exceptionalism.* New Haven: Yale University Press.

Holmes, Stephen. 2012. "Constitutions and Constitutionalism." In *The Oxford Handbook of Comparative Constitutionalism*, eds. Michel Rosenfeld and András Sajó. Oxford: Oxford University Press, 189–216.

Höreth, Marcus. 2010. "Der US Supreme Court als Agent des Verfassungswillens des Volkes?" In *Die hybride Republik. Die Federalist Papers und die politische Moderne*, ed. Roland Lhotta. Baden-Baden: Nomos, 127–50.

Horn, James, Jan E. Lewis, and Peter Onuf, eds. 2002. *The Revolution of 1800. Democracy, Race, and the New Republic.* Charlottesville, London: University of Virginia Press.

Hueglin, Thomas. 1985. "Yet the Age of Anarchism?" *Publius* 15 (2): 101–12.

Hueglin, Thomas, and Alan Fenna. 2015. *Comparative Federalism: A Systematic Inquiry.* 2nd ed. Toronto: University of Toronto Press.

Huntington, Samuel. 1982. "American Ideals versus American Institutions." *Political Science Quarterly* 97 (1): 1–37.

Hutson, James. 1981. "Country, Court, and Constitution: Antifederalism and the Historians." *William and Mary Quarterly* 38 (3): 337–68.

Ives, Anthony. 2018. "Frederick Douglass's Reform Textualism: An Alternative Jurisprudence Consistent with the Fundamental Purpose of Law." *Journal of Politics* 80 (1): 88–102.

Jensen, Merrill. 1950. *The New Nation. A History of the United States during the Confederation, 1781–1789.* New York: Random House.

Jillson, Calvin, and Cecil Eubanks. 1984. "The Political Structure of Constitution Making: The Federal Convention of 1787." *American Journal of Political Science* 28 (3): 435–58.

Jörke, Dirk. 2010. "Die Transformation des Republikbegriffs in den Federalist Papers." In *Die hybride Republik. Die Federalist Papers und die politische Moderne*, ed. Roland Lhotta. Baden-Baden: Nomos, 39–57.

——— 2011. *Kritik demokratischer Praxis: Eine ideengeschichtliche Studie.* Baden-Baden: Nomos.

Kammen, Michael. 2006. *A Machine that Would Go of Itself. The Constitution in American Culture.* New Brunswick: Transaction.

Kateb, Georg. 2003. "Democratic Individualism and its Critics." *Annual Review of Political Science* 6: 275–305.

Keller, Morton. 1987. "Powers and Rights: Two Centuries of American Constitutionalism." *Journal of American History* 74 (3): 675–94.

Kenyon, Cecelia. 1955. "Men of Little Faith: The Anti-Federalists on the Nature of Representative Government." *William and Mary Quarterly* 12 (1): 3–43.

——— 1962. "Republicanism and Radicalism in the American Revolution: An Old-Fashioned Interpretation." *William and Mary Quarterly* 19 (2): 154–82.

Kidd, Thomas. 2007. *The Great Awakening. The Roots of Evangelical Christianity in Colonial America*. New Haven: Yale University Press.

Kleingeld, Pauline. 2008. "Kant on Historiography and the use of Regulative Ideas." *Studies in History and Philosophy of Science* 39 (4): 523–28.

Koselleck, Reinhart. 1982. "Begriffsgeschichte and Social History." *Economy and Society* 11 (4): 409–27.

Kramer, Larry. 2004. *The People Themselves. Popular Constitutionalism and Judicial Review*. Oxford: Oxford University Press.

LaCroix, Alison. 2010a. "The Authority for Federalism: Madison's Negative and the Origins of Federal Ideology." *Law and History Review* 28 (2): 451–505.

——— 2010b. *The Ideological Origins of American Federalism*. Cambridge, MA: Harvard University Press.

Lahat, Golan. 2013. *The Political Implications of Kant's Theory of Knowledge*. London: Palgrave Macmillan.

Landes, David. 1999. *The Wealth and Poverty of Nations. Why Some Are so Rich and Some so Poor*. New York: W.W. Norton.

Langley, Lester. 1996. *The Americas in the Age of Revolution 1750-1850*. New Haven: Yale University Press.

Laserson, Max. 1947. "Democracy as a Regulative Idea and as an Established Regime: The Democratic Tradition in Russia and Germany." *Journal of the History of Ideas* 8 (3): 342–362.

Lepsius, Oliver. 2006. "Die Religionsfreiheit als Minderheitenrecht in Deutschland, Frankreich und den USA." *Leviathan* 34 (3): 321–49.

Levi, Margaret. 1998. "A State of Trust." In *Trust and Governance*, eds. Valerie Braithwaite and Margaret Levi. New York: Russell Sage Foundation, 77–101.

Levinson, Daryl. 2005. "Empire-Building Government in Constitutional Law." *Harvard Law Review* 118 (3): 915–72.

——— 2011. "Parchment and Politics: The Positive Puzzle of Constitutional Commitment." *Harvard Law Review* 124 (3): 657–746.

Levinson, Sanford. 1979. ""The Constitution" in American Civil Religion." *The Supreme Court Review* 1979: 123–51.

——— 1988. *Constitutional Faith*. Princeton: Princeton University Press.

——— 2006. *Our Undemocratic Constitution. Where the Constitution Goes Wrong (and how We the People Can Correct it)*. Oxford: Oxford University Press.

Levy, Jacob. 2006. "Beyond Publius: Montesquieu, Liberal Republicanism, and the Small-Republic Thesis." *History of Political Thought* 27 (1): 50–90.

Lhotta, Roland. 2010a. "Die Federalist Papers und die moderne Politikwissenschaft: Der republikanische Institutionalismus von Hamilton, Madison und Jay." In *Die hybride Republik. Die Federalist Papers und die politische Moderne*, ed. Roland Lhotta. Baden-Baden: Nomos, 99–123.

———, ed. 2010b. *Die hybride Republik. Die Federalist Papers und die politische Moderne*. Baden-Baden: Nomos.

Lindberg, Carter. 2010. *The European Reformations*. 2nd ed. West Sussex: Wiley-Blackwell.

Lipset, Seymour M. 1991. *Continental Divide: The Values and Institutions of the United States and Canada*. New York: Routledge.

Locke, John. 1689 [2000]. *Two Treatises of Government*. London: J. M. Dent.

Loughlin, Martin. 2010. "What is Constitutionalism." In *The Twilight of Constitutionalism*, eds. Petra Dobner and Martin Loughlin. Oxford: Oxford University Press, 47–69.

Lutz, Donald. 1980. "From Covenant to Constitution in American Political Thought." *Publius* 10 (4): 101–33.

——— 1984. "The Relative Influence of European Writers on Late Eighteenth-Century American Political Thought." *American Political Science Review* 78 (1): 189–97.

———, ed. 1998. *The Colonial Origins of the American Constitution*. Indianapolis: Liberty Fund.

Mahoney, Dennis. 1987. "The Newer Science of Politics: The Federalist and American Political Science in the Progressive Era." In *Saving the Revolution: The Federalist Papers and the American Founding*, ed. Charles Kessler. New York: Free Press, 250–64.

Main, Jackson T. 2004. *The Antifederalists. Critics of the Constitution 1781–1788*. Chapel Hill: University of North Carolina Press.

Manning, John. 1997. "Textualism as a Nondelegation Doctrine." *Columbia Law Review* 97 (3): 673–739.

McDonald, Forrest. 1958. *We the People. The Economic Origins of the Constitution*. Chicago: University of Chicago Press.

——— 1985. *Novus Ordo Seclorem. The Intellectual Origins of the Constitution*. Lawrence: University Press of Kansas.

McGuire, Robert. 2003. *To Form a More Perfect Union. A New Economic Interpretation of the United States Constitution*. New York: Oxford University Press.

Michelman, Frank. 1999. "Constitutional Authorship by the People." *Notre Dame Law Review* 74 (5): 1605–30.

Mitchell, Joshua. 1992. "Protestant Thought and Republican Spirit: How Luther Enchanted the World." *American Political Science Review* 86 (3): 688–95.

Molot, Jonathan. 2006. "The Rise and Fall of Textualism." *Columbia Law Review* 106 (1): 1–69.

Montesquieu, Charles d. S. 1748 [1989]. *Spirit of the Laws*. Cambridge: Cambridge University Press.

Morgan, Edmund. 1948. "Colonial Ideas of Parliamentary Power 1764–1766." *William and Mary Quarterly* 5 (3): 311–41.

——— 1957. "The American Revolution: Revisions in Need of Revising." *William and Mary Quarterly* 14 (1): 3–15.

——— 1967. "The Puritan Ethic and the American Revolution." *William and Mary Quarterly* 24 (1): 3–43.

——— 1972. "Slavery and Freedom: The American Paradox." *Journal of American History* 59 (1): 5–29.

——— 1983. "The World and William Penn." *Proceedings of the American Philosophical Society* 127 (5): 291–315.

——— 1989. *Inventing the People. The Rise of Popular Sovereignty in England and America*. New York: W.W. Norton.

Morillo, Stephen. 2003. "A "Feudal Mutation"? Conceptual Tools and Historical Patterns in World History." *Journal of World History* 14 (4): 531–50.

Murkens, Jo E. K. 2007. "The Future of Staatsrecht: Dominance, Demise or Demystification?" *The Modern Law Review* 70 (5): 731–58.

Myrdal, Gunnar. 1944 [1996]. *An American Dilemma. The Negro Problem and Modern Democracy*. New York: Routledge.

Neem, Johann. 2013. "Developing Freedom: Thomas Jefferson, the State, and Human Capability." *Studies in American Political Development* 27 (1): 36–50.

Onuf, Peter. 1989. "Reflections on the Founding: Constitutional Historiography in Bicentennial Perspective." *William and Mary Quarterly* 46 (2): 341–75.

Oved, Yaacov. 1993. *Two Hundred Years of American Communes*. London: Routledge.

Owen, J. J. 2007. "The Struggle between "Religion and Nonreligion": Jefferson, Backus, and the Dissonance of America's Founding Principles." *American Political Science Review* 101 (3): 493–503.

Palonen, Kari. 2002. "The History of Concepts as a Style of Political Theorizing: Quentin Skinner's and Reinhart Koselleck's Subversion of Normative Political Theory." *European Journal of Political Theory* 1 (1): 91–106.

Pocock, J.G.A. 1957 [reprint 1987, 2009]. *The Ancient Constitution and the Feudal Law. A Study of English Historical Thought in the 17th Century*. Cambridge: Cambridge University Press.

Pole, J. R., ed. 2005. *The Federalist. Alexander Hamilton, James Madison, John Jay*. Indianapolis: Hart.

Pope, Jeremy, and Shawn Treier. 2015. "Voting for a Founding: Testing the Effect of Economic Interests at the Federal Convention of 1787." *Journal of Politics* 77 (2): 519–34.

Posner, Richard. 2010. *How Judges Think*. Cambridge, MA: Harvard University Press.

——— 2013. *Reflections on Judging*. Cambridge, MA: Harvard University Press.

Post, Robert. 1990. "Theories of Constitutional Interpretation." *Representations* 30 (Spring): 13–41.

——— 2006. "Democracy and Equality." *Annals of the American Academy of Political and Social Science* 603 (1): 24–36.

Post, Robert, and Reva Siegel. 2006. "Originalism as a Political Practice: The Right's Living Constitution." *Fordham Law Review* 75: 545–74.

Post, Robert. 2009. "Democratic Constitutionalism." In *The Constitution in 2020*, eds. Jack Balkin and Reva Siegel. Oxford: Oxford University Press, 25–34.

Powell, H. J. 1985. "The Original Understanding of Original Intent." *Harvard Law Review* 98 (5): 885.

Quine, W.V. 1991. "Immanence and Validity." *Dialectica* 45 (2-3): 219–30.

Rakove, Jack. 1997. *Original Meanings. Politics and Ideas in the Making of the Constitution*. New York: Alfred A. Knopf.

——— 2011. "Joe the Ploughman Reads the Constitution, or, the Poverty of Public Meaning Originalism." *San Diego Law Review* 48: 575–600.

Rappaport, Michael. 1999. "Reconciling Textualism and Federalism: The Proper Textual Basis of the Supreme Court's Tenth and Eleventh Amendment Decisions." *Northwestern University Law Review* (93): 819–76.

Rawls, John. 1971. *A Theory of Justice*. Oxford: Oxford University Press.

Requejo, Ferran, and Miquel Caminal, eds. 2010. *Political Liberalism and Plurinational Democracies*. London: Routledge.

Richards, David. 1989. *Foundations of American Constitutionalism*. Oxford: Oxford University Press.

——— 1993. *Conscience and the Constitution. History, Theory, and Law of the Reconstruction Amendments*. Princeton: Princeton University Press.

Riker, William. 1987. "The Lessons of 1787." *Public Choice* 55 (1/2): 5–34.

Rossiter, Clinton. 1966 [1987]. *1787: The Grand Convention*. New York: W.W. Norton.

Rothman, Adam. 2005. *Slave Country. American Expansion and the Origins of the Deep South*. Cambridge, MA: Harvard University Press.

Rublack, Ulinka. 2017. *Reformation Europe*. 2nd ed. Cambridge: Cambridge University Press.

Russell, Bertrand. 1905. "On Denoting." *Mind* 14 (56): 479–93.

Sargent, Mark. 1988. "The Conservant Covenant. The Rise of the Mayflower Compact in American Myth." *New England Quarterly* 61 (2): 233–51.

Sauer, Elizabeth. 2005. *'Paper-contestations' and Textual Communities in England, 1640–1675*. Toronto: University of Toronto Press.

Scalia, Antonin. 1989. "The Rule of Law as a Law of Rules." *University of Chicago Law Review* 56 (4): 1175–88.

——— 1997. *A Matter of Interpretation. Federal Courts and the Law*. Princeton: Princeton University Press.

Scharpf, Fritz. 1970. *Demokratietheorie zwischen Utopie und Anpassung*. Konstanz: Universitätsverlag.

Schönecker, Dieter. 2005. *Kants Begriff transzendentaler und praktischer Freiheit. Eine entwicklungsgeschichtliche Studie*. Berlin: Walter de Gruyter.

Schultz, David. 1993. "Political Theory and Legal History: Conflicting Depictions of Property in the American Political Founding." *American Journal of Legal History* 37 (4): 464–95.

Shain, Barry. 1994. *The Myth of American Individualism. The Protestant Origins of American Political Thought*. Princeton: Princeton University Press.

Shalhope, Robert. 1972. "Toward a Republican Synthesis: The Emergence of an Understanding of Republicanism in American Historiography." *William and Mary Quarterly* 29 (1): 49–80.

Shklar, Judith. 1991a. *American Citizenship. The Quest for Inclusion*. Cambridge, MA: Harvard University Press.

——— 1991b. "Redeeming American Political Theory." *American Political Science Review* 85 (1): 3–15.

Skinner, Quentin. 1969. "Meaning and Understanding in the History of Ideas." *History and Theory* 8 (1): 3–53.

Smith, Rogers M. 1988. "The "American Creed" and American Identity: The Limits of Liberal Citizenship in the United States." *Political Research Quarterly* 41 (2): 225–51.

——— 2001. "Citizenship and the Politics of People-Building." *Citizenship Studies* 5 (1): 73–96.

——— 2009. "An Almost-Christian Nation? Constitutional Consequences of the Rise of the Religious Right." In *Evangelicals and Democracy in America, Volume 1: Religion and Society*, eds. Steven Brint and Jean R. Schroedel. New York: Russell Sage Foundation, 329–55.

Soifer, Aviam. 1995. *Law and the Company We Keep*. Cambridge, MA: Harvard University Press.

Sonnicksen, Jared. 2010. "'That Unity is Conducive to Energy will not be Disputed': Die Einheit der Exekutive als problematisches Erbe der Federalist Papers." In *Die hybride Republik. Die Federalist Papers und die politische Moderne*, ed. Roland Lhotta. Baden-Baden: Nomos, 151–70.

Sørensen, Eva, and Jacob Torfing. 2005. "The Democratic Anchorage of Governance Networks." *Scandinavian Political Studies* 28 (3): 195–218.

Spiekermann, Kai, and Robert E. Goodin. 2012. "Courts of Many Minds." *British Journal of Political Science* 42 (03): 555–71.

Storing, Herbert. 1981. *What the Anti-Federalists Were For: The Political Thought of the Opponents of the Constitution*. Chicago: University of Chicago Press.

Stout, Harry. 1977. "Religion, Communications, and the Ideological Origins of the American Revolution." *William and Mary Quarterly* 34 (4): 519–41.

Strauss, David. 1996. "Common Law Constitutional Interpretation." *University of Chicago Law Review* 63 (3): 877–935.

Sunstein, Cass. 2009. *A Constitution of Many Minds. Why the Founding Document Doesn't Mean What It Meant Before*. Princeton: Princeton University Press.

Sunstein, Cass, and Adrian Vermeule. 2003. "Interpretation and Institutions." *Michigan Law Review* 101 (4): 885–951.

Tocqueville, Alexis d. 1835-40 [2003]. *Democracy in America. And Two Essays on America*. London: Penguin.

Troper, Michel. 2012. "Sovereignty." In *The Oxford Handbook of Comparative Constitutionalism*, eds. Michel Rosenfeld and András Sajó. Oxford: Oxford University Press, 350–69.

Tuckness, Alex. 2003. "Discourses of Resistance in the American Revolution." *Journal of the History of Ideas* 64 (4): 547–63.
Turley, Jonathan. 2015. "Madisonian Tectonics: How Form Follows Function in Constitutional Architectural Interpretation." *George Washington Law Review* 83 (2): 305–79.
Tushnet, Mark. 1985. "A Note on the Revival of Textualism in Constitutional Theory." *Southern California Law Review* 58 (1-2): 683–700.
——— 1999. *Taking the Constitution Away from the Courts*. Princeton: Princeton University Press.
——— 2015. *The Constitution of the United States of America. A Contextual Analysis*. 2nd ed. Oxford: Hart.
Urban, Wilbur. 1944. "The Dialectic of Meaning and Truth: Truth as Immanent in Discourse." *Philosophy and Phenomenological Research* 4 (3): 377–400.
Urbinati, Nadia. 2006. *Representative Democracy. Principles and Genealogy*. Chicago: University of Chicago Press.
Vaihinger, Hans. 1924 [2000]. *The Philosophy of "As If"*. Abingdon: Routledge.
van Cleve, George. 2010. *A Slaveholders' Union: Slavery, Politics and the Constitution in the Early American Republic*. Chicago: Chicago University Press.
Wald, Kenneth, and Allison Calhoun-Brown. 2014. *Religion and Politics in the United States*. 7th ed. Lanham: Rowman & Littlefield.
Weber, Max. 1905/06 [2010]. *Die Protestantische Ethik und der Geist des Kapitalismus*. Munich: Beck.
West, Robin. 1988. "Communities, Texts, and Law. Reflections on the Law and Literature Movement." *Yale Journal of Law and Humanities* 1 (1): 129–56.
——— 1990. "Progressive and Conservative Constitutionalism." *Michigan Law Review* 88 (4): 641–721.
Wood, Gordon. 1969. *The Creation of the American Republic 1776–1787*. Chapel Hill: University of North Carolina Press.
Woodberry, Robert. 2012. "The Missionary Roots of Liberal Democracy." *American Political Science Review* 106 (2): 244–74.
Wright, Benjamin. 1949. "The Federalist. On the Nature of Political Man." *Ethics* 59 (2): 1–31.
Young, James. 1996. *Reconsidering American Liberalism. The Troubled Odyssey of the Liberal Idea*. New York: Routledge.
Zander, Helmut. 2016. *"Europäische" Religionsgeschichte. Religiöse Zugehörigkeit durch Entscheidung - Konsequenzen im interkulturellen Vergleich*. Berlin: De Gruyter.
Zehnpfennig, Barbara. 2010. "Liberaler Republikanismus? Das politische Konzept der Federalists." In *Die hybride Republik. Die Federalist Papers und die politische Moderne*, ed. Roland Lhotta. Baden-Baden: Nomos, 81–97.
Zink, James. 2009. "The Language of Liberty and Law: James Wilson on America's Written Constitution." *American Political Science Review* 103 (3): 442–55.
Zuckert, Michael. 1992. "The Virtuous Polity, the Accountable Polity: Liberty and Responsibility in "The Federalist"." *Publius* 22 (1): 123–42.

4

THE STATE OF AMERICAN FEDERAL DEMOCRACY

It has been said that sovereignty is everywhere and nowhere to be found in the Constitution of the United States.[1] This terse dictum appears to convey something. Most obviously, the word "sovereignty" is missing in the constitutional text. It is however much more telling than that. This poses for several reasons an appropriate point of departure to explore the American state, its Constitution, and the dimensions of self- and shared rule in US federal democracy. How are these institutional arrangements coupled with one another as well as with ideas and with constitutional interpretation, and how does their compounded development lead to the immanent fragmentation of the US limited state? To answer this, the subsequent three chapters will explore the democratic and the federal dimensions of government, and strands of constitutional political contestation. This chapter examines first the state and statehood. It begins with a brief re-reading of the US Constitution, and then explores the development of the state in the USA between expansion and limitation.

A constitutional overture

A noticeable mark of the US Constitution is its literal absence of sovereignty. Taken *prima facie*, one could presume that this void possibly derived from some conceptual or terminological constraints at the time of drafting the Constitution in the late 18th century. The point in time predated, after all, other concepts and practices that only later became typical to modern government, such as intergovernmental relations in federalism, or political parties and partisan competition in democracy. Such a constraint on sovereignty is, however, easily ruled out. One need not look back far before the Constitutional Convention at Philadelphia of 1787 to do so. The Articles of Confederation, the preceding constitution drafted less than ten years prior, were actually rather unequivocal in this respect. Already Article 2 stipulated

DOI: 10.4324/9781003203674-4

that "Each state retains its *sovereignty*" as well as every "power, Jurisdiction and right", except with regard to those "expressly delegated to the United States".[2] The 10th Amendment of the US Constitution sets forth a nearly identically phrased residual power, reserving powers neither delegated to the USA nor prohibited by the Constitution to the states or the people. It omits sovereignty, though it also fails to specify *which* of those reserved powers belong to the states *or* the people.

Alternatively, as with other concepts such as republic and federalism, perhaps the framers of the US Constitution were in the midst of transforming the concept of sovereignty by its replacement with references to power. However, were that the case, it would be politically irrelevant. In contrast, for example the French Constitution of 1791, following the second democratic revolution (as of 1789) in modern history, declares straightforwardly in Article 1 of Section III that national sovereignty is indivisible and vested in the entire people. The Constitution of the Swiss Confederation – Switzerland representing since 1848 the longest standing federal democracy[3] – declares in Article 1 that the people and the cantons form the Swiss Confederation, and explicitly defines sovereignty in Article 3 as lying with the cantons, akin to Article 2 of the US Articles of Confederation. A lack of explicit formulation of sovereignty in the US Constitution is quite uncommon compared with other modern constitutions, but not entirely unique either (see e.g. Troper 2012: 350ff.). The Basic Law of the Federal Republic of Germany (1949) for instance states that "all state authority is derived from the people" (Art. 20 (2)), and in the preamble that the "German people, in exercise of their constituent power," adopt the Basic Law, as people in the sixteen enumerated states (*Länder*) in free self-determination. Those provisions still express the gist of popular as well as constituent-unit sovereignty. The same could be asserted with regard to the US Constitution. Its omission, however, is hardly a minor detail, especially since it relates to other constitutional features, or rather omissions.

One of the Constitution's acclaimed innovations, judicial review, which also carries extensive implications for federalism and even sovereignty in general, remains neither named nor defined in Article 3 on the judiciary. The power of judicial review could be deduced, for instance, by combining the judiciary's competence of arbitration in cases involving states and their laws as indicated in Article 3(2) on the Supreme Court and its areas of original and appellate jurisdiction, with the "Supremacy Clause" of Article 6 ("This Constitution, and all Laws of the United States … shall be the supreme Law of the Land"). Nonetheless, there is nothing anywhere in the US Constitution delineating a power to rule acts of Congress or the President unconstitutional. It is unequivocally not there in strict constitutional terms.

The implicit division of sovereignty links to one of the most fundamental constitutional principles in the US Constitution and one that has widely been deemed its most genuine innovation: federalism. Federalism in name is nowhere to be found in the constitutional text. There are dozens of references to the states. This at least suggests the relevance of federalism, though it also underlines, as Lutz points out, why the Constitution comprises an "incomplete text", that is because one actually can only fully understand many of the provisions by also reading the early state constitutions (Lutz 1988). As for the government established by the Constitution, there are only references to the "United States" and its respective branches of government, but not to the *federal government*, or the *central* or *national* level. The only self-references in the Constitution to what the federal or national government is are to a *Union*. Yet this comes up only two or three times,[4] most notably in the Preamble regarding the purpose of the Constitution, that is, among other things, "to form a more perfect Union". The latter implies that the predecessor Articles of Confederation were less than perfect, but nothing more concrete than that. The Constitution has left a great deal open to interpretation, wittingly or not, with regard to the nature of this union and even to its own government.

Unlike many modern constitutions, but even contrary to the previously established Articles of Confederation,[5] the US Constitution fails to declare what type of government it establishes at all. Only in Article 4(4) does one find a specific provision that the United States "shall guarantee to every State in this Union a Republican Form of Government". However, it remains unclear whether the US government implicates itself here as a republic, or commits itself rather to ensure that the states remain republics and newly admitted states become or are already established republics. The latter is more plausible when reading the rest of Article 4(4), as it entails commitments on the part of the "United States" to protect the states against "invasion" and "domestic violence" – i.e. they pertain more to what the US government (and implicitly the states together) guarantees *to do* vis-à-vis the individual states and *not* what the US government itself *is*. Explicit referents of popular sovereignty and democracy in the Union government are lacking, as are ones with regard to state sovereignty and federalism. In contrast again, while the German Constitution refrains from allocating "sovereignty" explicitly, its preamble underscores the constituent power and free self-determination of the *Länder* and the people, while Article 20 declares that "*all state authority* is derived from *the people*", fairly clear-cut formulations of both popular and state sovereignty in other words. The Swiss Constitution literally refers to both. Incidentally, Swiss federal democracy is well over one-and-a-half centuries old, so that the US Constitution, despite its age, demonstrates even more peculiar ambivalences.

What the US Constitution does ultimately provide are numerous *fragments* of text from which – individually or in combination – one can infer the respective constituent powers, ideas, and principles of federalism and democracy. The above review of primary examples of constitutional wording as well as lacunae could resemble at first glance semantic hair-splitting or similar. Processes and practices in federal and democratic governance surely depend on much more than literal phrases in constitutional provisions. The same goes for the inverse, that is explicit or verbatim codifications of sovereignty, federalism, and democracy, which can foster, but not realize on their own, the respective principles and regulative ideas. However, the above points already to ironies in political development and in the dynamics of immanent interpretation of a constitution that expresses so little about its own core features. While obviously not entirely, federal and democratic dynamics in the

USA unfold through recurring constitutional political contestation. They revolve frequently and intensely around textual fragments, and again this often *literally*.

The interpretation of these fragments has not only characterized, but also been decisive for, the dynamics and development of government in the USA at multiple levels. Two places in the Constitution are particularly critical for federalism and democracy, namely "We the People" and the powers "reserved to the States". The Preamble with its formulation of "We the People" who "ordain and establish this Constitution" has been taken to provide a fundamental signifier for popular sovereignty as well as the national sovereignty compounded in the federal government. The 10th Amendment reservation of powers not delegated to the "United States" nor prohibited to the states serves as a fundamental demonstration and justification of state sovereignty. Both comprise pivotal referents for the two main constituent powers constituting a federal democracy as well as for interpreting the Constitution with changing meanings over time and competing ones at times. Coinciding with this ambiguity of constitutional provisions is a host of ambiguities for the horizontal and vertical division of powers in practice.

The constitutional text comprises more than fragments and inconclusive provisions. The document continues to serve largely unaltered as the framework of powers and limits of federal and democratic government and rights of citizens – that is, aside from twenty-seven amendments, the first ten of which though (alias the "Bill of Rights", which is yet another synonym or nickname and not a constitutional denotation proper) were added at once immediately after the ratification, and another two of which cancel each other out (the 18th and 21st on alcohol prohibition and its repeal). This framework has been sustained despite a comparatively short constitutional corpus, that is in comparison with later constitutions in the world of modern states but even vis-à-vis the thirteen articles of its predecessor, the Articles of Confederation. The US Constitution encompasses only seven original articles. The last one, stipulating the number of state ratifications required (nine of thirteen) for approval of the Constitution, has been obsolete since the original ratification succeeded and thus for well over two centuries now.

At a number of places, some quite important for democratic and federal government no less, the Constitution actually leaves little room for interpretive uncertainty. Unequivocal rules include for example those on the legislative periods for both chambers of the Congress (i.e. House of Representatives and Senate), and, for the most part, the four-year term of office of the head of the executive branch, the President. These rules have not changed since 1789.[6] The prohibition on granting titles of nobility and on their acceptance by officers of the USA from foreign entities (Art. 1(9)) are plainly stated. Their direct implications have been considered unambiguous from the outset, that is medals, honors, and similar, but no noble title or privilege can be conferred by any level or branch of government. These provisions can be, and indeed have been, construed as a consequential expression of the republican form of government established by the Constitution (see e.g. Rossiter 1961 [1999]: No. 39).

Despite the interpretive uncertainty and multiple meanings of many provisions, the Constitution has demonstrated a remarkable continuity since its inception. There have been, for instance, extensive interpretations of the constitutional division of powers and checks and balances between the executive and legislative branches and between the House of Representatives and the Senate within the legislative branch. Yet for all of the apparent ambiguities that can be identified in the text and the contestations that have transpired, *not a single one* of the fifteen effective amendments, nor the first ten amendments nicknamed the "Bill of Rights" has addressed them, and thus have left entirely unaltered the original provisions in these respects. That is to say more specifically: no amendment has transferred a single power from the Senate to the House of Representatives or from the latter to the former, nor has there been a transfer of competences from the President to the Congress or vice versa by formal amendment.[7] These circumstances are not just worth noting, they should actually seem baffling. They are explainable to an extent on account of the high thresholds for successfully amending the Constitution, but insufficiently so.

Amendments introducing the power to raise an income tax, expanding civil rights and enfranchisement, and prohibiting discrimination based on race and sex have coincided with a tremendous expansion of Congressional, and thus federal, powers of legislation and regulation as well as executive administration. For instance, the "Reconstruction Amendments" each set forth in nearly identical wording that the Congress has the power to "enforce this article by appropriate legislation" (see Amendments 13(2) (1865), 14(5) (1868), and 15(2) (1870)). Commensurate provisions were adopted later and almost verbatim in the introduction of women's suffrage (Amendment 19 (1920)), the conferral of the right to vote in presidential elections to the District of Columbia (i.e. Washington D.C.) and to appoint (three) electors to the Electoral College (Amendment 23(2) (1961)), the ban on a poll tax or the imposition of any other tax as a requisite to vote in any federal election (Amendment 24(2) (1964)), and the reduction of the eligible voting age to eighteen (Amendment 26(2) (1971)). Over time, presidential powers as well as the position and influence of the Supreme Court have likewise grown substantially. These developments have not transpired via any specific formal constitutional amendment. Instead, they interconnect with constitutional *interpretation* and political *practice*, whether in courts or in the processes and arenas of politics, and their interplay with each other and society. Hence, a constitutional political pattern can be detected: in each case of the above amendments, the introduction of a new federal power or citizen right into the US Constitution matches the pattern already established in the original enumerated powers in Article 1: that is, by and large, *federal* powers are allocated expressly to the *Congress*. This warrants revisiting further on.

For the most part, the powers, functions, and roles enumerated in the first three articles of the Constitution regarding the legislative, executive, and judiciary branches of the USA have not changed in the constitutionally strict sense. Similar applies to the vertical division of powers between the US government and the states.

The original constitutional arrangement prescribes, in a strict constitutional sense, virtually no joint or concurrent powers of the US and state governments, and certainly not in the sense of ones they *must* exercise *together*.[8] There have also been no new constitutional rules referring to joint tasks, fiscal equalization, and the reallocation of the enumerated powers in Article 1, and no redefinition of the distribution of tasks between the federal and state governments pertaining to the administration of federal laws.

Equivalent processes and changes have certainly occurred and to different extents over time and by policy area. But other than taxation, there have been no constitutional amendments introduced related to the numerously increased specific policy areas in which the federal government meanwhile co-governs, such as education, environment, criminal law, welfare, healthcare, or modern communications and transportation. These developments in governing practice entail joint or concurrent, parallel, and "redundant" exercise of various government powers at federal and state levels. They have not resulted from formal constitutional change. One exception in this regard emerged with the 18th Amendment (1919) banning the manufacture, import, export, sale, transport, and consumption of alcohol ("intoxicating liquors"). In addition to the prohibitions, a constitutional provision was included by which both Congress and the states expressly "have *concurrent* power to enforce this article by appropriate legislation" (Amendment 18(2); emphasis added). As a result, the US Constitution formally prescribed a joint governmental task for the first time. It was also the only and last time. The Amendment was repealed, moreover, relatively soon thereafter (21st Amendment (1933)), making it an exception that no longer is, nor was, for very long.

The introduction of direct taxation, especially the federal income tax, and the amendments expanding rights and prohibiting discrimination, on the other hand, contributed to altering the scope of federal powers. They amounted in a strict sense to *unilateral* changes. The prohibitions, for example on various discriminations, pertain to and thus restrict *all* levels of the polity,[9] while the respective amendment provisions conferring legislative powers to enforce those rights and protections have referred *solely* to Congress. Otherwise, akin to the horizontal division of powers between the US branches of government, not much has changed in more than two hundred years regarding the vertical distribution of powers between the US government and the states in the strict constitutional sense.

Formally, the amendments have not legally altered state powers, though they have by implication, as they endowed the federal level with a substantial potential to intervene in the states, particularly when their laws and regulations could be deemed incompatible with the Constitution or with constitutionally compatible federal law, as underpinned by the Supremacy Clause (Art. 6). The amendments do not, however, prescribe that states lose authority per se in the potentially affected ambits or policy areas, but rather only that Congress *can* enforce the amended provisions through legislation. This is not the same as a complete transfer of authority. Even the introduction of the power to raise income tax does not amount to a full reallocation of powers in fiscal federalism. Income tax was not transferred to the federal level.

This change was rather a unilateral increase in Congressional authority, and thus a potential redundancy, as states can still levy their own income taxes. These remarks touch upon, can be conceived and contested with, the nature of the Union and thus the tensions between state and popular sovereignty. The amendments constitute significant changes that extend the potential scope and trajectory of the federal government. This potential has been used. However, it can equally be left dormant, resisted and repulsed, depending on different interpretations of the provisions by the courts, but also by states, political parties, and others.

Another constitutional pattern can be detected in light of constitutional amendments. One apparent feature is ambivalence. The recurring formulation that "Congress shall have power to enforce the provisions of this article" appears fairly straightforward, but also somewhat indeterminate. This connects to a second, but widely overlooked, feature, namely the sheer terseness of these provisions. More elaboration of *how* or *in which ways* new limits or extensions apply is consistently and altogether lacking: for example with regard to concrete policy areas or with specific references to the enumerated powers, not to mention the lack of bothering to specify further the powers of the US government enumerated in Art. 1(8). Congress *can* pass legislation to enforce non-discrimination and rights, while the "rest" is left not just unspecified, but simply unmentioned at all. As noted from the start, the original US Constitution is comparably short, much shorter than most modern constitutions, at many places much less specific, and by consequence tremendously ambivalent and open to interpretation. Whether this is a good thing or not is debatable. However, one should wonder why this manifest pattern of formulating ambivalent, unspecific constitutional provisions did not change. This seemingly begs for explanation, or at least some attention.

The persistent terseness and imprecision should seem obvious. Most modern constitutions encompass broad principles, but they also entail more numerous articles, details, specifics, and, over time, they usually tend toward concretization, especially when amendments are undertaken. The USA under the Constitution has experienced intense contestation over the authority of the US government from the outset, most poignantly illustrated in a devastating Civil War in the mid-19th century to resolve some of its original ambivalences. Thus, brevity or keeping it short and simple in constitutional rules may be more or less understandable with regard to articles drafted in the late 18th century – even though it had become immediately apparent already then that many of the original constitutional provisions, and the nature of the Union, were confronted with multiple and fundamentally divergent interpretations. The original constitution is admittedly old. However, not all amendments are. All the more so, why the subsequent amendments should refrain from further specification appears puzzling, though also problematic.

Because constitutional amendments require supermajorities in general and almost superlatively so in the USA, it is no surprise that their formulations can wind up broad, even vague. The isomorphism in the US Constitution on the other hand suggests an ideational-institutional boundedness of "thinking in the box". The constitutional amendments maintain a certain consistency with the original constitution. They repeatedly reproduce its textual character, in those instances when the window of opportunity opened, or was entered and engaged, to achieve formal constitutional change. The US Constitution throughout its sequence of development could have been concluded as having worked, that things ultimately worked out because they somehow appeared to in the aggregate. Yet, numerous historical events, developments, and conflicts so patently demonstrated that they often did not. For instance, the Reconstruction Amendments did not succeed, for almost an entire century, as a basis for guaranteeing the rights they enshrined. The Supreme Court in 1898 still managed to read a right of the states to practice segregation, creating the infamous doctrine of "separate but equal" in the Plessy v. Ferguson case. And yet in 1919, when states were still enforcing racial segregation and the utter disenfranchisement of citizens, and many even tolerating, if not sanctioning, domestic terrorism by the Ku Klux Klan, in order to achieve women's suffrage and guarantee its fulfillment, the authors of the 19th Amendment sufficed with emulating the formulation found in the Reconstruction Amendments pursuant to which Congress has the power to enforce its provisions by legislation. No further specifications were apparently required. The utter lack of concretization of constitutional amendments is consistent with the precedents. This pattern continued despite ample historical experience, but also prolific egregious violations of constitutional rights prescribed by the Reconstruction Amendments occurring at the very same time of introducing the right to women's suffrage.

Facing ambivalences in the original constitution, in order to assess what different provisions and phrasings related to sovereignty, federalism and democracy are meant to implicate, one recourse could be to revisit the past by reading the Convention debates and the *Federalist Papers* (Rossiter 1961 [1999]). This is precisely what countless people do. For one, though, the previous analysis of the Convention and the contention in the ratification debate revealed that these sources represent only one side of the founding. For another, much of the writing and terminology in the *Federalist Papers* can end up confusing more than clarifying, especially given the transformations in concepts, practices, and even nomenclature that have meanwhile occurred. While inventing, or rather reinventing, redefining, and tinkering with, federalism and the republic, the framers left explicit references and definitions of these governmental dimensions out of the Constitution. The *Federalist Papers* use these terms in ways that comply with, but also would diverge considerably from, what tends to be understood as federalism and democracy nowadays, even in the USA. *Federal* often refers to differences to *national* as well as to components of the Constitution involving primarily the states, such as the equal representation in the Senate or the ratification process. The terms "consolidated" and "national" refer to the US government, mixtures of "national", "consolidated", and "federal" to the composition and operation of the Electoral College, while at other times the national government is referred to as federal, or the entire arrangement of government as a federal one or at other times even as a confederacy and an association of states. This terminological melange appears even within one Federalist Paper like

No. 39, which may reveal complex thinking, but renders the conception of federalism there "messy" and a "jumble" (Rakove 1999: 43).

To resolve what parts of the Constitution are meant to mean, one could return then to the Constitution itself, examine the division of powers prescribed there, and compare their description and contestation in other period writings as well as with the state constitutions of the founding era. This could allow for reaching more conceptual clarity. The question remains however, for whom would this provide any binding interpretation. In the democratic federal polity of the USA, the Constitution says not only what various scholars or judges, but also what politicians and citizens, think and say it says.

The Constitution establishes a complex political order from the outset, one that encompasses a separation of powers in multiple dimensions – horizontal, vertical, as well as temporal. These various dimensions become compounded in the Constitution in its strict as well as broad sense. Fragmentation at the same time represents an overarching feature and logic: within the dimensions of government, the individual branches of government, and the textual corpus itself. The above constitutional reading began with reference to sovereignty along with its ubiquitous presence and absence in the Constitution. Federalism and democracy are equally everywhere and nowhere to be found in the US Constitution. They have emerged, operated, and changed over time through evolving practices in tensions between change and continuity as well as contested interpretations of the related constitutional fragments. The US political order has constitutional tensions, which connect with the overarching, but limited American state.

The contours of the American state

The USA is in a peculiar state. The US polity stands out in one immediately noticeable facet, in that "the state" tends to be associated with the subnational level, in common parlance and in the Constitution, and thus from the outset. The US state stands out further especially in broad comparison with the European continent. There the modern state has originated in multiple senses and dimensions. They range from the very term of the state itself (terminologically reaching as far back as Antiquity) to institutional features, and legal and philosophical notions conventionally associated with statehood in general. State sovereignty, intertwined with transitions from ecclesiastical and temporal orders to nations and states, had been compounding in Western Europe since the end of its Middle Ages (Dyson 2009; Ertman 2008; Kalmo and Skinner 2010). How one gets from there to here, from the origins of the modern state to the state in the USA, and the state of its state, entails making a long story short. However, this short story is important for capturing the US limited state. This demands a concept of the state itself for determining what poses the peculiar features and patterns of the USA, and what does not. Along these lines, it is possible to delineate meaningfully the contours of the US state in its bounded development, and what then constitutes its limited, and in multiple respects, ambivalent character.

Towards a state synopsis

The state strictly as term and broadly as concept rests upon a long and varied history. The modern understanding of the state can be abridged to comprise a, however constituted, overarching incorporation of legal, ideational, and structural-functional dimensions of a political order that is both bound to and binding for a rather fixed territory and its population. The state carries an assortment of additional, many still relevant, referents: from status and condition to estate. This provides clues for several complexities embedded in the evolution of the state.

The estate in the feudal or otherwise social-class-based *status* sense is largely obsolete as the basis for organizing the state, though its remnants still loom.[10] Further revealing is the juxtaposition with the term *politics*. This has a varied history and transformation, but with particular relevance to the state. The *political* connects with the "Western"-type differentiation of spheres (e.g. social, political, economic, religious, ethical) that turned the political into something quite different than its original meaning a few millennia ago (Sartori 1973). The institutional and ideational evolution spans in parts a congruous and in parts divergent differentiation, and thus conjuncture and disjuncture of conceptual fragments and threads. A state-political "knot" became suspended in a historically evolved ideational "sphere". Its strands relate to for example authority, constitution, rule, order, rights, government, citizenship, and territory (cf. *polis* and "city-state"). They are each distinct and yet all tied up in the political and the state. Many of these ambivalences are reflected in the American state, as will be shown. The actual transition to modern statehood warrants specific attention first.

Like constitutionalism, sovereignty and its emergence and development interlink with the historical, institutional, and ideational development of the modern state (Held 1989: 218–28; Skinner 2010). State and sovereignty rest on a multidimensional boundedness to society and its development on the one hand, and the tensions and mutual constitutiveness between them and "peoples" as well as "citizenship" on the other (see e.g. Habermas 1996; Hay 2014; Migdal 2001; Mitchell 1991). Nation and state building have often been connected historically, and often used synonymously, as concepts, as *nation-state* saliently reflects. However, the two are not identical processes, nor are they congruent in all states (if any at all), and certainly not in multilevel and multinational polities (see e.g. Anderson 1983; Fabbrini 2003; Tilly 1975).

For the emergence of state and sovereignty specifically, the Treaty of Westphalia of 1648 ending the Thirty Years' War holds a central conceptual place.[11] It has been widely construed as signifying the onset of the modern nation-state and state sovereignty in Europe: for example with regard to establishing the principle of recognition of the *internal* authority of temporal rulers over their territory, and their *external* independence from outside interference (Farr 2005). There is much reason to doubt that Westphalia as a critical juncture was "all that" (Krasner 1993): for example concerning how much state sovereignty in terms of internal control and external independence were actually achieved there, though also concerning the alleged inauguration of the "secular state" (Piirimäe 2010; Scheuerman 2004). The state–church establishment continued for centuries among the treaty signatory parties alone, while modern states were already developing among several belligerents like France and Sweden, or in countries outside the treaty framework like England. The period in time provides nonetheless an anchor for framing the sequence of development and multiple components, institutions, and ideas underlying the modern state and state sovereignty. One relevant, though often overlooked part of the Treaty of Westphalia in political analyses, pertains to restrictions on "letters of marque and reprisal" for the hire and deployment of privateers to commandeer foreign vessels at sea. The regulation of church–state–society relations and the often-referenced principle of *cuius regio, eius religio*[12] is conventionally treated as the main achievement and of far-reaching significance. There are several reasons though to zoom in briefly instead on the rules regarding the sovereign license of "private" subjects to seize property from hostile combatants.

These Westphalian provisions alone did not change inter-state conflict, even in Europe, at least not immediately. However, they signify an important legal precedent and emergent regulative idea for the development of international law, by which armed conflict becomes conceived in terms of external matters carried out between states, and internal matters organized and mobilized within states. This also underlines a transition from the reliance on mercenaries and other "soldiers of fortune" toward the establishment and proliferation of professional militaries of the state (Huntington 1957; Kempe 2010). This bears direct relevance to the American War of Independence nearly 130 years later as well as the US Constitution. For instance, mercenaries, most famously the "Hessians" (from Hesse-Cassel and Hesse-Hanau), were engaged by England in the war against the rebellious American colonies (Atwood 1980; Mauch 2003), and "Letters of Marque and Reprisal" were regulated in both the Articles of Confederation (Art. 9) and the enumerated powers in Article 1 of the US Constitution. That power was used in several armed conflicts of the early federal republic, but would soon fall into obsolescence with the establishment of a professional and eventually standing army in the USA. The development of "inter-state" conflicts ties in fundamentally with the evolving state apparatus and core state functions.

Without delving into complex and often controversial scholarly debates on the environmental, cultural, material, or technical determinants of state development (Acemoglu and Robinson 2012; Diamond 1997; Landes 1999; Schmidt 2006; Stokes 2001), it is necessary to zoom out again and underline here the interlinkage with broader political developments such as the organization of political rule and especially administration.[13] This points most fundamentally to *institutions* as distinguishing features of the modern state.

With the emergence and consolidation of rule of law, bureaucracy, coercion and the monopoly of legitimate violence, or market creation and regulation (see e.g. Benz 2008; Fukuyama 2012; Steinmo 2010), the modern state developed functional and structural differentiation and, as an overarching feature, processes of *rationalization* in the exercise of collectively binding authority and its legitimation (see also seminally

Weber 1921 [1976]). The concept of rationalization by Weber has been further elaborated with regard to structural, functional, processual, and power dimensions, and linked to bureaucratization, the division of labor, rules and rule-making, and legal implementation and interpretation (see e.g. Bendix 1977; Dowding 2004; Mayntz 1993). These features have been elemental to definitions of the modern state and government and their distinctions from more traditional political rule, whether based on hereditary, ecclesiastical, or other sources of legitimacy. The state and statehood comprise a set of functions, structures, and norms, and thus institutions and ideas. They pertain to law and legal order (e.g. worldly sovereignty and authority) within a particular territory, the regulation of its internal and external affairs on the basis of legal rules and procedures, the domestication of peace and order underpinned by the institution of police power (and similar, externally, through military armed forces), and the construction and operation of a public administration (see the works by Bendix, Dowding, and Mayntz, cited just above; also Finer 1980; von der Muhll 2003). There remains the cross-cutting question of finance, or, akin to the classic definition of politics as "who gets what, when and how" (Lasswell 1936), of what are the sources, objects, and modes of public finance in the modern state.

Different patterns of developing "rule and revenue" (Levi 1988) run more or less in parallel with different paths of state development. Revenue raising by taxation, as opposed to resource extraction via tribute or violent seizure, constitutes a hallmark of the state as a means to finance state functions and political administrative infrastructures (ibid.). Outliers, exceptions, and corruption aside, the institutionalization of tax authority and fiscal administration coincides with the development of the state apparatus, while the scope of public revenues and expenditures tends to reflect the extension of governmental functions (see e.g. Benz 2008: 215–58; Steinmo 1993, 2010). Taxation also interlinks society to state power and order in a delimited territory (see e.g. Huhnholz 2015). That the exercise of the "power of the purse" would require consent and representation of those taxed was relevant to developments toward representative government. In England and later colonial America, the evolving institution of rendering public finance subject to representative-democratic co-determination (e.g. no taxation without representation) also coupled with the evolution of popular sovereignty.

Sovereign authority was dislodged from divinity or otherwise transcendental sources toward the "solitude" of state sovereignty. This transition did not inaugurate an utter de-personalization of the "body politic". Nor did it come with the immediate unbridled establishment of the liberal constitutional state. This shift could usher in the *concentration* of authority toward absolutism and centralization in some political contexts as much as the *limitation* of government toward the separation of powers in others. The state can be generalized in institutional and ideational terms. The concrete manifestations of features and notions differ by context and historical development. This applies already to one critical state-formation phase of the mid-17th century in Western Europe alone. The origins and evolution of the state did not move unilaterally toward centralization in a nation-state. Clearly the early USA came to confirm this point, but so did much of early modern Europe, given the continuation of various leagues, proto-federal and multinational orders (Spruyt 1996), in addition to the monocratic and centralizing ones.

Finally, the constituent power in a democratically constituted state has built on popular sovereignty, the ideational and institutional transfer of sovereignty to the people. Thus re-enters the emergence of popular sovereignty in the mid-17th-century English case. A contingent contestation between Parliament and Monarch triggered a dynamic evolution of popular sovereignty. It transmuted by the early 18th century in England into *parliamentary* sovereignty, though not quite yet *parliamentary government*, which Bagehot (1867 [1974]) notably framed as the "efficient secret" of the English Constitution in the next century. In the USA, popular sovereignty developed on a different path of organizing government, and its horizontal and vertical division of powers.

England and the USA came early on to stand for veritable prototypes of unitary and federal organization of the state respectively. They shared, however, a fundamental common ground in the development of the state, one that connects to the ideational and institutional development of popular sovereignty. In both cases of early statehood evolution, *the state* served less as the concept and imagination of the overarching institution of political order, but was rather conceived as *government* (Benz 2008: 49–53; Nettl 1968). The relatively early onset of the separation of powers – between the legislature and executive, notions and practices of representative government linked to the legislative assembly, the proliferation and sanctification of private property and the coupling of taxation with the consent of the taxed, and last but not least, the transfer of sovereignty not to the state but rather to the *people and Parliament* – compound into the prevailing of *government* as the referent of collectively binding institutions of public authority. Political development in England and the nascent USA still generated a pattern of *state* building, even by other means or names. In the USA on the other hand, the state did become a concrete and prolific referent of political organization. But it attached primarily to the constituent units of the constitutional political order. And that is no small thing for the state of the American state, either then or now.

The states in the USA

Ideational and institutional tensions across the history of politics in the USA make it difficult to generalize a pattern of state development. A lack of one coherent pattern of the state or statehood over time is not solely unique to the American state. Political systems or modern states (or "the state") experience different phases of fluctuations in competences and the degree of central-state authority over time. The state, while terminologically suggestive of something "static", is neither immutable nor monolithic (Benz 2012). Federally constituted polities are especially predisposed to dynamic political development on account of the division of authority and the corresponding political contestation (see e.g. Bakvis and Chandler 1987; Benz 2013; Broschek 2015). Ambiguities may result in any case and at different times. In the USA, however, ambiguities of the state appear constituted from the outset and are recurring.

The USA demonstrates several particularities that indicate a problematic and conflict-laden relationship to the state and the federal government. This has been surely witnessed in the past, as revealed by a long history of common perceptions of government as a "necessary evil" (see e.g. Wills 1999). Widespread antagonism, distrust, and even anti-statism vis-à-vis the federal government have grown in recent decades again (Kamarck 2009; Quadango and Street 2005). As of the 1980s, the re-emergence and intensifying opposition to "big government" make up one of the most significant sources of dynamics in American politics, rendering the federal government "under constant siege" (Gerstle 2015: 8; see also 1–54). Already the US Constitution in the strict sense as well as in seemingly common understandings allude to an idiosyncratic notion of the state and seem to invite state ambivalences as well as contestation.

In contrast to the constituent units of other federal systems, designated as *communities* or *regions* (e.g. Belgium and Spain), *provinces* (e.g. Canada), *cantons* (e.g. Switzerland), or *Länder* (e.g. Austria and Germany), they carry the same legal denomination as *states* in the USA. In the discourse on the legitimate and necessary tasks, rights, and powers of *the* state, reference need not necessarily be limited to the *federal government*. *The state* can equally, if not more so, refer to states. The "empirical" state of the USA extends further in the broad constitutional sense, but in the strict constitutional sense, the state is primarily incorporated in individual states (see e.g. Fain 1972). Strictly and literally drawn from the Constitution, the compound order of *government* and its superordinate (federal or national) level are the "United States". This may invite the attribution of state sovereignty to the constituent-unit states and, prima facie, allow the federal or "Union" government to appear more as a compact among the constituent states. Some form of stateness, whether nominally signified as such or not, belongs to the constituent units of any federal order. The USA is not alone, either, in the designation of the sub-units of the federation as states (see e.g. Australia, Brazil, India, or Mexico). However, even more indicative of the US state-idiosyncrasy is the term *statehood* itself. This links the state ideationally and institutionally, and not just nominally, to the states.

US statehood

Statehood may generally imply "stateness", *Staatlichkeit*, or *étaticité* as in the functional-structural and ideational senses of the modern state (see e.g. Weber 1921 [1976]: esp. 27–32), or in the international legal sense of the recognition of a sovereign unit's territory, people, and government. In the USA, however, *statehood* in constitutional-legal and political terms has long referred specifically to *accession* to the USA as a full-fledged state. Accession has occurred by former territories, by the partition or dismemberment of a part of one pre-existing state, like Maine from Massachusetts or West Virginia from Virginia,[14] or of previously unincorporated areas as in the case of California (1850) and the Republic of Texas (1845). Statehood thus means becoming a US state. Disregarding the readmissions of states that seceded and joined the Confederation of the United States (1861–1865), there have been thirty-seven instances of new statehood since the ratification of the US Constitution by the original thirteen states.[15] Both aforementioned core dimensions of statehood – the institutional and ideational sense of stateness (e.g. with own state apparatus and constitutionality) and in the sense of an external recognition of a territorial political unit – refer to the states from the outset. While these conditions are often overlooked or forgotten, they are constitutive of subsequent American political development.

The historical contingencies of originating American federalism in the late 18th century entailed a great deal of conceptual contestation among supporters and opponents of the then "new" Constitution. Already with the Articles of Confederation and especially the US Constitution, forging a constitution coincided with the sheer uncertainty on the proper organization of a federal republic and the allocation of authority between levels of government (see e.g. LaCroix 2010). Ambiguity on statehood and the location of sovereignty remained, not only in the transition from former colonies into independent republics, but also in the Constitution (see e.g. Farrand 1908; Morgan 1948). Several constitutional provisions signify corresponding principles of statehood as well as the nature of interstate relations and comity among the states and the Union as a whole. Though again, formulated as they were in the late 18th century, neither the contemporary concept of intergovernmental relations, nor even comity, are explicitly laid down. Above all, Article 4 is pertinent in this context of the states: it prescribes mutual recognition and reciprocity between the states (Art. 4(1), "Full Faith and Credit" clause), the guarantee of rights and protections to be enjoyed by citizens of each state across the states (Art. 4(2), "Privileges and Immunities" clause), while Article 4(3) prescribes the rules for admitting new states and Article 4(4) guarantees a "Republican Form of government" to the states. In addition, Article 1(3) prescribes the representation of states, irrespective of population, in the second chamber of Congress with two senators each, both of whom have one vote each. The conjunction of these rules is crucial.

It was perhaps only through constitutional interpretation compounding these rules early on that the notion of state equality came to be understood as applying or "counting" for new states as well (see e.g. Davila-Colon 1981). This understanding is not self-evident, precisely since the Constitution endowed Congress with the responsibility and power for administering territories as well as admitting new states. This by consequence rendered Congressional recognition and regulation – of new states, boundaries, and the resolution of boundary disputes in frontiers and hinterlands – pivotal for the development of statehood (see e.g. Onuf 1982). These constitutional political circumstances invited different interpretations of sovereignty. The position of Congress seemingly conformed, in simplified dichotomy, to the Federalists' understanding of national sovereignty and the supremacy of federal government, yet could support the Antifederalists' idea of a preponderance of constituent-unit state sovereignty (see e.g. Aleinikoff 2002; Zick 2005). There was a fairly swift consensus in the course of independence that the original thirteen colonies would succeed as territorial units that constitute "states". But how to manage their Western territories and the acquisition of new territories immediately confronted the federal republic with fundamental issues of statehood and of regulating competing claims among individual states.[16]

As colonies in British North America, the conventional mode of mediation of such disputes would have resorted to appeals to the Crown in England, as continued to be the case for Canada well into the 20th century prior to the "patriation" of its constitution (Broschek 2009; Lhotta 1995). The early USA was well familiar with extensive local self-government, as has widely been pointed out, but also with institutions and dynamics of center–periphery relations, including on this specific issue of managing boundaries and territory. In lieu of the English Crown and Privy Council, both the Articles of Confederation and the Constitution prescribed the US Congress as arbiter. In the Constitution, Congress – no longer an assembly of states, but rather the legislative branch of US government – also became "manager" and rule-setter for statehood politics. This reveals a curious, but fundamental, disjunction in the Constitution from the outset. On the one hand, Congress was endowed with the primary competence for regulating center–periphery relations toward incorporated territories and in the politics of statehood. This underlines the new supremacy of the national government, especially since another approach could have been taken, that is simply to continue the initial arrangement under the Articles of Confederation of allowing individual states their own territories and, in expanding westward, to expand *their* territories rather than create new states under conditions and terms stipulated by Congress. On the other hand, Congress was not granted competence to arbitrate conflicts on the supremacy of law between the USA and the states, for example through a special committee of states or other configured sub-body, which was thus another divergence from the Articles of Confederation. This competence instead fell under the ambit of a federal judiciary (see e.g. LaCroix 2010), thus restoring a mode of arbitration resembling more the arrangement familiar from the colonial era (i.e. the Privy Council).

Regarding US territories and statehood aspirants, the US Constitution appears by and large to resolve the question of authority as resting with Congress. Authority over the relations between states and Congress or the US government, in contrast, were far from resolved. This ambivalence pertains to subsequently admitted states. The US government dictated rules and requirements for their admission, but they would join as *equal* states nevertheless. Several of these "newcomers" (e.g. Alabama, Arkansas, Florida, Louisiana, Mississippi, Tennessee, Texas), incidentally if not ironically, would call the authority of the US government, which established their statehood, into question over the first half of the 19th century, and eventually join in seceding from the Union and the ensuing Civil War. They justified this with a starkly contrasted idea of the nature of the Union as one of sovereign states. While Congressional authority for statehood politics may appear clear-cut, Congress compounded the representation of the people *and* the states, granting the latter equal representation in the Senate. Congressional powers over statehood were an expression of federal-level or "national" authority. At the same time, Congress served in the context of statehood politics (and of course other policy areas) as an arena of interstate politics and contestation among states. This revolved not least around the divide between slave-holding and "free" states.

In addition to the transition from colonies to republics and the constitutionalization of statehood in the late 18th century, American statehood transformed through the immediate onset of territorial expansion. The Louisiana Purchase (1803) from France had already doubled US territory far beyond the Mississippi River and into the Rocky Mountains. This also confronted the early federal republic with a host of challenges. It not only amplified tensions between Northern and Southern States, with controversy over whether and in which cases slavery would be allowed to expand, reignited multiple times until the Civil War. Additional contested questions arose concerning governmental-level competences for infrastructure over such a vast space, while issues of external protection and defense were intensified and exacerbated by the further intrusion into "Indian" territories. Challenges also pertained to the settlement of the territories, the monitoring and even guiding of their own state-making processes in order to become experienced in republican self-government as an eligibility criterion for statehood (e.g. the guarantee of a "Republican Form of government", Art. 4 (4)) (see also e.g. Biber 2004). Thus, expansion and statehood compounded with profound questions of whether state making should entail building an "empire of liberty" and thus concerns of how to uphold and implement the American Revolutionary principles themselves (Hammond 2003; Hill 1988; Horsman 1989; Johnson 2009a; Kastor 2004; Knowles 2003; Levinson and Sparrow 2005; Onuf 1981, 1982; Sparrow 2017). These challenges persisted and augmented through further expansions, increasing displacements of Native Americans and several wars. Armed conflicts occurred with Mexico over Texas and then again for nearly the rest of the Southwestern USA, as did numerous conflicts prompted by the USA's violation of nearly every treaty and agreement made with Native American tribes throughout the 19th century (see e.g. Aleinikoff 2002). Together these developments extended US territory by the advent of the Civil War from its original space between the Appalachian Mountains and the Atlantic eastern seaboard in the 1770s all the way to the Pacific.

To refer to the USA as a limited state appears misplaced. The opposite seems to apply on account of its enormous growth in political and military power by the mid-20th century for sure. Yet, already in light of developments throughout the entire 19th century, the USA became not only one of the largest countries in the world, but also an imperial power (see e.g. Ferguson 2005; Sparrow 2017), appropriating and settling vast territories, at times by purchase and at times by violent force. Dilemmas emerged in the sense that, to conform to US constitutional principles, statehood aspirants needed their own constitutions and experience in republican self-government. The US government often managed them, somewhat akin to former British Royal Governors, by installing their own governors in the territories (see e.g. Eblen 1968). They were thus in effect settled and colonized by the USA. From the earliest years of the federal republic, the US government engaged in the regulation of statehood as well as the very *invention* of future states. The attribution of a limited state still fits for other reasons, foremost with regard to limiting the national level of government *within* the Union and *among* the federal government and the states. This limitation applies far less with regard to the external expansion of the USA from the beginning of Independence onward.

The peculiar dynamics of state-making and territorial governance persisted well after the Civil War and into the 20th century with the admission of more states, though also the dominion over multiple territories to this day. Akin to the pre-Civil War dynamics, the politics of admitting new states often revolved around national political interests and ideas as well, and were conditioned asymmetrically by Congress: for example in the creation of North and South Dakota out of the Dakota Territory for the mere purpose of increasing the likely share of Republican senators; the postponement of Utah's statehood until it banned the Mormon practice of polygamy (although marriage was and still is primarily a state-regulated policy); the reservation as "federal lands" of large to gigantic shares of the territories of e.g. Alaska, Arizona, Colorado, Idaho, New Mexico, or Nevada (in the latter case, more than 80 percent of its land); not to mention the conquering of the Kingdom of Hawaii. These developments indicate in some cases expressions of popular or state sovereignty (e.g. when Western States held state constitutional and ratification conventions), but much more the preponderance of the federal government and national democratic political logics in the regulation of statehood, the creation of states, and extensive reach into their territories (see e.g. Bridges 2015; Clawson 2011; Hanson 2017; Sparrow 2017; Stewart and Weingast 1992; Tillin 2015; Weaver 1969). The peculiar division of Dakota into two states even reveals the artificial creation of two "state peoples" for national political purposes following an "ordinary" partisan political logic.

Finally, the development and dynamics of statehood have implications with regard to two influential concepts of American federalism and federalization. The USA as a case of Stepan's "coming together" federalism (Stepan 1999) and the prototype of Riker's federal bargain (Riker 1964) requires substantial modification. These concepts may hold some validity for the USA at the time of gaining independence. Yet even there, the amount of time the original thirteen states spent as truly independent ones is actually remarkably short: after declaring independence and in the midst of the War for Independence, they formed a Union under the Articles of Confederation, only to be replaced less than a decade later by the US Constitution that has remained in effect to this day. They spent decades more time as separate units of local self-government as English colonies, with colonial charters serving as the chief basis for determining boundaries between the new states. Their moment of coming together and reaching a "federal bargain" lies *not* with the Constitution, but the Articles of Confederation. But the latter involved an aggregation of territories that were only immediately before declared as independent states. The US Constitution on the other hand entails the remaining together of states in an attempt at a "renegotiation". These states were already together in the Union (see e.g. Preamble on the purpose of forming "a *more perfect* Union") and had been previously bound as British colonies as well. It was as *colonies* that they could be conceived as having been separate from one another to some extent. The original thirteen states drafted their own constitutions and indeed enjoyed a broad latitude of autonomy in the early republic and for a large part thereafter. For all intents and purposes, the amount of time they *really* spent as *independent republics* appears negligible.

The subsequent dynamics of statehood in the sense of admission to the Union, the dominant meaning of statehood in the USA – i.e. for all other thirty-seven and thus the vast majority of states in the USA – reveal a variety of patterns. They range from "joining in" federalism and territorial expansion leading to state manufacturing under conditions stipulated by the federal government, moreover by and large pursuant to ideas and conflicts of interests within the established states, to instances of coercive "holding together" as witnessed in the reaction of the Union to the secession of the Southern States, as well as several cases of new statehoods by dismemberment and partition. The notions of "federal bargain" and "coming together" federalism, each of which have been conceptualized precisely with the US case in mind, fail to capture accurately the character of its federation or its actual institutionalization in the US Constitution. They are empirically applicable, and this only partially, to the time of the founding, itself encompassing various constitutional moments, not just the Convention and the ratification of the US Constitution, and much less so for the institutional rules and dynamics of statehood development afterward – i.e. the actual dynamics at play for all but thirteen of the fifty states. All the more ambivalent then is the limited state in the USA given the ongoing and recurring uncertainty regarding constitutional authority granted to the US government in general and for multiple state functions. The concepts of coming together through a federal bargain do prove profoundly informative, but rather of regulative ideas and patterns of "what people think" about the constitution of the US federal republic. These *ideas* matter tremendously for American political development.

Another curiosity of the American state becomes apparent. On the one hand, multiple manifestations of federal supremacy are evident, like Congress steering westward expansion over the decades of the US's own "long 19th century" (Gerstle 2009). It mobilized for multiple military conflicts to these ends (e.g. wars against Mexico, Native Americans, slave uprisings, the seceding states), undertook expansionary endeavors with "Manifest Destiny" overtones and imperial undertones, stipulated conditions of admission to the Union for aspirant states, and even artificially created states on the basis of political ideas and preferences, for example in drawing straight "lines in the sand" or soil to be followed for admitting territories north thereof as free and south thereof as slave holding, or creating two Dakotas instead of one. All of the above could point to an actual superior, if not imperial, authority of the federal government. On the other hand, the idea that states' consent to the constitutional contract as both an expression of their authority and a rational-choice entry into a bargain and, with this, ideas of states' rights and sovereignty, persist all the same into the present. From this disjunction follows a fundamental ambivalence of the American state. It compounds to an overarching pattern of ambiguities of further dimensions, dynamics and tensions in developing the state in the USA.

Between a state uniting people and a Union of states

There is much reason to suppose that the US Constitution forged a "Union of States" (Forsyth 1981). A great deal of American political development at least lent credence to this premise for more than seven decades through the mid-19th century (see e.g. Deudney 1995). On the other hand, the historical development and dynamics of federalism, the early onset of cooperative patterns and their intensification already in the 19th century, as well as their linkage with the dynamics of democratic politics, foremost the permeation of national politics and parties across the multilevel system, provide ample reason for concluding instead a "myth of State autonomy" (Gardner 2013; cf. also Elazar 1962, 1964). Nonetheless the constitutional-political idea of *states' rights* has undoubtedly influenced political development and statehood in the USA. This maintains recurrent virulence and controversy as a legal political idea against shifts in authority toward the national level (see e.g. Orren and Skowronek 2004), and can be found in nearly every constructible epoch: from the Constitutional Convention of 1787, throughout the Antebellum years up to the Civil War of 1861–1865 and its aftermath, to the dispute over desegregation a century later, up to more recent politics in the areas of welfare and healthcare reform. In addition to the interests of different groups and parties, at the heart of scores of conflicts lies the contestation of constitutional understandings.

A key notion concerns the reference to the states as creators of the federal government, and not the other way around. State sovereignty and the "compact theory" of the Constitution are manifest in appeals to the Union as one created by the states, observable in John C. Calhoun, the leading political thinker and politician from the Antebellum South and a main theoretician of the concept of *nullification*,[17] to President Ronald Reagan's program of a New Federalism in the 1980s, aspiring to retrench the federal government and reinvigorate the states (Mann 2012: 59–65). The compact theory had also supported the claims to a constitutionally legitimate right to state secession throughout a large part of the 19th century (see e.g. Anderson 2004; Farber 2003; Stampp 1978; Whittington 1996). The issue of secession, like so many other things, is wholly absent from the Constitution. However, this omission does not implicate that, for the framers, withdrawal from the Union would have been inconceivable.

The USA, most obviously, was born itself out of "secession", and its own Declaration of Independence invoked a democratic right of revolution.[18] There also had been previous instances of secessions or splits in colonial America, like the separation of Rhode Island and Providence Plantations from Massachusetts. The predecessor constitution, the Articles of Confederation, was already in name a compact of *Perpetual* Union. Moreover, threats of secession from the Union had loomed in the immediate run-up to the Constitutional Convention. This body produced a new constitution, so that the Perpetual Union of the Confederation lasted less than a decade. Consequently, there were many available ideational, legal, and historical precedents as well as recent and contemporaneous incidents warranting an explicit address of secession in the US Constitution.

One could assume that the framers opposed any right to secession. Such could be inferred, for instance, from the amendment process delineated in Article 5, as implying the solely legitimate mode of forming and reforming a "more perfect Union". Alas, the residual ambiguities of the Constitution do not compel this interpretation. Divergent interpretations seem plausible, especially since the 10th Amendment reserves all powers – not delegated to the USA *nor prohibited* to the states by the Constitution – to the states or the people. It would be hardly far-fetched to conclude that the lack of an express prohibition of secession suggests its status as a right reserved to the states.

The omission of rules on regulating secession or prescribing its prohibition should seem curious, but also of serious consequence. It would apparently take a Civil War to resolve this constitutional question. Even more curious is that no formal constitutional regulation – either prohibiting secession, or establishing a formal process to that end – was undertaken in the period of Reconstruction, that is in the immediate wake of an actual secession. Nor have any constitutional political developments observable in other multilevel orders[19] prompted the USA to think outside its box on this matter. Instead the justification or proof for a prohibition of secession is not the Constitution, which remains silent on this issue, but rather the brute fact of the Northern military victory over the Southern seceding states. The constitutional (non-)regulation of secession points to contingencies, bounds, and limits of learning and adaptation within institutional settings. What this also reveals is another fundamental *ambivalence* underlying the state in the USA. Its path-dependent development in tensions between state-building and the limiting of (national) government becomes even more comprehensible, with a view to later developments of the American state.

States' rights and the compact theory, or their mobilization, have often helped thwart and at times retrench, but not utterly hinder, the expansion of powers, legislative and regulative activities of the federal government, and the development of an American state. Its modernization has been associated seminally by Beer with the rise of intergovernmental relations and changing political dynamics between the levels of government over two centuries (Beer 1973, 1978). Power sharing and cooperation intensified further into the 20th century, along with more functional interlocking between multiple levels and branches of government and increasing activities of the branches of the federal government, backed by a corresponding "loose" and "living" interpretation of the Constitution. On the other hand, cooperative federalism was confronted as of the late 20th century with resurgent challenges to "Washington's" perceived encroachment into the ambit and sovereignty of states, an implicit and often explicit revival of the compact theory, and demands for more political latitude for states. These trends of growing and combatting "big" federal government can be said to have generated a mixed pattern of dynamics of "ambiguous" (Elazar 1990; Walker 1996) and "janus-faced federalism", with states-oriented federalism backed up by a corresponding strict and literal interpretation of the Constitution (Conlan and de Chantal 2001; Conlan and Dudley 2005).

These ambiguities of US federalism connect more generally to an "ambiguous polity" (cf. Roelofs 1986). Numerous political developments and constitutional provisions provide referents that can be used to legitimize the competing notions of compounded popular sovereignty versus state sovereignty in political contestations. The preamble proclamation of "We the People", as much as the compact theory, can be taken as fiction or a historically constructed regulative idea. Both can be inferred from historical referents as much as the ambivalence – textual fragments and lacunae – of the Constitution. The dynamics of interpretation over time, and the *ex post* rationalization and justification of these two competing notions have made them ultimately mean more over time than they originally meant (cf. Munzer and Nickel 1977).

The phrase *We the People* could, and probably should, have included "We the People of the States of ...", for example the thirteen original states, as was the case in the preamble to the Articles of Confederation. Explicit reference to popular and constituent-unit authority would be consistent, and typical, in the constitution of a *federal* republic (cf. again German and Swiss constitutions). The duality of sovereign authority in people and states, moreover, was already expressed in the USA itself, in the Articles of Confederation and the Declaration of Independence.[20] During the ratification debates though, it became uncertain which states would actually ratify the new constitution.[21] The decision was made to cut the states out, which simply made practical and tactical sense (Farrand 1908: 543ff.). All the same, the wording of "We the People" *sans* the states winds up becoming the fundamental referent of popular sovereignty. This meaning has even come to be widely interpreted as the actual intent of the framers (cf. e.g. Amar 2005). Whether they meant this or not is debatable. What ultimately matters for subsequent political development is that people believe the idea or the text expressing it to mean that, and in this case, to "imagine" that they have been constituted as a people. Compound popular sovereignty may also be suggested by the process of state conventions and ratification acts to join the Union. Gaining statehood was stipulated and often managed by the US Congress for all but the thirteen original states. With few exceptions,[22] they were "states" that had not even existed as such before their admission to the Union, but instead as parts of US territories.

On the other hand, the same acts of state conventions and ratifications of the Constitution in statehood admissions can be viewed fundamentally differently. They have provided a basis for an – empirical or *ex post* imagined – demonstration of the sovereign consent of states. This principle of inherently requisite state consent could furthermore be drawn from the provisions of the amendment process. In addition to two-thirds approval of both chambers of Congress, one of them representing the states no less, a high threshold of three-fourths of the states is required for amendments to succeed (Monaghan 1996). From this perspective, admissions to the Union and the constitutional amendments represent not creations of the federal government, but rather renewals of the state creation of the Union compact. Both competing notions of the character of the US state and the Constitution binding federal and state governments and people(s) become effective regulative ideas. They ultimately appear to entail more belief than proof.

The state in the USA has rested primarily in conceptual and ideational terms with *the states*, while the US *government* stands terminologically for the national or "federal" state apparatus, and *nation*, instead, commonly for the polity as whole (see e.g. Benz 2008: 49–54; Fain 1972; Nettl 1968). "Nation" is also ambivalent. At least two basic concepts or dimensions can be summarized, one pertaining to an ethnic-national or otherwise culturally defined sense, and one to peoplehood as the *demos* or citizenry in a constitutional sense. The USA has witnessed ethnic nationalism in a caustic form, like "white nationalism", particularly in the 19th century and in recurring waves into the present. However, the USA, as argued by Kincaid, unlike several multinational federations (e.g. Belgium, Canada, India, Spain), lacks "peripheral" or regionally concentrated nationalisms (Kincaid 2016).[23] Of course nationalism and patriotism, and the mobilization and dedication to national "icons", are salient in the USA and its political history (see e.g. O'Leary 1999). Nevertheless, its nation is not properly defined along ethnic lines. And yet while the USA does not constitute a *nation-state* per se, nation and state have managed to blend, albeit idiosyncratically.

Ideas and institutions of nationhood and citizenship in the USA have, on the other hand, long built on inherited cultural and especially Anglo-Saxon legacies (see e.g. Huntington 1982, 2005) and thus also a profound *bias* (see e.g. Smith 1988). Their development surely coincided with legacies of profound racial bias as well (see e.g. King and Smith 2014; Morgan 1972; Shklar 1991a, 1991b). The US citizenship–nation-state nexus encompasses foundational political ideational legacies, which are also relevant to notions of the state and its political development, or its apparent absence as *the* state. Several such fundamental strands can be framed as a set of ideas attached to liberalism, individualism, and egalitarianism in the USA, which connect to individualistic political, economic, and religious freedoms, as well as widely shared beliefs in popular but limited *government* (see e.g. Hart 1907; Lipset 1975; Morgan 1989; Riker 1987; Roelofs 1986). They entangle with an American "creed" that harbors both trust in individual and egalitarian principles and practices as well as an inclination to distrust government. And yet ideological and religious-type moralist as well as missionary tendencies contribute to the exercise and expansion of political power and coercion, in pursuit or in the name of democratizing and equality-promoting reforms but also quests for domination over others (see also Hartz 1955; Hofstadter 1964; Kloppenburg 1987, 2001; Myrdal 1944 [1996]; Niebuhr 1952 [2008]; Smith 1993; Tocqueville 1835–1840 [2003]). Progressivism, populism, reformism, moralism, economic self-interested pursuit of wealth and property, republicanism, and libertarianism are compounded in ongoing tensions. They span between "institutions and ideals" (Huntington 1982), between the different institutional and societal "antinomies" embedded in the American constitution (Fabbrini 1999a), and between "contradictions" and "paradoxes" of these strands, generating an overall "ambiguous" US polity (Roelofs 1992). The processes of state and people building result in a mutually enabling and constraining interlinkage (see e.g. Smith 2001; cf. also Stepan 1999) within the bounds of the institutional framework of the US political order. The fragmented constitution of the polity, also in the broader sense of ideational and institutional developments, have contributed to a pattern of a limited, supposedly absent state. Neglect of *the* state is evident in political discourse, even though it is "there" and has expanded.

Evolution of state limiting and state building in the USA

In structural-functional institutional senses, the state has not only existed, but expanded over the course of American political development. The democratic and federal governmental dimensions entail multiple divisions of authority. They have nevertheless allowed for an extensive, even imperial, as well as a warfare, welfare, and regulatory state to emerge that can appear, almost paradoxically, "submerged" (Mettler 2011) or that "Americans can't see" (Sheingate 2009). Its development and trajectory, change and continuity, have invited "bringing it back in" to social science scholarship and the US case in particular (Evans, Rueschemeyer, and Skocpol 1985; Leuchtenburg 1986; cf. also e.g. Lowi 1992; Nordlinger, Lowi, and Fabbrini 1988). The federal governmental level was long throttled in developing the extent of administrative power, police power, direct taxation, regulatory activities, and capacities characteristic of many other modern states. But this is not the same as outright non-existence.

Despite contestation on the nature of the Union, the development of core state functions at federal level commenced from the outset, and were intensified already as of the 19th century. Examples include:

- Construction of a US postal system, promotion and financing of, or allocating territorial lands for, canals, roads, and railroads, and fostering together the infrastructural "seams of the state" (Callen 2009, 2012);
- The "building of a new American state" through establishing an own federal bureaucracy and as of the later 19th century its professionalization and expansion (Skowronek 1982);
- The shift from reliance on ad hoc mobilized militia and the outsourcing of military functions (e.g. granting Letters of Marque and Reprisal) to the establishment of standing and increasingly professionalized armies from the Civil War onward (Frye 2005; Huntington 1957);
- Progressive Era "state building" with the expansion of market regulation, "anti-trust" policy, and labor union protection, but also intervention in several domains like electoral regulations and rights, not least women's suffrage, as well as domestic issues under state jurisdiction, most (in)famously alcohol consumption and its eventual prohibition (McDonagh 1992; Pisani 1987);
- The development toward a "modern fiscal state" through e.g. using original Congressional power to regulate and impose indirect taxes like tariffs, customs and excise taxes, the formation of several federal banks and the permanent establishment of the Federal Reserve system in 1913, the introduction of direct taxation power (16th Amendment), and a federal income tax in the same year (Mehrotra 2013);

- The shift from state to federal control over immigration policy for regulating entry into and free movement of persons in the USA after the Civil War (i.e. when also prior fugitive slave laws became inapplicable) (Law 2014);
- In addition to the westward expansion steered by Congress in the politics of statehood, the "colonization", settlement, and regulation of vast territories enabled Congress to intervene in otherwise state ambits via governance over territories, one notable area being education in the mid-19th century and the provision of land grants to foster the establishment of higher education institutions (Johnson 2009a).

The late 19th century Gilded Age and the Progressive Era transition to the early 20th century have even been deemed in retrospect the first "New Federalism" (Johnson 2007; 2009b), but with a general pattern of state expansion and modernization rather than its limitation and retrenchment.

The development and exercise of these state functions entailed, to a large extent, practices and processes of governance and regulation rather than direct service provision. In the early to mid-20th century, the US state stands out in its restraint from assuming many functions directly, in contrast with other modern states which owned and operated for example railroads, telecommunications, universities, airlines, or broadcasting companies (King 1973b). The USA carried out state building from the earliest years of the federal republic and in intensifying fashion in the 19th and early 20th centuries. While adapting to functional necessities in the transition from primarily agrarian and merchant to an industrializing economy and society, singularities or idiosyncrasies persisted: whether due to ideational patterns linked to support for private property, capitalism, and the market economy; or due to institutional and constitutional limits linked to the federal distribution of powers.

The depiction of the US government as "stateless" for much of its pre-20th-century history is a simplification that makes some metaphorical sense, if by comparison to other political systems and in reference to the federal level. Such characterization of the state in the USA becomes oversimplified and untenable with a view to state building at the subnational level in the states and to for example: the development of police powers, policies and institutions regulating early welfare, public education, and social control. The states comprised arenas where the tensions and dynamics between "liberty and coercion" as a "paradox of American government" (Gerstle 2015: 55–87) are especially observable. This is most salient in connection with the "American paradox" of "slavery and freedom" (Morgan 1972), that is the dual expansions of democratic citizenship and republican government in tandem with institutions for the utmost suppression and subjugation of people.

Despite differences to other modern states, as in Europe in particular, the USA in the early to mid-20th century undertook major steps toward expanding the regulatory and redistributive competences of the federal level as was the case with the New Deal in the 1930s. Federal public works and infrastructure programs and a national welfare regime including unemployment insurance and social security as a retirement insurance program were introduced, spurring the intensification of cooperative federalism (see e.g. Beer 1973, 1993; Kincaid 1990, 2012; Zimmerman 1992, 2001). These changes coincided or were followed by the emergence of a "military-industrial complex", the intensifying pursuit of "national security" with a global trajectory, and an astronomic expansion in budget and capacity for military, defense, and space exploration in the course of the world wars and the Cold War (Gerstle 2015). The 1930s has generally counted as a critical juncture and even a "constitutional moment" (see e.g. Ackerman 1991) for US government and its ensuing tremendous growth. Though again, not a single formal constitutional change in federal powers in welfare, defense, commerce, or taxation policy occurred at that time (or ever since). This was not a big bang in state transformation in the sense of acquiring hitherto unknown or missing state powers (see e.g. Lewis-Beck and Squire 1991). The corresponding federal-level statehood capacities were already incrementally emerging, as elaborated above. There were manifold antecedent developments in "American partnership" in state building, whether through public and private partnerships or federal and state government cooperation and coordination, as well as intergovernmental relations in the 19th century (Elazar 1962).

Meanwhile the arm of the state reaches far into numerous spheres of the polity and social, political, and economic life *within* the USA. The expansion of the American state, if indicated by the public sector growth, was also mirrored by government growth at the state level, with large public-finance shares thereof allocated by the federal government (see e.g. Garand 1988). In the criminal penal system, the scope and extent of the US state spans even further. This is indicated most saliently and brutally by the continued exercise of capital punishment, but also an extent of incarceration which is unparalleled around the world, including in authoritarian and otherwise non-democratic or non-rule-of-law states (see e.g. Dhami and Cruise 2013; Gottschalk 2006; Weaver and Lerman 2010). On the other hand, the expanding trajectory of federal governance, regulation, and enforcement from the mid-19th century and increasingly in the 20th century has also pursued the protection and realization of civil rights, political and social equality, combatting multiple forms of discrimination, requiring "affirmative action" to ensure the inclusion of women and minorities at multiple levels of the polity and areas, from public and private workplaces and education institutions to electoral processes and district design (see e.g. King 2007, 2017; King and Smith 2014; Lieberman 2011). The expansion of federal authority precisely in these areas and exercised by all three branches of government represents perhaps one of the most peculiar "ironies" of American state building given its entanglement with the institution and legacies of slavery (King and Lieberman 2009): for example slavery had determining effects on the dynamics of statehood politics, the limitation of the federal government, and the composition of its three main branches of government (see again the three-fifths clause) in the first three-quarter century of American political development under the US Constitution.

The statelessness of US government can be deemed an "illusion" (King and Lieberman 2009) that is powerful nonetheless. Comparison with other modern states allows for inferring a generally more limited state in the USA, especially with regard to *how* conventional state functions were organized and carried out. This surely links to ideational patterns as well. To quote from another comparative study:

> the State plays a more limited role in America than elsewhere because Americans, more than other people, want it to play a limited role. In other words, the most satisfactory explanation is one in terms of Americans' beliefs and assumptions, especially their beliefs and assumptions about government.
>
> (King 1973a: 418 (original emphasis))

This conclusion is plausible and resonates with the analytical framework here. However, institutions matter more extensively. Various ideas oriented toward limited government only capture one, albeit profound and extensive, ideational pattern. These beliefs and "wants" neither persist in a vacuum, nor emerge autopoetically. A constitutional-political ideational pattern oriented to limiting the state and the federal government has evolved in tensions and dynamics between change and continuity. It is also embedded in and bounded by institutional settings. However, the same applies *too* for the inverse pattern: that is the dynamics toward state building, expanding federal governance, as well as democratic practices, rights, and equality predicated, among other things, on the actualization of "We the People" and the "more perfect Union". Both limitation and expansion, and thus *ambiguity*, appear to capture the overarching pattern of developing the US state.

Patterns of dynamics differ, broadly conceived, between other modern states and the US state and the states. This may suggest the need to moderate or relativize American "exceptionalism" (Fabbrini 1999a: 466ff.; 1999b): how developmental patterns of polity, policy regimes, and politics combine makes, in sum, any case unique. This conclusion notwithstanding, the preceding survey has pinpointed peculiarities, ambiguities, and even ironies tied to the US state and its development. It reaffirms the often purported limited role of and opposition to government, the federal level in particular. What should also become apparent is that this applies neither at all times nor unequivocally across the board at any given time in the US polity. Expansion of federal level and multilevel coordination as well as retrenchment and further fragmentation can and do unfold in formal and informal democratic and federal institutions readily available and conducive to these opposing ends. The different directions, moreover, can each find constitutional provisions to support competing interpretations. Fragmentation remains immanent to the US constitution in its strict sense. Ideas about limited government and separation of powers are easy to read out of the institutional provisions related to federalism and democracy. They may support prescribing and reinforcing the fragmentation already inherent in these institutional settings, which can render interlinkage and cooperation between branches and levels of government difficult.

A preface on the dynamics and constants of US federal democracy

The constitution and the state in the USA reveal multiple ambivalences. They relate to the complexities of division of powers in different dimensions of the polity and their paths of development over time. The dynamics of democratic and federal politics are generated in political processes revolving around interest conflicts. They also arise on account of interpretation and ideational contestation on the nature of the Union itself: for example either as one founded on the basis of the entire people as a compounded whole in a federal republic, or rather as one comprising a nation bound together but with a limited government consented and subject to limitation by the sovereign states. The institutional parameters are multidimensional. The following explores these governmental dimensions, in search of a composite pattern of democracy and federalism, their institutional arrangements and development. Their historical evolution reveals, as with the constitution in general, ambivalences, ambiguities, as well as contradictions.

The US system of government has come to be known as a presidential democracy. The Constitution prescribes a strict separation between the legislative and executive branches in the horizontal dimension of government. The vertical dimension is constituted with a strict separation between levels of government, commonly known as dual federalism. Hence two dimensions of government are rather geared toward stricter separation. By comparison with other federal democracies, for instance other longer established ones like Canada, Germany, and Switzerland, the composite model would appear to be a clear-cut case of an *uncoupled* federal democracy, at least in formal constitutional terms (Benz and Sonnicksen 2017). Moreover, the constitution, in a strict sense, has not changed much since the founding.

The constitution of the US polity in the broad sense reveals a much more complex picture. The dynamics of statehood and state building, as well as changing and contested constitutional interpretation, have altered patterns of government and politics in democratic and federal practice extensively, though not steadily. The pattern of coupling evolves within the multiple dimensions of government and multiple constituted fragments in the US federal-democratic political order. The evolution of federalism and democracy – akin to that of the state, statehood, and the Constitution – transpires over time in bounds and interactions of ideational and institutional path dependencies. Ambiguities may persist all the same on account of the interplay between old, changing, new, as well as "renewed" democratic and federal practices and interpretations.

Against the backdrop of the Constitution and the state of the USA, the following three chapters explore the tensions and immanent fragmentation of American federal democracy. To be determined are the *horizontal* and the *vertical* dimensions of the division of powers, their "dynamics and constants" in the coupling within and between federalism and democracy for one, and with political-constitutional contestation in the USA for another.

Notes

1 For a dense and comprehensive treatment of this "anomaly" of the ubiquity of sovereignty, yet lack of explicit delineation in the US constitutional case, see e.g. Rakove (1999).

2 All references to the Articles of Confederation are taken from the printed edition (United States 1781 [2005]); the same compendium is used for references to the US Constitution (United States 1787 [2005]).

3 While its constitution is younger than that of the USA (1848, but with major revisions in the decades to come and a total revision in effect as of 1999), Switzerland may represent a case of a longer-standing, *continuous* federal democracy than the USA. Its federal constitution was established about fifty years later than the US Constitution and after a civil war, the *Sonderbund War* of 1847 (though its extent pales in comparison to the US Civil War, lasting less than one month and with very few fatalities) (see e.g. Hueglin and Fenna 2015: 120ff.) – and thus thirteen years *prior* to the Secession of Southern States and their formation of a Confederate States of America and seventeen years *before* the end of the American Civil War.

4 Another reference to Union is the report on the "State of the Union" which the President is to provide to Congress (Article 2(3)), thus revealing nothing more about the character of the Union government itself.

5 This is apparent e.g. already nominally, "Articles of Confederation". Other examples include the first article, "The style of this *confederacy* shall be the 'United States of America'", and Article 13, "… the Articles of this *confederation* shall be inviolably observed by every state" (emphasis added).

6 The 20th Amendment (1933) rescheduled the starting dates of the session of Congress (Art. 1(4)) and the term of office of the President (Art. 2(1)), but not the duration of the terms, which have remained fixed at two, six, and four years for the representatives, senators, and the President (and Vice President) respectively.

7 An exception could be made, though only a slight one, with the 25th Amendment (1967) on presidential succession, which regulates, or specifies, procedures of succession originally set forth in Art. 2(1) for cases of vacancy in the offices of the President and Vice President (whether on account of removal, resignation, incapacitation, or death), as well as the role of and obligations to the Congress in these cases.

8 This poses a simplification, but not overly so. This strict constitutional dualistic arrangement can be said to apply by and large to governmental powers and processes. In contrast, one fundamentally relevant area of the joint exercise of functions prescribed in the Constitution refers to the most obvious one, namely the constitutional amendment procedures (Article 5), but also to elections, especially of the presidency (addressed further on).

9 However, the application of rights and prohibitions on discriminations to e.g. the states was contested, certainly up to the Civil War, only after which many civil rights and liberties, and their binding effect on the federal *and* state governments, could be implemented, though contestation continued for decades to come.

10 This is evident nominally: e.g. in the *Staten-Generaal*, the first and second chamber of the Dutch national parliament, or the semantic "split" mirrored in the Swiss second chamber of parliament representing the cantons, the Council of States, called *Conseil des États* in French (*état* meaning both "estate" and "state"), but *Ständerat* in German (*Stand* being understood in contemporary terms as "estate" or "social status", and *Staat* as "state").

11 In short, it broke out in 1618 in the wake of the Reformation from the mid-15th century, the internal strife within the Holy Roman Empire, the split between predominantly Catholic-led and Protestant-led "countries" (i.e. if one can use that term retrospectively),

and their increasing conflicts culminating in the eventual multinational and multi-confessional thirty-year embroilment (see e.g. Parker 1997; Whaley 2011).

12 The rule "whose region (or realm), their religion" was actually already set in the Peace of Augsburg of 1555.

13 For an illuminating comparative study, see also e.g. Morillo (1995).

14 The case of West Virginia's admission to the Union as a state in 1863 is particularly complex, for it occurred after the secession of Virginia from the USA and its joining the Confederacy in 1861, which prompted it to leave Virginia. West Virginian statehood was thus born out of back-to-back secessions, making its recognition by the US Congress and President Lincoln constitutionally dubious, no less since the counties of western Virginia were occupied by the Union Army almost immediately following the secession of Virginia (though this was welcomed by "Unionists" there); for a further exploration of this complex case, see e.g. Curry (1962, 1964).

15 For a comprehensive overview, see Shearer (2004). For a compact (and amusingly portrayed) compendium of the history of political boundaries in the USA with short reviews on each of the fifty states, see Stein (2009).

16 This is visible in the Northwest Ordinances of 1784 and 1787 pertaining to the region later known as the "Midwest" (between the Appalachians the Mississippi and bordering the Great Lakes); see e.g. Onuf (1982, 1983).

17 The theory purports that states have the right to nullify federal laws deemed incompatible with the constitutional authority of the federal government.

18 See in the Declaration of Independence, e.g. in the first paragraphs: "When in the Course of human Events, it becomes necessary for one People to dissolve the Political Bands which have connected them with another ... they should declare the causes which impel them to the Separation"; as well as: "[T]hat whenever any Form of Government becomes destructive of these Ends [i.e. previously elaborated inalienable rights], *it is the Right of the People to alter or to abolish it, and to institute new Government*" (emphasis added).

19 One such instance lies just across the border, i.e. in Canada with the "Clarity Act", passed after the marginally defeated Quebec secession referendum in the 1990s (Hueglin and Fenna 2015: 304 ff.).

20 See e.g. the concluding paragraph: "We, therefore, the Representatives of the United States of America ... by the Authority of the *People* of these Colonies, solemnly Publish and Declare, That these United Colonies are, and of Right out to be, Free and *Independent States*" (emphasis added).

21 Again, the framers of the Constitution added to this uncertainty by changing the rules of ratification to nine states instead of unanimity.

22 E.g. the short-lived Republic of Texas, though its "independence", or rather forced acquisition from Mexico, was sanctioned with political and military support by the USA.

23 The reference to Native American tribes as "nations" on the other hand represents an ambivalent case, also with a complicated to atrocious history of massacres and expulsions to reservations.

References

Acemoglu, Daron, and James Robinson. 2012. *Why Nations Fail. The Origins of Power, Prosperity and Poverty*. New York: Crown Business.

Ackerman, Bruce. 1991. *We the People. Volume 1, Foundations*. Cambridge, MA: Belknap, Harvard University Press.

Aleinikoff, T. A. 2002. *Semblances of Sovereignty. The Constitution, the State, and American Citizenship*. Cambridge, MA: Harvard University Press.

Amar, Akhil R. 2005. *America's Constitution. A Biography*. New York: Random House.

Anderson, Benedict. 1983. *Imagined Communities. Reflections on the Origin and Spread of Nationalism*. London: Verso.

Anderson, Lawrence. 2004. "The Institutional Basis of Secessionist Politics: Federalism and Secession in the United States." *Publius* 34 (2): 1–18.

Atwood, Rodney. 1980. *The Hessians. Mercenaries from Hessen-Kassel in the American Revolution*. Cambridge: Cambridge University Press.

Bagehot, Walter. 1867 [1974]. *The English Constitution: The Collected Works of Walter Bagehot, Vol. 5*. London: The Economist.

Bakvis, Herman, and William Chandler, eds. 1987. *Federalism and the Role of the State*. Toronto: University of Toronto Press.

Beer, Samuel. 1973. "The Modernization of American Federalism." *Publius* 3 (2): 49–95.

——— 1978. "Federalism, Nationalism, and Democracy in America." *American Political Science Review* 72 (1): 9–21.

——— 1993. *To Make A Nation. The Rediscovery of American Federalism*. Cambridge, MA: Belknap, Harvard University Press.

Bendix, Reinhard. 1977. *Max Weber. An Intellectual Portrait*. Berkeley: University of California Press.

Benz, Arthur. 2008. *Der Moderne Staat: Grundlagen der politologischen Analyse*. 2nd ed. Munich: Oldenbourg.

——— 2012. "Eine Gestalt, die alt geworden ist? Thesen zum Wandel des Staates." *Leviathan* 40 (2): 223–47.

——— 2013. "Balancing Rigidity and Flexibility: Constitutional Dynamics in Federal Systems." *West European Politics* 36 (4): 726–49.

Benz, Arthur, and Jared Sonnicksen. 2017. "Patterns of Federal Democracy: Tensions, Friction, or Balance between Two Government Dimensions." *European Political Science Review* 9 (1): 3–25.

Biber, Eric. 2004. "The Price of Admission: Causes, Effects, and Patterns of Conditions Imposed on States Entering the Union." *American Journal of Legal History* 46 (2): 119–208.

Bridges, Amy. 2015. *Democratic Beginnings: Founding the Western States*. Lawrence: University Press of Kansas.

Broschek, Jörg. 2009. *Der Kanadische Föderalismus. Eine historisch-institutionalistische Analyse*. Wiesbaden: VS Verlag.

——— 2015. "Exploring Authority Migration in Multilevel Architectures: A Historical-institutionalist Framework." *Comparative European Politics* 15 (6): 656–81.

Callen, Zachary. 2009. *The Seams of the State: Infrastructure and Intergovernmental Relations in American State Building: (Dissertation)*. Chicago, Ann Arbor: ProQuest.

——— 2012. "Congress and the Railroads: Federalism, American Political Development, and the Migration of Policy Responsibility." *American Politics Research* 40 (2): 293–326.

Clawson, Marion. 2011. *The Federal Lands Revisited*. New York: RFF Press.

Conlan, Timothy, and François V. de Chantal. 2001. "The Rehnquist Court and Contemporary American Federalism." *Political Science Quarterly* 116 (2): 253–75.

Conlan, Timothy, and Robert Dudley. 2005. "Janus-Faced Federalism: State Sovereignty and Federal Preemption in the Rehnquist Court." *PS: Political Science & Politics* 38 (3): 363–66.

Curry, Richard. 1962. "A Reappraisal of Statehood Politics in West Virginia." *Journal of Southern History* 28 (4): 403–21.

——— 1964. *A House Divided. A Study of Statehood Politics and the Copperhead Movement in West Virginia*. Pittsburgh: University of Pittsburgh Press.

Davila-Colon, Luis. 1981. "Equal Citizenship, Self-Determination, and the U.S. Statehood Process: A Constitutional and Historical Analysis." *Case Western Reserve Journal of International Law* 13 (2): 315–74.

Deudney, Daniel. 1995. "The Philadelphian System: Sovereignty, Arms Control, and Balance of Power in the American States-union, circa 1787–1861." *International Organization* 49 (2): 191–228.

Dhami, Mandeep K., and Paula A. Cruise. 2013. "Prisoner Disenfranchisement: Prisoner and Public Views of an Invisible Punishment." *Analyses of Social Issues and Public Policy* 13 (1): 211–27.

Diamond, Jared. 1997. *Guns, Germs, and Steel. The Fates of Human Societies*. New York: W.W. Norton.

Dowding, Keith. 2004. "Thoughts on Modelling the State." *Government and Opposition* 39 (1): 101–18.

Dyson, Kenneth. 2009. *The State Tradition in Western Europe: A Study of an Idea and Institution*. Colchester: ECPR Press.

Eblen, Jack. 1968. *The First and Second United States Empires. Governors and Territorial Government, 1784–1912*. Pittsburgh: University of Pittsburgh Press.

Elazar, Daniel. 1962. *American Partnership: Intergovernmental Co-Operation in the Nineteenth-Century United States*. Chicago: University of Chicago Press.

——— 1964. "Federal-State Collaboration in the Nineteenth-Century United States." *Political Science Quarterly* 79 (2): 248–81.

——— 1990. "Opening the Third Century of American Federalism: Issues and Prospects." *Annals of the American Academy* 509 (1): 11–21.

Ertman, Thomas. 2008. *The Birth of Leviathan. Building States and Regimes in Medieval and Early Modern Europe*. Cambridge: Cambridge University Press.

Evans, Peter, Dietrich Rueschemeyer, and Theda Skocpol, eds. 1985. *Bringing the State Back in*. Cambridge: Cambridge University Press.

Fabbrini, Sergio. 1999a. "American Democracy from a European Perspective." *Annual Review of Political Science* 2: 465–91.

——— 1999b. "The American System of Separated Government: An Historical-Institutional Interpretation." *International Political Science Review* 20 (1): 95–116.

——— 2003. "A Single Western State Model?: Differential Development and Constrained Convergence of Public Authority Organization in Europe and America." *Comparative Political Studies* 36 (6): 653–78.

Fain, Haskell. 1972. "The Idea of the State." *Nous* 6 (1): 15–26.

Farber, Daniel. 2003. *Lincoln's Constitution*. Chicago: University of Chicago Press.

Farr, Jason. 2005. "Point: The Westphalia Legacy and the Modern Nation-State." *International Political Science Review* 80 (3-4): 156–59.

Farrand, Max. 1908. "The Federal Constitution and the Defects of The Confederation." *American Political Science Review* 2 (4): 532–44.

Ferguson, Niall. 2005. *Colossus. The Rise and Fall of the American Empire*. New York: Penguin.

Finer, Samuel. 1980. "Princes, Parliaments, and the Public Service." *Parliamentary Affairs* 33 (1): 353–72.

Forsyth, Murray. 1981. *A Union of States. The Theory and Practice of Confederation*. New York: Leicester University Press.

Frye, Ellen. 2005. "Private Military Firms in the New World Order: How Redefining Mercenary Can Tame the Dogs of War." *Fordham Law Review* 73 (6): 2607–64.

Fukuyama, Francis. 2012. *The Origins of Political Order. From Prehuman Times to the French Revolution*. London: Profile Books.

Garand, James. 1988. "Explaining Government Growth in the U.S. States." *American Political Science Review* 82 (3): 837–49.

——— 2013. "The Myth of State Autonomy: Federalism, Political Parties, and the National Colonization of State Politics." *Journal of Law and Politics* 29 (1): 1–68.

Gerstle, Gary. 2009. "The Resilient Power of the States across the Long Nineteenth Century: An Inquiry into a Pattern of American Governance." In *The Unsustainable American State*, eds. Lawrence Jacobs and Desmond King. Oxford: Oxford University Press, 61–87.

——— 2015. *Liberty and Coercion. The Paradox of American Government*. Princeton: Princeton University Press.

Gottschalk, Marie. 2006. *The Prison and the Gallows. The Politics of Mass Incarceration in America*. New York: Cambridge University Press.

Habermas, Jürgen. 1996. "The European Nation State. Its Achievements and Limitations. On the Past and Future of Sovereignty and Citizenship." *Ratio Juris* 9 (2): 125–37.

Hammond, John. 2003. ""They Are Very Much Interested in Obtaining an Unlimited Slavery": Rethinking the Expansion of Slavery in the Louisiana Purchase Territories, 1803–1805." *Journal of the Early Republic* 23 (3): 353–80.

Hanson, Russell. 2017. "Distending the Republic." *Perspectives on Politics* 15 (4): 1082–86.

Hart, Albert B. 1907. "Growth of American Theories of Popular Government." *American Political Science Review* 1 (4): 531–60.

Hartz, Louis. 1955. *The Liberal Tradition in America. An Interpretation of American Political Thought since the Revolution*. New York: Harcourt, Brace and Co.

Hay, Colin. 2014. "Neither Real Nor Fictitious but 'as if real'? A Political Ontology of the State." *British Journal of Sociology* 65 (3): 459–80.

Held, David. 1989. *Political Theory and the Modern State: Essays on State, Power, and Democracy*. Stanford: Stanford University Press.

Hill, Robert. 1988. "Federalism, Republicanism, and the Northwest Ordinance." *Publius* 18 (4): 41–52.

Hofstadter, Richard. 1964. "The Paranoid Style in American Politics." *Harper's Magazine November*. 77–86.

Horsman, Reginald. 1989. "The Dimensions of an "Empire for Liberty": Expansion and Republicanism, 1775-1825." *Journal of the Early Republic* 9 (1): 1–20.

Hueglin, Thomas, and Alan Fenna. 2015. *Comparative Federalism: A Systematic Inquiry*. 2nd ed. Toronto: University of Toronto Press.

Huhnholz, Sebastian. 2015. "Refeudalisierung des Steuerstaates?: Vorüberlegungen zu einer politischen Theorie der Steuerdemokratie." In *Verfassung und Verteilung: Beiträge zu einer Grundfrage des Verfassungsverständnisses*, eds. Sigrid Boysen, Anna-Bettina Kaiser and Florian Meinel. Tübingen: Mohr Siebeck, 175–216.

Huntington, Samuel. 1957. *The Soldier and the State. The Theory and Politics of Civil-Military Relations*. Cambridge, MA: Belknap, Harvard University Press.

——— 1982. "American Ideals versus American Institutions." *Political Science Quarterly* 97 (1): 1–37.

——— 2005. *Who are We? America's Great Debate*. London: Simon and Schuster.

Johnson, Dennis. 2009a. *The Laws that Shaped America. Fifteen Acts of Congress and their Lasting Impact*. New York: Routledge.

Johnson, Kimberley. 2007. *Governing the American State. Congress and the New Federalism, 1877–1929*. Princeton: Princeton University Press.

——— 2009b. "The First New Federalism and the Development of the Modern American State: Patchwork, Reconstitution, or Transition?" In *The Unsustainable American State*, eds. L. Jacobs and D. King. Oxford: Oxford University Press, 88–115.

Kalmo, Hent, and Quentin Skinner, eds. 2010. *Sovereignty in Fragments. The Past, Present and Future of a Contested Concept*. Cambridge: Cambridge University Press.

Kamarck, Elaine. 2009. "The Evolving American State: The Trust Challenge." *The Forum* 7 (4): 1–11 (Article 9).

Kastor, Peter. 2004. *The Nation's Crucible. The Louisiana Purchase and the Creation of America.* New Haven: Yale University Press.
Kempe, Michael. 2010. "'Even in the Remotest Corners of the World': Globalized Piracy and International Law, 1500–1900." *Journal of Global History* 5 (3): 353–72.
Kincaid, John. 1990. "From Cooperative to Coercive Federalism." *Annals of the American Academy of Political and Social Science* 509: 139–52.
——— 2012. "The Rise of Coercive Federalism in the United States: Dynamic Change with Little Formal Reform." In *The Future of Australian Federalism*, eds. Gabrielle Appleby, Nicholas Aroney and Thomas John. Cambridge: Cambridge University Press, 157–79.
——— 2016. "Territorial Neutrality and Cultural Pluralism in American Federalism: Is the United States the Archenemy of Peripheral Nationalism?" *Swiss Political Science Review* 22 (4): 565–84.
King, Anthony. 1973a. "Ideas, Institutions and Policies of Governments: a Comparative Analysis: Part III." *British Journal of Political Science* 3 (4): 409–23.
——— 1973b. "Ideas, Institutions and the Policies of Governments: a Comparative Analysis: Parts I and II." *British Journal of Political Science* 3 (3): 291–313.
King, Desmond. 2007. "The American State and Social Engineering: Policy Instruments in Affirmative Action." *Governance* 20 (1): 109–26.
——— 2017. "Forceful Federalism against American Racial Inequality." *Government and Opposition* 52 (2): 356–82.
King, Desmond, and Robert Lieberman. 2009. "Ironies of State Building: A Comparative Perspective on the American State." *World Politics* 61 (3): 547–88.
King, Desmond, and Rogers M. Smith. 2014. ""Without Regard to Race": Critical Ideational Development in Modern American Politics." *Journal of Politics* 76 (4): 958–71.
Kloppenburg, James. 1987. "The Virtues of Liberalism: Christianity, Republicanism, and Ethics in Early American Political Discourse." *Journal of American History* 74 (1): 9–33.
——— 2001. "Review: In Retrospect: Louis Hartz's 'The Liberal Tradition in America'." *Reviews in American History* 29 (3): 460–78.
Knowles, Robert. 2003. "The Balance of Forces and the Empire of Liberty. States' Rights and the Louisiana Purchase." *Iowa Law Review* 88: 343–419.
Krasner, Stephen. 1993. "Westphalia and All That." In *Ideas and Foreign Policy. Beliefs, Institutions, and Political Change*, eds. Judith Goldstein and Robert Keohane. Ithaca: Cornell University Press, 235–64.
LaCroix, Alison. 2010. "The Authority for Federalism: Madison's Negative and the Origins of Federal Ideology." *Law and History Review* 28 (2): 451–505.
Landes, David. 1999. *The Wealth and Poverty of Nations. Why Some Are so Rich and Some so Poor.* New York: W.W. Norton.
Lasswell, Harold. 1936. *Politics: Who Gets What, When, How.* New York/London: Whittlesey House, McGraw-Hill.
Law, Ann. 2014. "Lunatics, Idiots, Paupers, and Negro Seamen-Immigration Federalism and the Early American State." *Studies in American Political Development* 28 (2): 107–28.
Leuchtenburg, William. 1986. "The Pertinence of Political History: Reflections on the Significance of the State in America." *Journal of American History* 73 (3): 585–600.
Levi, Margaret. 1988. *Of Rule and Revenue.* Berkeley: University of California Press.
Levinson, Sanford, and Bartholomew Sparrow, eds. 2005. *The Louisiana Purchase and American Expansion, 1803-1898.* Lanham: Rowman & Littlefield.
Lewis-Beck, Michael, and Peverill Squire. 1991. "The Transformation of the American State: The New Era-New Deal Test." *Journal of Politics* 53 (1): 106–21.
Lhotta, Roland. 1995. *Imperiale Verfassungsgerichtsbarkeit und Föderalismus. Das Judicial Committee of the Privy Council und der BNA Act.* Baden-Baden: Nomos.

Lieberman, Robert. 2011. "Ideas and Institutions in Race Politics." In *Ideas and Politics in Social Science Research*, eds. Daniel Béland and Robert H. Cox. Oxford: Oxford University Press, 209–27.

Lipset, Seymour M. 1975. "The Paradox of American Politics." *The Public Interest* Fall: 142–65.

Lowi, Theodore. 1992. "The State in Political Science: How We Become What We Study." *American Political Science Review* 86 (1): 1–7.

Lutz, Donald. 1988. "The United States Constitution as an Incomplete Text." *Annals of the American Academy of Political and Social Science* 496 (1): 23–32.

Mann, Dennis-Jonathan. 2012. *'We, the People' vs. 'We, the Peoples' - the Debate over the Nature of the Union in the USA and Canada and its Lessons for European Integration*. Florence: European University Institute.

Mauch, Christof. 2003. "Images of America-Political Myths-Historiography: "Hessians" in the War of Independence." *Amerikastudien/American Studies* 48 (3): 411–23.

Mayntz, Renate. 1993. "Modernization and the Logic of Interorganizational Networks." *Knowledge and Policy* 6 (1): 3–16.

McDonagh, Eileen L. 1992. "Representative Democracy and State Building in the Progressive Era." *American Political Science Review* 86 (4): 938–50.

Mehrotra, Ajay. 2013. *Making the Modern American Fiscal State. Law, Politics, and the Rise of Progressive Taxation, 1877–1929*. New York: Cambridge University Press.

Mettler, Suzanne. 2011. *The Submerged State: How Invisible Government Policies Undermine American Democracy*. Chicago: University of Chicago Press.

Migdal, Joel. 2001. *The State in Society. Studying How States and Societies Transform and Constitute One Another*. Cambridge: Cambridge University Press.

Mitchell, Timothy. 1991. "The Limits of the State: Beyond Statist Approaches and Their Critics." *American Political Science Review* 85 (1): 77–96.

Monaghan, Henry. 1996. "We the People[s], Original Understanding, and Constitutional Amendment." *Columbia Law Review* 96 (1): 121–77.

Morgan, Edmund. 1948. "Colonial Ideas of Parliamentary Power 1764-1766." *William and Mary Quarterly* 5 (3): 311–41.

——— 1972. "Slavery and Freedom: The American Paradox." *Journal of American History* 59 (1): 5–29.

——— 1989. *Inventing the People. The Rise of Popular Sovereignty in England and America*. New York: W.W. Norton.

Morillo, Stephen. 1995. "Guns and Government: A Comparative Study of Europe and Japan." *Journal of World History* 6 (1): 75–106.

von der Muhll, George. 2003. "Ancient Empires, Modern States, and the Study of Government." *Annual Review of Political Science* 6: 345–76.

Munzer, Stephen, and James Nickel. 1977. "Does the Constitution Mean What it Always Meant?" *Columbia Law Review* 77 (7): 1029–62.

Myrdal, Gunnar. 1944 [1996]. *An American Dilemma. The Negro Problem and Modern Democracy*. New York: Routledge.

Nettl, J. P. 1968. "The State as a Conceptual Variable." *World Politics* 20 (4): 559–92.

Niebuhr, Reinhold. 1952 [2008]. *The Irony of American History: With a New Introduction by Andrew J. Bacevich*. Chicago: University of Chicago Press.

Nordlinger, Eric, Theodore Lowi, and Sergio Fabbrini. 1988. "The Return to the State: Critiques." *American Political Science Review* 82 (3): 875–901.

O'Leary, Cecilia. 1999. *To Die For. The Paradox of American Patriotism*. Princeton: Princeton University Press.

Onuf, Peter. 1981. "State-Making in Revolutionary America: Independent Vermont as a Case Study." *Journal of American History* 67 (4): 797–815.

——— 1982. "From Colony to Territory: Changing Concepts of Statehood in Revolutionary America." *Political Science Quarterly* 97 (3): 447–59.

——— 1983. *The Origins of the Federal Republic. Jurisdictional Controversies in the United States 1775–1787*. Philadelphia: University of Pennsylvania Press.

Orren, Karen, and Stephen Skowronek. 2004. *The Search for American Political Development*. Cambridge: Cambridge University Press.

Parker, Geoffrey, ed. 1997. *The Thirty Years' War*. 2nd ed. Abingdon: Routledge.

Piirimäe, Pärtel. 2010. "The Westphalian Myth and the Idea of External Sovereignty." In *Sovereignty in Fragments. The Past, Present and Future of a Contested Concept*, eds. Hent Kalmo and Quentin Skinner. Cambridge: Cambridge University Press.

Pisani, Donald. 1987. "Promotion and Regulation: Constitutionalism and the American Economy." *Journal of American History* 74 (3): 740–68.

Quadango, Jill, and Debra Street. 2005. "Ideology and Public Policy: Antistatism in American Welfare State Transformation." *Journal of Policy History* 17 (1): 52–71.

Rakove, Jack. 1999. "Making a Hash of Sovereignty, Part I." *Green Bag* 2 (1): 35–44.

Riker, William. 1964. *Federalism: Origin, Operation, Significance*. Boston: Little, Brown and Co.

——— 1987. "The Lessons of 1787." *Public Choice* 55 (1/2): 5–34.

Roelofs, H. M. 1986. "The American Polity: A Systematic Ambiguity." *Review of Politics* 48 (3): 323–48.

——— 1992. *The Poverty of American Politics. A Theoretical Interpretation*. Philadelphia: Temple University Press.

Rossiter, Clinton, ed. 1961 [1999]. *The Federalist Papers. Alexander Hamilton, James Madison, John Jay.: With a new introduction and notes by Charles R. Kessler. New York*. New York: Penguin.

Sartori, Giovanni. 1973. "What is 'Politics'." *Political Theory* 1 (3): 5–26.

Scheuerman, William. 2004. "International Law as Historical Myth." *Constellations* 11 (4): 537–50.

Schmidt, Volker. 2006. "Multiple Modernities or Varieties of Modernity?" *Current Sociology* 54 (1): 77–97.

Shearer, Benjamin, ed. 2004. *The Uniting States. The Story of Statehood for the Fifty United States*. Westport, CT: Greenwood.

Sheingate, Adam. 2009. "Why Can't Americans See the State?" *The Forum* 7 (4): 1–14 (Article 1).

Shklar, Judith. 1991a. *American Citizenship. The Quest for Inclusion*. Cambridge, MA: Harvard University Press.

——— 1991b. "Redeeming American Political Theory." *American Political Science Review* 85 (1): 3–15.

Skinner, Quentin. 2010. "The Sovereign State: a Genealogy." In *Sovereignty in Fragments. The Past, Present and Future of a Contested Concept*, eds. Hent Kalmo and Quentin Skinner. Cambridge: Cambridge University Press, 26–46.

Skowronek, Stephen. 1982. *Building a New American State: The Expansion of Administrative Capacities, 1877–1920*. Cambridge: Cambridge University Press.

Smith, Rogers M. 1988. "The "American Creed" and American Identity: The Limits of Liberal Citizenship in the United States." *Political Research Quarterly* 41 (2): 225–51.

——— 1993. "Beyond Tocqueville, Myrdal, and Hartz: The Multiple Traditions in America." *American Political Science Review* 87 (3): 549–66.

——— 2001. "Citizenship and the Politics of People-Building." *Citizenship Studies* 5 (1): 73–96.

Sparrow, Bartholomew. 2017. "A Territorial State: Geographic Expansion, the US Territories, and 'Introduction to American Politics'." *PS: Political Science & Politics* 50 (2): 492–96.

Spruyt, Hendrik. 1996. *The Sovereign State and its Competitors. An Analysis of Systems Change*. Princeton: Princeton University Press.

Stampp, Kenneth. 1978. "The Concept of a Perpetual Union." *Journal of American History* 65 (1): 5–33.

Stein, Mark. 2009. *How the States Got Their Shapes*. New York: Harper Collins.

Steinmo, Sven. 1993. *Taxation and Democracy: Swedish, British and American Approaches to Financing the Modern State*. New Haven: Yale University Press.

——— 2010. *The Evolution of Modern States: Sweden, Japan, and the United States*. Cambridge: Cambridge University Press.

Stepan, Alfred. 1999. "Federalism and Democracy: Beyond the U.S. Model." *Journal of Democracy* 10 (4): 19–34.

Stewart, Charles, and Barry Weingast. 1992. "Stacking the Senate, Changing the Nation: Republican Rotten Boroughs, Statehood Politics, and American Political Development." *Studies in American Political Development* 6 (2): 223–71.

Stokes, Gale. 2001. "The Fates of Human Societies: A Review of Recent Macrohistories." *American Historical Review* 106 (2): 508–25.

Tillin, Louise. 2015. "Explaining Territorial Change in Federal Democracies: A Comparative Historical Institutionalist Approach." *Political Studies* 63 (3): 626–41.

Tilly, Charles, ed. 1975. *The Formation of National States in Western Europe*. Princeton: Princeton University Press.

Tocqueville, Alexis d. 1835–40 [2003]. *Democracy in America. And Two Essays on America*. London: Penguin.

Troper, Michel. 2012. "Sovereignty." In *The Oxford Handbook of Comparative Constitutionalism*, eds. Michel Rosenfeld and András Sajó. Oxford: Oxford University Press, 350–69.

United States. 1781 [2005]. *The Articles of Confederation*. New York: Barnes & Noble.

———. 1787 [2005]. *The Constitution of the United States of America*. New York: Barnes & Noble.

Walker, David. 1996. "The Advent of an Ambiguous Federalism and the Emergence of New Federalism III." *Public Administration Review* 56 (3): 271–80.

Weaver, Glen. 1969. "Nevada's Federal Lands." *Annals of the Association of American Geographers* 59 (1): 27–49.

Weaver, Vesla, and Amy Lerman. 2010. "Political Consequences of the Carceral State." *American Political Science Review* 104 (4): 817–33.

Weber, Max. 1921 [1976]. *Wirtschaft und Gesellschaft*. Tübingen: Mohr Siebeck.

Whaley, Joachim. 2011. *Germany and the Holy Roman Empire: Volume I: Maximilian I to the Peace of Westphalia, 1493-1648*. Oxford: Oxford University Press.

Whittington, Keith. 1996. "The Political Constitution of Federalism in Antebellum America: The Nullification Debate as an Illustration of Informal Mechanisms of Constitutional Change." *Publius* 26 (2): 1–24.

Wills, Garry. 1999. *A Necessary Evil: A History of American Distrust of Government*. New York: Touchstone.

Zick, Timothy. 2005. "Are the States Sovereign?" *Washington University Law Review* 83 (1): 229–337.

Zimmerman, Joseph. 1992. *Contemporary American Federalism: The Growth of National Power*. New York: State University of New York Press.

——— 2001. "National-State Relations in the Twentieth Century." *Publius* 31 (2): 15–30.

5

DEMOCRATIC DIVIDED GOVERNMENT

The US system of government and its division of powers is the prototype of "presidential democracy". This model is conceptualized in basic distinction to parliamentary ones in the classic typology of democratic forms of government (see e.g. Steffani 1979; Verney 1959). To a certain extent, US presidential democracy provides a rather unambiguous *form* or *design*. The Constitution translates the separation of powers between the legislative, executive, and judicial into three distinct *branches* consisting of the Congress, the presidency, and the federal judiciary respectively. Moreover, the first two branches are installed via separate elections and enjoy fixed periods of office. One exception is the power of Congress to impeach and remove the President for "High Crimes and Misdemeanors" or incapacitation. Conversely, the chief executive lacks any power to dissolve either chamber of the legislature. This structural design may ease formal attribution of authority to discernible institutions, a feature that even staunch critics of presidentialism have noted as one potential advantage (see e.g. Linz 1990). While complex, these formal features evoke a relative clarity in their dualism between *the* executive and *the* legislative. However, the dualism can invite contestation that is difficult to cope with in cases of irreconcilable political differences between and within branches of government.

Parliamentary democracy diverges from the classic separation between executive and legislative: by fusing the head of government and cabinet with the majority in parliament for one, which typically become pitted against a parliamentary minority relegated to the status of "opposition", for another. There is a major discrepancy between the formal and "dignified parts" of head of state, the government, and the parliament as a whole vis-à-vis the "efficient secret" of parliamentary government at work (Bagehot 1867 [1974]). The latter implies "confidence", the linchpin between government and parliament which is underpinned by party discipline. The functional division of powers runs largely within the governing party or parties instead of between *the* executive and *the* parliament. Both branches are internally

DOI: 10.4324/9781003203674-5

divided through the heads of state and government in the executive and the government and opposition parties in the legislative branch. Executive and legislative fit less neatly than in the presidential case. Cabinet members often simultaneously hold seats and vote on legislation in the parliament, and take over a sizeable to predominant share of proposing bills. These typical parliamentary features have been constitutionally excluded in the USA.

For the British case, institutional and ideational developments of popular sovereignty followed a path toward *parliamentary* sovereignty by the early 18th century. It headed further toward parliamentary democracy by the mid-19th century, with prime ministers and cabinets responsible to the majority of the House of Commons, coupled with the declining stature of the House of Lords and the reduction of the monarch to symbolic figurehead. Formal institutions persist, but the preponderance of political power, representation, and legitimacy rest with the lower house of Parliament. Democratic governance is led by the prime minister plus the cabinet who emanate from and remain dependent on the confidence of Parliament's majority. In cases of irreconcilable differences between government and parliamentary majority, votes of confidence and no confidence can enable early elections or changing the premier. These differences prove revealing for the current US government, but also its historical path dependencies.

US presidential and divided government

The division of authority constituted in the USA in 1789 is predisposed to tensions between the branches of government from the outset. The term "presidential government", like "parliamentary government" but for inverse reasons, is ambivalent, if not misleading. The US President forms but one part of government, and not necessarily the predominant one. This is already inherent in the Constitution. The original enumerated powers of the federal government and the new ones introduced via amendments are allocated expressly to Congress, that is the *legislative* branch. Presidents may often dominate public and press attention, and even enjoy a potential reservoir of popular legitimacy to lend weight to their political demands and proposals. Nonetheless, they remain multiply bounded in the constitutional framework, and not one amendment has augmented their powers. Presidents can propose legislative action, but must rely on Congress to initiate and pass it. At the same time, there exists a multiplicity of electoral mandates. Electoral linkages extend neither to Congress as a whole, nor from the people at large, but rather between individual members of the House of Representatives and individual district constituencies, and between individual senators and their state electorates. The popular electoral linkage to the presidency in turn is mediated through a states-based Electoral College.

Consequently, the US government builds on not only a separation of powers, but also a fragmentation of linkages. It multiplies and disperses chains of legitimacy, representation, and accountability, and thus ultimately popular sovereignty. For US government to work, it requires inter-branch interactions, negotiations, and agreements. This generally needs to occur on a case-by-case basis, since there are no "coalition agreements" between *a* government and *a* legislative majority. What follows from the *structural* independence between the executive and legislative branches is rather a wide range of *functional* interdependencies.

This flipside to the separation-prone framework of US government is reflected by the mutual checks and balances. The Constitution proclaims that "all legislative Powers" are "vested in a Congress of the United States" (Art. 1(1)), the same with regard to "executive Power" in a President of the United States (Art. 2(1)) and the judicial power in "one Supreme Court" (Art. 3(1)). However, while these provisions are formulated in absolute terms (e.g. "*all* legislative powers"), the Constitution contradicts or moderates them at multiple points. Already in its strict sense, the Constitution invests parts of each branch's powers mutually in each of the others: for example the President is made head of the military (Commander in Chief), but the power to declare war and regulate militia belongs to Congress; Congress has all the legislative powers, but the President has veto power over legislation, while the Vice President can cast a vote in the Senate in cases of a tie; Congress can exercise supervision over the executive, has powers of "advise and consent" over presidential nominees to the upper echelons of the executive branch, and judges for the federal judiciary.

The coupling of the separation of powers with checks and balances generates a power *sharing* arrangement. It may be conceived as a "Madisonian" or "plural" model of democracy (Dahl 1956), or as "separate institutions sharing powers" (Neustadt 1960) whereby sharing serves cooperation and reaching a broad consensus. These notions emphasize the *balances* counterpart to the separation of powers. However, the institutional arrangement could just as well be construed as power sharing by means of *dispersion* and *constraints* (on this conceptual differentiation, see Strøm et al. 2017) and thus a necessarily power-*limiting* arrangement, in which, as phrased by Madison, individual and institutional "ambition must be made to counteract ambition" (Rossiter 1961 [1999]: No. 51). These notions emphasize the *checks* counterpart to the separation of powers. Taken together, this indicates a fundamental ambivalence in the horizontal dimension of the division of powers of US government.

Tensions between organizational principles and the logics of politics are, per se, nothing exceptional. Both parliamentary and presidential democratic governments must cope with a simultaneity of constitutional and political demands of representation, responsibility, and accountability, and of fulfilling concrete policy agenda under conditions of more or less institutional complexity. However, the propensities for tensions in the USA are especially complex, not only by constitutional design, but also on account of particular historical developments. Its governmental arrangement requires, if not by normative expectations of common welfare, good governance, or similar, then at latest by functional necessity cross-institutional negotiation, consensus-seeking, and balancing. This stands at odds with the ideas and intentions of "ambitions *counteracting* ambitions" and making governing difficult, albeit less so than had been under the Articles of Confederation. Furthermore, tensions inherent in the constitution of US government can turn into severe frictions on account of both political party and popular democratic dynamics. Indeed, "sharing isn't easy", as Aberbach has succinctly phrased, since the Constitution conjuncts rival institutional logics with rival democratic constituencies into a compounded federal government, one that requires cooperation to operate and yet invites competition and conflict between the two Houses of Congress, and between the Congress and the President (Aberbach 1998; see also Aberbach 2003; Aberbach and Rockman 1997).

The idea of the need to constrain the "tyrannies" and "evil" of government, though also of majorities and "factions", in order to protect liberty and yet enable effective governing has been pervasive in the USA from the outset. These motives were at play in drafting and debating the Constitution as a whole. This becomes apparent with a view to the presidency: its design as a "unitary executive", as opposed to a collective body, is to enable effective administration, but multiply checked by the bicameral legislature and moderated through its installment via the Electoral College, a selection procedure that combines and channels yet limits both popular and state electoral linkage to the federal executive (see e.g. Sonnicksen 2010). This constellation can encumber government responsivity as the conversion of electoral linkages, and the "inputs" they generate, into governmental "outputs".

One could surmise, and it seems that many have, that conflicts and complications affirm what was actually the very point of the Constitution and the framers' intentions from the beginning.[1] This makes it tempting to conclude that that there is no ambivalence, contradiction, or irony in US polity development, and thus case closed. However, such inference would surely and grossly miss another, more important, analytical point. There is a much deeper lying crux to be found. It lies precisely between the origins of the constitutional design bound to a political context of the late 18th century, and the development of US democratic government into the present.

An 'old' separation-of-powers arrangement

The Constitution forged by the framers', and the Federalists in particular, involved an often acclaimed "new science of politics", a design intended to foster limited, but effective national government for promoting general welfare by which the compounding of linkages, powers, and decision-making rules were supposed to integrate but also filter out "factional", provincial, and majoritarian self-interest (see e.g. Lhotta 2010; Rossiter 1961 [1999]). The historical accuracy, no less the normative desirability, of all or some of these original intents and motives are debatable. What seems certain though is that they were not just naïve wishful thinking. They connect at least to cautious but contingent lessons about dual tyrannies of despotism and majorities that contemporaries drew from their immediate and antecedent context. Overly powerful majorities and factions and overly powerful governmental actors were supposed to be prevented or tempered, not by reliance on republican civic virtues of enlightened rulers, nor on the citizenry at large alone. It was rather a separation of powers and checks and balances based on competition that would breed "virtue" by cancelling "ambitions" out, leaving actors and institutions no choice but to seek compromises for the public interest and common good (cf. e.g. the elaboration in Goodin 1996; Sonnicksen 2010). While the common focus on the "negative" is applicable, for example constitutional features designed to throttle decision making to protect liberty and prevent tyrannies, it is also overly one-sided (Zvesper 1999). It overlooks precisely the division of powers for the purposes of their joint exercise.

As of the 20th century, in contrast, the presidency and Congress would become more democratized, but also a superlative case among modern democracies for recurrent gridlock and divided government (Binder 2015; Coleman 1999; Mayhew 2005; Ware 2011). Ironically, this pattern gets generated not least by rival "factions": in terms updated since the late 18th century, *political parties* on the one hand, and *interest groups* and "pork barreling" or "logrolling" to secure allocations of federal funding for local constituent and special interests, on the other hand (see e.g. Fiorina 1991; Krehbiel 1996; Lancaster 1986; Lowi 1969; Schattschneider 1960). Multiple constitutional "veto players" (Tsebelis 1995) surely contribute to this pattern too. Still, the complexity of factors lies deeper. The Constitution inaugurated a *modern* republic for representative democratic government, but it did so in an *unmodern* late-18th-century context. While original election rules have been amended in several places, the original horizontal division of powers has not. In strict constitutional sense to this day, neither the distribution of powers between President and Congress, nor within Congress between its branches, nor of the office of the presidency have changed.

There may be reasons to contend that frequent occurrences of divided government were intended by the US Constitution (see e.g. Connelly 2015; Wilson 1987). President and Congress also can and do find ways to "navigate the divide" (Beckmann and McGann 2008; see also e.g. Gordon and Landa 2017). However, *how things turned out* are not necessarily *how they were meant to be*. Gridlock for instance may or may not have been what the framers wanted. Either way, gridlock would have been more anticipated under widely different conditions and understandings in the late 1780s than compared with how politics and government would develop over the next two centuries. Moreover, how things turn out can evolve *in spite of* how they were meant to be.

The original constitution of a republican form of government connects with the state of the USA and its development. The prior comparison with parliamentary government helps elucidate the character of the democratic separation of powers in the USA. However, the contrast also bears significance regarding the formative dynamics and circumstances. The founding era was path-setting as much as path-diverging for democratic government and the constitution of the state. The framers' invention of presidential democracy – more precisely, the framework within which this form of government would later democratize – could be construed as a purposive choice to achieve closer approximation with the doctrine of the separation of powers, and thus a choice against the parliamentary form. There is a case to make for that storyline, at least in part, but without reading history backwards.

The US Constitution continued and, for a time, modernized an ages-old legacy of "mixed constitutions" (see e.g. Almond 1966: 871ff.). By that time, in both the

British and US cases, historical developments had led to the early emergence and institutionalization of popular sovereignty, as well as the proliferation of *government* rather than "state" as the referent incorporation of the political order. However, the USA took a pivotal path-divergence from Britain – and almost all of Europe and many other modern democracies worldwide – which is reflected in another difference in *government*. In parliamentary systems, government has come to be synonymized with the current party or coalition in power, its executive cabinet in particular, evident in the dualism of *government and opposition*. In the USA, government to this day is synonymous neither with Congress, nor its majority in either House, nor with the President, but rather with multiple branches together and the state.

The 18th-century US Constitution modernized mixed constitutions foremost by its exclusion of both monarchy and "estates"-based representation. *How* and *when* the USA did so proves decisive. Independence had cut the USA off from Britain. With the strict separation of powers between the executive and legislative, the USA in effect cut itself off from later political modernization processes in Europe. The Constitution fixated an 18th-century – and even older – division of powers arrangement, one Huntington referred to as approximating the English pre-Glorious Revolution *Tudor* constitution (Huntington 1966; see also Nettl 1968). In translating sovereignty into a mixed constitution during its formative critical juncture, the US Constitution lodged popular sovereignty in the legislative and the executive branch, and compounded further both branches to various extents with state sovereignty in the emerging federal order. A manifold popular-state sovereignty mix results, with each compounded yet dispersed in the President and Congress, their separation of powers, and their respective electoral linkages.

Furthermore, the US Constitution actually ended a brief experiment with national assembly government under the Articles of Confederation. The Congress of the USA under the Articles already had "presidents", who served rather as chairs of congressional sessions, and special committees for administering affairs (a proto-cabinet), including when Congress was out of session (Morris 1987). A reform under that government arrangement could have logically proceeded along the parliamentary government path – again, the one most modern democracies end up taking.[2] For instance, these initial presidents of Congress could have gained the head of government-type functions assisted by an administrative committee, while remaining dependent on the support and control or "confidence" of the legislature. The original "Virginia Plan" proposed by Madison for the Philadelphia Convention even put forward the election of a president by Congress (Buckley 2012; Clinton 1990).[3] Had the Articles of Confederation been reformed or Madison's Virginia Plan adopted, the resultant arrangement may or may not have set the path of American government toward the "efficient secret" of parliamentary government. Madison likely did not have this in mind given the federalists' aversion to "factions", one also shared by most Antifederalists (see e.g. Reichley 1992). Moreover, parliamentary democratic government had not yet emerged, not even in England, which had transitioned to a system of parliamentary *sovereignty*, but not yet parliamentary *government*. Thus, by establishing an independent unitary executive, the Constitution, rather than revolutionize, *restored* government with the dualistic division of powers.

This formative step in the developmental path of American government had antecedents within the USA as well. A dualistic pattern of dividing governmental powers was already institutionalized during the colonial era. The divide ran between increasingly powerful assemblies vis-à-vis an assembly-independent executive, formerly the colonial governors serving as representatives of the monarch as "King in Colonial Assembly" (Coleman 2016: 17–38). The early US states' institutions and practices in local self-government evolved during their decades of experience as colonies, not just the very short-lived phase as independent republics. The latter phase surely had impact on ideational and institutional path-dependencies. However, that formative legacies extended further back becomes apparent precisely with a view to the choice for an assembly-independent executive in the US Constitution. This diverged from no less than eight of those thirteen "early republics" that actually had replaced colonial governors with state-legislature elected ones in their new constitutions after independence (see e.g. Morris 1987: 679). Hence, the Constitution rejected those recent innovations, and *re-established* the stricter, and much longer and familiar, dualistic separation of powers. The abolishment of monarchy at national level, in turn, was not the republican innovation of the Constitution, but rather already in the Articles of Confederation.

Consequently, the Constitution's strict separation of powers between branches of government was also a product of institutional-ideational thinking in the box. This box was bound to the immediate late-18th-century context, but also its antecedent evolution. The strict separation of the executive and legislative branches, later referred to as a presidential system of government, became constitutionally fixated in that box of space and time. This is of fundamental relevance for subsequent political developments in democratic government. Two are of particular note: the development of the "plebiscitary", popular presidency, and of modern political parties. Both of them are coupled with representative-democratic and electoral dynamics over time. Representative democratic and electoral rules, in turn, are predominantly simple majoritarian ones in the USA. The elections of representatives by rules of majority in territorially decoupled districts are elemental to American representative democracy. However, their foundation too was already laid in that late-18th-century box, that is likewise inherited from British colonial legacy (see e.g. Caramani 2017: 55ff.). Political parties were nascent but, in contemporary senses (e.g. terms, organization, functions), yet to develop.

The US form of government corresponds to an early modern constitutional arrangement. It may even be viewed as an anachronism in the world of contemporary government. However, extensive adaptations, not least in the sense of *democratization*, have transpired since its (re-)invention as a republican version of older mixed constitutions over two hundred years ago. Many adaptations and changes correlate with electoral dynamics in the US polity over time. They are also reflected in the dynamics of the party system and political parties. How they develop connects with their evolution within the presidential democratic form of government.

A tale of two parties

Two features of democratic politics in the USA are fundamentally constitutional in the broad sense, though in parts the strict sense as well: elections by simple majority rules, for one, and two-party dominance, for another. Both features, moreover, apply virtually to all levels and branches of government throughout the US polity.

The connection between plurality, first past the post, or winner takes all electoral rules in single-member districts, and the predominance of two large parties, represents a pattern of democratic politics long familiar to the study of parties and elections. This correlation is reflected in the perhaps only theorem in political science to have been donned with the epithet "law", that is Duverger's Law (see originally in Duverger 1951).[4] The USA has clearly conformed to this co-relational pattern between electoral simple majoritarianism and a two-party system (see e.g. Riker 1976). However, US politics diverges from other countries with similar electoral systems, also in quite idiosyncratic ways.

The predominance of Democrats and Republicans for more than one and a half centuries is of such commonplace familiarity that it seems easy to overlook what is actually puzzling behind these circumstances. On the one hand, the USA uses at multiple levels practically the same electoral rules (plurality) for electing representatives adopted from Britain and still practiced in other political systems, especially Commonwealth ones, including its northern neighbor Canada, which is likewise federal. On the other hand, the UK and Canada reveal that, under winner takes all conditions, not only can smaller parties still manage to become competitive and dominant at regional levels, but also gain status as minor parties with legislative representation at national level (see e.g. Gaines 1999; Singer 2013). Even higher multipartyism is demonstrated by the enormously diverse democratic-federal case of India, even though its Lower House (Lok Sabha) elections are likewise organized in single-member districts determined by simple majority (plurality) rules (Chhibber and Kollman 1998). The USA, in stark contrast, exhibits neither regionally concentrated "other" significant parties, nor any other "minor parties", but rather the *same* two parties at all levels. This constitutes thus a major and peculiar difference.

One potential explanation could be traced back to a lock-in effect of the Civil War and thus an ensuing path-dependent political development of Democratic and Republican dominance. This enduring duopoly was certainly reflected in the so-called "Solid South" (i.e. the former seceded Confederate States), that is the dominance of the Democratic Party there since the Reconstruction Era up to the mid-20th century, as decades of resentment of the Republicans as the "party of Lincoln" (Grantham 1988; Key 1949). However, this could not explain the persistence *and* proliferation of isomorphism in the party system across the *entire* polity. The isomorphic US party system is not explainable by the post-Civil War legacy alone, nor by the electoral system alone. The expansion of the USA, again, continued well into the 20th century.[5] The institutional and political dynamics of the North–South divide around slavery, while applicable to states admitted up to the mid-19th century, was no longer relevant for the growing number of Western states. The resultant increasing regional diversity of the USA made the success of "other" parties reasonably probable.[6] The persistence of decentralized state dominance in organizing party politics only added to the permissive conditions for new and other parties.

The position of parties as organizations, including notorious "party machines", was rather weakened by the late 19th century onward in the course of the Progressive-era reform movement through, for example: the introduction and expansion of primaries, so that parties increasingly lost their hold over candidate selection to the voters themselves; the replacement of the appointment of senators by state legislatures with direct popular election (17th Amendment, US Constitution (1913)); the "Australian ballot" rules of ballot secrecy, and with that, the transfer of responsibility for designing ballots from party to state officials; and the introduction of women's suffrage (19th Amendment (1920)), tremendously expanding and diversifying the electorate (see e.g. Andersen 2012; Ansolabehere et al. 2010; Bowler and Donovan 2006; Teele 2018; Ware 2004). Taken together, while reducing party control over candidate selection and elections, these changes expanded democratic rights and participation opportunities as well as the electorate, thus also creating favorable conditions for new parties. Notable "third" parties such as progressives, populists, and socialists did emerge and compete, often with sizeable electoral gains into the early 20th century, albeit in stark disproportion to the amount of seats or offices they gained (see e.g. Hirano and Snyder 2007).

There have been occasional exceptions of "independents" gaining political offices, such as the occasional Senate seat or state governorship (see e.g. Best and Lem 2011). However, the sheer irrelevance of third parties, not just at national but also, indeed *especially*, at regional level, should pose an anomaly given the actually multiple permissive conditions for establishing at least state or regional other parties. This becomes all the more astonishing, again, in comparison to other political systems.

The puzzle of the American two-party system is reflected in one particularly famous phenomenon, namely the question of: why no socialism in the USA? This example proves revealing for the party system as well as its interconnection with democracy and federalism in the USA. Two of the most well-known explanations for a lack of a socialist party, the Hartz and the Sombart theses, are rather sociological and conceived in contrast to European modernization processes. The two theories point to a lack of feudalism in US history and society, as a country that was "born free" with a profound institutionalization of liberalism, and that exhibited a comparatively well-off and propertied mass society from the outset (Hartz 1955; Sombart 1906) (cf. also e.g. Lipset and Marks 2001). Both theories point to a comparative lack of the socio-economic conditions as well as citizen demands and even mindsets theoretically conducive to supporting the emergence, establishment, and competitiveness of a socialist or otherwise distinctly leftist labor party.

These explanations seem plausible. The contrast with the UK and Canada as well as Australia raises several doubts on their reliability. In these three cases, mass enfranchisement of males at least had already been achieved along with a comparatively high degree of property ownership in the course of the 19th century, while Canada and Australia, like the USA, shared features of immigrant or settler societies that likewise displaced indigenous peoples no less and that also have little to no "feudal" history of their own, strictly conceived. Moreover, industrialization disrupted the societies of Australia, Canada, and the UK as well as the USA.[7] Yet the UK developed a Labour Party as did Australia at national level by the early 20th century, no less under first-past-the-post electoral rules, while Canada witnessed at the Western regional level the rise of "agrarian socialism" with the Cooperative Commonwealth Federation and its social democratic New Democratic Party successor (Archer 2007; Broschek 2009: 198ff.; Lipset 1950). The Sombart thesis that plenty of "roast beef and apple pie" served as a bulwark against socialism for American workers is surely misleading. The position of US workers relative to workers in other countries cannot solve the puzzle. With the onset of industrialization, a great deal *within* the USA changed dramatically relative to its previous societal and economic relations, for example impoverished working conditions and exploitation, and extensive changes in production, socio-economic relations, and the distribution of wealth.

The "no socialism" question is misleading since the actual question is "why is there no established or successful socialist or labor *party*?", which is not the same question as "why is there no socialism or no socialism-affine movements *partout*?". There were actually quite significant ones in the USA, including for example trade union movements, labor demonstrations, protests and strikes, the emergence of the "Knights of Labor" and the "Workingmen Party" already before the Civil War and thus one of the first labor parties in the world, as well as a nominal Socialist Party whose leading candidate Eugene Debs competed in five presidential elections (see e.g. Archer 2007; Gourevitch 2011; Lipset and Marks 2001; McDonagh 1992; Orren 1995; Shafer 1999). The supposed "American exceptionalism" is also in this context much less applicable than the often presumed and purported loatheness to social democratic thinking. Moreover, widespread beliefs in egalitarianism in the USA could not have functioned *only* as a hindrance to social justice politics, as the Hartz thesis implied. It rather could also serve as motive and mobilization toward a politics of socio-economic equality promotion.

Democratic government preceded to an extent the establishment of a modern state in the USA, particularly a rationalized bureaucratic one as of the late 19th century onward and in particular with regard to the *national* level (see e.g. Skowronek 1982). Against this backdrop, Lowi for instance places the answer in the federal system and the location of the *state* with the states, especially before the New Deal and the post-World War II era, as the main arena of democratic politics and party competition (Lowi 1985). This federalism thesis demythologizes the theories of a lack of feudalism and class-consciousness in American history. There are many reasons to do so; for example: the long institutionalization of slavery and the continued marginalization of African Americans into the 20th century; the ever creeping closure of the frontier in the USA, coupled with drastic changes in societal and economic relations ensuing with industrialization that rendered the USA no longer a merchant, pioneer, and agrarian-based egalitarian society. Accordingly, the federal order in the USA made the *state* that was to be contested, for example by labor movements, parties, and organizations, more *the states* than the federal government. The disjunction between the cross-territorial contestation of capital-and-labor issues and the vertical distribution of governmental powers most certainly applied in the pre-New Deal era. Federalism and the highly decentralized character of the American polity well into the early 20th century are of course relevant to the dynamics of democratic politics in the USA in general. But then one should expect *all the more* so the establishment of "other parties", if not at the national, then at the regional level.

The question posed as "why no socialism?" in the USA, as prefaced above, is ultimately reflective of a much more general phenomenon that extends further. For instance:

- Why no Christian Democracy in such a profoundly religious society?
- Why no electorally significant Liberal (i.e. Libertarian) parties?
- Why no green party, or no ethnic-identity or sub-national party?
- Why no regional identity-based parties?

In short: why not *any other* party in office? Minor or "third" parties face lower thresholds in proportional electoral systems and thus higher chances of success in gaining public offices or seats in parliaments. However, again, examples of such parties still manage to persist in democratic countries even with similar to almost identical electoral systems, including in highly diverse societies and federal systems. This leaves by process of comparative elimination one distinguishing factor in the USA: a presidential, *not a parliamentary*, form of government with *a polity-wide, popularly elected head of government at the national level.*

Electoral linkages, political parties, and compound majoritarianism

Elections in the USA have a multiply fragmented predisposition, in both horizontal and vertical as well as temporal terms: *horizontally*, with a bicameral legislature of representatives elected in single-member districts for each seat of the House of Representatives and senators elected in separate at-large state-wide elections, virtually all of which follow first-past-the-post, winner-takes-all rules, as do elections for the separately elected chief executive;[8] *vertically*, a highly decentralized electoral regime where states still enjoy a wide scope of jurisdiction over organizing elections, including federal ones, while parties have exceptionally limited control on candidate selection – *the* otherwise distinguishing characteristic of modern political parties – but voters instead largely determine this process in primaries held and widely organized separately in the states; *temporally*, with different terms of office for representatives (two years), senators (six years, but with staggered elections of one-third of senators every two years), and President (four years), with all of their elections divided between a primary and a general election. Under these complex institutional conditions, *presidential government* provides a missing link as to why the *same two* parties dominate. This represents an unintended consequence of American political development for several reasons.

The election of the President was not conceived as a direct election by the people. The Constitution prescribed instead an Electoral College[9] as a means of selecting electors from across the states, based on their number of representatives and senators, to assemble in their states and choose among the candidates for President. Nor was the government conceived as a "presidential government". Explicitly, the US Constitution does not even declare what type of government it has, other than a *Union*. The executive branch is headed by one president rather than a committee, and the *unitary executive* was surely designed with an effective administration in mind (Morris 1987; Sonnicksen 2010). However, this does not implicate the necessity of presidential leadership over governing at the national level. Rather, Congress holds a constitutionally pre-eminent position for lawmaking and regulation, not least given the predominant attribution of federal powers to the federal legislature.

However, it did not take long at all for a democratization process to set in (see e.g. Boudreaux 2004; Ross 2016). The electoral "Revolution of 1800" resulted in a sweeping victory for Thomas Jefferson and the Democrat-Republicans, a resounding defeat of the "Federalists", and a groundbreaking peaceful alternation in power. This critical juncture ushered in the transition from the popular election of electors to a "plebiscitary" election of presidential candidates (see e.g. Ackerman 2005). Moreover, it coincided with the advent of political parties, party competition, and "party government", to which Madison no less – by then a Democrat-Republican now opposing the Federalists party – also contributed. These shifts in the path of American political development can be conceived together as "two Madisonian" legacies in the US Constitution (Zvesper 1984): for example one in the constitutional strict sense (e.g. separation of powers with checks and balances) and one in the broad sense (e.g. the emergence and consolidation of political parties as main intermediaries in modern representative democracy).

During the ensuing 19th century, the US polity was still characterized by limited federal government on the whole, but also Congressional pre-dominance at the national level. However, the 19th century not only witnessed occasional periods of stronger presidents in times of crises like the Civil War, but also presidents elected on decidedly popular mandates. These dynamics became institutionalized following the 'Jeffersonian' (1800) and 'Jacksonian' (1828) electoral revolutions in the early federal republic. These elections influenced the development of the party system. They likewise set precedents for presidents to pursue (party) political governing and policy-making agenda backed by claims to popular mandates (see e.g. John 1997; Rogowski 2016; Skowronek 1997: 61–195; 2011). In short, from the outset, the President has been a key "partisan actor" (Milkis 2010) for politics and for the development of the party system.

The rise of a plebiscitary presidency led to endowing the President with a nationwide democratic mandate. Interpreting the constitutional position of the unitary executive and its legitimate scope of powers would become all the more complex and contentious (see e.g. Bailey 2008). The shift in conceiving presidential government as a "presidential democracy" was assessed by Lowi to be an evolved "pathology" of the US political system (Lowi 1994), intensifying further the institutional rivalry and tendencies toward divided government and gridlock already inherent in the Constitution's separation-of-powers system (see also Ackerman 2000, 2013). Whether conceived as irony or pathology or not though, what is clear is that these changes emerged precisely on account of *democratizing* dynamics. Unlike democratization processes in other federations that led to parliamentary systems (e.g. Australia, Canada, Germany, or India), the American head of government is elected popularly (albeit still *indirectly*) and separately from Congress, and remains independent of the latter's confidence for a fixed term. As Aldrich and Lee have argued, partisan and policy ambitions render the presidency *the* "opportunity structure" that incentivized the evolution and persistence of the two-party duopoly in the USA (Aldrich and Lee 2016; cf. also Jones 2009: 29–84). However, this ambition theory only works when also considering the evolution of other patterns of dynamics. They stem from the bounded path of democratization within the presidential division of powers arrangement and under plurality electoral rules, but also a compounded pattern of thinking in the box.

Through this compounded development, capturing the presidency follows not just political-power and policy-programmatic but also democratic-representative logics with centripetal effects across branches and levels of government over time. In parliamentary cases, a minor party, even a regionally concentrated one, may not likely ascend to the head of government. It can, however, become a coalition partner and thus part of the government majority in the parliament. With this option precluded in the USA, the only path to forming the head of government and state is to win the separately elected, *unitary executive* presidency. That this goal unites both major parties irrespective of their political programs appears self-evident only because it *became* that way. It points to how parties and voters, whether consciously or not, also treat the USA as a *national* Union. Were the USA only a compound of states, then winning the White House should seem less important. The presidency is one cause of this development of the USA toward a "nation" (state), but the presidency's own evolution is also a result of it.

The results for American political development have been manifold. They include mutually reinforcing effects of expanding representative and policy-agenda claims of presidential candidates. They make electoral promises and thus stimulate the expansion of expectations on the presidency, for one, and can turn competitive democratic dynamics subsequently into institutional ones, for another: horizontally between Congress and President, and vertically between President and the states. Moreover, the federal dimension has implications for parties to compete with presidential candidates under one party label that is on the ballot in all of the states. After all, presidential aspirants, while seemingly elected by the people at large, must ultimately gain the majority of *state-based* electoral votes.

States according to the Constitution to this day may appoint electors "in such Manner as the [State] Legislature" chooses. All states nonetheless have come to base their *electoral* vote on the *popular* vote in accordance with the incremental democratization of the USA – and thus in fundamental divergence from the original intents. This path of democratization has apparently transpired within the already long-established institutional-ideational box: that is almost wholly pursuant to simple majoritarian, winner-takes-all rules. At the same time there is no such thing as *the* Electoral College in the USA, nor has there ever been *one*. Aside from Maine and Nebraska, which divvy up electoral votes according to their states' popular electoral results, a presidential candidate can only win all or nothing of the electoral votes awarded by the other 49 separate but simultaneous electoral contests (i.e. the other forty-eight states plus the District of Columbia). Practically all states have adopted such similar rules, despite their constitutionally protected leverage for deviations and divergences. The incentive of winning the presidency does not explain how isomorphism has evolved *also* in this respect. This points rather to an evolved institutional-ideational thinking in the box.

This evolution includes the coupling of the advent and intensification of the plebiscitary presidency with the institutionalization of party competition in representative democracy. Presidential candidates in the USA have had to rely on politically *and* geographically broad based catch-all political parties – or, I submit as a more appropriate term in the US plurality, winner-takes-all context, *catch enough* political parties. Against this backdrop, and oddly enough, the hopes of some of the framers that the Constitution would bring about *national government* and *nationalized* politics were eventually achieved. The oddness or irony relates to the circumstance that two pivotal factors conducive to this outcome have involved precisely two sets of means they unequivocally attempted to avoid, the plebiscitarization of the presidency through a *popularly* elected head of state and government, and the evolution of modern political parties and party competition. And yet these changes transpired without a single amendment to the US Constitution in order to achieve them – not a single new presidential power, nor anything at all about parties can be found in there.

Regarding the coupled evolution between the two-party dominance and the presidency, the case of the so-called "Dixiecrats" provides another example indicating a wider pattern of institutionalized thinking in the box. This short-lived splinter party emerged in the "Solid South" (i.e. the former Confederate States) stronghold of the Democratic Party in the late 1940s (see e.g. Frederickson 2001). Their opposition was not to the Democrats' socio-economic, redistributive, and welfare inclined New Deal coalition. Their split was triggered rather by the increasingly pro-desegregation policies beginning in and especially after World War II, one fought against several fascist-racist regimes no less (see e.g. King and Smith 2014: 962; Polsby 1969: 120). The critical election of 1948 and the Dixiecrats contributed to breaking the Solid South, instigating a realignment as of the 1950s and 1960s toward the more currently familiar pattern of the electorate and the two parties (see e.g. Aldrich 2011: 255–78). What could be easily overlooked is what should actually read like a sizeable success of the Dixiecrats. The new party managed to win four states in the first presidential election in which it competed. Thus it had a significant regional base of support and competitiveness it could have built upon and consolidated even under plurality election rules; that is, if it had made do with being a regional party, one that could win public office at local and state level as well as some seats in Congress. Partisan dynamics in other federal democracies reveal that this would have constituted a wholly "rational choice" for third parties to make. As such, the Dixiecrats did not fail, but rather gave up and then switched parties by joining the Republicans.

There is nothing self-evident in and of itself to this pattern. It only makes sense under the institutional conditions *and* patterns of thinking within the institutional settings of the USA. The capacity to capture the presidency has become apparently the yardstick for determining the viability of a party – even for a party like the Dixiecrats that was attached to strong historical and regional identity as well as adamantly supportive of states' rights and antagonistic toward the federal government. The fate of this short-lived and perhaps last potentially significant third party conforms to a wider pattern in the USA. Barring the occasionally successful "independent" (i.e. party-less) candidate, newcomers opt for one of the two main parties, not by rising through the ranks, but by running in primaries. This is reflected most recently and saliently in the Tea Party. This loose conservative populist social movement (see e.g. Courser 2012) did not lead to a single instance of a new party formation, even though it explicitly donned the name *party*. Nevertheless, its candidates competed under the banner of the Republican Party, in many cases defeating established and incumbent office holders in primaries (see e.g. Miller and Burton 2014; Rapaport, Dost, and Stone 2014).

The US party system has gone through various phases of "de-alignment" and "re-alignment" between voters and parties. They have coincided with dynamics in government–societal relations as well as new social and political movements inducing reactions by parties and shifts in their party programs (on "electoral cycles", see e.g. Merrill, Grofman, and Brunell 2008; see also Sundquist 1983). Nevertheless, the same two parties have persisted. Since the late 19th century, their respective ideological orientations have nearly switched wholesale in the course of the 20th century (see e.g. Lewis 2018). Furthermore, the two parties have (re-)consolidated as well as increasingly polarized in recent decades (see e.g. Brewer and Maisel 2013; Green, Coffey, and Cohen 2014; Stonecash 2010). The progressive-era reforms – e.g. primary elections, ballot secrecy, direct election of senators, expansion of women's suffrage, the improved realization of suffrage rights especially for African Americans later following desegregation – contributed to weakening parties as organizations.

The ideological shifts in the first half of the 20th century produced the once familiar pattern of two rather incoherent, amorphous political parties.[10] Claims that the "party is over" (Broder 1972; cf. also e.g. Pomper 1977) or that Congress consists of only "weak parties" (Mayhew 1974) became commonplace. Not long thereafter though, the Democrat and Republican realignment was quite underway, and the broad spectrum spanning conservatives and liberals found in both parties was diminishing (see e.g. Hare and Poole 2014: 415ff.). Already by the 1980s, the weak political party theses no longer held, with partisanship steadily increasing. In many ways, the same factors that had initially weakened parties in the late 19th and early

20th centuries contributed to the emerging "new American parties" (Schlesinger 1985). Primaries, intended by progressive reformers to weaken party control over candidate selection and politics more generally, seem rather over time to have reinforced the incumbency advantage and contributed to the partisan "purification" of the parties that facilitates partisan polarization (see e.g. Ansolabehere et al. 2010; Hirano et al. 2010; Layman et al. 2010). The intraparty homogeneity within and interparty heterogeneity between Democrats and Republicans have increased, reflective in electoral results for and voting patterns within Congress, as well as the continued absence of any "other" parties, which have not vanished from the land, but from all public offices across the country (see e.g. Hare and Poole 2014; Hirano and Snyder 2007; Rohde and Aldrich 2010; Schraufnagel and Milita 2010). The result is a curious mixture between the inherent fragmentation of the division of powers in democratic government and the corresponding separate electoral systems, and yet the consolidation of two parties and their apparent nationalization cum polarization in the present.

The coupling of institutional fragmentation with partisan polarization

The resurgence and increase in partisanship in terms of party voting and two-party coherence does not equate with stronger parties as *organizations*, nor necessarily with stronger party identification on the part of the electorate (see e.g. Fiorina 2002). The factors of primaries, the state-dominant organization of elections, and their design of electoral districts following plurality winner-takes-all rules, but also strategies of "gerrymandering" districts to partisan advantage (see e.g. Edwards et al. 2017), have reinforced the dualistic, partisan composition of the US polity. The *same* two-party consolidation, that is only Democrats and Republicans, across the polity links to the plebiscitary evolution of the presidency as well. In addition to partisan politics having become *increasingly* nationalized, the multitude of electoral districts have become *decreasingly* competitive (i.e. more safe seats), so that while voters have become increasingly polarized too, the intensified dualism renders the institutional make-up of the polity more divided and polarized along two-party lines than the electorate itself (Carson et al. 2007; Flavin and Shufeldt 2016; Hare and Poole 2014; Abramowitz and Saunders 2008). The now familiar binary of Red (Republican) and Blue (Democrat) states and districts reflect the polarization of the party system and of the political system on the whole. However, they also *amplify* this divide in US politics and polity. The voters themselves also contribute to this pattern, obviously. The following shows, however, the structural-functional *immanent fragmentation* that is not just conducive but also reinforcing in effect.

The two chambers of Congress and the chief executive are each endowed with linkages to their respective constituencies that are at once complex and yet over simplified – or rather *over-simplifying*. Firstly, Figure 5.1[11] shows that the House of Representatives reflects the typical party distribution of seats won by either Democrats or Republicans in recent decades. Given the single-member,

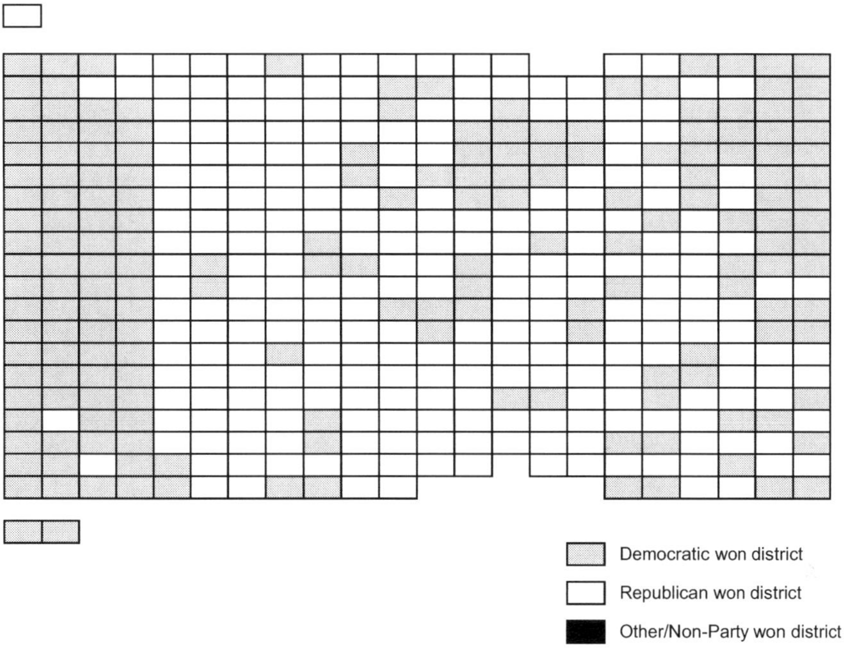

FIGURE 5.1 Partisan distribution of seats for the House of Representatives by district

winner-takes-all system followed in all states and thus for all 435 electoral districts linked to the individual seats of the popular chamber of Congress, the electoral map of the USA tends to appear as shown in the figure.

The partisan make-up of the House of Representatives reflects, but also augments and reinforces, the two-party dualism of the party system and particularly elected institutions in the USA. This applies not least since the 435 separate districts (435 boxes in Figure 5.1), given their plurality elections, are determined by winner-takes-all rules, which also produces "loser loses all" results. The political map repeatedly, that is every two years (Representatives' term of office), generates a composite set of hundreds of either–ors, that is a district is Democrat or Republican. One remarkable flipside to this pattern is how it easily masks the respective shares of votes in each separate contest for the "loser(s)". US elections are thus fundamentally predisposed to distortion, even with regard to the population-based chamber of the House of Representatives. These tendencies toward a distorted dualism have intensified on account of a series of institutional rules and their developments in recent decades – e.g. the nationalization of electoral and partisan competition, the primaries, the manufacture of "safe" districts that are more inclined to be "catch-enough" constituencies for one or the other party.

The electoral-partisan map of US Senate elections can be depicted in analogous fashion. For the election of senators, by direct popular vote since the 17th Amendment (1913) instead of by state legislatures, a state always comprises an

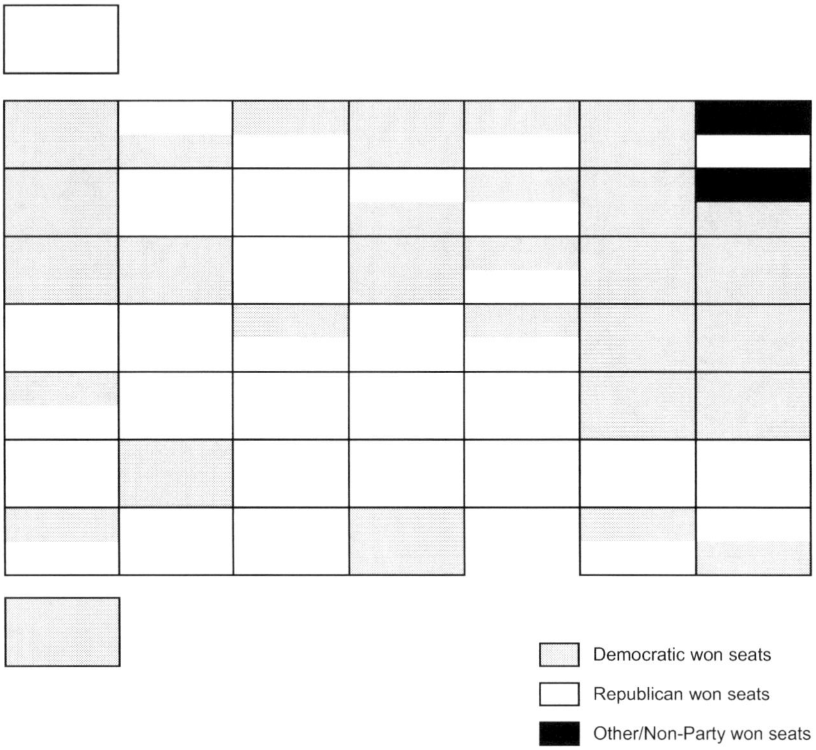

FIGURE 5.2 Partisan distribution of seats for the Senate by states

at-large, statewide district. The two senators are each elected for six-year terms, but staggered in two-year intervals (one-third of 100 senators every two years). Each statewide election (save in Georgia and Louisiana) is also a plurality, winner-takes-all (and loser-loses-all) contest (Figure 5.2).

The electoral map of the Senate (the fifty boxes approximating the fifty states in Figure 5.2), akin to the partisan pattern linked to the House of Representatives, reflects the two-party dominance (save the occasional exception of an "independent") and elections by simple majority rules. At the same time, the states' equal representation, that is two senators per state irrespective of population, generates a quite different map as the states appear equal in size, in contrast to the population-based number of constituencies elected to the House of Representatives per state. The dualistic representative distortion linked to the Senate is thus amplified even further than vis-à-vis the popular chamber. For instance, individual senators get elected by a variable range of percentages of the vote, but also vastly different numbers of voters, for example from a few hundred thousand in the least populous to tens of millions in the most populous states.

The elections for the US presidency on the other hand compound majoritarian systems and logics with the popular and electoral votes. Again, there is no such thing

FIGURE 5.3 Partisan distribution of electoral (presidential election) votes

as *the* Electoral College, but rather fifty-one (fifty States + Washington D.C.) separate presidential general elections held simultaneously. The popular vote in a state has come to determine by plurality (save in Maine and Nebraska) which candidate receives *all* of its electoral votes (Figure 5.3).

The electoral map of typical presidential election (Figure 5.3) results illustrates the disproportions[12] underlying this system. It reflects yet again a strictly dualistic or rather duopolistic partisan make-up of the polity, in this case, linked to the federal executive branch, but with a compounded linkage to the states and the citizenry, though the latter is actually organized as fifty-one separate electorates. The compounded majoritarianism is predisposed to distortion by amplifying relative majorities into wholly either–or constituencies. Much like the different elections and constituent linkages to the bicameral federal legislature, the political map easily conceals shares of votes received by the "losers" in the separate presidential contests.

In contrast to all other elections in the USA, the electoral arithmetic underlying the system for electing the President (and Vice President) does not only magnify electoral majorities, but can lead to manufacturing electoral victories for candidates garnering a lower share of the *aggregate* popular vote. Ironically, precisely the *democratization of presidential elections* according to the established winner-takes-all logic of democratic politics in the USA have increased the possibility of *undemocratic* electoral outcomes. The potential for "wrong winners" under these *democratized* circumstances that was hypothesized in the early 1990s (Abbot and Levine 1991) has come to fruition already twice in recent years, the 2000 (George W. Bush) and 2016 (Donald Trump) presidential elections in which the winner of the majority of electoral votes had less total popular votes than the main opposing candidate. Nevertheless, through competitive dualism and simple majoritarianism, presidential elections correspond with the general patterns and rules of US representative democracy.

The horizontal, democratic dimension of government in the USA encompasses a variety of patterns. They are linked to its institutional configuration and its constitutional predisposition from the outset, and the bounded institutional and ideational evolution within these settings. Regarding coupling within the democratic dimension of US government, the institutional arrangement is *uncoupled* on account of the strict separation of powers. On the other hand, the various checks and balances prescribed by the Constitution provide for several linkages between the President and Congress. This implies, by functional necessity at the least, the requirements of negotiation and cooperation, and thus at least on a case-by-case or decision-by-decision basis the need for loose coupling. The tensions within democracy inherent to this arrangement can be coped with in governmental practice, or they wind up intensified into veritable frictions. The different propensities may coincide with constellations of either "unified government" (i.e. the White House and both chambers of Congress are led by the same party) or "divided government" (i.e. countervailing majorities between them). However, whether cooperation or contestation occurs in governing processes is contingent on more than that. The fragmented disposition of the US polity, here with a focus on the federal legislature and executive, stems not only from the separation of powers among branches of governments. It also emanates from the multiplicity of different and distinctive electoral linkages, and thus is also intertwined with the vertical dimension of the division of powers. All the more significant, indeed peculiar in comparative perspective, is how the party system has managed to consolidate over time into a two-party duopoly across all branches and levels of government.

One overarching anomaly against this backdrop is that the presidency was rather intended to function as a non-, or at least cross-partisan, institution, and its electoral arrangement – commonly and erroneously referred to as the Electoral College – as a filter of "factions". The presidency has instead served a major partisan-fostering and consolidating role in the development of the American polity. Compared with other countries, for example federal ones and also those with plurality elections, the US presidency constitutes the distinguishing institutional feature that facilitates the dominance of the *same* two parties in all branches and at all levels of government. Furthermore, the Constitution invested several contradictions into the presidency that have only grown due to its political development: the union of head of state with head of government, two widely different roles and positions in most democracies, into one office; the tensions between the Constitution in the strict sense of a limited chief executive and in the broad sense of a plebiscitary president with an at-large popular mandate and with numerous, extensive expectations which include proposing and asserting a policy agenda while still serving as the head of state who must achieve cross-institutional and cross-party agreements; and the necessity of partisanship for winning both primary and general elections across the country in the first place in order to become a president that represents the people or Union as a whole (Cronin and Genovese 2004; see also Skowronek 2014). The transformation toward a *perceived* pre-eminence of the presidency, but which has absolutely no basis thus far in formal constitutional change, has gone so far that elections held in non-presidential election years are referred to as "midterm elections" –that is the two-year intervals in the midst of a four-year presidential term for all members of the House of Representatives and a third of the senators. Like many seemingly self-evident, "common knowledge" features of the US polity, this concept is at once significantly *indicative* and yet fundamentally *contradictive* of the political system. For again, contrary to parliamentary systems, Congressional elections are *not* indirect executive elections. The strict separation of powers adopted in the late 18th century that constituted US government has not changed to this day. Complications and contradictions become all the more apparent, in turn, precisely on account of changes to the party system and partisan dynamics.

Inter-branch and multilevel politics have been characterized by tensions and frictions, but also relatively incoherent political parties for a larger share of American political development. These parties were, however, key to so-called "bi-partisanship" that facilitated federal governance irrespective of the constellations of unified or divided government. The lack of "responsible parties", familiar to most other modern (parliamentary) governments, in the USA for much of the 20th century met with a normative-democratic critique. Those circumstances in retrospect most likely eased cross-partisan, cross-branch, and cross-level negotiation and consensus-seeking. The consolidation, increasing coherence, discipline, and thus growing "responsibility" of the two parties may now ironically warrant the caution to "be careful what you wish for" (Rae 2007; cf. e.g. White 1992). Rigidly disciplined, dual-partisan competitive politics have increased in parts despite (e.g. hundreds of decoupled, single-member districts for both Congressional chambers; fifty-one separate electoral constituencies for electing the President) and in parts due to (e.g. plurality rules, primaries, incumbency advantages, partisan-favored gerrymandering of districts) the fragmented disposition of the multitude of electoral linkages. Consequently, the "middle ground" has gradually diminished as well (Masket 2012), in the citizenry as a whole, but even more so among parties and elected officials.

Given the enduring separation of powers in US government, neither the Congress nor the President have the means to "discipline" one another in order to overcome political impasses and governmental deadlocks, other than mutual vetoes and threats thereof. The constitutional default settings of the US government ultimately imply necessities of power sharing and consensus-seeking or possibilities of standoffs and stalemate. The Constitution in the strict sense and its development in the broad sense have led to the coupling of partisan integration and political polarization with structurally divided branches of government and a multiplicity of separated electoral linkages. How the dynamics of democratic governance and political development unfold in the USA are not determined at the national level alone. They also interlink with the federal dimension of government and its dynamic development.

Notes

1 For a compelling analysis of this line of thinking in much of American political development, see Zvesper (1999). A particularly revealing example provided is the quote by Supreme Court Justice Brandeis on the original separation of powers designed by the Constitution as intended "not to promote efficiency, but to preclude the exercise of arbitrary power. The purpose was *not to avoid friction*" (own emphasis added), (Zvesper 1999: 6). For a much different reading of the constitutional intents, including the Convention debates, and explicitly against the Brandeis thesis, see e.g. Barber (2001) and again Zvesper (1999).

2 The denominations of premiers in several parliamentary systems like Italy (*Presidente del Consiglio*), the Netherlands (*Minister-president*), or at state level in Germany (*Ministerpräsident*) attest to this institutional evolution by which the "presiding" officer over a council of ministers became the head of government.

3 To an extent, the Electoral College by design in the US Constitution implies this possibility, though only for cases when no candidate wins a majority of electoral votes and the selection then shifts to Congress – a situation that already came up in the critical election of 1800 (see e.g. Ackerman 2005), while the voting procedure is by state delegation and not the regular majority of Congress members (see Art. 2(1) and the 12th Amendment).

4 The typical inverse side of this "law" (which incidentally Duverger did not refer to as such) is that electoral systems following rules of proportional representation tend to foster multiparty systems. That this connection between electoral and party systems is more complex was already suggested by Duverger (1951), but was more systematically explored in the seminal study by Rae (1967) – e.g. taking further factors into consideration like ballots, district magnitude, and formula for converting votes into seats. See also e.g. Colomer (2005).

5 Fourteen and thus more than one-fourth of the entire fifty states were admitted to the Union after the Civil War. The first state to be admitted was Nebraska (1867), followed by Colorado (1876), Montana (1889), North Dakota (1889), South Dakota (1889), Washington (1889), Idaho (1890), Wyoming (1890), Utah (1896), Oklahoma (1907), Arizona (1912), New Mexico (1912), Alaska (1959), and Hawaii (1959); with regard to the history of statehood admissions, and for a comprehensive overview, see Sheridan (1985).

6 Western states did prove innovative for democratic politics, but more through introducing direct democratic instruments like the referendum, popular initiative, and recall procedures (see e.g. Persily 1997) than new parties.

7 On Anglo-American democracies and linkages between societal and party development, see Alford (1963).

8 Exceptions are elections in the states of Georgia and Louisiana, which require a simple (50+x) majority, while for presidential elections, a plurality of the popular vote suffices to win all of the electoral votes of nearly all states, but the simple majority of electoral votes is required to win the presidency.

9 Note though that here – *yet again*, like many other features in the US Constitution – the *Electoral College* is not denoted as such. Article 2(1) is rather ambivalent, and only prescribes that "Each State shall appoint, in such Manner as the Legislature thereof may

direct, a Number of Electors, equal to the whole Number of Senators and Representatives to which the State may be entitled in Congress". The 12th Amendment (1804) specified the procedure for how and when the electors meet, which is in their individual states separately and not as one assembly, but also here there is no mention of an "Electoral College".

10 These circumstances also met with critique in political science, exemplified by the American Political Science Association in its report calling for a system of two more coherent, "responsible political parties" (American Political Science Association 1950; cf. also e.g. Schattschneider 1960).

11 The figures depicting the US House of Representatives' constituencies, and of the US Senate and the presidential electoral votes, do not replicate one particular election, but rather typical patterns of federal election results in the last two decades. Using gray (Dem.), white (Rep.), and black (Other) emphasizes the *binary* distribution of Democrat and Republican electoral successes and especially the *amplification* of this dualism.

12 Akin to the prior figures, this presidential election map refrains from naming the states. The point again is to emphasize the binary disposition of the electoral map. Moreover, a much different image than the territorial map of the states is generated, based on the magnitude of electoral votes from the fifty-one different constituencies.

References

Abbot, David, and James Levine. 1991. *Wrong Winner: The Coming Debacle in the Electoral College*. Westport, CT: Praeger.

Aberbach, Joel. 1998. "Sharing Isn't Easy: When Separate Institutions Clash." *Governance* 11 (2): 137–52.

——— 2003. "The U.S. Federal Executive in an Era of Change." *Governance* 16 (3): 373–99.

Aberbach, Joel, and Bert Rockman. 1997. "Back to the Future? Senior Federal Executives in the United States." *Governance* 10 (4): 323–49.

Abramowitz, Alan, and Kyle Saunders. 2008. "Is Polarization a Myth?" *Journal of Politics* 70 (2): 542–55.

Ackerman, Bruce. 2000. "The Separation of Powers." *Harvard Law Review* 113 (3): 633–729.

——— 2005. *The Failure of the Founding Fathers. Jefferson, Marshall, and the Rise of Presidential Democracy*. Cambridge, MA: Belknap, Harvard University Press.

——— 2013. *The Decline and Fall of the American Republic*. Cambridge, MA: Belknap, Harvard University Press.

Aldrich, John. 2011. *Why Parties? A Second Look*. Chicago: University of Chicago Press.

Aldrich, John, and Daniel Lee. 2016. "Why Two Parties?: Ambition, Policy, and the Presidency." *Political Science and Research Methods* 4 (2): 275–92.

Alford, Robert. 1963. *Party and Society: The Anglo-American Democracies*. Chicago: Rand McNally.

Almond, Gabriel. 1966. "Political Theory and Political Science." *American Political Science Review* 60 (4): 869–79.

American Political Science Association. 1950. "Toward a More Responsible Two-Party System: A Report of the Committee on Political Parties." *American Political Science Review* 44 (3 (Supplement 2)): 1–99.

Andersen, Lisa. 2012. "From Unpopular to Excluded: Prohibitionists and the Ascendancy of a Democratic-Republican System, 1888-1912." *Journal of Policy History* 24 (2): 288–318.

Ansolabehere, Stephen, John M. Hansen, Shigeo Hirano, and James M. Snyder. 2010. "More Democracy: The Direct Primary and Competition in U.S. Elections." *Studies in American Political Development* 24 (2): 190–205.

Archer, Robin. 2007. *Why Is There No Labor Party in the United States?* Princeton: Princeton University Press.

Bagehot, Walter. 1867 [1974]. *The English Constitution: The Collected Works of Walter Bagehot, Vol. 5*. London: The Economist.

Bailey, Jeremy. 2008. "The New Unitary Executive and Democratic Theory: The Problem of Alexander Hamilton." *American Political Science Review* 102 (4): 453–65.

Barber, N. W. 2001. "Prelude to the Separation of Powers." *Cambridge Law Journal* 60 (1): 59–88.

Beckmann, Matthew, and Anthony McGann. 2008. "Navigating the Legislative Divide: Polarization, Presidents and Policymaking in the United States." *Journal of Theoretical Politics* 20 (2): 201–20.

Best, Robert, and Steve Lem. 2011. "Electoral Volatility, Competition and Third-Party Candidates in US Gubernatorial Elections." *Party Politics* 17 (5): 611–28.

Binder, Sarah. 2015. "The Dysfunctional Congress." *Annual Review of Political Science* 18: 85–101.

Boudreaux, Paul. 2004. "The Electoral College and Its Meager Federalism." *Marquette Law Review* 88 (2): 195–249.

Bowler, Shaun, and Todd Donovan. 2006. "Direct Democracy and Political Parties in America." *Party Politics* 12 (5): 649–69.

Brewer, Mark, and L. S. Maisel, eds. 2013. *The Parties Respond: Changes in American Parties and Campaigns*. 5th ed. Boulder: Westview Press.

Broder, David. 1972. *The Party's Over: The Failure of Politics in America*. New York: Harper & Row.

Broschek, Jörg. 2009. *Der Kanadische Föderalismus. Eine historisch-institutionalistische Analyse*. Wiesbaden: VS Verlag.

Buckley, F. H. 2012. "The Efficient Secret: How America Nearly Adopted a Parliamentary System, and Why it Should Have Done So." *British Journal of American Legal Studies* 1 (1): 349–410.

Caramani, Daniele. 2017. "Will vs. Reason: The Populist and Technocratic Forms of Political Representation and Their Critique to Party Government." *American Political Science Review* 111 (1): 54–67.

Carson, Jamie, Michael Crespin, Charles Finocchiaro, and David Rohde. 2007. "Redistricting and Party Polarization in the U.S. House of Representatives." *American Politics Research* 35 (6): 878–904.

Chhibber, Pradeep, and Ken Kollman. 1998. "Party Aggregation and the Number of Parties in India and the United States." *American Political Science Review* 92 (2): 329–342.

Clinton, Robert. 1990. "A Brief History of the Adoption of the United States Constitution." *Iowa Law Review* 75 (4): 891–915.

Coleman, Aaron. 2016. *The American Revolution, State Sovereignty, and the American Constitutional Settlement, 1765-1800*. Lanham: Rowman & Littlefield.

Coleman, John. 1999. "Unified Government, Divided Government, and Party Responsiveness." *American Political Science Review* 93 (4): 821–35.

Colomer, Josep. 2005. "It's Parties that Choose Electoral Systems (Or, Duverger's Law Upside Down)." *Political Studies* 53 (1): 1–21.

Connelly, William. 2015. "American Politics: "Broken" Since 1885." *The Forum* 13 (3): 507–24.

Courser, Zachary. 2012. "The Tea 'Party' as a Conservative Social Movement." *Society* 49 (1): 43–53.

Cronin, Thomas, and Michael Genovese. 2004. *The Paradoxes of the American Presidency*. 2nd ed. Oxford: Oxford University Press.

Dahl, Robert. 1956. *A Preface to Democratic Theory*. Chicago: University of Chicago Press.
Duverger, Maurice. 1951. *Les Partis Politiques*. Paris: Armand Colin.
Edwards, Barry, Michael Crespin, Ryan Williamson, and Maxwell Palmer. 2017. "Institutional Control of Redistricting and the Geography of Representation." *Journal of Politics* 79 (2): 722–26.
Fiorina, Morris. 1991. "Coalition Government, Divided Governments, and Electoral Theory." *Governance* 4 (3): 236–49.
——— 2002. "Parties and Partisanship: A 40-Year Relationship." *Political Behavior* 24 (2): 93–115.
Flavin, Patrick, and Gregory Shufeldt. 2016. "Party Competition and Citizens' Political Attitudes in American States." *Electoral Studies* 44: 235–44.
Frederickson, Kari. 2001. *The Dixiecrat Revolt and the End of the Solid South, 1932-1968*. Chapel Hill: University of North Carolina Press.
Gaines, Brian. 1999. "Duverger's Law and the Meaning of Canadian Exceptionalism." *Comparative Political Studies* 32 (7): 835–61.
Goodin, Robert. 1996. "Institutionalizing the Public Interest: The Defense of Deadlock and Beyond." *American Political Science Review* 90 (2): 331–43.
Gordon, Sanford, and Dimitri Landa. 2017. "Common Problems: (or, What's Missing from the Conventional Wisdom on Polarization and Gridlock)." *Journal of Politics* 79 (4): 1433–37.
Gourevitch, Alex. 2011. "The Contradictions of Progressive Constitutionalism." *Ohio State Law Review* 72 (6): 1159–82.
Grantham, Dewey. 1988. *The Life and Death of the Solid South. A Political History*. Lexington: University of Kentucky Press.
Green, John, Daniel Coffey, and David Cohen, eds. 2014. *The State of the Parties. The Changing Role of Contemporary American Parties*. London: Rowman & Littlefield.
Hare, Christopher, and Keith Poole. 2014. "The Polarization of Contemporary American Politics." *Polity* 46 (3): 411–29.
Hartz, Louis. 1955. *The Liberal Tradition in America. An Interpretation of American Political Thought since the Revolution*. New York: Harcourt, Brace and Co.
Hirano, Shigeo, and James Snyder. 2007. "The Decline of Third-Party Voting in the United States." *Journal of Politics* 69 (1): 1–16.
Hirano, Shigeo, James Snyder, Stephen Ansolabehere, and John M. Hansen. 2010. "Primary Elections and Partisan Polarization in the U.S. Congress." *Quarterly Journal of Political Science* 5 (2): 169–91.
Huntington, Samuel. 1966. "Political Modernization: America vs. Europe." *World Politics* 18 (03): 378–414.
John, Richard. 1997. "Governmental Institutions as Agents of Change: Rethinking American Political Development in the Early Republic, 1787–1835." *Studies in American Political Development* 11 (2): 347–80.
Jones, Charles. 2009. *The American Presidency*. New York: Sterling.
Key, V. O. 1949. *Southern Politics in State and Nation*. New York: Alfred A. Knopf.
King, Desmond, and Rogers M. Smith. 2014. ""Without Regard to Race": Critical Ideational Development in Modern American Politics." *Journal of Politics* 76 (4): 958–71.
Krehbiel, Keith. 1996. "Institutional and Partisan Sources of Gridlock: A Theory of Divided and Unified Government." *Journal of Theoretical Politics* 8 (1): 7–40.
Lancaster, Thomas. 1986. "Electoral Structures and Pork Barrel Politics." *International Political Science Review* 7 (1): 67–81.
Layman, Geoffrey, Thomas Carsey, John Green, Richard Herrera, and Rosalyn Cooperman. 2010. "Activists and Conflict Extension in American Party Politics." *American Political Science Review* 104 (2): 324–46.

Lewis, Verlan. 2018. "Party Control of Government and American Party Ideology Development." *Studies in American Political Development* 32 (2): 188–216.
Lhotta, Roland. 2010. "Die Federalist Papers und die moderne Politikwissenschaft: Der republikanische Institutionalismus von Hamilton, Madison und Jay." In *Die hybride Republik. Die Federalist Papers und die politische Moderne*, ed. Roland Lhotta. Baden-Baden: Nomos, 99–123.
Linz, Juan. 1990. "The Perils of Presidentialism." *Journal of Democracy* 1 (1): 51–69.
Lipset, Seymour M. 1950. *Agrarian Socialism: The Cooperative Commonwealth Federation in Saskatchewan. A Study in Political Sociology*. Berkeley: University of California Press.
Lipset, Seymour M., and Gary Marks. 2001. *It Didn't Happen Here. Why Socialism Failed in the United States*. New York: W.W. Norton.
Lowi, Theodore. 1969. *The End of Liberalism*. New York: W.W. Norton.
——— 1985. "Why is There No Socialism in the United States?" *Society* 22 (2): 34–42.
——— 1994. "Presidential Democracy in America: Toward the Homogenized Regime." *Political Science Quarterly* 109 (3): 401–15.
Masket, Seth. 2012. *No Middle Ground: How Informal Party Organizations Control Nominations and Polarize Legislatures*. Ann Arbor: University of Michigan Press.
Mayhew, David. 1974. *Congress. The Electoral Connection*. New Haven: Yale University Press.
——— 2005. *Divided We Govern: Party Control, Lawmaking, and Investigations, 1946-2002*. 2nd ed. New Haven: Yale University Press.
McDonagh, Eileen L. 1992. "Representative Democracy and State Building in the Progressive Era." *American Political Science Review* 86 (4): 938–50.
Merrill, Samuel, Bernard Grofman, and Thomas Brunell. 2008. "Cycles in American National Electoral Politics, 1854–2006: Statistical Evidence and an Explanatory Model." *American Political Science Review* 102 (1): 1–17.
Milkis, Sidney. 2010. "The President as a Partisan Actor." In *New Directions in American Political Parties*, ed. Jeffrey Stonecash. Abingdon/New York: Routledge, 205–33.
Miller, William, and Michael Burton. 2014. "Allies and Antagonists: The Tea Party Impact on the Republican Party." In *The State of the Parties. The Changing Role of Contemporary American Parties*, eds. John Green, Daniel Coffey and David Cohen. London: Rowman & Littlefield, 191–204.
Morris, Richard. 1987. "The Origins of the Presidency." *Presidential Studies Quarterly* 17 (4): 673–87.
Nettl, J. P. 1968. "The State as a Conceptual Variable." *World Politics* 20 (4): 559–92.
Neustadt, Richard. 1960. *Presidential Power. The Politics of Leadership*. New York: Wiley.
Orren, Karen. 1995. "The Primacy of Labor in American Constitutional Development." *American Political Science Review* 89 (2): 377–88.
Persily, Nathaniel. 1997. "The Peculiar Geography of Direct Democracy: Why the Initiative, Referendum and Recall Developed in the American West." *Michigan Law and Policy Review* 2: 11–42.
Polsby, Nelson. 1969. "An Emerging Republican Majority?" *The Public Interest* 0 (17): 119–26.
Pomper, Gerald. 1977. "The Decline of the Party in American Elections." *Political Science Quarterly* 92 (1): 21–41.
Rae, Douglas. 1967. *The Political Consequences of Electoral Laws*. New Haven: Yale University Press.
Rae, Nicol. 2007. "Be Careful What You Wish For: The Rise of Responsible Parties in American National Politics." *Annual Review of Political Science* 10: 169–91.
Rapaport, Ronald, Meredith Dost, and Walter Stone. 2014. "The Tea Party, Republican Factionalism, and the 2012 Election." In *The State of the Parties. The Changing Role of Contemporary American Parties*, eds. John Green, Daniel Coffey and David Cohen. London: Rowman & Littlefield, 157–74.

Reichley, A. J. 1992. *The Life of the Parties: A History of American Political Parties*. Lanham: Rowman & Littlefield.

Riker, William. 1976. "The Number of Political Parties: A Reexamination of Duverger's Law." *Comparative Politics* 9 (1): 93–106.

Rogowski, Jon. 2016. "Presidential Influence in an Era of Congressional Dominance." *American Political Science Review* 110 (2): 325–41.

Rohde, David, and John Aldrich. 2010. "Consequences of Electoral and Institutional Change: The Evolution of Conditional Party Government in the U.S. House of Representatives." In *New Directions in American Political Parties*, ed. Jeffrey Stonecash. Abingdon/New York: Routledge, 234–50.

Ross, Robert. 2016. "Federalism and the Electoral College: The Development of the General Ticket Method for Selecting Presidential Electors: Table A1." *Publius* 46 (2): 147–69.

Rossiter, Clinton, ed. 1961 [1999]. *The Federalist Papers. Alexander Hamilton, James Madison, John Jay.: With a new introduction and notes by Charles R. Kessler. New York*. New York: Penguin.

Schattschneider, Elmer E. 1960. *The Semisovereign People: A Realist's View of Democracy in America*. Chicago: Holt, Rinehart and Winston.

Schlesinger, Joseph. 1985. "The New American Political Party." *American Political Science Review* 79 (4): 1152–69.

Schraufnagel, Scot, and Kerri Milita. 2010. "The Partisan Duopoly in US House Elections: An Analysis of Minor Party Failure." *Representation* 46 (2): 241–53.

Shafer, Byron. 1999. "American Exceptionalism." *Annual Review of Political Science* 2: 445–63.

Sheridan, Peter. 1985. *Admission of States into the Union after the Original Thirteen. A Brief History and Analysis of the Statehood Process*. Washington, DC: Library of Congress.

Singer, Matthew. 2013. "Was Duverger Correct? Single-Member District Election Outcomes in Fifty-Three Countries." *British Journal of Political Science* 43 (1): 201–20.

Skowronek, Stephen. 1982. *Building a New American State: The Expansion of Administrative Capacities, 1877-1920*. Cambridge: Cambridge University Press.

——— 1997. *The Politics Presidents Make: Leadership from John Adams to Bill Clinton*. Cambridge, MA: Belknap, Harvard University Press.

——— 2011. *Presidential Leadership in Political Time: Reprise and Reappraisal*. 2nd ed. Lawrence: University Press of Kansas.

——— 2014. "Twentieth-Century Remedies." *Boston University Law Review* 94 (3): 795–805.

Sombart, Werner. 1906. *Warum gibt es in den Vereinigten Staaten keinen Sozialismus?* Tübingen: Mohr Siebeck.

Sonnicksen, Jared. 2010. "'That Unity is Conducive to Energy will not be Disputed': Die Einheit der Exekutive als problematisches Erbe der Federalist Papers." In *Die hybride Republik. Die Federalist Papers und die politische Moderne*, ed. Roland Lhotta. Baden-Baden: Nomos, 151–70.

Steffani, Winfried. 1979. *Parlamentarische und Präsidentielle Demokratie*. Opladen: Westdeutscher Verlag.

Stonecash, Jeffrey, ed. 2010. *New Directions in American Political Parties*. Abingdon/New York: Routledge.

Strøm, Kaare, Scott Gates, Benjamin Graham, and Håvard Strand. 2017. "Inclusion, Dispersion, and Constraint: Powersharing the World's States, 1975-2010." *British Journal of Political Science* 47 (1): 165–85.

Sundquist, James. 1983. *Dynamics of the Party System: Alignment and Realignment of Political Parties in the United States*. Washington, DC: Brookings Institute.

Teele, Dawn. 2018. "How the West Was Won: Competition, Mobilization, and Women's Enfranchisement in the United States." *Journal of Politics* 80 (2): 442–61.

Tsebelis, George. 1995. "Decision Making in Political Systems: Veto Players in Presidentialism, Parliamentarism, Multicameralism and Multipartyism." *British Journal of Political Science* 25 (3): 289–325.

Verney, Douglas. 1959. *The Analysis of Political Systems*. London: Routledge.

Ware, Alan. 2004. *The American Direct Primary. Party Institutionalization and Transformation in the North*. Cambridge: Cambridge University Press.

——— 2011. *Political Conflict in America*. New York: Palgrave Macmillan.

White, John. 1992. "Responsible Party Government in America." *Perspectives on Politics* 21 (2): 80–90.

Wilson, James. 1987. "Does the Separation of Powers Still Work?" *The Public Interest* 86 ((Winter)): 36–52.

Zvesper, John. 1984. "The Madisonian Systems." *Political Research Quarterly* 37 (2): 236–56.

——— 1999. "The Separation of Powers in American Politics: Why We Fail to Accentuate the Positive." *Government and Opposition* 34 (1): 3–23.

6

MULTILEVEL DIVIDED GOVERNMENT

Federalism in the USA rests principally on the separation of powers. It also exhibits checks and balances and, as such, various rules, norms, and arrangements involving the sharing of powers. Ambivalence is typical of federalism in general. The federal division of powers comes with an indeterminacy in the proper balance between self- and shared rule, one that is never settled or fixated permanently, but rather requires (re-)balancing pursued on a continuing basis. However, the USA has a particularly ambivalent federal order in its constitutional formation from the outset and in its political development over time.

The USA has served as a model for a modern federal system. US federalism, like the presidential system of government also introduced by the Constitution of 1789, represents the first of its kind in the world of modern states. Its modernity lies especially with the conjunction of a federal order with republican forms of government – albeit ones yet to democratize more consistently in the decades to follow. This republican character contrasts with earlier proto-federal cases like Ancient Greek and Medieval city-state leagues or more contemporaneous examples around the 18th century like the United Provinces of the Netherlands, which the US framers referenced frequently (though often inaccurately) in constitutional debates (see e.g. Diamond 1973: 131ff.; Elazar 1987: 130–38; Riker 1957). On the other hand, the US federal model continues to diverge from other modern-day federal systems, in structural-institutional as well as functional respects (see e.g. Weissert 2011). At the same time, US federalism has represented the prototype of *dual* federalism with its strict vertical separation of powers by constitutional design. Yet the evolution of US federal practice also served by the early 20th century as the originator of the *cooperative* federalism concept (see e.g. Clark 1938; Corwin 1937; Grodzins 1966; Strong 1938).

In the preceding chapters, the re-reading of the Constitution and the development of the *state* and the *states* already revealed a fundamental ambivalence in the

DOI: 10.4324/9781003203674-6

US polity between a union of people or states, and thus between popular and state sovereignty, for which the Constitution allows considerably different competing interpretations. In the democratic-governmental dimension too, it became apparent that federalism permeates multiple facets of democratic politics and electoral linkages. As the following explores, the original constitution of American federalism established a strict structural and functional division between levels of government. Through processes of adaptation, including changing and competing constitutional interpretations, interlinkages between the levels and processes of government emerged and later intensified over time, but also remained fragile and contested.

Federalism by separating power but compounding the republic

The Union constitution replaced the short-lived Articles of Confederation as the first federal compact of the USA after independence. In strict or formal terms, this original constitution of federalism has largely persisted into the present. This early establishment of a "league of their own" invited the long-held equation of the US variant with the principles and design of modern federalism more generally, although it was and has remained distinct in many regards (see e.g. Hueglin 2013). The distinctiveness links to institutional features, but also historical context. The Constitution's separation between the national and state levels did not derive from, nor seek to provide, a model per se. The USA could be conceived as a *dual* federal model only in comparison with earlier and especially latter-day federal systems. This corresponds with a pattern in the democratic–government division of powers as well. For it too only becomes a model of presidential government after the evolution of democratic parliamentary government, both later and elsewhere.

Akin to the establishment of republican government, the "revolutionary" founding of US federalism transpired at a time that preceded much of the development and expansion of the modern state. Institutions of modern bureaucracy, public administration, and large-scale representative democracy evolved significantly *after* the formation of the federal republic. The founding era spans from the run-up to independence to the drafting and ratification of the Constitution, though also the first decades afterwards. In this early context, American institutions of and experience in government revolved predominantly around local self-government (see e.g. Derthick 2001: 11ff.; Edling 2003; Moreno 2005). The original constitution of US federalism, which was intensely contested, may reflect a conscious effort to translate ideas of separation of powers into concrete institutional arrangements to secure effective but limited government. This captures an important, but only one, part of the formative picture. The separation-of-powers federalism was bound to limited government not just on purpose, but also necessarily on account of specific temporal contingencies, that is the space and context of the time, when in general the scope of governmental institutions, responsibilities, and activities themselves were limited.

The political realities of the late 18th century differed tremendously from the present ones. However, core functions of government like taxation, defense, domestic order, transportation, and even market regulation were on the immediate constitutional agenda. In the course of deliberating them, of fundamental concern were not only the division of powers among branches, but especially the distribution of responsibilities between *levels* of government. Again, according to a widely influential concept, the Constitution has been conceived as a *federal bargain* (Riker 1964) by which the states consent to the partial transfer of powers and authority to fulfill particular goals: a reliable rule-of-law order conducive to internal peace and commerce as well as external security and defense. On the other hand, the making of the original federal bargain in the USA, as in other cases to be sure, extends deeper and wider than the rational choice for fulfilling political interests. Federal questions were particularly complex and contentious on account of value orientations like securing liberty or upholding state and popular sovereignty.

Liberty, equality, and division of powers appear to have been attached to widely shared convictions. They were substantiated by historical experience in local self-government and reinforced by resistance to and independence from a colonial power perceived as unrepresentative, arbitrary, and despotic. There were obviously controversial differences in the late-18th-century constitutional debates on how to construct a proper union. In brief reiteration: the Federalists apparently deemed the Articles of Confederation and, with that, both the enormous latitude of the state and the rigid restriction of national powers ineffective for meeting governmental demands and maintaining a union; the Antifederalists deemed the then-draft Constitution as destined to erode state and local government and thus be ineffective for protecting liberty. However, there was broad general consensus on principles and shared values of *republican* liberty (see e.g. Moreno 2005). It is rather because than in spite of this nexus that the task of organizing federalism in the Constitution in accordance with republican government would – and recurrently still does – prove so contentious.

Neither the federalism of the Articles of Confederation nor of the new Constitution amounted to full-fledged inventions. Both could build on a multidimensional legacy of many decades of practice in self-government in the colonies. Another foundational dimension of US federalism is an ideational one, including accustomed ideas, and norms and ways of thinking. Familiarity with history and political-philosophical writings on the part of erudite participants in the early constitutional debates makes up one part of the "ideological origins" of the American Revolution as well as of federalism (Bailyn 1992; LaCroix 2010b). There was also mass familiarity with covenants, not only through covenant theology, but especially given the institutionalization of consent-based compacts and proto-constitutions for collective self-government in local communities (see e.g. Lutz 1980, 1998; McCoy 2001). In short, the recasting of federalism in the US Constitution rested upon the antecedent evolution of ideas and institutions coupling egalitarian popular and local or state self-rule.

The opponents of the Union constitution like the Antifederalists were anything but "against" federalism. In retrospect they were referred to for instance as "men of little faith" (Kenyon 1955) due to their suspicion against transferring power and majoritarian institutions to the national level. However, they espoused a large number of preferences closer to ideas linking federal unions to small republics *and* republican-democratic practices that had long been developing in colonial America (see e.g. Jörke 2010; LaCroix 2010a; Peterson 1985; Storing 1981). It would be inaccurate to depict the Federalists as having invented federalism. A veritable innovation much rather involved the attempted transformation of the federal order – previously one predicated on a compact of equal and sovereign states in a confederal "league of friendship" – into a hybrid or *compound* republic (see e.g. Derthick 2001; Diamond 1973: 132–35; Epstein 1984; Hail and Lange 2010; Lhotta 2010a, 2010b; Zvesper 1999). Many Federalist Papers make this departure from previous federal government clear, elaborating explicitly on the Constitution's *mixture* of (con)federal and national features. This is succinctly captured by Madison's well-known characterization of the Constitution as one that is "neither wholly federal" nor "wholly national" (see No. 39 in Rossiter 1961 [1999]).

The centrality of *republic* to the Federalists, and especially to Madison (see e.g. Greene 1994), is reflected in this composite of national and federal elements in the constitution, which connect many issues of allocation of powers to issues of *representation*. There was thought to be an inextricable link between representation as a pivotal republican institution for one and territorial size and constituency for another (see e.g. Squire 2012; Zagarrie 1987). In light of this, deliberation and debate on, but also many provisions and *omissions* in, the Constitution become more comprehensible. The ambiguity of the vertical distribution of powers is also in parts explainable by the assumptions and expectations of the time that most duties of government are carried out at local level, which fell, and predominantly still fall, under the ambit of the states (for an overview, see e.g. Karch 2016; Moncrief and Squire 2013: 3–23). Against this backdrop, provisions in the US Constitution on competences refer almost solely to the Union government and the US Congress in particular (Article 1). Conversely, certain powers are prohibited to the states, but almost none are positively specified, also reflected in the 10th Amendment residual power of the states. Moreover, given the context and constraints of the time, numerous modern institutions of federalism are missing in the original Constitution: for example intergovernmental relations, shared tasks and revenues, fiscal equalization schemes, or numerous policy areas. Astounding is rather their lack of constitutional regulation or prescription to this day. In contrast, the Constitution is concrete in setting forth a series of institutional rules and procedures concerned with *representation* of the *states*. These provisions may constitute the products of bargaining, but they are also indicative of the notion of a compound republic.

The balancing act to reconcile federalism with a large-scale, polycentric republic is embodied in another innovation, namely the "invention of the Senate" (Wirls and Wirls 2004). The Senate is an institutional compromise. It is surely *also* an interest-based one, with questionable democratic merit no less, between large and low populated as well as, infamously, between "free" and "slave holding" states (ibid.; Dahl 2003). However, the Senate is likewise part of the multifaceted balancing act between for example endowing the national level with effective and representative government but limiting it by the separation of powers and checks and balances linked to the people and the states, while accommodating states with equal representation, secured participation, and a voice in the compounded whole. As summarized by Gardner:

> the design of the U.S. Senate also was conceived in part as a mechanism for securing the independence and autonomy of the states. According to Publius [No. 62], representation in the Senate would "giv[e] to the State governments such an agency in the formation of the federal government as must secure the authority of the former." Even the equality of state representation in the Senate was understood in these terms. [...] Representation of states in the Senate was thus more than a method for influencing policy outcomes, although of course it was that as well; it was in addition a means by which states could ensure their own power, survival, and continuing autonomous role in the constitutional system.
>
> (Gardner 2013: 9)

Whether or to which extent the Senate could actually fulfill these purposes is one question (addressed below further). More importantly here, the linkage between federal or compound republic and representation of states serves as an organizational principle in the original constitutional design of US federalism. In addition to equal representation of states, this is underlined by the original *instalment* of senators through appointment by state legislatures for one, and the *powers* of the second chamber for another. The Senate is placed on a par with the House of Representatives in legislative matters, establishing a symmetric bicameralism. Moreover, the Constitution endowed the Senate with several sole competences vis-à-vis the executive branch such as "advice and consent" on presidential nominees and international treaties (Article 2(2)). These instances approximate a joint-decision-making arrangement, by providing the second chamber representing states, with members delegated by state legislatures, the sole powers of assent vis-à-vis the federal executive (e.g. nominations) and on international legal changes that would bind the compound union (e.g. treaty ratification) – or rather this was the *institutional* case until 1913 before the 17th Amendment's uncoupling of senators from state government by introducing their popular election. While the prerogatives of the US Senate continue to apply all the same, its institutional linkage to state governments does not.

The other, and perhaps closest, cross-level joint-decision-making arrangement in the Constitution concerns the provisions on amendments (Art. 5). Pursuant to these rules, which have also remained unaltered, amendments can be proposed either by a two-thirds majority of both houses of Congress or in a convention called by Congress upon the initiative of two-thirds of state legislatures. Amendment proposals require in either case ratification by at least three-fourths of the states, which may transpire via either their legislatures or special conventions. In the context of federalism, and in formal terms, the amendment rules suggest a prominent and strong status of the states in several ways: for example a high threshold (three-fourths) of their requisite approval for amendment, and their bottom-up right to initiate proposals. The latter feature had been viewed as an important reservoir of influence of the states, as a path to redressing illegitimate over-extensions or otherwise problematic developments of the federal government (see e.g. Kauper 1968; Monaghan 1996). However, in over two hundred years, none of the twenty-seven amendments to the US Constitution have resulted from this procedure, nor have any of the amendment proposals forwarded to the states for ratification so far, that is of the total thirty-three to pass the requisite super-majority federal threshold. In all cases they transpired top-down upon proposals initiated and passed by Congress.[1]

Nevertheless, Article V may still be deemed a safeguard to the states, at least against encroachments of the national government taken via *formal* constitutional change (see e.g. Monaghan 1996). The rules stipulate, by either amendment approach, a super-majority ratification by the states. Another provision in Article V underlining the stature of the states is the Constitution's only enduring entrenchment clause, namely the guarantee of "equal suffrage" to the states in the Senate. Thus to a good extent at least, the rigidity of the US Constitution becomes explainable by the multiple super-majority rules of amendment (cf. e.g. Lorenz 2005; Lutz 1994). These thresholds also provide one likely answer as to why the bottom-up amendment attempts have failed so far, or why efforts to effect constitutional change have largely wound up circumventing altogether the formal – and, compared with many other provisions, rather *unambiguous* – amendment rules (see e.g. Albert 2014). At the same time, the feature of constitutional rigidity can be taken as indicative of the US federal order as either a compound republic or as a Union of states.

The centrality of the states comes to the fore especially with a view to the dualistic character of the Constitution. However, this dualism is ultimately implicit. The Constitution addresses predominantly the organization of the Union government and its branches, powers, responsibilities, and restrictions. Provisions with explicit reference to the states mostly pertain to powers and competences they *do not have* rather than which ones they have or may exercise, while the 10th amendment reserves a blanket, unspecified remainder to the states. Article 1 addresses the US Congress and enumerates in Section 8 its powers, while Section 10 expressly prohibits the states from exercising several powers. In addition to reiterating powers they do not have, which were expressly granted to Congress two sections prior (e.g. issuing letters of marque and reprisal, coining money), Section 10 prohibits states from entering into leagues or confederations, and from entering compacts with foreign entities but also with one another without "consent of Congress". This is particularly notable for dual federalism emphasizing the separation of powers between levels of government and among the states themselves.

Little to almost nothing is delineated on the actual execution of state powers. The Constitution also refrains from specifying multilevel administrative rules, so that, again *implicitly*, the states are to administer their own laws independently and the US government its own. Moreover, while state legislatures were originally charged with delegating senators, there are no provisions related to imperative mandates or other forms of instructions from state governments to "their" senators. The Constitution implies an uncoupled federal predisposition also in terms of fiscal federalism. Certain types of taxation are expressly granted to Congress in Article 1(8), but without provisions on sharing taxation revenues with the states, nor vice versa their sharing of revenues, such as those from sales and income taxes, with each other or with the national government. Aside from prohibitions on states against raising tariffs and customs (Art. 1(10)) or on the US government from raising "capitation and other direct" taxes (Art. 1(9)), the states retain their own and wide fiscal revenue raising and expenditure authorities.

The Constitution gears US federalism (see Figure 6.1) toward the strict vertical separation of powers between levels of government. This dual federalism also implies largely *concurrent* and many *redundant* powers and institutions at multiple levels. It generally prescribes comity and reciprocity in the relations among the states, their governments, and citizens (e.g. Art. 4(1) and (2)). These provisions entail commitments, foremost to mutually recognize state public acts and mutually grant privileges and protections, for example to citizens of other states. However, they do not express requirements for uniform regulations or even cooperation and coordination. As such, they emphasize the autonomy of the states and their latitude for governing. The uncoupled character of US federalism as framed by the US Constitution is exhibited furthermore by the original, and still valid, provision making of interstate compacts contingent upon Congressional approval (Art. 1 (10)).

Institutional features	(vertical / intergovernmental dimension) **separation of powers** ◄——► **sharing of powers**
Vertical distribution of powers (gov't levels)	enumerated powers (esp. Congress) residual powers (States) no joint/shared administration amendment procedures
Bicameralism	strong second chamber Senate appointment (pre-1913) Senate appointment (post-1913)
Horizontal relations	State equality mutual recognition ('full faith and credit') interstate compacts (subject to Congressional approval)
Fiscal relations	enumeration of tax powers no revenue sharing no equalization scheme

FIGURE 6.1 Constitutional order of US federalism

Consequently, interstate cooperation is not precluded, but it is not prescribed either. Elements of coupling or multilevel linkages, on the other hand, pertain mainly to electoral ones with regard to the Senate, the elections to presidency, as well as the far-reaching scope of state authority for organizing elections in general, including federal ones.

The constitutional arrangement of US federalism as dualistic and rather uncoupled has had a long trajectory of impact, for decades after its establishment and for recurring interpretations of these original default settings into the present. The federal order was to witness shifts from the stricter dualism to patterns of multilevel governance and cooperative federalism. These developments however have transpired largely without constitutional amendment, facilitating all the more their possible political contestation.

The onset of cooperative federalism under a dual federal framework

The dual federalism of the USA became defined as a model more "after the fact" (Stonecash 2015: 189) than by the ambiguous Constitution itself. The structural and functional separation between the US or federal and state levels represents an uncoupled federal order. However, the separation of powers is also partially elastic or mixed, and already so by the original constitution. This is evident in several formal institutional and electoral cross-level linkages elaborated previously.[2] Another original constitutional feature, also particularly relevant for federal and state political development, entails a functional multilevel interlinkage and even cooperative federalism, namely the domain of defense.

The Constitution prescribes for matters of defense both the separation of powers and checks and balances or rather power sharing. While Congress has powers and responsibilities for raising and regulating "land and naval"[3] forces, providing for a "common Defence", and the sole power to declare war (Art. 1(8)), the President is charged with serving as "Commander in Chief" of the military (Art. 2(2)). However, the shared-rule constellation extends further into the vertical dimension of government. For instance, the President serves not only as head of the US armed forces, but also the "*Militia of the several States*".[4] References to state militia are also among the enumerated powers of Congress: that is to summon the state militia to "execute Laws of the Union, suppress Insurrections and repel Invasions", to organize, arm, and discipline as well govern "such Part of them as may be employed in the Service of the United States", while the states retain the authority to appoint officers and train their militia, albeit "according to the discipline prescribed by Congress". Consequently, the tasks and infrastructure of defense are originally *federated* or joint ones. This is underlined further by Article 4 on the states and Section 4 especially, by which the USA guarantees a "Republican Form of Government" to every state, protection against "Invasion", and, upon application by the state, "domestic Violence". These constitutional rules and their institutional-ideational antecedent developments link to the complex, and ambivalent, evolution of the US federal order. They too have invited fundamentally opposing interpretations on the nature of the Union, providing constitutional referents both for the supremacy of the federal as well as the retained sovereignty of the state governments.

These constitutional provisions on national military and state militias, common defense, and protection of the states could suggest together the integrity and sovereignty of the states, with duties and powers to protect themselves, but also commitments by the Union as a whole to *their* preservation (cf. e.g. Zick 2005). Moreover, the inclusion of state militia derives from the context of drafting the Constitution and antecedent developments, which were compounded in the evolved "box" of republican-federal ideas and institutions. State militias were not only envisioned as a division-of-labor type of "assistance" in cases of external threat to the USA. Akin to the trial by jury of citizen peers in the judicial domain, militias were also supposed (i.e. also believed) to serve as a crucial linkage between "citizen and government" (Konig 2009; Moreno 2005: 717ff.; Shalhope 1986). Militias should also provide a bulwark against an overly powerful national government in the future – like they already supposedly did in the War for Independence, even though they proved on their own ineffective, and the "Continental Army" which relied on outside professional ones, most notably from France; but the idea of state militias as buttress of republican liberty persisted all the same. While some Convention participants preferred establishing a more coherent, centralized military under the ambit of the federal government, again given the insufficiency of the militia during the War for Independence, these rather negative-liberty (e.g. protection against tyranny) and positive-liberty (e.g. republican linchpin) notions of militias together constituted ideas generally shared by most Federalists and Antifederalists alike (see e.g. Gardner 2013: 7ff.; Hutson 1981: 364; Levy 2007: 464ff.).

While local and early state militias had become established by the onset of struggle for independence, the revolutionary period likewise set a precedent for their cross-state or proto-federal coordination and ultimately top-down direction by the then "Continental Congress" (see e.g. Hail and Lange 2010: 369ff.). Additional complexity emerges due to one of the most famous early additions to the US Constitution, namely the Second Amendment, adopted in 1791 with the first ten Amendments (alias Bill of Rights), guaranteeing the right of the people to "keep and bear arms". Its origins reach back at least to the political turmoil of mid-17th-century England and the predecessor adoption of this right in the Bill of Rights of 1689 there (see e.g. Malcolm 1994). Whether this amendment secured an individual or collective right, or one strictly bound to a "well regulated militia, being necessary to the security of a free State" and thus exercised by and part of state institutions alone or not, remain highly contested questions into the present (see e.g. Halbrook 2008; Konig 2009; Malcolm 1994). However, the amendment is surely entangled with the larger US evolutionary institutional-ideational box in general and the development of US federalism in particular.

The militia–military nexus connects to the state more broadly, and its development and fundamental, but complex to ambivalent, interlinkage with the states in the USA. As in numerous other country cases, the development of the military under state authority spurred by armed conflict became a "principal agent of state development" in the USA too, and this already as of the early 19th century onward. Up to the Civil War, military actions were frequently conquests intertwined with Westward and also slavery expansion as well as conflicts against and forced expulsions of Native Americans (Ericson 2017), though the latter continued well after the Civil War. The extension of the Union, from territorial expansion to outright colonization, was carried out from the outset by Federalists and then Democrat-Republicans after the critical election of 1800 (e.g. the Louisiana Purchase under President Jefferson) as well as throughout the populist "Jacksonian" administration and beyond (see e.g. John 1997). The military–militia dimension of statehood though, as in other ones, did not evolve through continuous centralization and professionalization. The development of a "Yankee Leviathan" continued to be a staggered one, while consolidation of central-state authority in Southern States and especially during the Confederacy period (1861–1865) appears to have exceeded that of the Union (Bensel 1987, 1990). The Union government lacked a "monopoly of legitimate violence" with regard to the military for much of the 19th century, though also for internal police power which resided predominantly in the states (see e.g. Deudney 1995). Vis-à-vis territories prior to their admissions to the Union and thus *statehood*, here the Union government could and often did exercise the respective defense and police authority.

Congress–state coordination of military service, despite constitutional provisions explicitly endowing Congress with regulatory and the President with leadership competences, long remained subject to controversial interpretation as to whether the state contributions were ultimately voluntary or compulsory cooperation (see e.g. Corwin 1937: 606ff.). However, Congress did commence from the outset with providing financial assistance to state militias. The federal military experienced enormous fluctuations between expansion in the course of several wars and the reduction to a limited "standing army" in peacetime – a recurring pattern until the post-World War II era. By the late 19th and early 20th centuries though, with many states until then harboring several different militias, some state-sanctioned, some bottom-up and civically organized, Congress steered the consolidation of state militias into the state National Guards (see e.g. Kaufman 2001). In short, rather than centralization, expansion and consolidation proceeded at multiple levels of the polity. These US Congress–state dynamics connect to more generalizable patterns in US federalism and its political development.

The formal constitution and the institutional predisposition to dual federalism still applied, also in the sense of *concurrent* powers and government institutions at multiple levels. However, *cooperation* and *collaboration* have likewise characterized federal–state relations, albeit with variable extents of institutionalization and practice. For one, collaboration between the federal government and states has involved financial grants provided by the former to the latter, coupled more or less with guidelines, standards, or other strings attached (for an overview, see e.g. Hale and Palley 1981; Maxwell 1952), a federal governance approach taken from the very beginning. Secondly, ambivalence has emerged on account of "government by proxy"

(Kettl 1988), US federal governance, and public administration by instead indirect regulation and public-good provision via other funding and land grants to states and localities as well as private actors. Thirdly, contestation arises when cooperative arrangements have turned into an asymmetric relationship with top-down coercive measures and by the national government over the states.

The establishment and expansion of cooperative relations by the federal government with the states includes a wide range of public projects already as of the late 18th and early 19th centuries. As Elazar showed (1964), the early federal government supported states in infrastructural projects like canal and road building, public education, through national banks – not least by debt relief or assumption, though a critical precedent to refrain from bailing out states in a fiscal crisis was set in the mid-19th century (see e.g. Wibbels 2003) – and early welfare projects. Federal cooperation and assistance involved measures like subsidies, land grants, supply of federal administrative and army engineer expertise, and investments or partnership in public–private joint stock companies (on "American Partnership" see also Elazar 1962). Such arrangements pertained to for example the postal system, the management of roads and rivers, and Congressional investment in and regulation of the railroad system (see esp. Callen 2009, 2011, 2012). Federal spending and its coupling with stipulations and regulations comprises one of the most significant elements undergirding cooperative federalism in the USA into the present, but already developed as a mode of federal governance in the 19th century.

These cooperative approaches were likewise entangled with another strand of US federal patterns, namely fluctuations in the functional distribution or exercise of powers between the federal and state governments. Aside from the extreme case of secession and the ensuing Civil War, there were multiple early political instances of states invoking constitutional rights to refuse cooperation with the federal government, for example: the Kentucky and Virginia Resolutions against the federal Alien and Sedition Act of 1798 (drafted by Thomas Jefferson and James Madison); the Hartford Convention of several New England states against Congress conscripting state militia for the War of 1812; or the Nullification Crisis of the 1830s fronted by John Calhoun and predicated on the compact theory of US federalism, grounded in the popular sovereignty of the people of the states from which *their* right to rule on the constitutionality of federal laws accordingly followed (Whittington 1996). Even with the emerging "new" administrative state by the late 19th and early 20th century (Skowronek 1982), extensions of federal activity into hitherto state policy ambits continued to face constitutional and political hurdles against having states serve as "agents of the nation" (Holcombe 1921) to fulfill federal policy goals and programs. The Constitution, with few exceptions, does not compel cooperation among the states and between levels of government. But it does not prohibit it either. Cooperative federalism by the early 20th century could intensify, especially when conforming with concurrent and "joint" activities to develop arrangements of *voluntary* interdependence, without having to amend the Constitution to these ends (Clark 1936; Corwin 1937; Johnson 2009; Koenig 1938).

As for specific policy domains, the development, expansion, and contestation of social and welfare policies are pivotal in the dynamics of cooperative federalism and intergovernmental relations. On the one hand, the Constitution generally commits the US government and Congress in particular to promote the "general Welfare" (Preamble, and Art. 1 (8)). On the other hand, debate on its meaning, whether it legitimizes and even calls for a national welfare policy, a welfare state or not, is almost "as old as the Constitution itself" (Lutz 1950). Over several centuries, the general welfare has been entangled with multiple and conflicting political traditions (e.g. republican, social-democratic, liberal, or individualist). This brings different understandings and potential implications for federal or state governments as well as localities, public and private actors, and individual citizens concerning the extent of social welfare obligations and the proper location (i.e. governmental level) of those responsibilities (see e.g. Barber 2003; Heclo 1986). Like many ideas and institutions in the USA, practices in welfare provision and public assistance extend back to the colonial era and local communities. Early forms encompassed a diversity of public institutions and private, religious, and civic organizations, and thus a fragmented, and in parts grass-roots, basis upon which chiefly the early states and, indirectly, the federal government could commence building welfare policies (see e.g. Trattner 1999).

The New Deal in the wake of the 1930s Great Depression represents a well-known critical juncture in multiple regards. In social and welfare policy specifically it ushered in a federal pension scheme of social security, unemployment insurance, labor regulations, agricultural support, and employment and economic stimulus programs. But prior to this critical juncture, a diverse spectrum of welfare-type programs had already developed within the USA by the early 20th century, though in rather decentralized fashion – e.g. in public safety and health, poor assistance, public education, labor regulations, worker compensation laws and funds, and many other social policies (Johnson 2007; Katz 1996; Law 2014; Novak 1996; Quadango and Street 2005; Trattner 1999). The federal government forayed into welfare programs from the outset, though sparingly until after the Civil War. Perhaps most significantly, and as seminally analyzed by Skocpol, an extensive policy regime for "protecting soldiers and mothers" (Skocpol 1992) emerged, establishing pensions and expanding hospitals for veterans as well as multiple assistance programs for women and children in need.

Of course federalism matters for the development of social policies, as does the particular type of federal order. Accordingly, and unsurprisingly, even new US federal programs in areas of veteran and family support did not become entirely nationally designed and implemented policies, but rather carried out in tandem, in supplement, or in the co-financing of state as well as private programs. Akin to the "myth of the weak American state" (Novak 2008), a more nuanced pattern becomes apparent regarding the welfare state that evolved in a "both weak and strong state" (Gerstle 2010). Welfare policies – such as old-age insurance, labor protections, and especially workers compensation, the most widely institutionalized social insurance program prior to the New Deal (and wholly state-based) – emerged and grew within the states and were also coupled with democratic political dynamics in the late 19th and early 20th century "progressive era", with diverse social groups, labor unions, and a plethora of civil society organizations mobilizing for reforms within states (see e.g. Crowley and Skocpol 2001; Glenn 2001; Howard 2002; McDonagh 1992; Robertson 1989; Sonnicksen 2018; Thurston 2015). Inversely though, the dual federal order also provided constraints that help explain why competitive politics and strong lobbies could succeed in preventing the introduction of a public unemployment insurance program anywhere (except Wisconsin) prior to the New Deal, or other worker protections perceived as threats to market competition (see e.g. Karch 2016; Karch and Rose 2017; Quadango and Street 2005). Many of these constraints were overcome by the New Deal under the F. D. Roosevelt administration (see e.g. Campbell and Morgan 2005) and later policy endeavors like the "Fair Deal" and the "Great Society" under the Truman and Johnson administrations respectively (see e.g. Fabbrini 1999: 109), but not necessarily on a sustained constitutional basis (see e.g. Sunstein 1987).

Between cooperative and coercive federalism

The structures and rules of American federalism were able to shape conflict but also cooperation in government throughout American political development (Robertson 2017). But how the patterns and dynamics of federalism unfold couple with political contestation and interpretation, which in turn have been shaped, if not bounded, by antecedent developments. Given the intensive shifts toward cooperative federalism by the mid-20th century, the "passing of dual federalism" was finally proclaimed (Corwin 1950). This assertion was premature in hindsight, but also in parts overstated at the time. Analogous to the view of the Civil War apparently settling issues on the nature of the federal union, the onset of the New Deal era has been deemed a "constitutional moment" (Ackerman 1991) and commonly viewed as inaugurating a different federalism in the USA (see e.g. Grodzins 1966). These views of course have substantial validity given the growing extent of cooperative federalism as well as functional and operative multilevel interdependence. However, these changes on their own did not entail an outright transformation of American federalism and the state.

Multiple features of modern statehood – e.g. bureaucracy; police power and the military; social, welfare, and economic control and regulation; and taxation, even federal direct taxation, introduced in 1913 with the 16th Amendment – were already established and consolidating by that time (see also Lewis-Beck and Squire 1991). These developments also continued the overall pattern of *concurrent* expansion of state capacity at the state and federal levels. Akin to Neustadt's thesis on the horizontal separation of powers as rather "separate institutions sharing powers" (Neustadt 1960), the constitutional framework of US federalism always could imply separate levels of government-sharing powers. A myriad of cooperative governmental arrangements did emerge, starting in the early federal republic and increasingly by the late 19th and early 20th century. Further changes occurred as of the mid-20th century. They included not just policy innovations, but also changes in how US government would work in general for the decades to follow. Accordingly, much indeed *evolved* through mutations and adaptations, also through continuation and intensification of pre-established institutions and patterns of governing in the division-of-powers US polity.

Regarding changes in cooperative federalism, as of the 1950s the number of federal grants in aid grew by the hundreds and the subnational governmental recipients – i.e. state but also local governments – from a few dozen into tens of thousands (Walker 2000: 2–6). The expansion of both the federal government and cooperative federalism has coincided with the enormous growth in the share of federal-government financial transfers as part of state budgets (on average more than 30 percent as of the 1960s to the present) and the state implementation of federal programs and regulations, for one, and with the development of a "picket fence federalism", a complex latticework of multilevel networks of administration, intergovernmental relations, and public lobbies, for another (see e.g. Peters 2019: 22–26). The growth in government at the federal level was paralleled, if not exceeded – and again indicative of *concurrent* powers and institutions in US federalism – at state as well as county, municipal, and further district levels (see e.g. Garand 1988; Wright 1975). The increased complexity was also reflected in the exponential growth in conceptual models and descriptors of US federalism – several hundred by one study's count – like "picket fence" or several cakes alone like "marble cake", "fruitcake", or "birthday cake" federalism, among others (Stewart 1982).

Changes in federal governance were permitted and propelled by further political institutional and developmental factors. They span the far-reaching nationalization of politics, linked to the presidency as well as party politics in general, or as of the late 1930s the Supreme Court's broader interpretation of Congressional enumerated powers to tax and spend, regulate interstate commerce, and to take "necessary and proper" measures to fulfill those powers and purposes including the "general Welfare" as well as civil rights, affirmative action, and anti-discrimination (see e.g. Beer 1973, 1978; Gardner 2013; Hueglin and Fenna 2015: 315–21; Smith 2015; Watts 2006). None of these ensuing changes to federalism involved new constitutional changes in the strict sense – i.e. equal rights and protection amendments (especially the 13th, 14th and 15th) by the mid-19th century, women's suffrage (19th) as of 1920, and the federal power of direct taxation by 1913 (16th) having already been introduced. The diversity and intensity of multilevel coupling increased. They remained on the whole nevertheless either loosely coupled arrangements and not, in strict constitutional terms, ones of compulsory cooperation or tightly coupled joint tasks, while in other cases federal governance proceeded rather through hierarchic top-down enforcement.

In addition to judicial review, the changes in cooperative federalism and federal governance transpired largely through political and administrative mechanisms without formal constitutional change. As alluded to above with the concept of the "picket fence", the extension and density of intergovernmental relations increased. Their structural and operational patterns coincided furthermore with the multidimensional division of powers in the US political order (see e.g. Agranoff and Radin 2015). As summarized by Watts:

> In the United States, the diffusion of authority within each order of government has promoted the development of many points of contact between the state and national orders of government. Furthermore, it has provided "multiple cracks" enhancing the access of interest groups to the political process. Intergovernmental cooperative arrangements have tended to be along programmatic lines, involving the interaction of congressional subcommittees, federal agencies, state bureaucrats and legislators, city officials, and interest groups in a *complex web of relationships*.
>
> (Watts 1987: 782, emphasis added)

Accordingly, the USA has not developed "ministerial conferences" as commonly found in parliamentary-democratic federal systems like Australia, Canada, or Germany (Bolleyer 2013; Poirier, Saunders, and Kincaid 2015; Simeon 1972; Watts 2008). Rather, the "intergovernmental lobby" between states and the federal government and the multilevel picket fence include for example: several state-legislative organizations like the National Conference of State Legislatures, multiple executive organizations like the National Governors' Association, the US Conference of Mayors or the National Association of State's Attorneys, and multiple cross-cutting organizations like the Council of State Governments (i.e. representing all three branches), the (meanwhile abolished) Advisory Commission on Intergovernmental Relations which included US Congress members, Metropolitan Planning Organizations, and numerous regional-based governmental forums and administrative networks (for an overview, see esp. Smith 2015). Hence the sphere of intergovernmental relations reflects the manifold separation-of-powers in the democratic and federal government dimensions of the US polity.

Under these complex conditions, multiple new federalism approaches did not replace, but rather added to, dual and cooperative federalism. Policy innovations by states as commensurate with dual federalism or states as "laboratories of democracy" have still been possible, as has also been "pragmatic federalism" (Glendening and Reeves 1977) in limited, specific, common, problem-solving endeavors. Cooperative federalism has also permitted and witnessed voluntary *horizontal* state-cooperative dynamics, notably through policy diffusion, in the sense of policy learning and adaptation in specific programs and in the larger sense of permeation of and convergence in institutional changes like new governmental bodies and rules of organizing government as well as elections across the states (see e.g. Karch et al. 2016; Rosenthal and Hoefler 1989; Walker 1969). The map of US federalism also changed through the intensification of interstate cooperation and a series of "compacts" and "councils" entered by states on their own, that is not necessarily on the basis of federal laws or directives and at times precisely in preemption of possible federal government actions (see e.g. Bowman 2004; Bowman 2017; Bowman and Woods 2007; Smith 2015: 428ff.; Zimmerman 2011). The multidimensional functional overlapping and institutionalizing of cooperation, coordination, and interdependence seem to support the conclusions of a "passing" or otherwise obsolescence of dual federalism. However, without constitutional amendments, the constitutional-legal order of dual federalism between levels of government remained mostly unaltered. These circumstances would prove fundamentally significant, especially for the recurring contestation of the federal government into the present.

The overall character of federalism became even more complex on account of several political developmental strands that have been entangled. For one, a multiplicity of democratic governmental and electoral linkages as well as political and partisan dynamics traverse the intricate network of intergovernmental, inter-administrative, and interstate relations across multiple levels. One particularly significant manifestation of this multi-strand nexus for several decades has been the exponential growth of "pork barreling" in the US Congress for securing national funding for specific constituencies and local districts but which are not part of a germane federal policy program, grant-in-aid arrangement, or similar (Frisch 1998; Lancaster 1986). One could view these practices in isolation from federalism – i.e. strictly in the context of Congress at the federal level alone, in which horse trading and logrolling help secure sufficient-winning voting coalitions in a symmetric bicameral legislature embedded in a presidential separation-of-powers government. However, Congress members' pursuit of federal funding for projects in their districts connects precisely to representative-democratic political dynamics, which again coincide with the multiplicity of the separated and distinct senators' state-based and representatives' district-based electoral linkages. The legislative branch is fragmented internally and in its vertical linkages to state and local constituencies. The democratic and federal governmental dimensions and political dynamics become intertwined, but with ambiguous federal implications.

Politics in the *national popular* chamber, the House of Representatives whose members are subject to frequent elections (every two years), *also* follow "geographic" (see e.g. Lee 2003) logics of representing and asserting state and local interests. These features increase the relevance of the House for subnational intergovernmental lobbies – whether for "bringing home the bacon", or more generally for channeling the input of local, regional, and state interests, needs, and wants into the federal lawmaking processes. On the other hand, the Senate as the chamber for *representing states* consists of members who enjoy much longer tenures (six years) and thus much longer detachment from their state constituencies. The Senate still poses an important institution for state and other intergovernmental lobby actors. However, it is precisely *lobbying* vis-à-vis the Senate that is noteworthy. The Senate became further detached institutionally from the states and state governments through the introduction of the popular election of senators in 1913 (17th Amendment), and thus another chamber to lobby, rather than instruct. The reform introduced a fundamental feature of *uncoupling*. This reinforced *separation* between federal and state governments, and this well before the supposed death knell of dual federalism rang as of the mid-20th century. The change rather formalized the evolving popular democratic trends over previous decades vis-à-vis senatorial selection, and may have served as another contributing factor to the *nationalization* of US politics as well as increasing partisan politics in the Senate over time (see e.g. Crook and Hibbing 1997; King and Ellis 1996; Meinke 2008; Wirls 1999). This formal institutional change reinforced the constitutional structural dualism of US federalism nonetheless.

Prior to this rather rare instance of formal constitutional change, state governments and their legislatures in particular were charged with appointing their state senators. They could by implication monitor, directly exert pressure, and even instruct their senators in order to channel interests and demands as well as elicit the responsiveness of senators on account of anticipation of their possible recall or failure to gain re-election by the state legislatures (see esp. Riker 1955). In turn, legislatures at the state level could likewise serve as relevant addressees for mediation of local and state interests vis-à-vis the federal government. Consequently before the 17th Amendment, there was extensive debate on possible ramifications of Senate popular elections for federalism in general and the stature of the states in particular (see e.g. Burgess 1902). The Progressive Era thrust for democratizing American politics in the late 19th and early 20th centuries targeted the popular election of the Senate, among other reforms. Though again, they corresponded with the evolved thinking in the box, reflected in the motives of weakening parties for one and holding elections by simple majority, winner-takes-all rules for another. However the issue of popular senatorial selection began to emerge even earlier. This occurred not least due to the *internal* governmental fragmentation of states given their presidential arrangement of separately elected governors and especially bicameral legislatures, so that the coupling of senators to states proved substantially more ambivalent, incoherent, and loose than the original constitutional design principles had implied (see e.g. Barnett 1915; Riker 1955; Schiller 2006; Schiller and Stewart 2014). As such, the coupling of democratizing dynamics with the institution of the Senate rather led to constitutionally sealing several antecedent developments linked with the multi-dimensional institutional fragmentation of the US polity: that is vertically between government levels, but also in *dual* or *two-fold* horizontal terms given the separation of powers at federal and state levels.

Viewed again with interest mediation, it becomes all the more comprehensible as to how intergovernmental relations in the USA have developed ultimately into a lobby "like everyone else" (Hueglin and Fenna 2015: 249). Subnational public interest associations must compete with private ones as well as with each other regarding the federal government, which rather means its two chambers of Congress as well as the President and the federal bureaucracy. The public ones face challenges to their coherence or uniformity given their institutional fragmentation, for example governors vs. state legislatures, which in turn are – save in Nebraska – all bicameral. However, subnational governmental actors have one sizeable advantage over private ones, namely through *party* linkages. This in turn connects with two institutions of modern federal and representative-democratic government that developed after the constitutional establishment of federalism, that is political parties and intergovernmental relations, which must operate under the same constitution that was designed before they were even conceived. Especially, and ironically, political parties can serve both as a multilevel interlinkage and political safeguard, if not more so than the originally intended Senate (see e.g. Bednar 2009; Gardner 2013; Kramer 2000; Schleicher 2016), and this especially due to their nationalization and permeation across all branches and levels of government despite their comparatively highly decentralized organization.

While the linkage between state-level governments and the federal-level Senate was uncoupled by the 17th Amendment, another significant feature is precisely that the linkage ran through the *legislative branches* of the states. Their *division* was structurally constituted by bicameralism, but the division becomes functionally deeper over time especially through competitive political party dynamics. The original coupling between the Senate and state governments was predisposed to diffusion given the separation of powers at state level that increased especially over time. Moreover, the constitution, again, does not prescribe implementation of federal laws and programs by the states, so that even senators selected by state legislatures never had a constitutional duty, nor a political mandate or role, to ensure top-down the implementation of federal legislation at state level. Such a duty or role would apply fundamentally less so for senators elected *popularly* by their state constituents. Yet the evolution of cooperative federalism in the USA, particularly as of the mid-20th century, has involved to a large extent exactly that: the implementation of federal programs by governments and administrations in the states. All the while, the constitutional dual federal order persists, reinforced by the uncoupling of the Senate from the states, thus leaving no formal institutional channel for democratically elected state legislatures and governors to have a say in matters. Of course federal funding – whether in policy programs including financial transfers to the states or in grants-in-aid – can incentivize and entice states to carry out federal policy decisions. The complex web of the intergovernmental lobby and multilevel partisan linkages also provide multiple spaces and places for mediating local and state input toward the federal branches of government. However, more federal ambivalence emerges on account of the federal government's augmented capacity and exercise of measures to *enforce* implementation of and compliance with national policies, standards, and regulations on the states.

The extension of federal policymaking, regulation, and funding would also enable growing intrusion through various mechanisms. Through grants-in-aid for instance, depending on design from broader block grants to more specific project ones, the federal government can attach stipulations to the funding in order to achieve political goals in areas outside of direct federal authority. The new or intensified cooperative federalism as of the mid-20th century already entailed the usage of federal spending power and grants to effect or pressure states to adopt uniform standards, welfare benefits, and with even greater force for ensuring civil rights and anti-discrimination protections (see e.g. Derthick 1970; Wright 1975). However, much of the national government activity vis-à-vis the states began to turn to hierarchic enforcement and with asymmetric national power, with patterns that have been conceived as "nation-centered", "forceful", or "coercive" federalism (Kincaid 1990; King 2017). Coercive federalism has encompassed a spectrum of mechanisms and instruments. They range from conditional grants with "crossover sanctions", for example tacking on stipulations to the states to introduce certain rules in other areas not directly related to the policy or project addressed by a grant, altogether "unfunded mandates", myriad regulatory actions, hundreds of statutes for the federal preemption of state actions in a particular policy area, to conscription and orders directed at state as well as local governments (see e.g. Conlan 1991; Kincaid 2012; Posner 1998, 2007; Smith 2015: 429–33; SoRelle and Walker 2016; Zimmerman 1992, 2005).

These approaches to federal governance apparently not only cross the party lines of Democrats or Republicans in the White House or the majority in Congress. They have contributed substantially to federal government involvement in numerous policy areas, including welfare, civil rights and anti-discrimination, housing and urban affairs, infrastructure and transportation, crime and punishment, the "wars" on poverty, drugs, or terrorism, occupational safety, environmental protection and regulations, and education. These changes have occurred on the basis of legal acts (e.g. laws and statutes, executive orders and regulations), and can be and have been justified by respective constitutional interpretations. Even though, not one of these new powers or policy responsibilities has been allocated to Congress, or the President for that matter, through an amendment to the Constitution for over one hundred years now, but rather on the basis of applying explicit and implied constitutional rules that were already there. Although a great deal of the federal government expansions and intrusions have transpired outside of various funding programs, the distributive and redistributive top-down federal revenue sharing has remained part and parcel even of coercive federalism, but without constitutional adaptation like fiscal equalization schemes otherwise characteristic of most other federal democracies (see e.g. Béland and Lecours 2014; Pierson 1995; Weissert 2011). As such, states lack a constitutional entitlement to federal revenue sharing. Cooperative federalism becomes all the more ambivalent given the uncertainty of the states' co-determination rights under these conditions for one, and given the tendencies for federal cooperation approaches to turn coercive for another.

In summary (see also Figure 6.2), the US federal order has evolved in multifaceted fashion toward cooperative, though in many parts coercive, federalism. Changing federal governance and intergovernmental relations on the whole has become superimposed upon and integrated within the structural-institutional constitutional framework of dual federalism. These federal dynamics, taken together, contribute to overarching patterns of "janus-faced" or "ambiguous federalism" (Conlan and Dudley 2005; Walker 1996). Almost any of the changes assessed above can invite opposition and contestation on the basis of the constitution or its respective interpretation. Nearly all of the substantial changes in cooperative federalism and federal government expansion as of the mid-20th century transpired without amendments to the Constitution and widely on the basis of continuing the pattern of *concurrent* powers and institutions at multiple government levels. These changes also remained dependent on a permissive interpretation of the Constitution.

The formal constitutional framework could still be *read* like dual federalism. This leaves a great deal of governmental change susceptible to contestation as well as retrenchment, and this likewise through means of "ordinary" politics rather than constitutional

Institutional features	(vertical / intergovernmental dimension) **separation of powers** ◄——► **sharing of powers**
Vertical distribution of powers (gov't levels)	Constitutional amendments expanding federal authority expansion of federal executive judicial review parallel growth of State governments
Bicameralism	local constituency services by Congress members Senate election (post-1913) joint IGR commissions
Interstate and State-federal relations	growing State and local admin. of federal programs administrative networks ('picket fence') intergovernmental lobby *interstate compacts** *w/o joint administration **w/ bi-/multilateral joint admin.
Fiscal relations	*federal grants-in-aid**, ° *block grants **grants with mandates °unfunded mandates no constitutional revenue sharing no equalization scheme

(esp. as of mid 20th century)

FIGURE 6.2 Development of US federal order toward cooperation

change in the strict sense. In short, one need not amend or abolish a constitutional rule or power that was never constitutionally created in the first place. Consequently, any thrusts towards "new federalism", reinvigorating states, and retrenching "big government" could proceed – as cooperative and coercive federalism have done – through various mechanisms in democratic and federal government that are underpinned by (re-)interpretation of the constitution, without having to coalesce the broad base of consensus needed to surmount the obstacles to amending the US Constitution. Constitutional judicial review precedents could still stand in the way, that is, unless new or renewed interpretations allow for overturning them as well. This brings us closer to the current state of US federal democracy and its evolved conditions.

Friction, adaptation, and the compounding of fragmentation

For much of the 20th century, democratic dynamics headed further toward the majoritarian democratization of multiple branches and levels of government and the consolidation of partisan realignment, and federal dynamics toward the expansion of the federal government as well as multilevel cooperation. These developments proceeded in parts by interruption and innovation to be sure. But they also entailed the continuation and expansion of trends like plebiscitary and popular democratic dynamics, cooperative and nationalizing federal dynamics, and state administrative building dynamics unfolding over many previous decades. Many antecedent features reach as far back as the formative early years of the federal republic. During the heyday of cooperative federalism as of the New Deal and the first successive decades, the countervailing majorities of divided government at the federal level were more typical than the occurrence of unified constellations (see e.g. Jones 1991; Sundquist 1988). Hence, neither divided government under the presidential system of government, nor the persistence of the constitutional dual federalism, hindered the wholesale emergence, evolution, and expansion of cooperation among branches and levels of government.

However, severe frictions and antagonisms have meanwhile come to abound. They impact on the ability to govern at the federal level, and to achieve intergovernmental and cross-level cooperation, tendencies which couple with competitive democratic dynamics. Gaining in political momentum with the New Federalism in the 1980s and increasingly as of the 1990s, a pattern of critical politicization has oriented toward disentangling arrangements of cooperative federalism and contesting the scope of powers and activities exercised by the federal government (see e.g. Conlan 1998). This is reflected in demands by many executive and legislative representatives of the Republicans in particular – but also, and just as importantly, in their electoral successes – to retrench the federal government, for example through extensive deregulation and flexibilization, and to restore the governing latitude of the states. Both thrusts are also backed by respective interpretations of the US Constitution.

The extended spectrum of federal government involvement, with more or less intensity across the policymaking board, has always met with opposition by different parties or groups at different phases of American political development. However, as of the latter half of the 20th century, the increases – especially in federal coercive measures, cross-over and unfunded mandates, preemptions and orders – imposed on state and local governments have fostered political backlashes on policy, partisan, and constitutional grounds (see e.g. Conlan 1991; Kincaid 2012; Moreno 2005: 712–15; Posner 1998; SoRelle and Walker 2016; Zimmerman 2001, 2005). What is more, intensified political competition under the separation-of-powers among branches at the federal level alone has had ramifications for federal governance and on fragmenting relations, between Congress and President, but also between one or both vis-à-vis the states. There are multiple factors behind this development, even irrespective of which party controls the White House and one or both chambers of Congress. They include (see e.g. Aberbach 2003; Conlan 2017b; Jacobs and King 2009; Sonnicksen 2010; Thompson 2013; Walker 1996), on the one hand, the federal bureaucracy under the expanding authority of the chief executive, in practice, has become both more professionalized and politicized over time, but nevertheless constrained by the horizontal and vertical separation and diffusion of powers, as well as subject to supervision and interventions by Congress, backed up by its constitutional legislative, investigative, budgetary, and nomination-confirmatory powers; and on the other hand, presidential constitutional authority and discretion over the execution of legal acts and the budget (once passed by Congress) have been used, also in predication of the president's evolved plebiscitarization, to steer the implementation and even conduct broad federal policy in numerous policy areas in circumvention of the Congress, not only via executive orders and signing statements, but also in negotiating with states directly on particulars of legal provisions, allowing waivers from parts of programs, or drawing from broadly allocated funds in one area to mold its own specific funding initiatives to entice states to adopt presidential policies. This represents together *one compounded source of the growing ambivalence and reinforcing fragmentation* of the federal order that links to the evolution of the democratic dimension of the US polity.

On the one hand, these developments indicate various and often sophisticated approaches to adapt to and to cope with the tensions and frictions within the democratic dimension of the US government. They have coincided with the consolidation with polarization of the two major, and effectively only, political parties on the one hand, and the nationalization and the augmented presidential-centeredness of politics on the other hand. These developments have transpired within a system of government that is already predisposed to the separation of powers among branches of federal government that are also coupled with a multiplicity of diverse and separated electoral linkages. Consequently, the pressure to succeed is further reinforced, and the chances of success are further constrained on account of the endogenous democratic logics of politics and the disjointed presidential and individual congressional constituency mandates and expectations. Within the constitutional default settings and their bounded evolution, fragmenting governance becomes a cause as much as a consequence over a time of adaptations to navigate the multiple institutional and meanwhile growing political divides. Such adaption strategies may follow not just power, policy, and problem-solving but also representative-democratic motives and logics.

On the other hand, the fragmenting shifts in federal governance are likewise reflections of and reactions to multilevel *federal* dynamics. In the recent past and present, federal political dynamics have witnessed growing opposition to perceived excessive federal government intervention on the one hand, and toward support for granting or safeguarding for the states more autonomy to govern as well as more leverage to implement federal policies in accordance with state and local needs and wants, on the other hand. These federal dynamics emanating from the states couple with the institutions and logics of democratic politics *within* the states.

Conflictive federal dynamics seem to have become all the more virulent – or rather their virulence enabled – on account of a discontinuity between strict constitutional structures and functional patterns of governing. The federal government has continued to rely predominantly on the state and local governmental implementation of a wide range of federal programs. However, state governments lack a guaranteed power or formal right of co-determination, save in the formal constitutional amendment procedures, in federal-level decision making. This mismatch has resulted from historical developments that followed different, but incongruent or opposing logics immanent in the US polity.

The federal government has always been rather uncoupled structurally from the state governments. The structural dislocation between levels of government was thus rendered more consistent by the 17th Amendment (1913) requiring the popular election of senators. It had already been an evolving constitutional change in the broad sense. Unlike most other constitutional change in the USA, it became a *formally* codified part of the Constitution. The evolution of the Constitution in the broad sense for over a century by that point included further popular democratization and the internal institutional fragmentation of the state governments that wound up inhibiting a coherent linkage between US senators and state legislatures. This multipart antecedent path of development pointed, or rather was *interpreted* as pointing, toward the need to switch to having senators elected *popularly* but still *in their states*. Different choices could have been made based on different consequences drawn. The option to abolish the US Senate altogether could, even should, have appeared as a viable reform commensurate with popular sovereignty in a national union of "We the People". But that would have been unthinkable – or rather a seemingly much too radical break with the revered constitutional system of the separation of powers and checks and balances. In the face of the double expansion of federal authority and cooperative federalism, it could, even should, have seemed at least equally appropriate to amend Senate appointments rather toward (re-)ensuring state governmental input into the federal legislature, and thus toward cooperation between state and federal governments on a more equal basis. The USA had after all constituted a "Union of States" for so many and for so long. Finding a consensus on how to achieve such a reform may have appeared too unfeasible given the institutional fragmentation of the states, or as a contradiction to the popular and *majoritarian* democratic norms, government institutions, and growing reform demands that had evolved there. Instead, in accordance with the compounded "institutional and ideational box", the 17th Amendment followed, not the explicit purpose, but an *immanent pattern of fragmentation*. It decoupled senators from the constituent states and their governments and thus the latter from the federal level of government, shifted the electoral linkage of senators directly to the constituent people, but on the established basis of distinct and separated electoral linkages to the states. In other words: the amendment conformed to the "old" dual federalism, contradicted the "new" cooperative federalism, and confirmed the "new" popular democracy only to contradict it at the same time by confirming the "old" checks and balances with a powerful Senate that continues to check the House of Representatives as the national popular chamber as well as the President. The reform was also at once commensurate with democracy (popular election) and fundamentally contradicting of democratic equality (one person, one vote of equal value) in upholding the constitutional principle of state equality irrespective of state population (one state, two senators).

The expansion of the federal government scope of powers was to continue nevertheless through both cooperation with and coercion of the states, while relying on them to carry out numerous federal policy programs. All the while though, the Constitution continued to lack joint tasks or rules prescribing intergovernmental collaborative administration. That is to say more precisely, generations of governments have either failed or refrained from integrating this spectrum of constitutional change in the broad sense into the constitution in the strict sense. *Interpretations* of the Constitution and the Congressional enumerated, elastic, and implied powers that were already there have read change into and superimposed it onto the Constitution. Constitutional interpretations at many points have confirmed the expanded federal authority, not only to cooperate with, but also to coerce, the states to adopt and implement legislative and administrative decisions taken at the federal level as well as to preempt them from doing otherwise. As equally immanent in the multidimensional bounded evolution of the US polity, inverse thrusts of politicization contesting federal authority can and often must be grounded in constitutional interpretation, no less an *immanent* one. Constitutional interpretative contestation is an approach states have taken in the past, increasingly into the present and in multiple arenas, whether in intergovernmental lobbying, legislative measures at the state level, or litigation in the federal courts (see e.g. Gleason and Provost 2016). Thus, new federal government measures in an area of contested authority still have to adapt to actual or expected resistance from states, their governments, or, as the case may be, individual branches or administrations in the states.

State governmental actors can maneuver the multidimensional "intergovernmental lobby" to channel interests and demands and pursue budgetary "pork" and "earmarks" vis-à-vis Congress, and procure waivers, tax breaks, or other exemptions and incentives from presidents. States have increasingly garnered both opt-ins and opt-outs,[5] and in numerous cases even refuse federal funding to evade federal policy stipulations, or pass their own laws, openly challenging federal laws and regulations (see e.g. Balla and Deering 2015; Bulman-Pozen and Metzger 2016; Conlan 2006; Conlan and Posner 2016; Dinan 2010; McGuinn 2016; Nicholson-Crotty 2012; Rose 2015; Saultz, Fusarelli, and McEachin 2017). Taken together, *state-based* policy, and democratic-political and constitutional-interpretive dynamics *compound to a further source of growing ambivalence and fragmentation* of the intergovernmental, multilevel dimension of the US polity.

Intensifying party-political competitive and nationalized politics have coincided with uncoupling – including "fend for yourself" and "going on one's own" unilateralism as well as splintering multilevel politics, captured conceptually together as patterns of "polarized" and "fragmented" federalism (see e.g. Bowling and Pickerill 2013; Bowling and Rose 2016; Conlan 2017a, 2017b; Conlan and Posner 2016; Pickerill and Bowling 2014; Rose and Bowling 2015). Commensurate with fragmenting patterns are not only the various tendencies in the development of federal inter-branch and vertical federal–state relations. Frictions and fragmentation have also permeated into *horizontal relations* among the states. Indicative of this is a gradual disintegration of the once dense "picket fence" of intergovernmental relations. This is particularly evident in the dissolution of the Advisory Commission on Intergovernmental Relations in 1996 (see e.g. Bowman 2017). This thus eliminated the only formally institutionalized intergovernmental forum in the USA that assembled representatives of different branches *and* levels of government for cooperative and coordinative efforts.

Moreover, additional governor and state legislature coordinative forums have emerged along party-political lines, reflecting the polarization and fragmentation among and within the states themselves (see e.g. Abramowitz and Webster 2016; Bolleyer 2006; Conlan 2017a; Conlan and Posner 2016; Smith 2015). Polarization and fragmentation also manifest in heightened tendencies to unilateral state actions and open refusals to implement federal statutes even at the cost of forfeiting federal funding, as well as voting patterns in state governorship and legislature elections (see e.g. Horst 2016). These tendencies are also evident in the increasing occurrence of coordination among state-level Attorney Generals, who usually are popularly and separately elected, along party lines to contest federal policies,[6] for example through joint amicus curiae briefs and litigation in federal courts, or in measures taken by state governments and their legislatures to preempt local level policies[7] that would diverge in a partisan fashion from state policy (see e.g. Gleason and Provost 2016; Nolette 2017; Riverstone-Newell 2017).

While it could appear as if the conduits of multilevel partisan interlinkages are short-circuiting, it is much rather that they are working and, in a sense, more effectively than ever and in multiple directions – i.e. top-down, bottom-up, and sideways. These composite developments not only stand in fundamental, and somewhat ironic, contradiction to the Progressive Era democratization reforms. As part of a wider program of reforming American politics and society, they originally aimed precisely at weakening *state* and *local* party patronage and control over elections and much of the operation of government. In a sense, the reforms actually achieved or at least contributed significantly to precisely that. However, the further weakening of subnational party organizations was succeeded over time by the national consolidation and polarization of an effectively duopolistic party system that remains, nevertheless, extensively decentralized in structure and organization. Consequently, there results yet another *compounded source of growing ambivalence and fragmentation* of the polity that links to inter- and intra-state institutions and dynamics coupling with multilevel ones. The result is a certain *simultaneity of incompatibilities*, with partisan multilevel consolidation and nationalization intensifying rather than attenuating polarization and fragmentation.

Summary

Multiple sources and mechanisms have been compounding to further fragment American federal democracy. The US Constitution and its interpretation crosscuts them. The multidimensional evolution toward compounded fragmentation has transpired widely under the same constitution. Federal and democratic contestations are already immanent in the constitutional order of the US polity. The US

Constitution was designed deliberately for multiple and conflicting ends: an effective but limited Union government that safeguards state and republican liberty, as seemingly evident in the multiplicity of the separation of powers and checks and balances. The purposive account is valid to an extent, especially if one succumbs to the temptation to read history backwards as a living proof of constitutional intentions; "ambitions made to counteract ambitions" as it were. Instead, contestation and fragmentation correlate to the constitutional design, but for complex, including unintended and some originally unimagined, reasons. The formative constitutional contingencies (i.e. at the time of its original drafting) range from the ambivalence and contestation of the very meanings and implications of "American Revolution" principles for designing a constitution, to the circumstances of pioneering a large-scale modern federal republic but before many of the central institutions and practices of modern representative democracy, federalism, and the state itself had evolved. This legacy is reflected in several concrete and contradictory changes in the constitution between the strict and broad senses.

The key features originally conceived to serve as state safeguards have either transformed or devolved into obsolescence: the state-based voting system (alias Electoral College) for electing the president, the state-legislature appointment of senators, and the constitutional amendment procedure. The first two *counter-majoritarian* features have mutated with their *majoritarian democratization* over time, still with the effect of reinforcing rather than reducing *divided government*. The amendment procedure has remained a path barely ever taken, and for several reasons. One lies with the original high thresholds for formal constitutional change, which multiplied further through the tremendous expansion of territory and a fourfold number of states. As for the amendments introduced so far, aside from the first ten (alias Bill of Rights) immediately after the Constitution's ratification, they were articles extending Congressional powers, adding clarifications of the presidency (e.g. term limits, presidential succession, but not a single presidential power), and endowing people with more rights, protections, and enfranchisements. In contrast, not one new article has ever involved formally specifying the vertical sharing of powers nor, barring express prohibitions, have they further specified or expanded those of the states.

The US Constitution enumerates powers of the federal government, predominantly of Congress, imposes a series of prohibitions on the states and on the federal government, and reserves the remainder to the states. The separation-of-powers character of the US Constitution could appear as a rather clear-cut arrangement of the federal division of powers. Additional civil rights and protections are later amended to the Constitution. These rights-extending amendments not only contribute to improving liberty and equality, they extend Congressional authority "to enforce this article by appropriate legislation". However, such provisions do not transfer power to Congress solely, but rather continue the *concurrence of powers* with the states, when not otherwise prohibited. Immanently read, the US Congress can raise and regulate an income tax, *but so can the states still*; Congress can enforce new rights and combat discrimination, and so can the states. State governments may extend welfare benefits, the rights of same-sex couples, or protections of freedom of religion and gun ownership further than the federal government. Given the dearth of formal constitutional change and specification, the persistent dualism and concurrence allow for ongoing expansions *at both levels* of government as well as *further contestation between them*, justified and legitimated by competing interpretations. A crux lies in the supremacy of federal government laws and, in case of conflict, the need to determine when state laws contravene government ones, and when they do, whether the federal ones contravene the Constitution. Answering these questions remains a matter of interpretation. And interpretations, unlike the constitutional text itself, actually change in the USA. Interpretive changes may involve new as much as renewed ones. Rather than settling the division of authority and responsibilities in the Constitution, the result over time has been an amplification of horizontal and vertical ambivalence, contestation and fragmentation.

The US Constitution itself, however flawed or faultless it may be deemed, cannot cause this result. It has evolved on account of the coupling between the bounded institutional development of democratic and federal government, the interplay of their respective political dynamics, and constitutional interpretation. Constitutional change in the broad sense connects to, for example, how the modern state, modern representative democracy, modern federalism, cross- and multilevel interdependence, interest mediation, and constitutional interpretation have developed. Institutions have contributed to the various directions of change that were and continue to be omitted from the constitution in the strict sense: for example political parties and judicial review, the popular election of the President, intergovernmental relations, as well as cooperative federalism. They have all evolved within the same constitutional framework that was established either before their evolution toward contemporary forms and practices or before they had emerged at all.

The explorations of the American state, democracy, and federalism help explain the evolution of multiple dimensions of US government, but also how the distending of constitutional ambiguity has coupled with fragmentation of the polity over time. What has also become clear is that the state limited in the USA has expanded enormously over time in capacity and functions, and this *at both federal and state levels*. Yet, these developments have transpired in the bounds of a constitution that facilitates multidimensional contestation *for limiting one or both levels of the state or states*. Mutual limitation and contestation is possible not only by the original constitution, but also by the evolved adaptations in federal and democratic government dimensions reinforcing immanent fragmentation.

This study could end on this note. But to figure out why the composite pattern could turn out the way it has requires exploring more closely the evolution of institutional-ideational thinking in the box in the politics of constitutional interpretation. That so many ambiguities, tensions, and conflicts have persisted, and even increased, reveals the truly constitutional relevance of interpretation. This applies, if anything, for the most obvious reason: the US Constitution *could* be amended at multiple places, thoroughly revised, or replaced altogether in order to address manifold policy and polity challenges, or at least some of them. That the option of constitutional revision remains a counterfactual should appear puzzling: in comparison to other constitutions in the democratic-federal world, for one; compared internally with the constitutions of the US states, which tend to be more frequently amended and specific, for another; or given that the US Constitution itself actually provides a living proof of the possibility to replace a constitution deemed insufficient for meeting the demands of the day. There have been amendments and important ones at that. They consist, however, almost only of these types: adjustments to the presidency such as the rules of succession, dozens of civil rights and protections including expansions of suffrage, and a federal income tax. These changes are also rare and growing older. The US legacy of constitutional amendment is a remarkably restricted one, and one that largely conforms with and *perpetuates the original framework* – with regard to the state in general, and the institutional arrangement of the democratic and federal dimensions of government in particular.

The final piece of the puzzle pertains to a peculiar synthesis, in which the federal government can be contested, not by calling the legitimacy of the original Constitution, its intents and meanings into question, but rather precisely through claims *based on them*. This evolved pattern can be simplified in terms of an Antifederalist constitution integrated into a Federalist one. One could deem this synthesis a cause for celebration: that is as putative testament to the reconciliation of different and once fundamentally opposing constitutional, democratic, and federal understandings. But how the USA got from there to here has been coupled with constitutional interpretation, the regulative idea of text immanence, and with that, various dynamics of contending, elevating and flattening, and distending the Constitution.

Notes

1 A number of proposals by Congress can be said to be in reaction to calls, political movements, and similar emanating from the state level. Nevertheless, all proposals forwarded to the states so far have been on the basis of proposals passed by Congress (see e. g. Albert 2014; Latham 2005; Monaghan 1996).
2 E.g.: the instalment of senators by state legislatures, the compound election procedures for the presidency, and the predominant state authority over organizing elections; the requirement of Senate approval for several federal executive competences like international treaty-making and appointments to the executive and judiciary branches; the rules and procedures of constitutional amendment, with high thresholds for approval by the states.
3 Unsurprisingly for the 18th century, neither branch is granted competence over aviation or air forces or other military branches. They become established and regulated later, but without explicit constitutional amendments.
4 The proviso here being "(…) when called into actual Service of the United States".
5 For instance, in the health care reform under the Obama presidency, or in public medical and unemployment insurance reforms, education, transportation, emissions' reduction, or voter ID and driver's license programs pursued by several recent administrations.
6 For instance in anti-discrimination, environmental, education, healthcare and welfare, immigration, gun, and drug related policy areas.
7 For instance by passing a stricter emissions ordinance or deciding to not enforce policing of illegal immigrants in a "sanctuary city".

References

Aberbach, Joel. 2003. "The U.S. Federal Executive in an Era of Change." *Governance* 16 (3): 373–99.

Abramowitz, Alan, and Steven Webster. 2016. "The Rise of Negative Partisanship and the Nationalization of U.S. Elections in the 21st Century." *Electoral Studies* 41 (1): 12–22.

Ackerman, Bruce. 1991. *We the People. Volume 1, Foundations.* Cambridge, MA: Belknap, Harvard University Press.

Agranoff, Robert, and Beryl A. Radin. 2015. "Deil Wright's Overlapping Model of Intergovernmental Relations: The Basis for Contemporary Intergovernmental Relationships." *Publius* 45 (1): 139–59.

Albert, Richard. 2014. "Constitutional Disuse or Desuetude: The Case of Article V." *Boston University Law Review* 94 (3): 1029–82.

Bailyn, Bernard. 1992. *The Ideological Origins of the American Revolution.* Cambridge: Belknap.

Balla, Steven J., and Christopher J. Deering. 2015. "Salience, Complexity and State Resistance to Federal Mandates." *Journal of Public Policy* 35 (3): 459–76.

Barber, Sortirios. 2003. *Welfare and the Constitution.* Princeton: Princeton University Press.

Barnett, James. 1915. "The Bicameral System in State Legislation." *American Political Science Review* 9 (3): 449–66.

Bednar, Jenna. 2009. *The Robust Federation: Principles of Design.* Cambridge: Cambridge University Press.

Beer, Samuel. 1973. "The Modernization of American Federalism." *Publius* 3 (2): 49–95.

——— 1978. "Federalism, Nationalism, and Democracy in America." *American Political Science Review* 72 (1): 9–21.

Béland, Daniel, and André Lecours. 2014. "Fiscal Federalism and American Exceptionalism: Why is there no Federal Equalisation System in the United States?" *Journal of Public Policy* 34 (2): 303–29.

Bensel, Richard. 1987. "Southern Leviathan: The Development of Central State Authority in the Confederate States of America." *Studies in American Political Development* 2 (1): 68–136.

——— 1990. *Yankee Leviathan. The Origins of Central-State Authority in America, 1859–1877.* Cambridge: Cambridge University Press.

Bolleyer, Nicole. 2006. "Federal Dynamics in Canada, the United States, and Switzerland: How Substates' Internal Organization Affects Intergovernmental Relations." *Publius* 36 (4): 471–502.

——— 2013. "Paradoxes of Self-coordination in Federal Systems." In *Federal Dynamics: Continuity, Change, and the Varieties of Federalism*, eds. Arthur Benz and Jörg Broschek. Oxford: Oxford University Press, 321–42.

Bowling, Cynthia, and J. M. Pickerill. 2013. "Fragmented Federalism: The State of American Federalism 2012-13." *Publius* 43 (3): 315–46.

Bowling, Cynthia, and Shanna Rose. 2016. "Introduction to the Special Issue." *Publius* 46 (3): 275–80.

Bowman, Ann O. 2004. "Horizontal Federalism: Exploring Interstate Interactions." *Journal of Public Administration Research and Theory* 14 (4): 535–46.

Bowman, Ann O.. 2017. "Intergovernmental Councils in the United States." *Regional & Federal Studies* 27 (5): 623–43.

Bowman, Ann O., and Neal Woods. 2007. "Strength in Numbers: Why States Join Interstate Compacts." *State Politics & Policy Quarterly* 7 (4): 347–68.

Bulman-Pozen, Jessica, and Gillian Metzger. 2016. "The President and the States: Patterns of Contestation and Collaboration under Obama." *Publius* 46 (3): 308–36.

Burgess, John. 1902. "The Election of United States Senators by Popular Vote." *Political Science Quarterly* 17 (4): 650–63.

Callen, Zachary. 2009. *The Seams of the State: Infrastructure and Intergovernmental Relations in American State Building: (Dissertation)*. Chicago, Ann Arbor: ProQuest.

——— 2011. "Local Rail Innovations: Antebellum States and Policy Diffusion." *Studies in American Political Development* 25 (2): 117–42.

——— 2012. "Congress and the Railroads: Federalism, American Political Development, and the Migration of Policy Responsibility." *American Politics Research* 40 (2): 293–326.

Campbell, Andrea, and Kimberly Morgan. 2005. "Financing the Welfare State: Elite Politics and the Decline of the Social Insurance Model in America." *Studies in American Political Development* 19 (2): 173–95.

Clark, Jane P. 1936. "Joint Activity between Federal and State Officials." *Political Science Quarterly* 51 (2): 230–69.

——— 1938. *The Rise of a New Federalism: Federal-State Cooperation in the United States*. New York: Columbia University Press.

Conlan, Timothy. 1991. "And the Beat Goes On: Intergovernmental Mandates and Preemption in an Era of Deregulation." *Publius* 21 (3): 43–57.

——— 1998. *From New Federalism to Devolution. Twenty-Five Years of Intergovernmental Reform*. Washington, DC: Brookings Institute.

——— 2006. "From Cooperative to Opportunistic Federalism: Reflections on the Half-Century Anniversary of the Commission on Intergovernmental Relations." *Public Administration Review* 66 (5): 663–76.

——— 2017a. "Intergovernmental Relations in a Compound Republic: The Journey from Cooperative to Polarized Federalism." *Publius* 47 (2): 171–87.

——— 2017b. "The Changing Politics of American Federalism." *State and Local Government Review* 49 (3): 170–83.

Conlan, Timothy, and Robert Dudley. 2005. "Janus-Faced Federalism: State Sovereignty and Federal Preemption in the Rehnquist Court." *PS: Political Science & Politics* 38 (3): 363–66.

Conlan, Timothy, and Paul Posner. 2016. "American Federalism in an Era of Partisan Polarization: The Intergovernmental Paradox of Obama's "New Nationalism"." *Publius* 46 (3): 281–307.

Corwin, Edward. 1937. "National-State Cooperation. Its Present Possibilities." *Yale Law Journal* 46 (4): 599–623.

——— 1950. "The Passing of Dual Federalism." *Virginia Law Review* 36 (1): 1–24.

Crook, Sara B., and John R. Hibbing. 1997. "A Not-so-distant Mirror: the 17th Amendment and Congressional Change." *American Political Science Review* 91 (4): 845–53.

Crowley, Jocelyn, and Theda Skocpol. 2001. "The Rush to Organize: Explaining Associational Formation in the United States, 1860s-1920s." *American Journal of Political Science* 45 (4): 813–29.

Dahl, Robert. 2003. *How Democratic is the American Constitution?* 2nd ed. New Haven: Yale University Press.

Derthick, Martha. 1970. *The Influence of Federal Grants. Public Assistance in Massachusetts*. Cambridge, MA: Harvard University Press.

——— 2001. *Keeping the Compound Republic: Essays on American Federalism*. Washington, DC: Brookings Institute.

Deudney, Daniel. 1995. "The Philadelphian System: Sovereignty, Arms Control, and Balance of Power in the American States-union, circa 1787–1861." *International Organization* 49 (2): 191–228.

Diamond, Martin. 1973. "The Ends of Federalism." *Publius* 3 (2): 129–52.

Dinan, John. 2010. "Contemporary Assertions of State Sovereignty and the Safeguards of American Federalism." *Albany Law Review* 74 (4): 1637–69.

Edling, Max. 2003. *A Revolution in Favor of Government. Origins of the US Constitution and the Making of the American State*. Oxford: Oxford University Press.

Elazar, Daniel. 1962. *American Partnership: Intergovernmental Co-Operation in the Nineteenth-Century United States*. Chicago: University of Chicago Press.

——— 1964. "Federal-State Collaboration in the Nineteenth-Century United States." *Political Science Quarterly* 79 (2): 248–81.

——— 1987. *Exploring Federalism*. Tuscaloosa: University of Alabama Press.

Epstein, David. 1984. *The Political Theory of the Federalist*. Chicago: University of Chicago Press.

Ericson, David. 2017. "The United States Military, State Development, and Slavery in the Early Republic." *Studies in American Political Development* 31 (1): 130–48.

Fabbrini, Sergio. 1999. "The American System of Separated Government: An Historical-Institutional Interpretation." *International Political Science Review* 20 (1): 95–116.

Frisch, Scott. 1998. *The Politics of Pork. A Study of Congressional Appropriation Earmarks*. New York: Routledge.

Garand, James. 1988. "Explaining Government Growth in the U.S. States." *American Political Science Review* 82 (3): 837–49.

Gardner, James. 2013. "The Myth of State Autonomy: Federalism, Political Parties, and the National Colonization of State Politics." *Journal of Law and Politics* 29 (1): 1–68.

Gerstle, Gary. 2010. "A State Both Strong and Weak." *American Historical Review* 115 (3): 779–85.

Gleason, Shane, and Colin Provost. 2016. "Representing the States Before the U.S. Supreme Court: State Amicus Brief Participation, the Policy-making Environment, and the Fourth Amendment." *Publius* 46 (2): 248–73.

Glendening, Parris, and Mavis Reeves. 1977. *Pragmatic Federalism. An Intergovernmental View of American Government*. Pacific Palisades, CA: Palisades Publishers.

Glenn, Brian. 2001. "The Rhetoric of Fraternalism: Its Influence on the Development of the Welfare State, 1900-1935." *Studies in American Political Development* 15 (2): 220–33.

Greene, Francis. 1994. "Madison's View of Federalism in "The Federalist"." *Publius* 24 (1): 47–61.

Grodzins, Morton. 1966. *The American System: A New View of Government in the United States*. Chicago: Rand McNally.

Hail, Michael, and Stephen Lange. 2010. "Federalism and Representation in the Theory of the Founding Fathers: A Comparative Study of U.S. and Canadian Constitutional Thought." *Publius* 40 (3): 366–88.

Halbrook, Stephen. 2008. *The Founders' Second Amendment. Origins of the Right to Bear Arms*. Chicago: Ivan R. Dee.

Hale, George, and Marian Palley. 1981. *The Politics of Federal Grants*. Washington D.C.: Congressional Quarterly Press.

Heclo, Hugh. 1986. "General Welfare and Two American Political Traditions." *Political Science Quarterly* 101 (2): 179–96.

Holcombe, Arthur. 1921. "The States as Agents of the Nation." *Southwestern Political Science Quarterly* 1 (4): 307–27.

Horst, Patrick. 2016. "Gouverneurs- und Legislativwahlen im fragmentierten Föderalismus der Obama-Jahre. Ringen um einzelstaatliche Autonomie." In *Die USA am Ende der Präsidentschaft Barack Obamas. Eine erste Bilanz*, eds. Winand Gellner and Patrick Horst. Wiesbaden: Springer VS, 53–83.

Howard, Christopher. 2002. "Workers' Compensation, Federalism, and the Heavy Hand of History." *Studies in American Political Development* 16 (1): 28–47.

Hueglin, Thomas. 2013. *"Comparing Federalism: Variations or Distinct Models?" In Federal Dynamics: Continuity, Change, and the Varieties of Federalism*, eds. Arthur Benz and Jörg Broschek. Oxford: Oxford University Press, 27–47.

Hueglin, Thomas, and Alan Fenna. 2015. *Comparative Federalism: A Systematic Inquiry*. 2nd ed. Toronto: University of Toronto Press.

Hutson, James. 1981. "Country, Court, and Constitution: Antifederalism and the Historians." *William and Mary Quarterly* 38 (3): 337–68.

Jacobs, Lawrence, and Desmond King. 2009. "The Political Crisis of the American State: The Unsustainable State in a Time of Unraveling." In *The Unsustainable American State*, eds. Lawrence Jacobs and Desmond King. Oxford: Oxford University Press, 3–33.

John, Richard. 1997. "Governmental Institutions as Agents of Change: Rethinking American Political Development in the Early Republic, 1787-1835." *Studies in American Political Development* 11 (2): 347–80.

Johnson, Kimberley. 2007. *Governing the American State. Congress and the New Federalism, 1877-1929*. Princeton: Princeton University Press.

——— 2009. "The First New Federalism and the Development of the Modern American State: Patchwork, Reconstitution, or Transition?" In *The Unsustainable American State*, eds. *Lawrence Jacobs and Desmond King*. Oxford: Oxford University Press, 88–115.

Jones, Charles. 1991. "The Diffusion of Responsibility: An Alternative Perspective for National Policy Politics in the US." *Governance* 4 (2): 150–67.

Jörke, Dirk. 2010. "Die Transformation des Republikbegriffs in den Federalist Papers." In *Die hybride Republik. Die Federalist Papers und die politische Moderne*, ed. Roland Lhotta. Baden-Baden: Nomos, 39–57.

Karch, Andrew. 2016. "The States and American Political Development." In *The Oxford Handbook of American Political Development*, eds. Richard Valelly, Suzanne Mettler and Robert Lieberman. Oxford: Oxford University Press, 361–80.

Karch, Andrew, Sean Nicholson-Crotty, Neal Woods, and Ann O. Bowman. 2016. "Policy Diffusion and the Pro-innovation Bias." *Political Research Quarterly* 69 (1): 83–95.

Karch, Andrew, and Shanna Rose. 2017. "States as Stakeholders: Federalism, Policy Feedback, and Government Elites." *Studies in American Political Development* 31 (1): 47–67.

Katz, Michael. 1996. *In the Shadow of the Poorhouse: A Social History of Welfare in America*. New York: Basic Books.

Kaufman, Jason. 2001. ""Americans and Their Guns": Civilian Military Organizations and the Destabilization of American National Security." *Studies in American Political Development* 15 (1): 88–102.

Kauper, Paul. 1968. "The Alternative Amendment: Some Observations." *Michigan Law Review* 66 (5): 903–20.

Kenyon, Cecelia. 1955. "Men of Little Faith: The Anti-Federalists on the Nature of Representative Government." *William and Mary Quarterly* 12 (1): 3–43.

Kettl, Donald. 1988. *Government by Proxy: (Mis?) Managing Federal Programs*. Washington, DC: CQ Press.

Kincaid, John. 1990. "From Cooperative to Coercive Federalism." *Annals of the American Academy of Political and Social Science* 509: 139–52.

——— 2012. "The Rise of Coercive Federalism in the United States: Dynamic Change with Little Formal Reform." In *The Future of Australian Federalism*, eds. Gabrielle Appleby, Nicholas Aroney and Thomas John. Cambridge: Cambridge University Press, 157–79.

King, Desmond. 2017. "Forceful Federalism against American Racial Inequality." *Government and Opposition* 52 (2): 356–82.

King, Ronald, and Susan Ellis. 1996. "Partisan Advantage and Constitutional Change: The Case of the Seventeenth Amendment." *Studies in American Political Development* 10 (1): 69–102.

Koenig, Louis. 1938. "Federal and State Cooperation under the Constitution." *Michigan Law Review* 36 (5): 752–85.

Konig, David. 2009. "Why the Second Amendment has a Preamble: Original Public Meaning and the Political Culture of Written Constitutions in Revolutionary America." *UCLA Law Review* 56 (5): 1295–1342.

Kramer, Larry. 2000. "Putting the Politics Back into the Political Safeguards of Federalism." *Columbia Law Review* 100 (1): 215–93.

LaCroix, Alison. 2010a. "The Authority for Federalism: Madison's Negative and the Origins of Federal Ideology." *Law and History Review* 28 (2): 451–505.

——— 2010b. *The Ideological Origins of American Federalism*. Cambridge, MA: Harvard University Press.

Lancaster, Thomas. 1986. "Electoral Structures and Pork Barrel Politics." *International Political Science Review* 7 (1): 67–81.

Latham, Darren. 2005. "The Historical Amendability of the American Constitution: Speculations on an Empirical Problematic." *American University Law Review* 55 (1): 145–266.

Law, Ann. 2014. "Lunatics, Idiots, Paupers, and Negro Seamen - Immigration Federalism and the Early American State." *Studies in American Political Development* 28 (2): 107–28.

Lee, Frances. 2003. "Geographic Politics in the U.S. House of Representatives: Coalition Building and Distribution of Benefits." *American Journal of Political Science* 47 (4): 714–28.

Levy, Jacob. 2007. "Federalism, Liberalism, and the Separation of Loyalties." *American Political Science Review* 101 (3): 459–77.

Lewis-Beck, Michael, and Peverill Squire. 1991. "The Transformation of the American State: The New Era-New Deal Test." *Journal of Politics* 53 (1): 106–21.

Lhotta, Roland. 2010a. "Die Federalist Papers und die moderne Politikwissenschaft: Der republikanische Institutionalismus von Hamilton, Madison und Jay." In *Die hybride Republik. Die Federalist Papers und die politische Moderne*, ed. Roland Lhotta. Baden-Baden: Nomos, 99–123.

———, ed. 2010b. *Die hybride Republik. Die Federalist Papers und die politische Moderne*. Baden-Baden: Nomos.

Lorenz, Astrid. 2005. "How to Measure Constitutional Rigidity." *Journal of Theoretical Politics* 17 (3): 339–61.

Lutz, Donald. 1980. "From Covenant to Constitution in American Political Thought." *Publius* 10 (4): 101–33.

——— 1994. "Toward a Theory of Constitutional Amendment." *American Political Science Review* 88 (2): 355–70.

———, ed. 1998. *The Colonial Origins of the American Constitution*. Indianapolis: Liberty Fund.

Lutz, Karl. 1950. "The General Welfare Clause: Does it Authorize a Welfare State?" *American Bar Association Journal* 36 (3): 196–98.

Malcolm, Joyce L. 1994. *To Keep and Bear Arms. The Origins of an Anglo-American Right*. Cambridge, MA: Harvard University Press.

Maxwell, James. 1952. *Federal Grants and the Business Cycle*. Cambridge, MA: National Bureau of Economic Research.

McCoy, Charles. 2001. "Federalism: The Lost Tradition?" *Publius* 31 (2): 1–14.

McDonagh, Eileen L. 1992. "Representative Democracy and State Building in the Progressive Era." *American Political Science Review* 86 (4): 938–50.

McGuinn, Patrick. 2016. "From No Child Left behind to the Every Student Succeeds Act: Federalism and the Education Legacy of the Obama Administration." *Publius* 46 (3): 392–415.

Meinke, Scott. 2008. "Institutional Change and the Electoral Connection in the Senate." *Political Research Quarterly* 61 (3): 445–57.
Monaghan, Henry. 1996. "We the People[s], Original Understanding, and Constitutional Amendment." *Columbia Law Review* 96 (1): 121–77.
Moncrief, Gary, and Peverill Squire. 2013. *Why States Matter: An Introduction to State Politics*. Lanham: Rowman & Littlefield.
Moreno, Paul. 2005. ""So Long as Our System Shall Exist": Myth, History, and the New Federalism." *William & Mary Bill of Rights Journal* 14 (2): 711–44.
Neustadt, Richard. 1960. *Presidential Power. The Politics of Leadership*. New York: Wiley.
Nicholson-Crotty, Sean. 2012. "Leaving Money on the Table: Learning from Recent Refusals of Federal Grants in the American States." *Publius* 42 (3): 449–66.
Nolette, Paul. 2017. "The Dual Role of State Attorneys General in American Federalism: Conflict and Cooperation in an Era of Partisan Polarization." *Publius* 47 (3): 342–77.
Novak, William. 1996. *The People's Welfare: Law and Regulation in 19th Century America*. Chapel Hill: University of North Carolina Press.
——— 2008. "The Myth of the "Weak" American State." *American Historical Review* 113 (3): 752–72.
Peters, B. G. 2019. *American Public Policy. Promise and Performance*. 11th ed. Thousand Oaks, CA: Sage.
Peterson, Paul. 1985. "Federalism at the American Founding: In Defense of the Diamond Theses." *Publius* 15 (1): 23–30.
Pickerill, J. M., and Cynthia Bowling. 2014. "Polarized Parties, Politics, and Policies: Fragmented Federalism in 2013-2014." *Publius* 44 (3): 369–98.
Pierson, Paul. 1995. "Fragmented Welfare States: Federal Institutions and the Development of Social Policy." *Governance* 8 (4): 449–78.
Poirier, Johanne, Cheryl Saunders, and John Kincaid, eds. 2015. *Intergovernmental Relations in Federal Systems: Comparative Structures and Dynamics*. Don Mills, Ontario: Oxford University Press.
Posner, Paul. 1998. *The Politics of Unfunded Mandates. Whither Federalism?* Washington, DC: Georgetown University Press.
——— 2007. "The Politics of Coercive Federalism in the Bush Era." *Publius* 37 (3): 390–412.
Quadango, Jill, and Debra Street. 2005. "Ideology and Public Policy: Antistatism in American Welfare State Transformation." *Journal of Policy History* 17 (1): 52–71.
Riker, William. 1955. "The Senate and American Federalism." *American Political Science Review* 49 (2): 452–69.
——— 1957. "Dutch and American Federalism." *Journal of the History of Ideas* 18 (4): 495–521.
——— 1964. *Federalism: Origin, Operation, Significance*. Boston: Little, Brown and Co.
Riverstone-Newell, Lori. 2017. "The Rise of State Preemption Laws in Response to Local Policy Innovation." *Publius* 47 (3): 403–25.
Robertson, David. 1989. "The Bias of American Federalism: The Limits of Welfare-State Development in the Progressive Era." *Journal of Policy History* 1 (3): 261–91.
——— 2017. *Federalism and the Making of America*. 2nd ed. New York: Routledge.
Rose, Shanna. 2015. "Opting In, Opting Out: The Politics of State Medicaid Expansion." *The Forum* 13 (1).
Rose, Shanna, and Cynthia Bowling. 2015. "The State of American Federalism 2014–15: Pathways to Policy in an Era of Party Polarization." *Publius* 45 (3): 351–79.
Rosenthal, Donald, and James Hoefler. 1989. "Competing Approaches to the Study of American Federalism and Intergovernmental Relations." *Publius* 19 (1): 1–23.
Rossiter, Clinton, ed. 1961 [1999]. *The Federalist Papers. Alexander Hamilton, James Madison, John Jay.: With a new introduction and notes by Charles R. Kessler. New York*. New York: Penguin.

Saultz, Andrew, Lance Fusarelli, and Andrew McEachin. 2017. "The Every Student Succeeds Act, the Decline of the Federal Role in Education Policy, and the Curbing of Executive Authority." *Publius* 47 (3): 426–44.

Schiller, Wendy. 2006. "Building Careers and Courting Constituents: U.S. Senate Representation 1889–1924." *Studies in American Political Development* 20 (2): 185–97.

Schiller, Wendy, and Charles Stewart. 2014. *Electing the Senate. Senate Elections before the 17th Amendment*. Princeton: Princeton University Press.

Schleicher, David. 2016. "Federalism and State Democracy." *Texas Law Review* 95: 763–820.

Shalhope, Robert. 1986. "The Armed Citizen in the Early Republic." *Law and Contemporary Problems* 49 (1): 143–50.

Simeon, Richard. 1972. *Federal-Provincial Diplomacy: The Making of Recent Policy in Canada*. Toronto: University of Toronto Press.

Skocpol, Theda. 1992. *Protecting Soldiers and Mothers: The Political Origins of Social Policy in the United States*. Cambridge, MA: Harvard University Press.

Skowronek, Stephen. 1982. *Building a New American State: The Expansion of Administrative Capacities, 1877-1920*. Cambridge: Cambridge University Press.

Smith, Troy. 2015. "Intergovernmental Relations in the United States in an Age of Partisanship and Executive Assertiveness." In *Intergovernmental Relations in Federal Systems: Comparative Structures and Dynamics*, eds. Johanne Poirier, Cheryl Saunders and John Kincaid. Don Mills, Ontario: Oxford University Press, 411–39.

Sonnicksen, Jared. 2010. "'That Unity is Conducive to Energy will not be Disputed': Die Einheit der Exekutive als problematisches Erbe der Federalist Papers." In *Die hybride Republik. Die Federalist Papers und die politische Moderne*, ed. Roland Lhotta. Baden-Baden: Nomos, 151–70.

Sonnicksen, Justin. 2018. "The Fire Rises…". *Workers' Compensation Quarterly* 31 (3): 2–4.

SoRelle, Mallory, and Alexis Walker. 2016. "Partisan Preemption: The Strategic use of Federal Preemption Legislation." *Publius* 46 (4): 486–509.

Squire, Peverill. 2012. *The Evolution of American Legislatures: Colonies, Territories, and States, 1619-2009*. Ann Arbor: University of Michigan Press.

Stewart, William. 1982. "Metaphors, Models, and the Development of Federal Theory." *Publius* 12 (2): 5–24.

Stonecash, Jeffrey. 2015. "Martha Derthick and the Influence of Federal Grants: Explaining Federalism." *The Forum* 13 (1): 189–91.

Storing, Herbert. 1981. *The Complete Anti-Federalist*. Chicago: University of Chicago Press.

Strong, Frank. 1938. "Cooperative Federalism." *Iowa Law Review* 23 (4): 459–518.

Sundquist, James. 1988. "Needed: A Political Theory for the New Era of Coalition Government in the United States." *Political Science Quarterly* 103 (4): 613–35.

Sunstein, Cass. 1987. "Constitutionalism after the New Deal." *Harvard Law Review* 101 (2): 421–510.

Thompson, Frank. 2013. "The Rise of Executive Federalism: Implications for the Picket Fence and IGM." *American Review of Public Administration* 43 (1): 3–25.

Thurston, Chloe. 2015. "Policy Feedback in the Public-Private Welfare State: Advocacy Groups and Access to Government Homeownership Programs, 1934-1954." *Studies in American Political Development* 29 (2): 250–67.

Trattner, Walter. 1999. *From Poor Law to Welfare State: A History of Social Welfare in America*. 6th ed. New York: Free Press.

Walker, David. 1996. "The Advent of an Ambiguous Federalism and the Emergence of New Federalism III." *Public Administration Review* 56 (3): 271–80.

——— 2000. *The Rebirth of Federalism. Slouching Toward Washington*. 2nd ed. New York: Chatham House.

Walker, Jack. 1969. "The Diffusion of Innovations among the American States." *American Political Science Review* 63 (3): 880–99.

Watts, Ronald. 1987. "The American Constitution in Comparative Perspective: A Comparison of Federalism in the United States and Canada." *Journal of American History* 74 (3): 769–92.

——— 2006. "Origins of Cooperative and Competitive Federalism." In *Territory, Democracy and Justice: Regionalism and Federalism in Western Democracies*, ed. Scott Greer. Basingstoke: Palgrave Macmillan, 201–23.

——— 2008. *Comparing Federal Systems*. 3rd ed. Montréal: McGill-Queen's University Press.

Weissert, Carol. 2011. "Beyond Marble Cakes and Picket Fences: What U.S. Federalism Scholars Can Learn from Comparative Work." *Journal of Politics* 73 (4): 965–79.

Whittington, Keith. 1996. "The Political Constitution of Federalism in Antebellum America: The Nullification Debate as an Illustration of Informal Mechanisms of Constitutional Change." *Publius* 26 (2): 1–24.

Wibbels, Erik. 2003. "Bailouts, Budget Constraints, and Leviathans: Comparative Federalism and Lessons From the Early United States." *Comparative Political Studies* 36 (5): 475–508.

Wirls, Daniel. 1999. "Regionalism, Rotten Boroughs, Race, and Realignment: The Seventeenth Amendment and the Politics of Representation." *Studies in American Political Development* 13 (1): 1–30.

Wirls, Daniel, and Stephen Wirls. 2004. *The Invention of the United States Senate*. Baltimore: Johns Hopkins University Press.

Wright, Deil. 1975. "Revenue Sharing and Structural Features of American Federalism." *Annals of the American Academy of Political and Social Science* 419 (1): 100–19.

Zagarrie, Rosemarie. 1987. *The Politics of Size: Representation in the United States, 1776–1850*. Ithaca: Cornell University Press.

Zick, Timothy. 2005. "Are the States Sovereign?" *Washington University Law Review* 83 (1): 229–337.

Zimmerman, Joseph. 1992. *Contemporary American Federalism: The Growth of National Power*. New York: State University of New York Press.

——— 2001. "National-State Relations in the Twentieth Century." *Publius* 31 (2): 15–30.

——— 2005. *Congressional Preemption. Regulatory Federalism*. Albany, NY: State University of New York Press.

——— 2011. *Horizontal Federalism. Interstate Relations*. Albany, NY: State University of New York Press.

Zvesper, John. 1999. "The Separation of Powers in American Politics: Why We Fail to Accentuate the Positive." *Government and Opposition* 34 (1): 3–23.

7

POLITICS OF THE CONSTITUTION

A peculiar synthesis has evolved over time, connecting various interpretations of a constitution that has not changed very much in the strict sense but that has a great deal in the broad sense. The evolved mixture of interpretive orientations, in abbreviated terms, combines one constitution oriented toward a more *Federalist* and *framer* vein, that is as one union out of many states with a foundation of legitimacy for a republican government by a compounded "We the People"; *but also* toward a more *Antifederalist* and *other founders* vein, that is as one establishing a limited federal government forged by equal states to secure state sovereignty, democracy, and civil rights and liberties. The resultant strict and broad mixed constitution accommodates an amalgamation of evidently and supposedly original text, ideas, intentions, and meanings into a *composite founding* embodied in the US Constitution. One may wonder how such a distending of constitutional ambivalence has resulted and what it entails. This requires capturing, finally, how constitutional immanent interpretation has become the cause and consequence of this multifaceted fragmentation, one moreover that perpetuates the American limited state.

Constitutional dynamics between contestation and veneration, tension and distension

In the beginning, there was the wording of "We the People", who ordained and established the Constitution of the United States in six articles, and the seventh article was to lay in eternal rest by the grace of nine of the thirteen States. And thus the Sovereign proclaimed, let there be "domestic Tranquility", "the common defence" as well as "Justice", "the general Welfare" and "the Blessings of Liberty" for the nation of America and generations of its "Posterity". For the Exodus had led Americans from the pharaohs of Europe to the shores of a Promised Land, where they fell into the bonds of tyranny

DOI: 10.4324/9781003203674-7

> imposed by an imperial Goliath, from which they rose through revolution to independence, only to be left then to wander through the wilderness. And so it had come that several Fathers of the Founding heeded the call to return to Philadelphia in an assembly that, they resolved, the people shall not look upon; and they reappeared with the New Covenant of vows and commandments of government framed; and these were presented to the States on a parchment, to which the people pledged their allegiance and to the Republic of, for and by the people for which it stands. Thereafter the Constitution and the Laws of the United States "shall be the supreme Law of the Land"; in the trinity of that government so consecrated for the New World Order, the legislative power "shall be vested in a Congress", the executive power in "a President", the judicial power in "one supreme Court"; and to the States shall be given "Full Faith and Credit"; and their citizens "shall be entitled to all Privileges and Immunities" of the several States; but a State shalt not "be deprived of its equal Suffrage in the Senate"; nor shall any person, "without due process of law", "be deprived of life, liberty and property" or the "pursuit of happiness"; and the Congress "shall make no Law" infringing on the freedoms of religion, speech, and assembly; nor shall it infringe on the "right of the people to keep and bear Arms"; and all powers "are reserved to the States" so long as they are not delegated to the United States, or prohibited to it or the States by the Constitution.
>
> And the past shall be a prologue.

The above narrative recounts the founding of the USA. It pays reference to the European colonization and settlement of North America that came to be dominated by Britain, the American War for Independence, the brief interregnum under the Articles of Confederation and its demise, the Constitutional Convention and its closed-door sessions, and the triumph of the US Constitution in the ratification debates in the early federal republic. It has dramatically abbreviated, exaggerated, and exalted, but not fabricated, the history of events. At the same time, it strings together constitutional referents in a roughly sequential order, starting with the preamble, followed by renowned verbatim fragments taken from the seven articles as well as some of the first ten amendments, while interweaving prominent bits of outer-constitutional sources: for example the Declaration of Independence (1776), the Great Seal of the United States (1782), the Gettysburg Address (1863), and the Pledge of Allegiance (late 1890s). This mock-biblical rendition truncates many details, omits even more, including and especially defects, contradictions, but also injustices and atrocities except in allusion to those committed by "others". It thus represents a fairly accurate reproduction of long-standing and widespread understandings, perceptions, and recitals of the American Founding and the US Constitution over time. This point transports a compounded analytical argument related to institutional frameworks as well as path-dependent and multidimensional bounded developments. They have led in the USA to persistent, even growing constitutional ambiguity and distension despite, or rather on account of, constitutional contestation, veneration, and varieties of immanent interpretation.

Before exploring the evolution of the politics of the Constitution, several key premises and points from the previous sections should be recapitulated. The analytical framework and its theoretical foundations allow for an overarching inference of path dependencies of ideas and institutions that, evolving together, do not cause predestined outcomes, but rather generate feedback loops of causality and meaning over time. This inference applies further to the coupling of federalism and democracy, which variably interlinks different governmental structures, logics, and ideas. Specifically to the US founding and Constitution, the third chapter on constitutional text immanence as regulative idea retraced, assessed, and conceptualized a compound puzzle piece. It entangles for its part the formative institutionalized settings in the early USA and their dynamic evolution with ideational orientations. These settings included, for example: local self-government; an exceptionally rapid increase in mass enfranchisement attached to property ownership including over *people*; widespread practices in constitution and covenant making and interpreting; and the coupling of egalitarianism to both *popular and state* sovereignty (i.e. equal people *and* equal states). These institutional settings also included religious institutions and dynamics, including processes of increasingly personalized interactions with *Scripture* and the attenuation of social hierarchy and control. What emerged was a comparatively early onset of compounded economic, social, and political leveling. This appears to have been so much the case that not even the American Revolution triggered principled or popular threats to the established sanctity of private property (the concern was rather how to protect it) otherwise so typical to the disruption of political order witnessed in revolutions in the world later and even earlier in the 17th-century English case.

From the latter case emerged, in turn, popular sovereignty out of a contingent contestation between King and Parliament. Here wider political dynamics were unleashed when the idea was taken seriously *and* literally, thus becoming partially "emptied" of original political intentions and yet "filled" or extended with new meaning. Popular sovereignty was transplanted to early colonial America to a new, evolving institutional context. This also illustrates regulative ideas and their related dynamics. A regulative idea, in short, was conceived functionally as an ideational construct that provides orientation – for action, interaction, decision and sense making – has institutional underpinnings and evolves out of a particular institutional context, but can change over time. Furthermore, the multilayered and many-sided "constitutional quandary" in founding the USA and its Constitution revealed the entanglement of *the* two exceptional institutional legacies of the American Constitution, the first modern federal republic for one and the only modern constitution to include and perpetuate the institution of slavery for another, with ramifications for decades, even centuries to come.

In revisiting the Constitutional Convention and constitutional debates, an obvious but easily overlooked pattern becomes apparent. Aside from the different and intensely contested views in the constitutional debates, a rather broad consensus on several general principles can be identified. This can be specified further as a *manifold consensus*: a *positive* federal republic, generally self-rule friendly, private-property sanctifying, and an individual *and* community liberty consensus; a *negative* consensus concerning government as necessary evil and the mutual fear of threat to order, life, liberty, and property posed by despots or masses; a consensus on a seemingly self-evident need for a constitution and a union in the first place; a most obvious, usually taken-for-granted, consensus implied by what was mostly missing, such as proposals for a dissolution of the states into a centralized unitary one, a reinstallation of some form of monarchy, or a disaggregation into "stateless" societies of collective-communal orders based also on common resource and property sharing. There had emerged thus a quite *restricted* scope of imaginably legitimate alternatives. This manifold consensus may seem unsurprising given the price paid for independence and the vested interest in its preservation. However, it also suggests that certain default settings were already prevalent and seemingly self-evident – in short: an established *institutional-ideational box*. This box still contained many possible options. Debate revolved around how to appropriately secure the principles and promises of the American Revolution and their implications for organizing government. In other words, the manifold consensus among the constitutional contestants entailed a general preference for "continuing the business they started", and thus for a constitutional (re-)experiment in (con-)federated and republican limited government within an already familiar laboratory.

It was the *submission to* colonial rule and to the King that was overthrown through independence. It was not a disposal of the monarchy or a conquest over the colonizers, but rather a divorce from them. The split may appear spectacular. But the American break with the past was more dramatic than drastic. Many institutional legacies from England and the colonial era found more continuity through reform, adaptation, and translation than by radically new inventions. Institutions and governmental features already established in England and at the time of drafting the US Constitution, and persisting in the US polity ever since, are numerous: the rule of law with statutory and common law, assemblies elected by simple majority in single-member districts and endowed with the "power of the purse", strong bicameralism, an extent of parliamentary control over the executive but without a confidence relationship between the chief executive and the majority in the lower house,[1] multilevel government, even the very demarcation of the original states' boundaries based on English colonial charter ones. Yet the fact that the endeavor in independence, which could have gone awry but ultimately went the rebels' way and the window of opportunity it opened for forging a "new world order", made for a powerful success story. Thus enter a first factor contributing to the reverence of the US Constitution, which eventually came to embody a profoundly revered American Revolution and its manifold legacy.

The adoration of the founding and constitutional veneration

The mere fact of gaining independence can be seen to transmute into the proof of a number of things. The past accomplishment of American independence has been able to serve as a demonstration of the resolve and rightfulness of the revolution, whether recalled without probabilistic and counterfactual thinking, but even more so *with it*, that is by weighing its own collective achievement against the odds in comparison with the far higher incidence of the failures of others as demonstrated in the past and repeatedly as time goes on. Moreover, a socially constructed "own" successful past – even though it inevitably becomes that of increasingly distant ancestors – could provide or be viewed as providing further grounds for justifying the established order.

From the early republic into the 19th century, and into the present, the legacy of independence has provided ongoing assurance in good things like the perceived rectitude of the principles of liberty and equality. American independence could further substantiate an ambivalent, though outlandish thing like the mythological folklore envisioning the divine "providence" cast over the USA, especially when later "manifestations of destiny" putatively revealed themselves, as in the westward expansion over the rest of the continent between Canada and Mexico, and beyond. At the same time, the legacy of independence by revolution long served an abhorrently perverse thing: the tautological rationale by which a lack of upheaval by slaves as well as the defeat of the revolts that did occur[2] was used and abused by many as proof of slaves' insufficient resolve to gain liberty. Moreover, slavery and the looming possibility of slave revolts provided a constant threat to southern slaveholders, among them Thomas Jefferson, James Madison, and George Washington, many of whom must have been aware of their own tyranny and every right to be despised by slaves. Slavery also gave a living and proximate reminder to *all* Americans of what it meant to be (un)free and thus a reinforcing acknowledgment of the "Blessings of Liberty" bestowed upon the white "Posterity" by the American Revolution (Furstenberg 2006; on the similar effect in colonial Virginia, see Morgan 1972). Reinforcement of appreciation for the humane principles of liberty and equality in the early federal republic unfolded, not despite, but *in connection with*, superlative inhumanity.

From the previous points follow an important conclusion. The institutionalization of a compounded set of institutional and ideational factors could strengthen the perceived exceptional legacy of the revolution as well as the need to continue defending it in the early federal republic onward – that is based on factors related to the operation of institutions as much as actors' thinking about them in their respective present contexts and in view of their origins from the past. A constitution, in turn, that could serve as a framework to secure a continuing legacy of the American Revolution – including liberty, and popular and state equality with order under limited government – could receive all the more so its further legitimation, no less so when the constitution also came to *symbolize* the continuation of this compounded legacy.

A civil-religious strand of legitimation to the revolution and the Constitution was alluded to above as the mythology of American providence. One may recall again the early pervasiveness of notions like divine fate, "city on the hill", "covenants", or the "new Jerusalem". Their interlinkage was explored previously with several religion-related institutions, practices, and dynamics of colonial America and the early USA, particularly in the context of local and state covenants, personalized interactions with *Scripture*, and social leveling in local communities. They reveal particular *institutional-ideational* underpinnings and implications for political development. The USA from the outset was not only highly decentralized, but also in its formative years – despite various flaws and egregious violations of its own principles – exceptionally democratic for the time. Given also that it was not a theocracy nor even had *a* state church, the early political usage of religious-type speech by political leaders could hardly be construed as an attempt to evade hard sanctions from *the* church or a religious council, though perhaps from church personnel and especially churchgoing voters. The prevalence of religious-type allusions and allegories should be conceived rather in their embeddedness in a *political* dimension of communication through a *popular* set of ideas and terminology for interactions not only among elites but also the public at large as well as constituents who were literate, if not fluent, in that language.

On the surface it is already easy to identify multiple, demigod-like patriarchal referents: from "Pilgrim Fathers" to "Founding Fathers", from the "Father of the Declaration of Independence" (for Jefferson), the "Father of Our (or His) Country" (for Washington) to the "Father of the Constitution" (for Madison),[3] and thus a quasi-deification or certainly adoration of the founders. Of further importance here, and in multifaceted respect, are the copious references and allusions to Moses. With his character associated with *exodus* and the *liberation* of a nation, explicit invocations of Moses permeated the founding era – for example the "pilgrims" and "puritans", in escaping persecution to found the Plymouth and Massachusetts Bay colonies, or George Washington as general in the War for Independence and first chief executive under the new Constitution (Hay 1969). The invocations traverse generations of political leaders like Abraham Lincoln (in connection with the Civil War to end slavery), Martin Luther King Jr. (in the struggle to end segregation and racial inequality) and Barack Obama, who referred to the civil rights' leaders as the "Moses generation" and his own commitment to serve the "Joshua generation" (see e.g. Murphy 2011), that is the one to complete the unfinished journey to the promised land of equality. However, this point of reference extends further and deeper to the founding and the Constitution.

Viewed through a institutional-theoretical lens, the question arises as to how Moses got "locked in" to the formative institutional-ideational space. The nexus is not only informative, but also pertinent in several regards. In light of all the extensive religious reference making, embedded no less in such a religiously charged socio-political context of the founding era, all the more puzzling should seem the lesser to marginal role played by the New Testament messiah-figure Jesus. Surely the latter's teachings and actions could have equally lent themselves to invocation in the context of liberty and the coming of a new world order. The charismatic orator's words and deeds were, however, unequivocally documented by others (i.e. the Gospels). Moses on the other hand signified both a liberator *and* a giver of written laws, *the* original legislator and servant of the law. Other factors central to this parable were that Moses stuttered, or had some form of speech impairment, was apparently self-conscious of this,[4] was thus hesitant to assume the responsibility to verbally promulgate divine laws, proceeded to negotiate with the Almighty, to which the latter, at first infuriated, then *consented* and prescribed a division of responsibilities, with Moses' brother primarily responsible for continuing oral traditions, and Moses charged with presenting laws written in a newly invented alphabet for the Hebrew language.[5] This still left Moses with the duty to read them aloud to the people who were as of yet illiterate in a new alphabet. But all the better to have them judiciously communicated by a modest speaker. For charismatic orators can be great communicators, but behind great orations may hide demagogues who can seduce and incite the masses. Unlike fiery speeches, or burning bushes, written laws can enlighten without blinding. These could pose potentially important post-liberation lessons, especially for drafters of a constitution who are profoundly concerned with re-establishing and maintaining order based on rules *and* the consent of the governed, but not on their mass influence and control.

The parables and their symbolism, including cautionary implications they had, apparently were well familiar to and rather cherished by many political leaders of the US founding. Furthermore, the invocations and recitals of the Israelite liberation narrative and its linkage with the formation of a covenant had appealed, in multiple senses, to colonialists and US citizens in the early federal republic, not least in areas heavily influenced by Puritan and covenant theology (see e.g. Dreisbach 2011; Gorski 2017: 37–82; Hay 1969; Wald and Calhoun-Brown 2014: 43ff.). None of this proves on its own a cause of one particular outcome. It does however provide explanatory indicators of a *context of causality*. That context included religious parables, no less ones that were read by many as truth, even literally, that permeated political discourse and concrete institutions (like "covenants"). The context also includes: *sources* from which political leaders were taking cues, whether as inspiration on account of socialization in churches, or simply their "beliefs"; *the recipients* (e.g. citizens) of the cues they were providing in mind; and the wider, already evolved *ideational-institutional box and space of meanings* within which such invocations, representations, and legitimations (some temporal, some transcendental, some both) were transpiring. Two additional factors of antecedent development and one of the immediate context of the early USA under the "new" Constitution warrant brief attention.

Without revisiting the religious origins of the (or some) colonies or the "Great Awakening", the above-depicted Moses lock-in entails rather an interlocking one, also with antecedent developments. First, the Reformation in Europe had already revived the Old Testament and, in connection with the dogma of *sola scriptura* and practices of personal Bible study of the New Testament, the dedication to learning also from Moses' Laws, their meaning and implications to the present political and social world (see e.g. Mitchell 1992). Second, the Great Awakening of the early to mid-18th century in America had contributed to considerable disruption (e.g. of local social hierarchies), but it also reinforced and energized evangelicalism across the colonies. In sum, Puritan and Covenant theology churches were most affected. They were concentrated in New England. That region was, in turn, *the* solid base of the Federalists, who persisted to act like a political party in denial during the first decade of government under the new US Constitution. Thus enters the immediate context under the new Constitution. The adoration of the founders and increasingly of George Washington as the "Moses of America" – meanwhile serving as the head of the executive branch – may have reflected a wider common pattern of communication, representation, and legitimation. It was also a pattern that former Antifederalists, turning by the late 1790s into a Democrat-Republican party, incidentally with Madison now a convert, could likely see right through.

Whether or to what extent Federalists (whether stemming from Puritan backgrounds or not) actually believed in the American providence and their station in life to fulfill it, need not be answered here. Nor is it necessary to determine here if they instrumentalized such beliefs and ideas in order to mobilize support for the Constitution they forged and for their own political program to bring a more national union to life. Perhaps another motivation or strategy was to discredit their popular-democratic oriented opponents, who were growing in strength in the run-up to the 1800 elections, in which Jefferson would ultimately win the presidency. It may also very well be the case that the Federalists refused to accept or simply could not grasp yet that they were a political party.

Against this backdrop, the adoration of the Constitution, the Founding Fathers, the framers, and the "American Moses" Washington takes on a more multifaceted, yet contingent, character. Adoration and quasi-providential invocations could serve as political strategy, as well as justification and (self-)reassurance in light of the uncertainty of the state of the Union.[6] This connects yet again to the providence cum allegorical Moses pattern. One lesson learned (emulated, used as inspiration, or similar) from Scripture was the significance of the repetition and recital of the inherited legacy of liberation. This should not only serve as a commemorative celebration, but also, indeed especially, the political consolidation of the established order. A concrete manifestation is found already on the Liberty Bell hung in Independence Hall (where the Constitutional Convention met), inscribed with "Proclaim Liberty throughout all the land and to all its inhabitants". It is an iconic phrase on a soon-to-become-mythical symbolic emblem[7] in the USA. It is also a direct quote from Leviticus 25:10, the context of which is the commandment, promulgated by Moses to the "chosen nation", to celebrate the gift of liberation every fifty years, also as a way of renewing the covenant that "constitutionalized" liberty. This points to several relevant facets. One is the blending of the instruments of the republic and its government with its symbols over time.[8] Another is the usage by political leaders in the early federal republic of such ritual performance and reiterated invocations of the constructed noble past for the purpose of "people making" (Smith 2001). Another is more immediately relevant to the new party in power as of 1800.

The Revolution of 1800 produced a resounding defeat for the Federalists, but it also inaugurated the more plebiscitary election of the president, a Democrat-Republican majority in Congress, and opened a path for converting their views into government practice. It was a peaceful transition in the end, despite tremendous political tensions, and the Revolution transpired under the same constitutional framework no less (see e.g. Ackerman 2005). All the more interesting is that the pattern of reverence and adoration would persist, as would the Constitution itself (see e.g. Brennan 2017: 939ff.), instead of formal constitutional change. Nor was a process unleashed of discrediting the US Constitution that, for the Democrat-Republicans and former Antifederalists in particular, had clearly represented a partisan affair and not an outright equation with American Revolution legacy. Unlike the Federalists who emphasized the national union, the rule-of-law, and the constraints on popular democracy, Democrat-Republicans should have likewise been expected to oppose the exaltation of political leaders, especially of presidents, as well as of the Constitution – an instrument of government, not a sacred document – as rather elitist tendencies evocative of royalty and thus incompatible with republican liberty.[9]

For a variety of reasons, the new President Jefferson and the Democrat-Republicans in Congress appeared instead to come to terms with the Constitution. For one, the fact that they managed to gain predominance at the federal level could actually reduce their misgivings about the Constitution and shift their attention instead toward a focused critique of the previous administration, its centralizing programs, and thus attempts to overturn *them*, not the Constitution. Consequently, the Democrat-Republicans set a precedent for transitions in government in a modern representative democracy. Moreover, the emerging party was diverse and included many supporters of the Constitution (even its "Father" Madison), but who preferred a stricter interpretation that placed emphasis on states, but also decentralized government in general, as well as popular sovereignty and individual liberty (see e.g. Dunn 2004; Schoenbachler 1998). It could thus be entirely useful to uphold the Constitution and govern according to their popular program within the constitutional framework.

Applying a stricter interpretation of the Constitution would be anything but difficult given the ambivalence of multiple constitutional provisions from the outset. After all, much if not most of the Federalist, national-union type intentions were literally detectable only outside (most notably in the *Federalist Papers*) rather than in the constitutional text itself. To govern accordingly would imply all the more so a need to refrain from delegitimizing the Constitution. *Using the Constitution*, through interpretation and respective application, *against the Constitution* (i.e. the Federalist version) offered multiple advantages: for partisan and strategic interest-based ends, but also as a strategy pursued to achieve principle-based ones, including a different version of federal democracy. The already widespread adoration of the Founders,[10] commemorations of the Revolution and recitals of the founding, the linking of the latter to the Constitution, and even a national public holiday on Washington's birthday not only ceased to pose a threat to Democrat-Republicans or their political and partisan programs, but could be tolerated and even supported (see e.g. Hay 1969: 789ff.). The veneration of the Constitution, underpinned by religious-providential and American Revolution-invoking legitimation, could also help stabilize the constitutional order as a safeguard for state autonomy. The same applied for the Southern States especially concerning the institution of slavery, with regard to which, incidentally, during the antebellum years political references to Scripture

– including from the very same chapter of Leviticus quoted on the Liberty Bell – were commonly invoked to claim that states' rights and slavery were constitutionally but also providentially sanctioned.[11] In addition, several challenges could underline the urgency to carry on with the business of government: for instance the expansion of US territory, which increased immediately under the new administration (e.g. the Louisiana Purchase) and elicited more responses by the US government to secure borders as well as monitor and steer the settlement and development of its own republican governments in the territories.

The critical juncture of 1800 ushered in major changes and implications for American political development, to be sure. However, this Revolution turned nothing around in the Constitution. There was no constitutional redrafting, nor even one single revision of the horizontal or vertical division of powers.[12] Formal constitutional change did not happen, even though it should have been expected, for example given the profound prior opposition and contestation of the Constitution and of the Federalists first decade of governing under it as well as the rather permissive conditions for change. Instead, *a pattern of constitutional change without changing the Constitution* set in that has continued into the present.

Constitutional contestation and change in the USA transpire predominantly, *almost solely*, through the politics of the Constitution without constitutional amendments. Contestation unfolds by democratic and party political or federal and multilevel dynamics, or both, and in response to and interaction with societal dynamics. Critical elections generating unified government may facilitate extensive changes. But their translation into actual change – whether to fulfill mandates or meet new public policy challenges – follows respective interpretations of the Constitution in the strict sense instead of amendments to secure the constitutional changes pursued or achieved in the broad sense. This generates a pattern of continuity in the sense of persisting constitutional text, but also of heightened veneration paired with distending ambiguity. The Constitution can appear all the more legitimate as it can seemingly uphold the legacy of independence and the revolution(s) by accommodating such widely different readings: from a union of states or a union of one people, as a charge for government or for limiting it, for limiting the federal government or the states. The different readings are engaged in variable intensity at different times and often at the same time.

Immanent interpretation between change and continuity, contestation and impoverishment

The elevation of a constitution to an adored and venerated embodiment can help consolidate the legitimacy of the Constitution itself in the strict sense, and of the polity in the broad sense. The US Constitution would come to be perceived as encompassing the revolutionary principles of American independence and a variety of immanent constitutional principles – e.g. democracy, federalism, separation of powers, limited government, and individual liberties and rights. They are implied and in parts literally expressed or legible based on concrete wordings. The US

Constitution does not realize any of its principles of course. But it can be *read* as having done so as well as implying or meaning an embodiment of substantially different governmental orders at once. In addition to the veneration of the founding, the Founders, Independence, and Revolution, this development was also enabled through the conversion of large political changes into constitutional ones. They started to be integrated, "read" into, and superimposed upon the same constitutional text practically from the outset. The dynamics of constitutional politics evolving in a feedback loop of multiple meanings and within the mostly same formal framework over time have continued, though with intermittent disruptions, into the present.

Integration with interpretation would turn out to be the case already for early notable critical junctures like the "Jeffersonian" (1800) and the later "Jacksonian" (1828) democratic "revolutions", as well as later ones like the New Deal of the 1930s, desegregation and the Civil Rights movement of the 1950s, and the New Federalism of the 1980s. Each of these would have or coincide with implications on the further development of the state, federalism, and democracy at work, yet with the persistence of the predominantly same formal constitution in writing. Drawing from Corwin on the transformation of the US Constitution from "instrument" to "symbol", the Constitution became by the early 19th century a powerful source of taboos for judging acts and policies of government, reflected in the critique by a senator in 1811 (merely one decade after the Revolution of 1800) that could have just as well been lodged nowadays:

> many of the various constructions given to the Constitution are the result of the belief that it is *absolutely perfect*. It has become so extremely fashionable to eulogize the Constitution, whether the object of the eulogy is *the extension or the contraction of the powers* of the government.
>
> (Corwin 1936: 1077; emphasis added)

Weighing new political proposals vis-à-vis the Constitution is inherent to the principles and dynamics of constitutionalism in general. There are nonetheless two distinctive facets in the USA illustrated by the excerpt above. One is the supposed equation of the US Constitution with perfection. It had already been elevated to the sublime within a short amount of time, and taken on the fundamental character of constraining what may pass for legitimate government, in an almost polar opposite position from its contestation in the ratification debates and in the first decade of government under it. This critical observation may capture the "actual beliefs" of the time. It may also indicate a pattern of expressed ideas strategically employed in pursuit of political interests, many of which apparently involve appeals to the same "perfect" source even when they are diametrically opposed – e.g. limiting (*contraction*) or expanding (*extension*) a branch or level of government, accommodating an augmented plebiscitary and popular-democratic oriented president, or a thrust to safeguard states from federal encroachments. These and numerous other similar instances already there in the 19th century demonstrate an institutionalized constitutional veneration as well as the use, and an abundance of mutual politically lodged indictments of "abuse", of the Constitution (see Corwin 1936; also e.g. Grey 1984; Wofford 1964). They suggest an early lock-in of political contestation bound to constitutional interpretation without formal constitutional change.

The exaltation of the US Constitution early on becomes an *institutionalized pattern of politics*, of political contestation, representation, and legitimation. This pattern can be spurred by adaptation strategies to disguise self-interests, but also by the dynamics of taking ideas seriously as well as literally. Constitutionally charged politics become invigorated no less on account of the democratic and federal institutional parameters of the polity as well as their further democratization over time – whether by increasingly de facto popularly elected presidents, elected representatives and senators, governors and state assemblies or citizens and reform movements. Constitutional principles and provisions can be invoked to discredit opponents or their ideas. They may just as well be taken wholeheartedly, seriously, and even literally, internalized as ideas regulating the interpretation of the Constitution weighed against political practice, by which the detection of injustices or inadequacies invite if not demand reform in order to bring practice in line with the respective, constitutionally immanent principle. Consequently, diverse policy issues wind up being entangled with polity ones bound to the Constitution and its interpretation.

Moreover, text immanence as interpretive orientation – a highly personal, individualized, leveled, and egalitarian one – had already been institutionalized in colonial America and the early federal republic, precisely with regard to interactions with *sacred* texts and *covenants*. Surely the precedents establishing judicial review by the federal courts and especially the Supreme Court have been pivotal in multiple regards and almost from the outset. The acceptance of judicial review does not contradict, but rather fundamentally shows, the institutionalization of the US Constitution as a closed document and a complete text, even though it is and was not complete,[13] nor a sort of destiny. It could only become construed so by its being treated that way over time. The closure and consecration as "supreme law" render it, in turn, wide open for textual *interpretive* contestations, adaptations, and renewals, by courts but also political actors, parties, and citizens.[14]

Matters become even more complicated and distended on account of recurring visitations to the original constitution, with searches for intents, purposes, and meanings. The impulse to do is reinforced by the venerated stature of the Constitution as manifold repository of immanent legacies, ideas, principles, and rules. Along these lines, constitutional text fragments, for example single articles, amendments, clauses therein, are viewed in later and altered contexts. Antecedent informal changes become integrated or superimposed upon the Constitution for one, and the terminology may persist but their meanings have changed – whether regarding "power", "commerce", "the right to bear arms", "an establishment of religion", "cruel and unusual punishment", or "the general welfare", to name a few (see e.g. Munzer and Nickel 1977; Rakove 1997). Nevertheless, those original words can be strictly read and construed to mean what one thinks they mean now – i.e. at any number of "nows" in the sequence of political development – or what one thinks they meant "then".[15] Consequently, a multitude of constituents can see in the same perfect source an array of widely different things. Meaning, in the end, necessarily involves an attribution. Such attribution is not solely determined, but complexly bound with historically evolved and socially constructed institutional settings, which likewise evolve in tensions between change and continuity.

An exalted US Constitution appears to have transformed into a repository for the assessment of meaning. Its formal change has tended to become off limits and instead the *sacred covenant* rather subject to interpretation by a multiplicity of constituent units and a constituent multitude. The result is not immunization against change, but rather compounding institutional and ideational paths that are bounded by and, in further evolution, bounding for the Constitution and the US polity on the whole. The evolved extension of the US Constitution – from instrument to stabilized document, venerated symbol, and worshipped scripture – contributes to entrenching the framework of government as well as patterns of textual orientation to interpreting it. In addition to high formal amendment thresholds, constitutional veneration and related constitutional politics and interpretation seem to reinforce the political "psychological" barriers to changing the US Constitution as well (see esp. Zink and Dawes 2016). Accordingly, to demand an overhaul of the US Constitution could amount to desecration, not just of the document itself but also the legacies and various promises of the founding the document protects. Consequently, deep and wide deference for the Constitution promotes and bolsters the formal *constitutional* status quo. This does not make altering the *political* status quo impossible, nor far-reaching changes unattainable.

Political developments on the contrary can and do change the US Constitution in the broad sense. This is evident in incremental changes in federal and democratic government as well as later "revolutions" like the New Deal and the Civil Rights movement in the 20th century. Both gradual and extensive adaptations may become triggered by critical elections, political mobilization, shifting modes of government, as well as litigation and constitutional interpretation in line with judicial review, which become integrated into the US Constitution in the broad sense (see e.g. Ackerman 2007; Strauss 1996; Tushnet 2015). Nevertheless, practically any change has to fulfil criteria of constitutionality, whether implicitly or explicitly, broadly or strictly interpreted. Numerous historical events and conflicts disclose the inaccuracies and inadequacies of the US Constitution time and again, so that the pursuit of certain changes could be expected to pursue changing the Constitution too. But unlike the constitutions of many other modern countries and even of the US states, amendments have been comparatively seldom pursued and even more rarely achieved. One reason lies again in the ability of myriad actors to interpret the Constitution so as to accommodate a wide spectrum of possible changes. Moreover, the institutional-ideational thinking in the box in constitutional politics and interpretation allows for regularly adapting and renewing the covenant without formally changing it. However, these dynamics have led over time to its *impoverishment*.

Extending and limiting the state and the states, and the immanent fragmentation of the polity, are facilitated by competing commitments to constitutional immanence, which can diminish or restrict the charge of governing to conform to a limited scope of constitutional readings. Under these evolved conditions, it has become entirely "normal" that proposals like the expansion of welfare programs or even the prohibition of child labor[16] hinge on whether they sufficiently pertain to matters of "interstate commerce" so as to conform to the wording of Congress's enumerated powers, whether gauged by the understandings of the framers, citizens at the time of ratification, or plain text, [17] rather than matters of realizing justice and equality.[18] Similar *limits* apply to recurring, indeed endless, contestations in the USA around women's reproduction rights and the myriad issues of market, financial, environmental, health care, and welfare regulations. They revolve around competing political, partisan, and principle-based ideas. Rules pertaining to the numerous policies and functions of modern government cannot be found in the Constitution explicitly, save in terms of the powers enumerated in 1789 and the individual rights and federal direct taxation added since. Political contestation, if not US government in general, ultimately depends on squaring political proposals and decisions with fragments of the Constitution, its implicit spirit or explicit text through one reading, or to oppose them with another reading.[19]

Constitutional amendments have occurred. However, the predominant pattern has been long periods of dormancy in formal constitutional revision – the current phase as of now lasting fifty years[20] (see e.g. Albert 2014). The first wave of formal constitutional change is especially notable, which did not come about until after the Civil War, and thus more than sixty years after the 12th Amendment (1804) or seventy years after the Bill of Rights (1791). Again, the "Reconstruction Amendments" (13th, 14th, and 15th) seemingly redefined or reconfirmed, depending on perspective, the nature of the Union as one extending beyond a compact of states, with direct application of citizen rights and protections throughout the USA (i.e. binding the federal or "national" level government and the states). For one though, these amendments were passed in the wake of the most drastic critical juncture since the War for Independence, but also under questionable constitutional conditions – i.e. imposed and in parts coerced upon occupied Southern States by a dominant Republican Party in power.[21] For another, it would still take decades for their intention or purpose to be fulfilled. Interpretation by various political actors, constituencies, state governments, and the Supreme Court could still apparently read continued racial segregation as constitutionally permissible (e.g. *Plessy v. Ferguson* (1896)), a precedent overturned, not by formal but rather interpretive revision or "restoration" (e.g. *Brown v. Board of Education* (1954)). For yet another, while these amendments settled several issues (e.g. the abolishment of slavery in the 13th Amendment and of the three-fifths clause in the 14th Amendment), the provisions on the whole reproduced the original character of vague, commandment-type provisions (e.g. "Congress shall have power to enforce … with appropriate legislation"). No further institutional specifications or adjustments were added then or later to those amendments, nor to other provisions such as the enumerated powers or the distribution of powers between branches or between levels of government.[22] Liberty and equality for instance is implied by the "spirit" of the Constitution. Its wording though could then and can now be read in much different directions:

equality of all citizens, but also states – indeed, *especially* for states, as "equal suffrage" in the original Constitution only comes up in reference to that of the states in the Senate (Art. 5); as a charge for the federal government to work towards these ends or to leave it mainly up to the states to do so; or the enshrinement of principles may be even read as the actualization of the respective principle itself.

An overarching pattern in the US polity can be captured as a complexly reinforcing institutional-ideational thinking in the box, and also in the domain of the politics of the Constitution. The Revolution of 1800, Jacksonian popular democracy, slavery, the Civil War, the success and failure of Reconstruction, the initial blockade of the New Deal reforms and the "switch" in the Supreme Court's decision making, or desegregation can be, and widely get, conceived as indications or "evidence" for the capacity for reform *within* the framework of the US Constitution. In other words, thinking in the box entails seeing phases of "bad politics" and multiple and repeated violations of its own constitutional principles as straying from the path, but which can be corrected precisely through bringing politics back in line with the Constitution, if only it were read and then abided by properly. Various adaptations become retrospectively conceived, even as actually implementing the original US Constitution. Rather than as merits of the Constitution, multiple changes and achievements could or rather should affirm constitutional inadequacies to which political actors adapted despite the Constitution.

What remains in place and can become overlooked, intensified, and bloated are multiple inherited legacies of ambivalence, ambiguity, and contradictions. They originate in an 18th-century context, in which constitutional authors as well as many consenters and dissenters (1) were not prepared for or did not yet foresee for example modern representative democracy, modern public administration, cooperative federalism, intergovernmental relations, and some form of state implementation of federal programs in numerous areas of public policy; (2) failed or did not bother to address for example judicial review of federal government laws and acts, rules or prohibition of secession, citizenship, immigration, or revenue sharing; (3) tried even to thwart for example political parties and popular democracy. Why almost none of these things[23] have come to be adopted into the written US Constitution, even though they have happened or developed over time, should seem puzzling, that is unless one takes the puzzle piece of politics of the Constitution and its evolution into account.

On the other hand, constitutional evolution in the USA has not been restricted to veneration and "worship" only. The secession of eleven states and the Civil War are perhaps the most obvious example. However, this is also exemplified by the second significant phase of formal constitutional change. In the early 20th century, and in a quite brief timespan, four amendments were ratified between 1913 and 1920, achieving the introduction of the federal income tax (16th), the direct election of senators (17th), the prohibition of alcohol (18th), and women's suffrage (19th). Unlike the first major and brief wave of formal constitutional change in the wake of the Civil War, this phase of political development reflects more a general thrust to *alter* rather than renew the original Constitution or bring politics back in line with supposedly original intents, purpose, or design. This shift in the path of development however winds up adding over time to constitutional distension as well as the reinforcement of the regulative idea of text immanence in the dynamics of constitutional interpretation.

These reforms were spearheaded by a diverse coalition of actors and parties in the context of surging anti-elitist, participatory-democratic populism movements, farmer alliances, a Populist Party, and a People's Party, among others (see e.g. Jörke and Selk 2017: 17–25; Lowndes 2017). The "Progressive era" reform movements also addressed a similarly diverse spectrum of social and democratic reforms including for more direct democracy and more social regulation, for example on alcohol, gambling, monopolies, and other societal "vices" in the late 19th and early 20th century (see e.g. Andersen 2012; Persily 1997). Variegated groups, parties, and movements followed, some concurring and many opposing reform aspirations, and their impact[24] had likewise disparate and in parts contradicting implications for the further development of American democracy, federalism, and the state (see e.g. Skowronek, Engel, and Ackerman 2016). Depending on the focus, a share of progressives and populists especially could be construed as the continuation or reemergence of the 'other Founders' Antifederalist and Democrat-Republican vein of constitutional political legacy (see e.g. Cornell 1990): for example emphasizing popular sovereignty and antagonism to elite government.

However, one significant strand of the Progressive era, the evangelical movements that resurged after the early to mid-19th-century revivals (e.g. Second and Third Great Awakenings), not only turned outward to reform society. Much of their reform advances were explicitly *against* the Founders' Constitution. They targeted particularly the "devilish" and corrupting features they saw in the Consttution, and sought their correction, as visible in the slavery abolition movement and later the women's suffrage movement, the temperance movement, and reform efforts against corruption, greed and materialism, and for property restrictions, antipoverty, and welfare measures (Compton 2014; see also e.g. Sweeney 2005). Thus emerges an intriguing contradiction, or rather several that would develop over time. These reform politics of formal constitutional change, if not invented, surely invigorated the idea and respective interpretive pattern of a "living" constitution (ibid.). This antecedent development would prove crucial for the socio-economic progressivism of the New Deal constitutional moment and its ensuing changes to government without amending the Constitution. On the other hand, the social-political conservative strand of the progressive era, particularly the evangelical emphasis *also* on morality policies, would become largely dislocated from the socio-economic one.[25]

As of the mid-20th century, support for conservative morality policies has tended rather to coincide with opposition to federal government and especially to "liberal"-progressive policies including social-welfare programs, and support *for* the original US Constitution (see e.g. Compton 2014; Conlan 1998; Walker 1996). This development has also coincided with party realignment in the USA, changes in judicial review restricting the scope and application of certain federal authorities, as well as the corresponding dynamics of party competition and political contestation (see e.g. Clayton and Pickerill 2004; Rappaport 1999; Rubenfeld 2002). With the onset of the New Federalism in the 1980s and the "devolution revolution" in the 1990s (see e.g. Conlan and de Chantal 2001; Moynihan and Ingraham 2010; West 1990), *originalism* and commitment to strict interpretation of *the Founders' constitution* has become a dominant orientation for social-political conservatism, but also for others supporting "small" limited *federal* government and emphasizing individual liberty and responsibility, state autonomy, and multiple forms of federal deregulation and decentralization. Thus reenter the peculiar synthesis of a Federalist and Antifederalist constitution.

Constitutional immanence and the competing constitutions

Political change to the Constitution in the broad sense but under a predominantly unchanged constitutional framework in the strict sense manifests in the (neo-)originalist political orientation. It (re-)emerged at least partially in reaction to the "living constitution" as of the mid-20th century. However, instead of altering the text itself to incorporate numerous and extensive changes, democratic and federal governance corresponding to the living constitution likewise built on constitutional interpretation: for example the "looser" interpretation of constitutional provisions like rights encoded in the amendments, the enumerated and implied powers of Congress, or presidents' democratic mandates. Cooperative federalism, which often turned coercive, the expansion of federal governance steered by Congress and President, as well as the growth of the American state and states have adapted the Constitution without formally changing it, thus keeping the original one alive. Hence, the peculiar synthesis of different constitutions works multiple ways. This synthesis does not entail a reconciliation, but rather multiple and variably evolved competing constitutions. Their juxtaposition into a dualism is still possible, but difficult because the Federalist and Antifederalist constitutions have morphed and even compounded. For instance, the modern, more national-Union and living-constitution orientation, rather affinitive to a Federalists' vision of the Constitution, came to incorporate a crucial element of Jeffersonianism, namely the idea that constitutions are "for the living", while the past and the "dead" should not unduly govern the present (see e.g. Goodheart 2013). Inversely, originalistic orientations drawing literally from the Constitution revive the Federalists' text but with many implications affinitive to Antifederalist-type restriction on federal government and support for states' rights. The politics of the Constitution, as a dimension of political development stemming from competing constitutional politics, provide for a major contribution to intensifying the *fragmentation* of the US polity into the present.

The original Constitution for establishing a national union of a compound republic can be conceived, from a general retrospective view, as the same original Constitution for uniting a nation but safeguarding states and limiting the federal government. However, such a composite understanding, interpretation, or belief in the origins of the US Constitution rests on the partial confirmation and partial contradiction of several constitutional-political legacies. There has been *synthesis* – of popular sovereignty, state sovereignty, majoritarian democracy, individual liberty – as much as *omission* – of manifold contestations and contradictions attached to the Constitution from its very beginning, not least its anti-democratic components. Processes of taking constitutional ideas and text strategically, seriously, or literally over time, and various motives simultaneously at different times build upon multiple antecedent developments. They include far-reaching political changes which became accommodated by and integrated in the formal constitutional framework, or more precisely, by myriad collective and individual political actors and at multiple times.

Constitutional ambiguity has derived from multidimensional – different federal, democratic, temporal – developments between change and continuity, contestation and disruptions, adaptations and veneration. Politics revolving around constitutional text immanence reproduces, yet constricts and decontextualizes, the US Constitution. Wider political development in constitutional political discourse has also revealed *impoverishment*, with one such trajectory of change broadly heading toward intensified emphasis on *individual rights* and seeing them as embedded in the US Constitution and derived from the American Revolution (see esp. Glendon 1991; Roelofs 1992). In the present tense, state and federal government acts are increasingly and frequently contested, from various directions of the political spectrum, and with appeal to explicit rights of "the people" but conceived as "individual" rights that limit multiple levels of government.[26] This pattern may seemingly confirm over-generalized concepts of the US polity, its system of government, and society as heavily slanted toward individual liberty and liberalism from the beginning. This inference is not utterly wrong but biased and deficient, and grossly oversimplifies the past as well as the present (see e.g. Smith 1993). To be sure, individual rights are anything but a "poor" thing. Impoverishment here insinuates neither right nor wrong, but rather implicates a part of the evolved conundrum or trap of fragmentation limiting the state in the USA.

Constitutional interpretation oriented to the text itself and grounded in appeal or "belief" in the legacies of the founding are usually far removed from and diminishing of the context of both Federalist and Antifederalist liberal and republican understandings. Theirs were certainly constrained by the context and horizons of the time yet, in many ways compared to the present, more ambiguous and complex, and variably compounded with civic responsibilities, commonweal and community orientations, and thus an even larger diversity of ideational origins of the US founding (see e.g. Bailyn 1992; Hemberger 1990; LaCroix 2010; Shain 1994; Shklar 1991; Wood 1969). From this it does not follow that one should pursue a more faithful realization of the Founders' ideas and understandings (*whose* would one adopt anyway?), but rather an indication of how institutional-ideational thinking in the box has evolved. An irony becomes apparent when constitutional politics grounds itself precisely in the interpretation of the original constitution that has come to compound "We the People" and "Union of States" dispositions, but which is bereft of their original context. That context encompassed: different ideational underpinnings but also intense contestations; a host of contradictions, not least of democracy and federalism; and multiple, patently obvious, egregious violations of its own principles, *especially* of liberty and equality. This renders it puzzling as to why all the appeal to the text itself with the invocation of the supposedly binding supremacy of its supposed origins became such an institutionalized pattern of politics.

Literal and text immanent interpretation of the Constitution is not only a current pattern of politics. It is a long-established one, intertwined with developments reaching far back to the founding era. The early *ideational and institutional context* had included a range of shared beliefs and practices of a highly individualized, personalized, and egalitarian interaction with *scriptures* of religiously and politically sublime texts. Exalting and religious-type invocations, representations, and legitimations were part and parcel of political discourse – and conflict[27] – from the outset. Furthermore, the institutionalization of an adoration of the founding and the elevation of the Constitution to a closed, perfect, complete, and sacred text have likewise evolved from the outset. At multiple points in the sequence of development though, constitutional veneration resulted not from explicit intention, but by implication, that is, on account of adaptation strategies[28] that helped to reinforce the rigidity of the formal constitutional status quo. Accordingly, constitutional faithfulness can become both elevated and flattened to textual faithfulness. Furthermore, *literal* translation of foundational texts offers one way of taking them seriously or of renewing them, for example through re-reading and reciting the covenant. High reverence tends to elevate the covenant's legitimacy and acceptance of its binding authority. This may lead, on the one hand, to inhibition against replacing or even revising it at all as well as against "contaminating" it with outside sources. On the other hand, believing in and reading the Constitution become not just warranted, but a constitutional part of citizenship. Moreover, the bounded evolution of constitutional politics in the USA connects precisely to egalitarianism, with constitutional faith in general and literalism in particular providing an easily, directly accessible *and popular* layperson's mode of interaction with the Constitution without reliance on elite authority, whether of the political, judicial, administrative, or scholarly type.

The surge in originalist cum literalist approaches to the US Constitution in recent decades has met with critique as well as attempts to debunk it as conservative political intention or ideology camouflaged in constitutional-judicial disguise (see e.g. Berman 2009; Tushnet 1985). The critique surely applies to certain, if not multiple, actors, instances, and motives. Nevertheless, originalistic orientations make up a salient and recurring part of constitutional political contestation throughout American political development. Ideas and invoking literal referents to substantiate them may be taken from a foundational *text*, taken out of *context*, or be "invented" in a context contingent on a particular dispute. Ideas and ideational orientations evolve dynamically in interplay with institutional settings and actor constellations, and in different directions. Taking them seriously does not necessarily preclude strategy or purpose – i.e. when the idea, or interpretation of the text read as capturing it, regulates individual or collective action toward further actualization of the idea or principle.[29] Critical analyses and political contestants may detect the sort of agenda that can be hidden behind a particular type of constitutional-political pattern. But the problem or dilemma seems more fundamental, indeed constitutional. The politics of the Constitution and adaptation through constitutional interpretation can *restrict* patterns of politics and governing in the USA. Moreover, respective approaches come from both sides – the condensation to *two* sides reflecting another multifaceted problem constitutive of the US polity – of the political spectrum.

Constitutional change can be exercised through interpretation committed to actualizing promises of liberty *and* equality deemed immanent in principles and even literal wordings like "general welfare" or "more perfect Union". A corresponding politics of the Constitution may appear more prone to political activism than originalistic, strict interpretations. However, and as critics already point out, the common notion that originalism and strict interpretations serve political restraint and constitutional preservation is misguided. They can prove at least as equally, if not more, conducive to interpretive intervention and even overturning precedents than is the case with loose and living constructions. Originalistic approaches demand revisiting the past, the original constitution, its meanings, and intentions. But a rendezvous with history always occurs from a different context whose differences magnify with the passage of time so that – again, wittingly or not, consciously or not – present and evolved meanings and orientations get read into what seems to be the plain text. Strict adherence to the text of the covenant can also foster fundamentalism and facilitate radical breaks with other conventions – i.e. as a way to remove a perceived accumulated ballast of imbalances or other developments that have taken the polity off the supposed proper path set forth by the original Constitution.

Consequently, there are multiple possible forms of *constitutional fidelity* orbiting the space of constitutional politics. They exhibit variable affinities to constitutional text immanence and have original and living elements, though they are distinguishable. Strict originalist orientations are more literal, which is not to say they are necessarily less selective than looser or progressive constitutional interpretation. A living constitutional approach upholds the original text by implication (i.e. by not amending it), but searches for ways of adopting and adapting immanent principles and promises in order to improve, reform, or fit the present. The originalist, strict-text approach fosters "reliving" the past or upholding the compact as it stands, also because, until it is formally changed, it continues to express *sovereign consent*. Incidentally, another form of fidelity, in keeping with the founding legacy of revolution, is one of the most obvious, yet most neglected, approaches: to revise, if not replace, the Constitution altogether. That this idea should seem unfeasible, if not preposterous to many, is in a word telling.[30] Limited to constitutional politics by interpretation as the USA has predominantly, almost solely, been, originalism-literalism carries all the more potentially extensive political implications, as have instances and phases of living constitutional politics.

Against the backdrop of the New Federalism, the new originalism, or the devolution revolution, calls for taking constitutional interpretation "away from the courts" (Tushnet 1999) and activating the "people themselves" (Kramer 2004) to engage in a "popular constitutionalism" may appear to favor a more progressive type of living constitutionalism. Such proposals have democratic merit and may constrain the judiciary from overturning laws and regulations enacted by representative-democratic institutions at multiple levels of the polity.[31] However, while they often get conflated, the categories of "progressive" and "popular" are different in political and constitutional terms (Balkin 1995). Moreover, it would appear that the renewed originalist literalism has already found "popular constitutionalism on the right" (Post and Siegel 2006; Schmidt 2011) in action. The implications are ambiguous. They do not necessarily point toward easing either democratic or federal governance, nor necessarily toward reinvigorating or safeguarding state governments. What appears certain is that they invite and will trigger even further political-constitutional contestation and more fragmentation of the polity.

The nexus between several constitutional-democratic-federal developments was on heated display in the intense opposition to the Patient Protection and Affordable Care Act (ACA or "Obamacare"), namely party politicization, but also the compounded evolution of constitutional veneration and interpretation, the politics of the Constitution, intensifying emphasis on individual rights, the distension of constitutional ambiguity, as well as a popular constitutionalism. In short, this warrants, as a final step, addressing this case further. The conflict seemingly climaxed in, though did not fully end with, the case of *National Federation of Independent Business v. Sebelius* (2012) before the Supreme Court. The ACA was mostly upheld as constitutional by the Supreme Court, including its most politically controversial element, the mandate on individuals to purchase health insurance. However, this was not upheld on the grounds put forward by the federal government – i.e. yet again, Congress's authority to regulate interstate commerce. Instead, it was permitted as falling under Congress's authority to tax. Among the dissenters, Justice Scalia, a renowned constitutional originalist, was a leading critic of Congress's attempt to impose an individual mandate for health insurance under the commerce clause as being tantamount to usurping unlimited power. The critique made during the oral proceedings received wide attention especially on account of his comparison of the mandate to compelling people to buy broccoli; that is obligating people to buy health insurance would be no different from forcing them to buy healthy vegetables. On the one hand, the Justice's comparison appears ridiculous, though that was surely part of the point. On the other hand, it could raise a serious federal issue on regulating interstate commerce, which implies barriers on direct regulation of individual economic activity and thus on the rather unprecedented thrust to regulate "inactivity", that is not buying health insurance. The mandate was upheld by reinterpreting it as a tax. But the decision actually followed the *dissenting* line of argumentation, even reiterating several times the potential broccoli apocalypse of unchecked federal power. Scalia's critique is important to the constitutional-political nexus of concern, and profoundly so for several reasons.

The first reason lies with the simple, but crucial, detail that he did not come up with the broccoli analogy. The analogy was adopted from *outside* the court, and precisely from the *popular constitutionalist* opposition to the ACA. The latter included the Tea Party but also virtually all Republican representatives and senators as well as opposition by roughly half of all state governments. The popular constitutional contestation had multiple and far-reaching implications. It not only influenced the court to borrow the broccoli analogy, having been reiterated hundreds of times in the press, in Congressional debates, by Tea Party activists or in protests. The dynamics apparently led the Supreme Court to deal with a fundamental *individual-liberty* issue, and thus confounded the issues at stake, turning a federal-authority interstate-commerce question into a decision of potentially massive consequence of what Congress may regulate at all without impinging on individual liberty (Rosen and Schmidt 2013).[32] That is to say: the Court not only considered, but also *answered*, questions[33] that the case, instigated by states at first in lower federal courts against a possible encroachment on state authority (see e.g. Dinan 2010: 1660ff.), did not primarily ask. They were interposed through *popular* constitutional contestation – carried out, debated, and mobilized by hundreds of politicians and mass citizen protests on the basis of fundamental constitutional individual rights and a question of freedom and liberty, not specifically federalism. It is *not* ridiculous at all for citizens to see a potential expansion of federal coercive power in a stipulation requiring citizens to purchase something. The provision was pursued in connection with the interstate-commerce and necessary-and-proper clauses, and thus actually a matter to resolve on the basis of federal authority vis-à-vis state governments. State governments exercise authority over individuals including legal requirements to purchase insurance, so that the constitutional-judicial question at stake would be, put simply, whether the federal government can do that too. It is not the duty, and it would be highly undemocratic, to demand of citizens participating in popular constitutionalism to distinguish such issues in formalistic constitutional-legal fashion. But it is interesting at the very least that many politicians and, most notably, the Supreme Court to an extent did not either.

Judicial review was not only drawn into, but assumed, the dynamics compressing federal issues of Congressional interstate regulatory authority with individual liberty ones emanating from popular politics of the Constitution. The Supreme Court has been responsive to societal and political movements, public opinions, and changing social, political, and economic conditions in the past, to be sure. The switch in judicial review in the New Deal era provides one of the most significant cases in point.[34] However, even a constitutional court so comparably highly politicized as the US Supreme Court still tends to discriminate popular political constitutional understandings from jurisprudential ones, whether in deciding to hear a case at all or in its official decisions. A partial judicial restraint was evident in reinterpreting the healthcare mandate as a tax and thus refraining from overruling the individual mandate wholesale, which indicates that the Court managed to strike a difficult balance. At the same time, the ruling was combined with a *principally* limiting intervention against Congress's exercise of the commerce clause that was reached, not on the primary federal question per se, but rather prompted by a popular constitutional interpretation that saw individual rights at stake. In *that* case though the Court should have dealt with issues of the "due process" and "equal protection" clause types, and yet these were not what the Court adjudicated and ruled on (Kahn 2013; Rosen and Schmidt 2013). This underlines the quite remarkable impact of recent popular constitutional dynamics.

In parallel, and likewise reflective of these constitutional-political dynamics, another major federal question at stake was deliberated and adjudicated accordingly, only to wind up being overshadowed by the pro-individual-liberty strand of the debate. This concerned whether Congress could cut federal Medicaid funding to states refusing to join in the Medicaid-expansion component of the ACA, designed to provide federal funds to states to support individuals with incomes marginally above the poverty line (and thus ineligible for Medicaid). This part of the reform was ruled unconstitutional for being overly coercive on the states,[35] which represents a big deal in deviating from the post-New Deal era. This less sensational (i.e. for constitutional or federal-legal laypersons), more seemingly technical constitutional-legal part of the ruling has already witnessed concrete, extensive, and diverse implications on federal–state relations in implementing the reforms that correspond with patterns of polarized and fragmented federalism (see e.g. Noh and Krane 2016; Oberlander and Weaver 2015; Rose 2015): for example from states volunteering to opt out, be all in, or only partially, others negotiating waivers or temporary exemptions, and many states facing subsequent *internal* differences between legislatures and governors on which route to take.

The contestation of the recent healthcare reform reveals a veritable collision between competing constitutions. The collision course has been in the (re-)making for some time. There was the seemingly established broad constitution that included an expanded social welfare regime, desegregation and affirmative action, intensified cooperative to coercive federalism, and "big" federal legislative and regulatory government. So certain were the Democrats apparently that the ACA reform rested securely on precedent laws (e.g. Medicaid and Medicare) and court rulings since the New Deal, exhibiting wide deference to Congress's exercise of the commerce clause and spending power (Somin 2016: 443), that they scarcely mentioned concerns of constitutionality in the course of drafting the legislation (Read 2016). They relied on judicial review precedents, and this even in the face of intensive and mounting political opposition. Under the US Constitution that does not include a single adoption of *any* of the changes that have developed in powers, policies, patterns, and modes of federal governance in over one hundred years, it had always remained a looming possibility that many changes could be modified and even undone if other things changed, namely judicial review, or political, partisan, and citizen preferences and interpretations. For what the interpretive authority giveth, the authority of interpretation can taketh away.

To do so becomes all the easier when stricter literal patterns of interpretation of the Constitution become (re-)activated and targeted against expanded governmental authority that had relied predominantly on permissive interpretation instead of adding concrete provisions to the Constitution. And in the case of healthcare reform, as well as in stark contrast to Democrats, progressive groups or a large share of the health and medical professional industry, the Republicans, libertarian groups, numerous state government actors, conservative media and talk radio, and the rising populist Tea Party movement were contesting the reform intensively *and explicitly* on constitutional grounds, with direct constitutional quotes as well as references to the founders and liberty abounding.[36] Upholding the Constitution and "restoring" government to its constitutionally envisaged original – taken to be synonymous with limited – scope represent the core referents and claims of many politicians, parties, judges, associations, and voters, but also for affinitive Constitution-studying citizens.[37]

The dynamics of an evangelized popular constitutionalism with limited government and individual liberty at its core could be construed as flattening constitutional theory and thought about government in a complex society and compound republic. The related politics of the Constitution are prone to take a great deal of text out of context in pursuit of restoring the supposedly original Constitution. Living progressive constitutional orientations also select or pick and choose from a repertoire of immanent constitutional principles, ideas, and concrete textual references. This serves less the purpose of upholding or restoring the original context, and more for enabling and advancing government toward fulfilling immanent goals, principles, or ideas, the overarching one being equality and thus toward *leveling*. On the other hand, the stricter originalist and literal constitutional orientation, as reflected by the dynamics of its own popular constitutionalism, exhibits a fundamental faith in liberty and independence, and an energetically non-elitist and *leveling* character. The thrust is toward flattening complexity but also elevating the people, many of whom in the USA profess to want to be left alone by the government, especially the big federal one.

Contestation along these lines and especially claims such as to take the government, the country, or the Constitution "back" – whether from the first black US president or the "underserving poor" – trigger suspicions or outright condemnations in return. Demands and slogans like these can signify objectionable discriminatory race, class, and gender overtones and undercurrents, inevitably embedded as they are in a history of American political development that undeniably offers far too much evidence corroborating their indictment.[38] But it would be normatively questionable and analytically distorted to lump New Federalism, new originalism, new "states' rights" and other more or less related constitutional politics and certainly all respective followers, supporters, and voters together with the places and people of the past in which state self-rule and the pursuit to limit the federal state served ignoble ends and inhumane institutions. One would wind up missing some potential warning signs, but also some legitimate concerns. The federal government, irrespective of the party in the majority, has not only cooperated with, but also come increasingly to coerce the states, whose democratically elected governments lack institutional linkages and constitutional guarantees to co-determine the myriad laws and regulations that bind them, including when they are imposed by presidents in evasion of Congress. As such, one would also miss much of what makes the clash of American constitutions a constitutional-political knot located in a multidimensional sphere, entangling multiple developmental strands of democracy, federalism, the state and states, and the Constitution itself over time.

The Constitution has predisposed the US polity to fragmentation. It does not cause the processes of further fragmentation over time. American governments, politics, and people do. And they do so not least by preserving and interpreting their Constitution.

Summary

Nearly four decades ago, one could ask the question "Were the Antifederalists right?" (McDowell 1982), and surmise that they predicted correctly the original US Constitution's disposition to bring forth a "consolidated" dominant national government, due to the immanent powers of the federal branches and constitutional interpretation by the courts. Going back one decade further, the modernization thesis on American federalism (Beer 1973, 1993) could assert that "the rhetoric of state sovereignty" and "states' rights" will have "dwindled into insignificance" (Beer 1973: 51), and expect that the modernization of federalism, with growing interdependence and national-political orientations "may produce a new positive phase of strength and integration" with the help of "American democracy ... to make the nation more a nation" (ibid.: 95). Viewing these two inquiries with the benefit of hindsight, they appear to provide exemplary insights into multiple aspects: into where things stood in American federal democracy at the time and how they had developed up to those respective points. However, they also reveal several counterintuitive and ironic developments that have transpired since. The two accounts on American federal democracy were each made in the context of critical junctures: the modernization thesis appeared in the dusk of the Nixon Presidency, which had seen its own New Federalism stifled and would end in a resignation preempting impeachment; The "Antifederalists were right" thesis came at the dawn of the New Federalism proposed by President Reagan, calling among other things for federal deregulation and retrenchment and reinvigorating state autonomy. Both junctures incidentally were surrounded by what had appeared to be low points in trust in government and highpoints in political disaffection, and thus times that could appear to be ripe for a change. Yet, the fear that the Antifederalists were right about national dominance over the states and the hope that federal integration would come about with the help of the nationalization of democracy have both been complicated, in parts confirmed and in parts contradicted, by how things have turned out.

From the prior analysis it may follow that the Antifederalists, on the one hand, were "wrong" on multiple counts. The factors and mechanisms that led to the expansion of federal government included precisely *popular democratic* and even some state sovereigntist antecedents to which successors of the Antifederalists contributed. What is more, not only the "national state", but *also the states themselves* have expanded in capacity and governmental activity exponentially over time. The intensifying multibranch and multilevel divides and polarization of recent years, on the other hand, have coincided precisely *with the nationalization of democracy*: the consolidation of a two-party duopoly across *all* levels and branches of government despite the decentralized, predominantly state-based organization of the party and electoral systems. This outcome has been coupled with nationally contested popular elections of the President despite the persistence of a state-based electoral vote system, which did democratize, but in disjointed fashion with simultaneous but *separated* winner-takes-all majoritarian contests. At the same time, or rather over time, the politics of the Constitution have developed in fundamentally different directions, including the dynamics of limiting the states and, especially in recent decades again, the "federal state". Patterns of constitutional interpretation, in turn, have evolved with processes of veneration, contestation, and amalgamation, of rather Federalist and Antifederalist living, original, and literal orientations. They have compounded over time, resulting in intense clashes rather than reconciliation of different constitutions. Together this has led to intensifying the fragmentation of the US polity.

Looking at how the American state has developed and at the state of its federal democracy, the above-postulated synthesis of Federalist and Antifederalist constitutions may still appear peculiar, but also now more comprehensible. This conceptual dualism has provided navigational assistance to explore several constitutional political orientations, and their further evolution with changing patterns of governance and recurring patterns of contestation and interpretation. The terms Federalist and Antifederalist constitution, however, actually pose an oversimplification for several reasons. For one, neither the one nor the other group – each of which was hardly monolithic anyway – could know how the American polity would develop. Hence their different visions may have proved correct or not, but when they have, then often in either different ways or with reasons, aims, or causes incompatible with their respective understandings and intentions. For another, obviously nobody can really predict the future, but the point of referring to the original supporters and dissenters of the US Constitution runs deeper. The Constitution they designed and disputed was forged at a time that preceded most of the features of the modern state, modern government, modern federalism, and modern democracy. This applies especially in comparative perspective, but even regarding institutions, procedures, and practices that developed *within* the USA, no less a USA that would colossally expand and multiply fourfold the already "extended compound republic" of the original thirteen states. As such, one could conclude that an analysis of constitutional development with the help of the terms Federalists and Antifederalists may distort more than it clarifies.

Another point though was to adopt, also here in this study, a pattern of American politics and constitutional interpretation that reflects primary contradictions, if not sheer dilemmas immanent to the US polity: the dilemma of a late 18th-century Constitution that has not changed much, but a constitution in the broad sense that has changed tremendously over time on account of, for example, democratization, bureaucratization, industrialization, globalization, immigration, and gender and race emancipation; and with the emergence and extension of, for example, suffrage, intergovernmental relations, cooperative and coercive administration and implementation, state *and* federal taxation, party competition, judicial review, and the plebiscitarization of elections. And yet all of this combines not only with the persistence of widely the same formal framework of government, but also with *the perpetuation of "thinking in the 18th-century box"*. Transpiring within the box is the endless usage of its vocabulary and wordings, the repeated invocation and quotation of the founders, and the seemingly eternal grapple with how to distill out and apply "their" principles and ideas toward a more perfect union or how to conjure up their past understandings and meanings in order to find guidance on how to govern as well as *to not govern* the present. Contestation and interpretation transpiring within the box spans across practically the entire spectrum of political issues and along the sequence of political development, from dealing with slavery and freedom to welfare and warfare; from debating myriad governmental limits on the state and the states, to granting one of the most conceivably coercive state powers to execute its citizens contingent on whether the *present* should or the *past* would have deemed this "cruel and unusual" or not; to determining whether numerous and meanwhile almost countless policy as well as rights questions can be (in)sufficiently construed as "commerce among the several states".

Consequently, the postulation of a peculiar synthesis of Federalist-Antifederalist constitutions can be taken as inaccurate with regard to most of the evolution of the American Constitution in the broad sense – i.e. as things went in directions neither of the camps could foresee and in some parts never really wanted. And yet it seems tremendously applicable on account of the evolution of patterns of constitutional interpretation – not least because so much of what "those guys" did and said a few centuries ago still matters. And the *democratic* enigma is: it matters because American governments, politics, and people make them matter.

When either side of political debates seeks recourse to either side of the Founding of the Founders in general for interpretations or legitimations, they almost inevitably get the story right as well as wrong. This applies already because it is simply difficult to clear up what they meant, evident already in ongoing disagreements among legal, historical, and social science scholars. This also applies on account of the complex evolution of the US Constitution, which incorporated limits, contradictions, and ambiguities from the outset and which have become further distended over time. All the while there remains a *negative* as well as a *positive* legacy of government embodied in the Constitution from the outset. It was undoubtedly committed to limited government as well as to a charge for governing. Already in the original debates and extending far beyond them, contestation revolves around constitutional interpretation, connected to specific principles and provisions, as well more general constitutional understandings. What unites the past with present in the USA further are the tensions running between rather popular and rather progressive orientations.

In contrasting the two, the progressive one can be compactly surmised, for instance, as less prone to "demonizing the state", tending "to embrace a positive vision of government power", rejecting "the libertarian belief that liberty and power are invariably competing", and accepts that "government has the ability, perhaps even the constitutional responsibility, to uproot entrenched inequalities and ensure certain minimum benefits for its citizens" (Schmidt 2011: 553). The populist variant in turn can be conceived, for instance, as not only wary of elitism, but also accepting of democratic popular culture as "the culture through which ordinary citizens express themselves" and "everybody gets to participate in it", but that it is "by nature unkempt and unruly, occasionally raucous and even vulgar …, by turns both eloquent and mawkish, noble and embarrassing, wise and foolish" and "is imperfect in precisely the same sense that democracy itself is imperfect" (Balkin 1995: 1948). These two concise, abridged depictions are only two ways to capture the differences. They provide however a valuable orientation for demarcating political as well as constitutional ideas of popular and state sovereignty, equality, and liberty that have traversed political contestation throughout American political development.

The popular and progressive as well as variable liberal and conservative constitutional political orientations need not entirely contradict one another. They can allow at the very least for various coalitions of individual and collective political actors to find common ground on certain issues, and recoalesce on other ones, sometimes even to achieve formal constitutional amendments. However, a predicament emerges when differences become or rather *are made* irreconcilable in political practice. This is to say: when individual and collective political actors increasingly fail to bridge these differences to negotiate a consensus; when the formal constitution of the polity makes it difficult to do so, especially under conditions of growing political polarization and fragmentation; and when the ensuing adaptation strategies involve, not broader "catch more" but rather "catch just enough" negotiations, and even further *constitutionalization* of political and policy debates built on competing and opposed interpretations of a constitution that has grown ever more ambivalent.

The path of analysis undertaken here has explored and reconstructed essentially four stories of genesis and evolution in the USA: of the state, democracy, federalism, and the Constitution. The analytical framework has been configured, not to audaciously cover these dimensions of the US polity in their entirety, but rather to traverse them to capture institutional and ideational path dependencies dynamically evolving in the multidimensional bounds of political space, time, rules, and meanings. It has attempted to figure out how fragmentation is immanent to each of these dimensions and constitutionally compounded in the US polity, in which multiple processes of further development may connect, collide, and collapse in ways that engender further fragmentation. The fragmentation we are witnessing – or appear to be seeing – in the current state of affairs of American federal democracy may very well be driven by other forces of alienation in an ever more complex world, latent to blatant racial discrimination and antagonism, persistent to growing socio-economic inequality, the individualization and atomization of the citizenry, or a mixture of them and more. Surely such forces are at play to one or the other extent in the USA as well as elsewhere. Even if one or more of them represent forces driving fragmentation, all the more necessary it becomes to capture *the constitutional* predicaments bounding them.

A major part of the quandary lies with the institutional framework of the polity: its branches and levels of government are geared toward strict horizontal and vertical separation of powers resulting in a *counter-majoritarian* arrangement of institutions for one, while having a multiplicity of separated electoral linkages each following simple *majoritarian* logics for another; these features comprise together a disjointed and uncoupled polity highly predisposed to fragmentation in the first place. Another major part of the predicament is the high susceptibility of this arrangement to variegated tensions and stalemates that, sooner or later, can only be relieved through either compromise or withdrawal. The US polity, its Constitution in particular, has proved resilient in being robust or resistant to change, while it also has at many times proved able to absorb shocks to the system. But under the given political circumstances, the US constitutional quandary that has emerged multiple times in the past is on full display today: the multidimensional division-of-powers system that demands compromise – whether in agreeing to work together or to leave each other alone – to make it work, with a multiplicity of separated electoral linkages based on a winner takes all and thus a loser loses all logic, can end up serving less as absorber or relay for various impulses, and more as an amplifier of them. Another complication of the quandary is the persistent coupling of all of the above to an outdated Constitution that almost only ever gets updated though constitutional interpretation. Interpretation in turn, unlike the Constitution itself, is fundamentally prone to change. The overarching crux lies finally with a constitution that, in the course of evolution through adaptation via interpretation, has become both increasingly venerated and distended, and yet impoverished over time. The abounding political contestation with competing constitutions reinforces the default settings of the Constitution that facilitate and even encourage dividing not only power, but also branches and levels of government as well as the constituent places and people against one another.

Notes

1 Again, parliamentary sovereignty had become established in England and then Great Britain, but not yet the "efficient secret" of parliamentary democratic government, which was consolidated in the course of the 19th century.

2 Suppression of these recurring revolts as well as against Indian raids and attacks frequently relied on US military support, as had the westward territorial expansionary endeavors, and thus also slavery (see esp. Ericson 2017).

3 One finds at least some matriarchal mystic balance with referents like "Lady Liberty" or "Columbia".

4 See e.g. Exodus 4:10 (King James English version): "Then Moses said to the Lord, 'O my Lord, *I am not eloquent*, neither before nor since You have spoken to Your servant; but I *am slow of speech* and *slow of tongue*.'' While one can infer that he stutters *in order to* avoid the call to duty because of some insecurity on being able to meet the challenge or the responsibility (and not the other way around) (see e.g. Baumgarten 1979), the chronic impediment of speech seems implied by the reference to "before" and "since" the encounter, and repeated reference to his speech and "tongue"; see also (Shell 2006).

5 On a side note, it is interesting to consider from an institutional-theoretical perspective that the parable may represent also an ancient attempt at a retrospective quasi-theorization of the origins of a written alphabet. It must have appeared as something of a puzzle, if not mysterious and "miraculous" to those contemplating where their alphabet came from. As such, the parable approximates a concept of path-dependence, given that the invention of this written alphabet was conceived as contingent on a historical context in which an adaptation became necessary to solve a specific problem (a perceived lack of good oratory skills), but with a far trajectory of impact – both enabling and constraining – on language communication and representation.

6 One particularly salient contestation of federal government authority was lodged by the Kentucky and Virginia Resolutions of the late 1790s (against the US government's Alien and Sedition Acts). Setting a precursor to the 1830s Nullification Crisis, it involved

declaring not only a federal government act unconstitutional, but also asserted a state's right to do so, thus challenging the Federalist-dominated government, as well as calling the very nature of the Union under the Constitution (or the Federalists' vision of it) into question.

7 On the recurring invocation of the Liberty Bell throughout multiple phases of American political development (e.g.in the Founding Era, for the abolitionist movement in the antebellum years, the parading of the bell across the country after the Civil War) (see e.g. Callahan 1999).

8 The Liberty Bell is but one case in point of these tendencies, commonly associated as it is with being forged and rung for the signing of the Declaration of Independence – both of which are simply false. It was built in Philadelphia in the 1750s to commemorate the 50th anniversary of the founding of Pennsylvania, and was likely out of commission in 1776 (see e.g. Hackett Fischer 2005: 54–60).

9 Democrat-Republican critiques had become increasingly frequent and caustic in the course of the 1790s, also because of the increasing royal-like ceremonial practices by Washington and increasingly frequent and lavish celebrations of him (like balls held in his honor), and even worse from their perspective of course his support for the Federalists' centralizing legislative and executive programs (see e.g. Newman 1992).

10 Many of them were still alive and even politically active. However Washington had died before the 1800 elections and thus was a most important rallying figure for the Federalists.

11 For a comprehensive study of Evangelicalism in the antebellum South and in connection with support for slavery, see e.g. Daly (2002). The passage on "Proclaim Liberty" is Leviticus 25:10. On the law regulating slavery, which, read strictly (literally), could be imposed only upon non-Israelites, see Leviticus 25: 39–54.

12 The only constitutional amendment brought on by the "Revolution of 1800" – and the last amendment until after the Civil War – specified the concurrent, but separate election of the President and the Vice President (12th Amendment, 1804). The implication is thus also a confirmation and reproduction of the original – and in terms of formal provisions, highly ambivalent – framework of government, distribution of powers, restraints, and rights. The state-based election of the President was left in place, so that not even under the administration of a president claiming to have been popularly elected was the popular election introduced.

13 See e.g. Lutz (1988) on the "incomplete" constitutional text or the prior discussion here on amendments concerning the original purposes as both safeguard as well as opportunity for corrections or adaptations.

14 This broad consensus of constitutional authority and perceived perfection can be postulated, I submit, even more so especially since, and ironically, judicial review is not even expressly granted in the Constitution, certainly not with regard to federal government acts (for a comprehensive review, see e.g. Kramer 2000). Precisely this contradiction – i.e. allowing an unelected branch of government a power it does not even have by the Constitution to overturn elected branches' decisions at multiple levels of the polity – thus points to the acceptance of the Constitution as "supreme law", and this by multiple and opposing parties and citizens.

15 One concrete case in point demonstrating how the dynamics of immanent constitutional interpretation, but taken in widely different directions, have played out, lies with capital punishment. In the mid-20th century, capital punishment or the "death penalty was abolished by almost all modern, rule-of-law, and democratic states, prompting reflection in the USA that state executions are now "unusual" and that standards of "cruelty" (and thus for humane treatment) in the penal system should be updated. Reforms by many state governments and several Supreme Court decisions put the USA even at the forefront of

constitutional protections for the rights of accused persons as well as convicted criminals, and even led to the (brief) suspension of the death penalty. While several different influences have been at work since the latter 20th century (e.g. economic inequality, racial discrimination, as well as law-and-order and tough-on-crime political campaigns; see e.g. Tonry 2009), a pattern of invoking "cruel and unusual punishment" to be interpreted as how the *framers* or the *early states* in the late 18th century would have understood this, has permitted multiple changes to pass constitutional muster: a drastic increase in the austerity of prison conditions, sentencing standards, and a globally unparalleled imprisonment rate, but also the reintroduction of capital punishment. Execution was hardly unusual in the late 18th century. But if this yardstick of constitutionality is applied, it seems impossible to resolve other issues such as whether electrocuting a convict to death would have been allowed by the framers, for whom rather firing squads, hanging, or beheading would have represented standard forms of execution and the electric chair would have been both "unusual" and impossible, if not unimaginable. This raises the altogether fundamental question as to why the understandings of punishment in the late 18th century, in which slavery and execution for numerous crimes (not just homicide) were considered sufficiently *uncruel* and *usual* to be deemed compatible with the Constitution, should trump higher developed standards of humanity and decency (on this discussion, see e.g. Goodheart 2013). This example reflects precisely the trap that the US polity has been caught in for some time, as variable political developments are coupled with changing immanent interpretation of a formally unchanging Constitution.

16 See e.g. *Hammer v. Dagenhart* (1918) which ruled unconstitutional a Congressional statute prohibiting the transportation of goods produced with child labor. On the significance of not only property but also labor issues in constitutional development more generally, see especially Orren (1995).

17 A *federal* constitution tends to pose particular challenges for social welfare policy given the vertical distribution of powers; see e.g. Simeon (2006). However, nearly all other federal democracies' constitutions include concrete provisions on the distribution of responsibilities also in this policy area as well as fiscal equalization schemes.

18 Political contestation, I submit, should address more fundamental questions such as commitments in communities bound together by a constitution, but also further principles. These sorts of questions obviously emerge, even permeate US federal democracy, but the bounded and bounding evolution of the politics of the Constitution frame and limit their trajectory.

19 Analogous impoverishment can be witnessed regarding constitutional-political contestation as to whether the right "to bear arms" applies to individuals or the "well regulated militia" rather than the need to find a sensible balance between liberty and security for contemporary purposes; or whether or not capital punishment should be considered "cruel and unusual" punishment by today's or yesterday's standard, rather than the question of what is appropriate usage of state coercive power and how to maintain higher humanitarian standards, irrespective of what the framers said or thought. Another problem though is that, also in these two examples, *there have been* multiple reforms in the USA (e.g. regulating gun ownership, limiting to suspending state executions, improving prison conditions and the rights of the accused), but without constitutional amendments, so that changes in politics and political-constitutional understandings *unsettle* these issues again and again across the polity.

20 The 26th Amendment lowering the voting age from twenty-one to eighteen was ratified in 1971. The one – and negligible – exception since then has been the 27th Amendment of 1992, which was more an uncontroversial gesture to adopt a proposal made in the 1790s, that was lost and forgotten for almost two hundred years, stipulating when Congressional pay increases can take effect (Ackerman 2007: 1740).

21 Again, Congress was clearly morally justified in doing so; it is rather analytically interesting to note that the amendment process succeeded under permissive conditions of party dominance.

22 Debate still persisted for several decades on whether the first ten amendments also now applied to state governments by implication of the 14th Amendment (see again e.g. Wofford 1964).

23 Citizenship represents a clear-cut exception, as defined by the 14th Amendment (1868).

24 Again, e.g. the introduction of primaries and direct democratic instruments (in numerous states), the expansion of public administration and regulation in multiple areas of social, economic, and political life.

25 At the same time, this split may have always been there, in that the Progressive movement (which overlapped with or followed, depending on definitions, the Populist movement) encompassed a diverse coalition or rather coalitions of groups that split variably on different issues. For a critique of the progressive movement as concept, i.e. that it never comprised *a* movement in the first place, see e.g. Filene (1970).

26 As just one highly pertinent example, one may take the 1st Amendment prohibition on Congress from making laws "respecting the establishment of religion" or abridging the "free exercise thereof", which has become understood as an *individual* freedom of religion. The interpretation of these provisions however evolved so as to serve as breaker of possibly any state or federal government act supporting any religious group or activity as much as, especially in recent years again, an individual right to discriminate against others on the basis of one's religious beliefs. Again, the Constitution may imply, but does not explicitly refer to, the "equality of people" or "individual rights" (exceptions being the 5th and 6th Amendments protecting the rights of accused *persons*). Of course multiple referents are unambiguous in implying individual rights. But it is not until the 14th Amendment (1868) that a provision makes this explicit, namely "equal protection of the laws" guaranteed to "any person" that shall not be violated (without due process) by either state or the federal governments. The Bill of Rights denotes either prohibitions on Congress, e.g. against making laws abridging freedom of speech or religion, but it was not clear until the 14th Amendment whether this meant protection against federal encroachments or of individuals against federal *and* state interventions. The right to bear arms, often and zealously construed as an individual right, is guaranteed to "the people", which is, unambiguously, a *collective* referent. This *collective* right is underlined in its linkage to the "well regulated Militia". It is only in the latter 20th century that the *individual-right* understanding has become established (though still contested), and its *activation* – by parties, citizens, interest groups, courts – has extensive implications, including the dismantling of prior regulations established at federal *and* state levels.

27 One should add the flipside to such patterns of discourse which was likewise prevalent in the Founding era, and recurs into the present, i.e. the mutual conjuring of "apocalyptic" scenarios against one's opponent.

28 This became evident for instance following electoral "revolutions", after which new majorities, presidents, or both pursued governmental changes of constitutional impact, but without any amendments.

29 As was shown previously, ideas or claims such as the proclamation that "all men are created equally" and with inalienable rights to "life, liberty and the pursuit of happiness" may have been wholeheartedly or partially believed. Either way, they were declared in a context of legitimating a right to independence and thus a sort of strategy, while continuing to exclude most of the population (e.g. the slave population, women, among many others). Despite their original contradiction, these referents in the Declaration

of Independence wind up getting invoked throughout numerous phases and reform movements for, e.g., the extension of suffrage, rights, political equality, citizenship, and democratization.

30 Again, this represents the actual origin of the US Constitution itself, born as it was out of intense contestation on *replacing* an established framework of government in order to serve the governmental needs of the time. Thus this possibility should already be imaginable within the *institutional-ideational* box of the USA, not to mention when one would take practically all other modern federal democracies into consideration that have not only younger, but also much more frequently amended, constitutions, as do mostly the US states.

31 Indeed, if one took the US Constitution *really* literally, judicial review over federal laws should cease altogether. Such a transition could encourage democratic popular constitutionalism. But it seems unlikely that the, or most, people in the USA (including originalists, ironically) would really want the institution of judicial review abolished.

32 In addition to their rich constitutional analysis, Rosen and Schmidt (2013) retrace the emergence of the broccoli analogy in depth, which dates back to a *Wall Street Journal* article, "Healthcare reform vs. the Founders", critiquing the Clinton-era foray into healthcare reform in the early 1990s (which ultimately failed to get passed), which the same author renewed in the context of the Obama Administration reform.

33 The precedent, if upheld, implicates that Congress may not in principle command individual purchase of *anything*, irrespective of any merit there may be to discern health insurance, or some other good of public-benefit or interstate-commerce relevance, from broccoli, fruit, or consumer goods. Some doubt that the decision will limit Congress significantly more in the future, see e.g. Tushnet (2015: 168ff.). But it codifies an emphasis on individual liberty linked to the commerce clause. It seems hardly far-fetched that the precedent could influence other kinds of conflicts in a *different* direction, see e.g. Kahn (2013), if the constitutional guaranteed individual liberty *not* to be compelled to purchase health insurance could also be used to invalidate state laws – like the Massachusetts' one (which had such a mandate) that had provided a precedent for the drafting of the ACA legislation.

34 On the *NLRB v. Jones and Laughlin Steel Corp* (1937) upholding of the "Wagner Act" and the further reaching decision on Congress's latitude in exercising the commerce clause, *Wickard v. Filburn* (1942), see e.g. Somin (2016: 443ff.) and Tushnet (2015: 27ff. and 163ff.). For a joint article uniting different analyses of the electoral and social protest factors behind the change in judicial review, see e.g. Skocpol, Finegold, and Goldfield (1990).

35 The excessiveness of the coercion lies in that states may decide to refuse to implement this section of the ACA so that the loss of the attached funding is forfeiture or "penalty" enough, but Congress may not extend the penalty to withhold additional or all Medicaid funding, an already long-established program. Consequently, the state implementation of the Medicaid-expansion section of the reform became voluntary, not obligatory.

36 Opposition by Republicans should not be over-generalized as conflating, *partout*, issues at hand in ACA with individual rights or overseeing the germane issue of federal authority. For instance, the then minority leader Boehner of the House of Representatives argued that a number of stipulations in the draft legislation were *fully within the constitutional scope of Congressional powers* in regulating the insurance market (e.g. regarding pre-existing conditions, coverage of children, or cost control measures), but that the individual mandate would exceed constitutional Congressional authority to regulate "commerce among the several States"; see Read (2016: 346ff.).

37 See again the exemplary in-depth study on Republican conservativism, especially with the Tea party changes, and the centrality of not only constitutional beliefs, but also widespread grass-roots "constitution-study" practices, in Skocpol and Williamson (2013: esp. 45–82).

An insightful example – reflecting many of the themes and developments in this section (the "adoration" of the Constitution and the Founding to name but one) – comes from an organization carrying out civic coursework, the National Center for Constitutional Studies, which has both a conservative political and religious outlook. One such course called "Proclaim Liberty throughout All the Land" promises the participant that "you will also become conversant with each part of the Constitution and understand … how *nearly every problem we face* in America today could be solved by *understanding and applying the wisdom of America's Founding Fathers*" (emphasis added). See: https://nccs.net/pages/proclaim-liberty-throughout-all-the-land.

38 On recent political opposition to the federal government, particularly linked with the Tea Party and/or "white backlash" (a phrase already used by Martin Luther King Jr. in the light of severe to violent reactions against the Civil Rights' movement), see e.g. Brown (2016); Courser (2012); Smith (2015); Uscinski, Klofstad, and Atkinson (2016).

References

Ackerman, Bruce. 2005. *The Failure of the Founding Fathers. Jefferson, Marshall, and the Rise of Presidential Democracy*. Cambridge, MA: Belknap, Harvard University Press.

——— 2007. "The Living Constitution." *Harvard Law Review* 120 (7): 1737–1812.

Albert, Richard. 2014. "Constitutional Disuse or Desuetude: The Case of Article V." *Boston University Law Review* 94 (3): 1029–82.

Andersen, Lisa. 2012. "From Unpopular to Excluded: Prohibitionists and the Ascendancy of a Democratic-Republican System, 1888–1912." *Journal of Policy History* 24 (2): 288–318.

Bailyn, Bernard. 1992. *The Ideological Origins of the American Revolution*. Cambridge: Belknap.

Balkin, Jack. 1995. "Review: Populism and Progressivism as Constitutional Categories." *Yale Law Journal* 104 (7): 1935–90.

Baumgarten, Murray. 1979. "That Stutterer Moses." *Western Political Quarterly* 32 (2): 150–53.

Beer, Samuel. 1973. "The Modernization of American Federalism." *Publius* 3 (2): 49–95.

——— 1993. *To Make A Nation. The Rediscovery of American Federalism*. Cambridge, MA: Belknap, Harvard University Press.

Berman, Mitchell. 2009. "Originalism is Bunk." *New York University Law Review* 84 (1): 1–96.

Brennan, Timothy. 2017. "Thomas Jefferson and the Living Constitution." *The Journal of Politics* 79 (3): 936–48.

Brown, David. 2016. *Assumptions of the Tea Party Movement*. New York: Palgrave Macmillan.

Callahan, Robey. 1999. "The Liberty Bell: From Commodity to Sacred Object." *Journal of Material Culture* 4 (1): 57–78.

Clayton, Cornell, and J. M. Pickerill. 2004. "Guess What Happened on the Way to Revolution? Precursors to the Supreme Court's Federalism Revolution." *Publius* 34 (3): 85–114.

Compton, John. 2014. *The Evangelical Origins of the Living Constitution*. Cambridge, MA: Harvard University Press.

Conlan, Timothy. 1998. *From New Federalism to Devolution. Twenty-Five Years of Intergovernmental Reform*. Washington, DC: Brookings Institute.

Conlan, Timothy, and François V. de Chantal. 2001. "The Rehnquist Court and Contemporary American Federalism." *Political Science Quarterly* 116 (2): 253–75.

Cornell, Saul. 1990. "Changing Historical Fortunes of the Anti-Federalists." *Northwestern University Law Review* 84 (1): 39–73.

Corwin, Edward. 1936. "The Constitution as Instrument and as Symbol." *American Political Science Review* 30 (6): 1071–85.
Courser, Zachary. 2012. "The Tea 'Party' as a Conservative Social Movement." *Society* 49 (1): 43–53.
Daly, John. 2002. *When Slavery Was Called Freedom: Evangelicalism, Proslavery, and the Causes of the Civil War*. Lexington: University of Kentucky Press.
Dinan, John. 2010. "Contemporary Assertions of State Sovereignty and the Safeguards of American Federalism." *Albany Law Review* 74 (4): 1637–69.
Dreisbach, Daniel. 2011. "The Bible in the Political Rhetoric of the American Founding." *Politics and Religion* 4 (3): 401–27.
Dunn, Susan. 2004. *Jefferson's Second Revolution. The Election Crisis of 1800 and the Triumph of Republicanism*. Boston: Houghton, Mifflin.
Ericson, David. 2017. "The United States Military, State Development, and Slavery in the Early Republic." *Studies in American Political Development* 31 (1): 130–48.
Filene, Peter. 1970. "An Obituary for "The Progressive Movement"." *American Quarterly* 22 (1): 20–34.
Furstenberg, François. 2006. *In the Name of the Father: Washington's Legacy, Slavery, and the Making of a Nation*. New York: Penguin.
Glendon, Mary. 1991. *Rights Talk. The Impoverishment of Political Discourse*. New York: Free Press.
Goodheart, Eugene. 2013. "The Constitution: Dead or Alive." *Society* 50 (6): 535–42.
Gorski, Philip. 2017. *American Covenant. A History of Civil Religion from the Puritans to the Present*. Princeton: Princeton University Press.
Grey, Thomas. 1984. "The Constitution as Scripture." *Stanford Law Review* 37 (1): 1–25.
Hackett Fischer, David. 2005. *Liberty and Freedom. A Visual History of America's Founding Ideas*. Oxford: Oxford University Press.
Hay, Robert. 1969. "George Washington: American Moses." *American Quarterly* 21 (4): 780–91.
Hemberger, Suzette. 1990. "Dead Stepfathers." *Northwestern University Law Review* 84 (1): 220–31.
Jörke, Dirk, and Veith Selk. 2017. *Theorien des Populismus zur Einführung*. Hamburg: Junius.
Kahn, Ronald. 2013. "The Commerce Clause and Executive Power: Exploring Nascent Individual Rights in National Federation of Independent Business v. Sebelius." *Maryland Law Review* 73 (1): 133–86.
Kramer, Larry. 2000. "Putting the Politics Back into the Political Safeguards of Federalism." *Columbia Law Review* 100 (1): 215–93.
——— 2004. *The People Themselves. Popular Constitutionalism and Judicial Review*. Oxford: Oxford University Press.
LaCroix, Alison. 2010. *The Ideological Origins of American Federalism*. Cambridge, MA: Harvard University Press.
Lowndes, Joseph. 2017. "Populism in the United States." In *The Oxford Handbook of Populism*, eds. Cristóbal Rovira Kaltwasser, Paul Taggart, Paulina Ochoa Espejo and Pierre Ostiguy. Oxford: Oxford University Press, 232–47.
Lutz, Donald. 1988. "The United States Constitution as an Incomplete Text." *Annals of the American Academy of Political and Social Science* 496 (1): 23–32.
McDowell, Gary. 1982. "Were the Anti-Federalists Right?: Judicial Activism and the Problem of Consolidated Government*." *Publius* 12 (3): 99–108.
Mitchell, Joshua. 1992. "Protestant Thought and Republican Spirit: How Luther Enchanted the World." *American Political Science Review* 86 (3): 688–95.
Morgan, Edmund. 1972. "Slavery and Freedom: The American Paradox." *Journal of American History* 59 (1): 5–29.

Moynihan, Donald, and Patricia Ingraham. 2010. "The Suspect Handmaiden: The Evolution of Politics and Administration in the American State." *Public Administration Review* 70: s229–s237.

Munzer, Stephen, and James Nickel. 1977. "Does the Constitution Mean What it Always Meant?" *Columbia Law Review* 77 (7): 1029–62.

Murphy, John. 2011. "Barack Obama, the Exodus Tradition, and the Joshua Generation." *Quarterly Journal of Speech* 97 (4): 387–410.

Newman, Simon. 1992. "Principles or Men? George Washington and the Political Culture of Leadership, 1776-1801." *Journal of the Early Republic* 12 (4): 477–507.

Noh, Shihyun, and Dale Krane. 2016. "Implementing the Affordable Care Act Health Insurance Exchanges: State Government Choices and Policy Outcomes." *Publius* 46 (3): 416–40.

Oberlander, Jonathan, and R. K. Weaver. 2015. "Unraveling from Within?: The Affordable Care Act and Self-Undermining Policy Feedbacks." *The Forum* 13 (1).

Orren, Karen. 1995. "The Primacy of Labor in American Constitutional Development." *American Political Science Review* 89 (2): 377–88.

Persily, Nathaniel. 1997. "The Peculiar Geography of Direct Democracy: Why the Initiative, Referendum and Recall Developed in the American West." *Michigan Law and Policy Review* 2: 11–42.

Post, Robert, and Reva Siegel. 2006. "Originalism as a Political Practice: The Right's Living Constitution." *Fordham Law Review* 75: 545–74.

Rakove, Jack. 1997. *Original Meanings. Politics and Ideas in the Making of the Constitution*. New York: Alfred A. Knopf.

Rappaport, Michael. 1999. "Reconciling Textualism and Federalism: The Proper Textual Basis of the Supreme Court's Tenth and Eleventh Amendment Decisions." *Northwestern University Law Review* (93): 819–76.

Read, James. 2016. "Constitutionalizing the Dispute: Federalism in Hyper-Partisan Times." *Publius* 46 (3): 337–65.

Roelofs, H. M. 1992. *The Poverty of American Politics. A Theoretical Interpretation*. Philadelphia: Temple University Press.

Rose, Shanna. 2015. "Opting In, Opting Out: The Politics of State Medicaid Expansion." *The Forum* 13 (1).

Rosen, Mark, and Christopher Schmidt. 2013. "Why Broccoli? Limiting Principles and Popular Constitutionalism in the Health Care Case." *UCLA Law Review* 66 (3): 67–145.

Rubenfeld, Jed. 2002. "The Anti-Antidiscrimination Agenda." *Yale Law Journal* 111 (5): 1141–78.

Schmidt, Christopher. 2011. "Popular Constitutionalism on the Right: Lessons from the Tea Party." *Denver University Law Review* 88: 523–57.

Schoenbachler, Matthew. 1998. "Republicanism in the Age of Democratic Revolution: The Democratic-Republican Societies of the 1790s." *Journal of the Early Republic* 18 (2): 237–61.

Shain, Barry. 1994. *The Myth of American Individualism. The Protestant Origins of American Political Thought*. Princeton: Princeton University Press.

Shell, Marc. 2006. "Moses' Tongue." *Common Knowledge* 12 (1): 150–76.

Shklar, Judith. 1991. "Redeeming American Political Theory." *American Political Science Review* 85 (1): 3–15.

Simeon, Richard. 2006. "Federalism and Social Justice: Thinking through the Tangle." In *Territory, Democracy and Justice: Regionalism and Federalism in Western Democracies*, ed. Scott Greer. Basingstoke: Palgrave Macmillan, 18–43.

Skocpol, Theda, Kenneth Finegold, and Michael Goldfield. 1990. "Explaining New Deal Labor Policy." *American Political Science Review* 84 (4): 1297–315.

Skocpol, Theda, and Vanessa Williamson. 2013. *The Tea Party and the Remaking of Republican Conservativism*. Oxford: Oxford University Press.

Skowronek, Stephen, Stephen Engel, and Bruce Ackerman, eds. 2016. *The Progressives' Century. Political Reform, Constitutional Government, and the Modern American State*. New Haven: Yale University Press.

Smith, Rogers M. 1993. "Beyond Tocqueville, Myrdal, and Hartz: The Multiple Traditions in America." *American Political Science Review* 87 (3): 549–66.

——— 2001. "Citizenship and the Politics of People-Building." *Citizenship Studies* 5 (1): 73–96.

Smith, Terry. 2015. "White Backlash in a Brown County." *Valparaiso University Law Review* 50 (1): 89–132.

Somin, Ilya. 2016. "Federalism and the Roberts Court." *Publius* 46 (3): 441–62.

Strauss, David. 1996. "Common Law Constitutional Interpretation." *University of Chicago Law Review* 63 (3): 877–935.

Sweeney, Douglas. 2005. *The American Evangelical Story. A History of the Movement*. Grand Rapids, MI: Baker Academic.

Tonry, Michael. 2009. "Explanations of American Punishment Policies: A National History." *Punishment & Society* 11 (3): 377–94.

Tushnet, Mark. 1985. "A Note on the Revival of Textualism in Constitutional Theory." *Southern California Law Review* 58 (1-2): 683–700.

——— 1999. *Taking the Constitution Away from the Courts*. Princeton: Princeton University Press.

——— 2015. *The Constitution of the United States of America. A Contextual Analysis*. 2nd ed. Oxford: Hart.

Uscinski, Joseph, Casey Klofstad, and Matthew Atkinson. 2016. "What Drives Conspiratorial Beliefs? The Role of Informational Cues and Predispositions." *Political Research Quarterly* 69 (1): 57–71.

Wald, Kenneth, and Allison Calhoun-Brown. 2014. *Religion and Politics in the United States*. 7th ed. Lanham: Rowman & Littlefield.

Walker, David. 1996. "The Advent of an Ambiguous Federalism and the Emergence of New Federalism III." *Public Administration Review* 56 (3): 271–80.

West, Robin. 1990. "Progressive and Conservative Constitutionalism." *Michigan Law Review* 88 (4): 641–721.

Wofford, John. 1964. "The Blinding Light: The Uses of History in Constitutional Interpretation." *University of Chicago Law Review* 31 (3): 502–33.

Wood, Gordon. 1969. *The Creation of the American Republic 1776–1787*. Chapel Hill: University of North Carolina Press.

Zink, James, and Christopher Dawes. 2016. "The Dead Hand of the Past? Toward an Understanding of 'Constitutional Veneration'." *Political Behavior* 38 (3): 535–60.

8

CONCLUSION

The decoupled polity

This study has explored many things that are already well known, while a number of its claims and conclusions will confirm what many people already know or think they already knew. To name just a few conventional wisdoms: the US state, its authority, and capacity are limited; government is limited in line with numerous separations of powers and checks and balances; presidents are predominant in elections and many political processes; American politics are at once highly competitive but thoroughly hostile to other parties outside the two major ones; American politics tends toward supporting self-rule, free enterprise, and the market over government intervention, regulation, and redistribution; the latter is unsurprising because American politics and society strongly support equality but tend to emphasize the individual liberty and freedom side of it; the relations between states and the federal government as well as among the states are heavily slanted toward decentralization; the latter is unsurprising because states in the USA are comparatively very strong units of government; the Constitution is old, rigid, and highly stable, also because it enjoys deep and wide support. All of these assertions appear to be true, or that is to say, quite valid and applicable. But none of them gets it quite right either. Either they fail to capture their respective referent in adequate differentiation, or miss important parts of their complexity, or both, and in any case may disregard the fact that things were once different in character as much as intention. Consequently, ambivalences, paradoxes, and several sheer ironies of political development could be all too easily neglected. With this come severe limits, not only on political science understanding and explanation, but also far-reaching political ones.

The US state, government, and multiple facets of American polity and politics in general overly appear to look according to the ways ascribed above. The points, configurations, mechanisms, and forces of *resistance* and *restriction* – and there are many – can overwhelm political practice. However, they may also overly skew *perception* toward overlooking how American political development in multiple dimensions

DOI: 10.4324/9781003203674-8

has actually experienced enormous expansion in state capacity and authority, government intervention as well as consolidation, integration, coordination, cooperation, and interdependence across levels and branches of government. These *other* patterns are easy to overlook because their respective features have not extended even further – e.g. as in so many other modern states in general and other modern federal democracies in particular. Limitation on the other hand becomes especially, repeatedly, and, as of recent, increasingly salient when these features of the *other* patterns are intensely resisted, repelled, retrenched, and refragmented. Some people, parties, and politicians want this to happen, some do not, while those who try to cope with *tensions* and *divides* in order to resolve or avoid *frictions* can wind up reinforcing all three of them, if not immediately, then by precedent, but followed later with different effects.

Furthermore, fragmentation connects to the division of powers *in*, as well as the politics *of*, the US Constitution. This piece of parchment cannot cause the complex outcome of fragmentation on its own. It does however provide a solid foundation conducive to enabling it. The foundation was already laid in a political, even partisan, conflict. The compromise that won out did include intentions of limiting government in comparison with other forms of government, but also *expanding* it in comparison with its own predecessor. But over time contingencies can be forgotten, neglected, rediscovered, infused with things and ideas that predominated later, and become gradually compounded to an apparent legacy of a general consensus that most, if not everyone, in the distant past agreed to and whose past continues to bestow commitments on the present. That is of course until their alleged consensus is thoroughly redesigned or replaced with a new one, that is a new constitution. But the chances of *that* happening look slim to none.

The reasons for this are arguably not the most obvious ones, namely the high *formal* thresholds for constitutional change, though this formal factor does weigh much heavier today than it did when it was originally binding for only thirteen states snuggled between the Appalachians and the Atlantic. However, the thresholds also derive from complex political developments by which the US Constitution transformed into a symbolic embodiment unifying different as well as contradicting legacies and purposes. It is still used as an, or *the*, instrument of government interpreted to permit or prohibit the pursuit of meanwhile even more fundamentally different and opposing ends. Ample incidences in political developments – with regard to the state and the states, to democracy and democratization, to federalism and intergovernmental relations – provide evidence or indicators that can be construed as substantiating different interpretations for the mutual contestation of the politics of opposing sides. All the while, the original structural arrangements of separation-of-powers presidential democracy and of separation-of-powers dual federalism have remained entirely in place, save for one single constitutional amendment, the direct election of senators, which institutionally detached state governments further from the federal government. Contingent on the point of reference or departure, focus, or perspective, it becomes possible to conclude that the US state continuously *is*, *gets*, *looks*, or *is supposed to be* limited. The complexity and ambivalence of the limited state actually indicates that *each one* of these conclusions is merited. This is not an evasion of a conclusion. It is the conclusion.

Confronting the puzzle raised at the beginning of this study has involved less a resort to a parsimonious theory in order to clarify a specific cause. It is a multidimensional jigsaw puzzle that the study has confronted. Piecing it together has required compiling an analytical lens drawn from multiple theoretical foundations and research strands. Given the defined scope and capacity of this study, which implies limits as with any study as well as its student, the puzzle pieces are treated each and together like chickens and eggs, instead of trying to resolve which came first, who produced what or what produced whom. A one-dimensional question is an altogether appropriate and necessary one to address for many phenomena and problems. However, it is not an appropriate inquiry when facing a jigsaw puzzle with multiple dimensions that also includes time. The joint evolutionary and mechanistic perspective pursued here attunes the exploration to search for whether at some point a mutation is born out of a predecessor that may resemble another, later, more familiar newborn. It also expects that whether the innovation or mutation persists – survives and can (re)produce – will depend not only on sufficiently permissive environmental conditions and an own capability to adapt, but also on how actors deal with it. In other incidences in space and time, other similar newborns may have not persisted. But looking at ones that *did* warrants an exploration of change and continuity. Its conclusion must remain open to whether the pattern will be explainable by for example: the result of an optimization by which the best or at least the better-adapted persisted, or rather an adaptation that persisted because others adapted to them; as an intention if it occurred through controlled "experiment"; as an outcome in an environment designed to reach it or possibly to prevent it; as an accident or perhaps also coincidence, for it could not occur without antecedent developments *and* favorable conditions; or a mixture of these possibilities. Of interest in this exploration is also whether the new "life forms" that managed to persist coexisted commodiously with pre-existing ones, complemented or contradicted them, or contributed to their demise, which may or may not have been bound to happen otherwise. The preceding remarks convey the analytical challenge as well as approach to solving the multidimensional jigsaw puzzle of immanent fragmentation and the limited state in the USA.

The composite pattern of the limited state entangles several strands. They are each for their own part complex. They are rendered even more complex through their interactions and linkages over time, and thus in compounded processes of dynamic evolution. Fragmentation as a composite condition endogenous to the US polity can become reduced, but it can also get reproduced and even reinforced. The dimensions and features engendering the limited state can be delineated by institutional factors, comprising chiefly structural and functional ones, and ideational factors comprising chiefly normative and perceptive ones. The latter – e.g. norms, beliefs, patterns of interpretation, regulative ideas – too can amount to institutions or be *institutionalized*. Cross-cutting these features is the dimension of temporality. And overarching them are the features of the constitution in the strict sense, with fragmentation as an immanent predisposition, and in the broad sense, with dynamics of evolution, contestation, adaptation, and interpretation. In short, the US polity is not only predisposed by the Constitution to fragmentation with the multidimensional separation of powers in democracy and federalism, time, and electoral linkages. Bounded developments in the democratic and federal dimensions of government – even when in contradiction to the default settings – can wind up fostering over time more competition, diffusion, and uncoupling among branches and levels of government.

These tendencies become all the more intensified – on account of being underpinned, supported,substantiated and legitimated – by competing interpretations of an ambivalent constitution in the strict sense, whose ambiguity has become more remarkably distended through the evolution of the Constitution in the broad sense. Interpretation oriented toward *text immanence*, affinitive to strict and literal reading especially, invites and can propel a politics of the Constitution contesting the "federal state" of the USA. For again, almost all constitutional change over time cannot be found in the US Constitution itself. The interpretive engagement of principles immanent to the Constitution likewise grounds itself in constitutional fragments of text. Appeals more to principles like equality and promoting the general welfare may be more conducive to federal governance, especially when its intended direction is toward actualization of the respective ideas and principles. But this may also lead to restricting the states. What has complicated matters more, the expansion of the federal government, its scope of assumed authority and activities, has actually tended to coincide rather with *concurring* expansion at the state level. Extensions of the federal government have transpired predominantly in reliance on the states to execute *its* programs and in reliance on interpreting the Constitution permissively to these ends, rather than amending the rules. Consequently, and inversely, it has become all the more feasible to contest, disentangle, and retrench federal authority and policy as well as established networks and practices of multilevel coordination and cooperation that are nowhere to be found prescribed in the Constitution. The combination of these institutional features, political processes, and dynamics reveals the preponderance of the American polity to *immanent fragmentation*, which contributes to the outcomes that the state(s) of the USA can expand, yet be, get, and look limited at nearly any given time in American political development and even at the same time.

These conclusions resonate with several other ones, according to which long-established modes of rather indirect governance and corresponding political governmental strategies have led to a "submerged" (Mettler 2011) state that Americans "can't see" (Sheingate 2009); that reveal an "American predicament" of government authority, capacity, activity, and even rights hidden by policymaking in a "policy state" (Orren and Skowronek 2017); and point to why US federalism "doesn't work" in the "divided States of America" (Kettl 2020). The concept of the state limited by immanent fragmentation shares in "seeing" *the state and the states* in a way that can otherwise appear deceptively "invisible". However, the concept here of the limited state also asserts that the federal state is, and the states are often, actually seen. Indeed, Americans see the emerged state "above the surface" all the time, certainly in their states, and often in the federal government – there is the Internal Revenue Service, where federal income tax declarations have to be filed, the Veterans' Affairs hospitals providing "socialized medicine" for veterans (of which, incidentally, there are many in the USA), and the tens of millions receiving retirement or disability payments from Social Security, to name a few. Many tend to dislike what they see, while patterns of governance, but also the politics of the Constitution, contribute to this. And this too plays a crucial part in the multidimensional active and reactive, in parts contradictory and ironic, dynamics of immanent fragmentation. With the limited state conceived in an implicitly comparative perspective, the "policy state" in turn then appears as more a phenomenon, and a problem in many ways, characterizing the transformations of government and governance in general. But *how* it has developed in multidimensional bounds over time entangling tensions and conflicts looks more like the perpetual American predicament. The "divided States of America" are indeed reinforced by the institutional settings of US federalism and their development, but also their coupling with democratic institutions, processes and dynamics, as well as, again, their interplay with the politics of the Constitution.

Immanent fragmentation makes up the composite pattern engendering the limited state. American federal democracy comprises a decoupled polity by constitutional predisposition. Fragmentation can also and fundamentally emanate from constitutional interpretation, various patterns of which are oriented toward constitutional text immanence. Factoring in this dimension is pivotal to resolving the jigsaw puzzle of American federal democracy and its limited state. As a regulative idea guiding patterns of interpretation, it is also coupled with – is interlinked, affected by, and affecting of – the institutional framework of the US polity. Its evolution is bounded in an institutional-ideational box, the bounds of which also evolve in interplay with the politics of the Constitution. Constitutional text immanence and its evolution as a pattern of interpretation is entangled, like the constituents of American federalism and democracy, with egalitarianism: institutionalized in structural-functional governmental parameters based on popular and state sovereignty on the one hand, and in personalized, leveled, and individualized reading of the Constitution on the other. The US Constitution has come to encompass, among others, a Federalist and an Antifederalist one, a Union of States, and a Union of "We the People" with the states, a Madisonian and a Jeffersonian one, a New Deal and a New Federalism one. This evolution has occurred through political adaptation converting constitutional changes in the democratic as well as the federal dimensions of government without changing the Constitution.

The evolution and institutionalization of constitutional interpretive patterns provides a key piece to the puzzle that helps explain how the pursuit and achievement of various, and frequently contested, changes *despite* the Constitution become widely construed over time as changes *because of* the Constitution. This may also help us to understand more fully how such a fragmented, decoupled polity by constitutional predisposition has witnessed so many complex and contradictory developments entangled with its federal multiple constituent units and its democratic constituent multitude. Indeed *constitutional politics* have always been *ordinary politics* in the USA. This has facilitated democratic and federal governance in the past, by supporting more horizontal and vertical *power sharing* or, when cooperation failed, permitting resort to more *self-rule*. The quandary that has emerged in the past, but has reemerged and has been intensifying into the present, is when *both self- and shared rule* become increasingly constrained by the contestation between substantially different constitutions.

Lessons from a peculiar case: toward a disjointed decision-making trap

Another implication to draw concerns patterns of federal democracy and the potential for further conceptualization of another pattern. To recapitulate briefly in terms of coupling in a federal democracy, the USA represents a generally uncoupled one by constitutional, structural-functional predisposition. However, this also implies in theory a potential flexibility and degree of slack for forms and modes of looser coupling, voluntary cooperation, and coordination between governments. Government in the USA has demonstrated these sorts of interactions and relations in practice as well. The heyday of cooperative federalism toward the late 19th to mid-20th century provides of course the most obvious example. Another, less obvious one is the nationalization of parties and presidential elections, precisely because they have come about despite the persistence of almost superlatively decentralized party organizations and state-based electoral systems. These factors did not cause alone, but certainly facilitated, the expansion and intensification of multilevel cooperation in numerous areas, even before the New Deal, and yet without adding prescriptions or requirements by the Constitution. The latter circumstance, a nearly complete lack of *Politikverflechtung* (Scharpf, Reissert, and Schnabel 1976) or compulsory multilevel cooperation and co-decision rules, save for amending the Constitution, has allowed states in turn to go their own way when consensus could not be reached. The default settings of presidential democracy and dual federalism may make cooperation and governing difficult, especially by comparison. But they also permit, in cases of impasses at the federal level or in intergovernmental arrangements and cooperation, *decoupling* as an internally logical, constitutionally immanent, coping mechanism.

On account of how they have developed over time, the democratic-government and the federal-government dimensions in the USA mutually complicate and perturb one another. It has become increasingly difficult to reach cross-level, cross-branch, and cross-party compromises *as well as* to resort back to more self-rule governing modes. The nationalization of politics has incentivized presidents and Congress to govern against each other as well as to govern the states more coercively, while the two-party consolidation and the polarization of national politics has permeated intergovernmental as well as interstate relations. Moreover, it has become commonplace in American politics for both political parties to call for a return to more bipartisanship and mutually criticize the other side for impeding it. The bipartisanship of a large share of the 20th century however was different. It was not necessarily bogus, as it worked frequently for reaching compromises. The parties themselves, though, differed in comparison to the present ones, being substantially less consolidated and disciplined, and substantially more disorderly and diffuse (see e.g. Lee 2016). This was no doubt less than ideal from a representative-democratic, responsible-party perspective. But it had some benefits for making American federal democracy work, especially given the circumstance of having only two political parties to work with throughout the entire polity.

In comparative federalism, the predominance of a bipolar antagonistic and disciplined party competition was originally conceptualized as structurally incompatible with federalism and intergovernmental cooperation in a parliamentary democracy (Lehmbruch 2000; Sharman 1990). It has turned out to be severely counterproductive in a presidential one too. However, the US case reveals that the parliamentary variant in a federal system may have a *productive contradiction* to its advantage withheld from federalism with presidential democracy. Parliamentary majorities or parliamentary governments (i.e. prime ministers or the cabinet collectively) at the national and subnational levels or together in the multilevel arena have constitutional instruments at their disposal for breaking an impasse in one or the other way, namely votes of (no) confidence. The usage of these instruments or their anticipation render the confidence relationship between executive and legislative rather a mechanism for governing. This may also carry potentially productive or conducive effects for multilevel and intergovernmental relations. The anticipation or threat of one of these types of votes in cases of conflicting political interests or preferences can lead either premiers to better accommodate parliamentary majorities into their negotiations in the intergovernmental arena, or the latter to muster "discipline" around the intergovernmental agreements reached by "their" government with other parliamentary executives. If both fail to work and impasse persists, there remains the possibility to dissolve the governing arrangement and hold new elections. This lesson or rather conceptual insight drawn by comparison of course should not overshadow the variety of potential problems and conflicts parliamentary democracy and federalism face (see, for comparative analyses, e.g. Benz and Sonnicksen 2021), but it does point to an often overlooked flipside to this arrangement of federal democracy.

These parliamentary potentials for federal governance are precluded in separation-of-powers government. In case of impasses in the USA, in short, presidents and Congress, governors and state assemblies remain stuck with one another until the next election. Moreover, with consolidated and polity-wide polarized parties operating in separated branches and levels of government in the USA, political dynamics of recent decades and increasingly into the present seem to be repeatedly heading into a trap of non-decision-making. The USA differs in multiple ways from federal-democratic cross-level arrangements theorized in the "joint-decision trap" (Scharpf 1985, 1988), which was originally conceived on the basis of the German and EU cases. In cases of joint decision-making, non-decisions may not only be likely, but also create a dilemma. As a consequence of the failure to reach a common decision, the status quo of the area or policy of concern cannot be changed at all because of the constitutional or treaty-based rule requiring its joint regulation; a unilateral decision is precluded under the given rules. Another institutional feature of the original joint-decision trap concept *implied* by its underlying cases is that the decision-makers are parliamentary governmental ones. While the EU is not a parliamentary democracy, its member states, like the *Länder* in the German case, are. That counts significantly. In these arrangements of joint decision-making, the decision-makers are parliamentary executives tied in a confidence relationship to the (majorities of) parliaments in the constituent-unit governments. Furthermore, they have to reach a common legislative decision in one arena (i.e. the second chamber) that they will subsequently be responsible for implementing in another one (i.e. within the jurisdiction of the respective government).

This points to several major differences to the US case: the institutional make-up of both the constituent-unit governments as well as the second chamber, for one, and the constitutional rules (or lack thereof) on constituent-unit implementation of decisions made in another arena or at another level, for another. Unlike an arrangement of joint decision-making and its potential trap, the trap of non-decisions is not a formal constitutional one in the US case. It emerges when political actors and dynamics push for a decision to be adopted across the polity. There are several, rather non-coercive or non-hierarchic ways of escaping the respective traps common to both types of arrangements such as agreement at the lowest common denominator or negotiating package deals and side payments.

To elaborate a more systematic concept, and potentially for further comparisons, the US case cannot be conceived as an arrangement of non-decision making. Non-decisions are a potential outcome of any federal-democratic arrangement, and indeed in any political system. However, drawing on its composite pattern as rather uncoupled federal democracy with a view to its federal and democratic governmental dimensions, the USA can provide for a model case for a concept of *disjointed decision-making*. The features are drawn from the US case for one, and based on comparison to institutional arrangements of joint decision-making for another. Parliamentary government at both federal and constituent-unit government level is added to the original concept of joint decision-making institutional arrangements. They are not necessary conditions, as neither are all the features demarcated in the following necessary to comprise or qualify as a *disjointed decision*-making arrangement. As with all models, other variants approximating the model will not share all of its features. Parliamentary government is a further abstraction of *jointed institutions*, as the separation between executive and legislative is substantially complemented or reduced by a structural-functional, shared-rule merger between the head of government and the majority in parliament. Also, electoral linkages should be figured in, as likewise indicative of, the *disjointing* or *jointing* character within the individual governmental institutions. Accordingly, the features of a disjointed decision-making arrangement can be delineated as follows:

- *At the federal level*: executive and legislative independence (lack of confidence relation); separate election of executive and legislative; election of legislature members in separate constituencies by plurality; symmetric bicameralism (all legislation subject to approval by two chambers).

- *Between levels*: separated levels of government (lack of cross-level interlocking); concurrence of powers (each level of government responsible for legislation and implementation within own jurisdiction); no constitutionally prescribed multilevel joint tasks.
- *At the state (constituent-unit) level*: mirrors the federal level – state level governments with separately elected executives and legislatures which are bicameral with members elected separately by plurality; no constitutionally prescribed horizontal joint tasks.

The potential traps of decision-making arrangements motivate this conceptualization as well. The following provides a brief, schematic version of the disjointed decision-making trap, preceded by a simplified version of the joint decision-making trap, not in its full complexity, but rather to serve as a contrast foil for the disjointed case.

The major problem or dilemma a *joint decision-making* arrangement faces is that it leaves little to no room for escape from the potential trap in which no agreement equals no change. The result is maintenance of the status quo throughout the polity since, given the rules of compulsory cooperation, no level and thus no government can alter it unilaterally. In short, apart from those preferring the status quo, the result would lead to nobody achieving their preferred outcome, or as the case may be, everybody gets what they do not want. The arrangement not only encourages, but also requires, governments to work together to address common problems, particularly those cross-cutting jurisdictions. The failure to reach agreements though imposes manifold frustrating implications across the polity.

The dilemma facing a *disjointed decision-making* arrangement is that it provides almost too much room for escape from an outcome of non-agreement concerning common, cross-level problems, which the governments are not constitutionally required to resolve together in the first place. However, given a failure to agree under this arrangement, a large variety of options still remain possible. The result can be maintenance of the status quo, for example no level or branch of government decides to unilaterally change it; or differentiation ensues, for example one, several, or many pursue change on their own way, be it a branch of government, or different units of government at different levels. This arrangement can help avoid intensifying frictions by allowing decision-makers, having failed to reach agreement, to go their separate ways and still have the possibility to (not) address the unsettled issue, also because they have the authority (not) to do so. But it may trigger new tensions if the separate, uncoordinated decisions produce externalities affecting other governments (i.e. their jurisdictions). This is highly likely when cross-cutting problems are at stake, or if branches on one level of government also then fail to reach an agreement and subsequently opt to circumvent each other to pursue changes – particularly separately elected executives may be prone to this strategy. Moreover, a *composite status quo* as the non-resolution of a *cross-cutting* problem would still persist. Without a common decision, either way then, some status quo is still the result. That is to say: there is no change *anywhere* or there is (some) change(s) but, viewed together, they are prone to comprise fragmented, disparate, or contradicting one(s).

The escape routes out of the trap of non-agreement in an arrangement of disjointed decision-making are principally similar to some of those taken in the joint-decision case, namely to come back to cooperation but without coercion, for instance to allow for side payments, to work out package deals, to partition the decision-making process and construct a temporally negotiated consensus (i.e. *do ut des* as giving now, and receiving later, or vice versa). To an extent, they represent modes of coordination, negotiation, and cooperation that have been typical to governing in the USA, not only in negotiations on terms of agreement in grant programs, but include even "pork-barreling" and log-rolling. But even under less polarized conditions than in the current state of affairs, and unlike a joint decision-making arrangement, a common decision, once reached, remains highly uncertain with regard to its implementation. This applies due to the lack of prescription of interstate and multilevel joint tasks and by consequence a lack of constitutional rules concerning how intergovernmental agreements reached at one level are to be handled at another level. This uncertainty also stems from the separation-of-powers of the state governments, whose legislatures are not required to follow and are not necessarily prone to suffer from dishonoring the agreements reached by the chief executive (they may even have incentives not to do so).

In addition to strictly separated branches of government, the multiplicity of separated, distinct electoral linkages to decoupled constituencies that magnify majorities by plurality rules, and are thus highly predisposed to distortion, can make it all the more difficult to reach common, multi-, and cross-level agreements in a disjointed decision-making system. The likelihood appears to diminish further when there are only two parties, and thus a comparatively limited potential for variable coalitions on a case-by-case basis at one level of government of separated institutions, and particularly in decision-making between levels of government – that is, unless the two parties are internally diffuse and low in discipline. If those two parties on the other hand become thoroughly cohesive internally and unified more by intense competition against one another, the capacity for reaching cross-level and cross-branch common agreement seems even more improbable.

Against the backdrop of recent patterns of politics and governing in the USA, it thus may seem unsurprising when a political party in the disjointed decision-making system meanwhile rather tends to sit it out until the next presidential election in the hope of *unified federal* government with the same party in the majority in both legislative chambers and its presidential candidate becoming the chief executive. This could appear to be a sensible, workable approach to escape the trap of non-decisions, even though experience – like the Prologue to this study – keeps showing again and again that it is not.

References

Benz, Arthur, and Jared Sonnicksen, eds. 2021. *Federal Democracies at Work. Varieties of Complex Government.* Toronto: University of Toronto Press.

Kettl, Donald. 2020. *Divided States of America. Why Federalism Doesn't Work.* Princeton: Princeton University Press.

Lee, Frances. 2016. *Insecure Majorities. Congress and the Perpetual Campaign*. Chicago: University of Chicago Press.

Lehmbruch, Gerhard. 2000. *Parteienwettbewerb im Bundesstaat. Regelsysteme und Spannungslagen im politischen System der Bundesrepublik Deutschland*. 3rd ed. Wiesbaden: Westdeutscher Verlag.

Mettler, Suzanne. 2011. *The Submerged State: How Invisible Government Policies Undermine American Democracy*. Chicago: University of Chicago Press.

Orren, Karen, and Stephen Skowronek. 2017. *The Policy State. An American Predicament*. Cambridge, MA: Harvard University Press.

Scharpf, Fritz. 1985. "Die Politikverflechtungs-Falle: Europäische Integration und deutscher Föderalismus im Vergleich." *Politische Vierteljahresschrift* 26 (4): 323–56.

——— 1988. "The Joint-Decision Trap: Lessons from German Federalism and European Integration." *Public Administration* 66 (3): 239–78.

Scharpf, Fritz, Bernd Reissert, and Fritz Schnabel. 1976. *Politikverflechtung. Theorie und Empirie des kooperativen Föderalismus in der Bundesrepublik Deutschland*. Kronberg: Scriptor.

Sharman, Campbell. 1990. "Parliamentary Federations and Limited Government: Constitutional Design and Redesign in Australia and Canada." *Journal of Theoretical Politics* 2 (2): 205–30.

Sheingate, Adam. 2009. "Why Can't Americans See the State?" *The Forum* 7 (4): 1–14 (Article 1).

EPILOGUE

It perhaps no longer seems puzzling that the Obama Presidency produced a much more limited extent of reform than could have been expected at first. These years witnessed intense institutional conflicts between branches and levels of government, polarization among the parties, many policymaking and budget deadlocks, and even multiple government "shutdowns" (see e.g. Abramowitz and Webster 2016; Bowling and Rose 2016; Gordon and Landa 2017; Mann and Ornstein 2013). The political landscape was marked by deep divides, brinkmanship and gridlock in politics, growing political and socio-economic differences and discrepancies, as well as distrust and voter anger toward the establishment, especially at the federal level (Goelzhauser and Rose 2017; see e.g. Grumbach 2018; Holbrook 2016; Jacobson 2017; Sides, Tesler, and Vavreck 2017; Uslaner 2015). In the run-up to the 2016 elections, calls for fundamental change returned.

The national mood provided fertile ground for political outsiders fighting Washington and demanding "restoration", whether of social, economic, democratic, federal, or international balance. The candidacy and campaign of Donald Trump to "make America great again" can be viewed in line with another continuity or legacy of the "populist persuasion" (Kazin 1998) and recurring waves of populism in American politics (see e.g. Brewer 2016; Mead 2017). However, Trump won the Republican primaries and the presidential election, defying the odds and multiple conventions. Like the start position of Barack Obama in 2008, the new president could enjoy a *unified government*, with its own-party majorities in both Houses of Congress and thus with conditions seemingly favorable for governing and even achieving larger reforms.

For various reasons, not only ones related to the controversial president, plagued no less by an unprecedented series of scandals, the administration produced only quite limited policy and especially legislative results. Even under the two-year period of unified government, the charge to repeal the healthcare reform, one of the

DOI: 10.4324/9781003203674-9

most vociferous Republican demands for several years, faltered. The complexities of "immigration federalism" that had evolved and frustrated the previous Obama but also Clinton and Bush presidencies, likewise constrained the realization of the immigration policy of the Trump administration, for which an anti-immigration stance, mostly saliently and notoriously expressed by the demands to "build a wall" alongside Mexico, had served as the veritable centerpiece of the electoral platform (Reich 2018). These impasses revealed once more how a federal and democratic separation of powers, coupled with a multiplicity of district- and state-based electoral linkages, can frustrate governing under otherwise seemingly favorable political conditions. And it did not take long for these conditions to change as well, as the federal elections two years later in 2018, in which Democrats won the majority of seats in the House of Representatives, also reinstated *divided government*. At the end of the Trump presidency, in the midst of the COVID-19 pandemic (Kettl 2020), and not least in the wake of the most tumultuous White House transition since the Civil War that brought the warnings of "how democracies die" (Levitsky and Ziblatt 2018) to life, it would appear that there are no signs of decline in partisan polarization and political friction confronting the current Biden Administration, between federal branches of government, as well as between levels of government and among the states.

Despite the extraordinary longevity and rigidity of its constitution, American federal democracy is not static. On the contrary the USA, like any federal democracy, is dynamic, not least because the adaptations to social, economic, and political challenges continuously touch upon arrangements of responsibility and decision-making constituted in the multiple division of powers in federal and democratic government. In short, *policy* change in federal democratic systems frequently triggers *polity* change as well. A "robust federation" (Bednar 2009), moreover, may require an endowment with sufficient corrective and protective institutional features that enable the balancing act between the capacity for political adaptation and polity resilience. As such, an occurrence of diverse dynamics in US federal and democratic government need not signify in principle anything peculiar or pathological. But the ongoing polarization and fragmentation of the US polity do.

It is impossible to forecast a single, distinct direction that US federal democracy will take. Drawn from the long term of historical development, gauging by the recent past, and as things stand now though, several patterns of dynamics are identifiable. They range from the national consolidation and polarization of both the major and only political parties, the unwavering and unrealistic political expectations placed on the president – and the campaigns for the 2020 presidential elections only continued the conventional escalation of campaign promises – the fragmentation of governance and of cross-level coordination and cooperation, paired with contestation around interpretation of an increasingly ambiguous US Constitution that continues to eschew amendment. Thus, in all likelihood, given the persistence of thinking in the box and the improbability of formal constitutional change, the immanent fragmentation of the US polity is to be continued.

References

Abramowitz, Alan, and Steven Webster. 2016. "The Rise of Negative Partisanship and the Nationalization of U.S. Elections in the 21st Century." *Electoral Studies* 41 (1): 12–22.

Bednar, Jenna. 2009. *The Robust Federation: Principles of Design*. Cambridge: Cambridge University Press.

Bowling, Cynthia, and Shanna Rose. 2016. "Introduction to the Special Issue." *Publius* 46 (3): 275–80.

Brewer, Mark. 2016. "Populism in American Politics." *The Forum* 14 (3): 249–64.

Goelzhauser, Greg, and Shanna Rose. 2017. "The State of American Federalism 2016–2017: Policy Reversals and Partisan Perspectives on Intergovernmental Relations." *Publius* 47 (3): 285–313.

Gordon, Sanford, and Dimitri Landa. 2017. "Common Problems: (or, What's Missing from the Conventional Wisdom on Polarization and Gridlock)." *Journal of Politics* 79 (4): 1433–37.

Grumbach, Jacob. 2018. "From Backwaters to Major Policymakers: Policy Polarization in the States, 1970–2014." *Perspectives on Politics* 16 (2): 416–35.

Holbrook, Thomas. 2016. *Altered States. Changing Populations, Changing Parties, and the Transformation of the American Political Landscape*. Oxford: Oxford University Press.

Jacobson, Gary. 2017. "The Triumph of Polarized Partisanship in 2016: Donald Trump's Improbable Victory." *Political Science Quarterly* 132 (1): 9–41.

Kazin, Michael. 1998. *The Populist Persuasion: An American History*. Ithaca: Cornell University Press.

Kettl, Donald. 2020. "States Divided: The Implications of American Federalism for COVID-19." *Public Administration Review* 80 (4): 595–602.

Levitsky, Steven, and Daniel Ziblatt. 2018. *How Democracies Die*. New York: Crown.

Mann, Thomas, and Norman Ornstein. 2013. *It's Even Worse than It Looks. How the American Constitutional System Collided with the New Politics of Extremism*. New York: Basic Books.

Mead, Walter R. 2017. "The Jacksonian Revolt: American Populism and the Liberal Order." *Foreign Affairs* 96 (2): 2–7.

Reich, Gary. 2018. "Hitting a Wall? The Trump Administration Meets Immigration Federalism." *Publius* 48 (3): 372–95.

Sides, John, Michael Tesler, and Lynn Vavreck. 2017. "How Trump Lost and Won." *Journal of Democracy* 28 (2): 33–44.

Uslaner, Eric. 2015. "Congressional Polarization and Political Trust." *The Forum* 13 (3): 361–74.

INDEX